MVS Power Programming

Ranade IBM Series

K. BOSLER • *CLIST Programming*, 0-07-006551-9

H. MURPHY • *Assembler for Cobol Programmers: MVS, VM*, 0-07-044129-4

H. BOOKMAN • *Cobol II*, 0-7-006533-0

J. RANADE • *DB2: Concepts, Programming, and Design*, 0-07-051265-5

J. SANCHEZ AND M. CANTON • *IBM Microcomputers*, 0-07-054594-4

M. ARONSON • *SAS: A Programmer's Guide*, 0-07-002467-7

J. AZEVEDO • *ISPF: The Strategic Dialog Manager*, 0-07-002673-4

K. BRATHWAITE • *System Design in a Database Environment*, 0-07-007250-7

M. CARATHANASSIS • *Expert MVS/XA JCL: A Complete Guide to Advanced Techniques*, 0-07-009816-6

P. DONOFRIO • *CICS: Debugging, Dump Reading and Problem Determination*, 0-07-017606-X

T. EDDOLLS • *VM Performance Management*, 0-07-018966-8

P. KAVANAGH • *VS Cobol II for Cobol Programmers*, 0-07-033571-0

T. MARTYN • *DB2/SQL: A Professional Programmer's Guide*, 0-07-040666-9

S. PIGGOTT • *CICS: A Practical Guide to System Fine Tuning*, 0-07-050054-1

N. PRASAD • *IBM Mainframes: Architecture and Design*, 0-07-050686-8

J. RANADE • *Introduction to SNA Networking: A Guide to VTAM/NCP*, 0-07-051144-6

J. RANADE • *Advanced SNA Networking: A Professional's Guide for Using VTAM/NCP*, 0-07-051143-8

P. J. TOWNER • *CASE*, 0-07-065086-1

S. SAMSON • *MVS: Performance Management*, 0-07-054528-6

B. JOHNSON • *MVS Concepts and Facilities*, 0-07-032673-8

P. McGREW • *On-Line Text Management: Hypertext*, 0-07-046263-1

L. TOWNER • *IDMS/R*, 0-07-065087-X

A. WIPFLER • *Distributed Processing in the CICS Environment*, 0-07-071136-4

A. WIPFLER • *CICS Application Development Programming*, 0-07-071139-9

J. RANADE • *VSAM: Concepts, Programming, and Design, Second Edition*, 0-07-051244-2

J. RANADE • *VSAM Performance, Design, and Fine Tuning, Second Edition*, 0-07-051245-0

J. SANCHEZ AND CANTON • *Programming Solutions Handbook for IBM Microcomputers*,

L. TOWNER • *CASE*, 0-07-065086-1

P. DONOFRIO • *CICS Programmer's Reference*, 0-07-017607-8

M. CARATHANASSIS • *Expert MVS/ESA JCL: A Guide to Advanced Techniques*, 0-07-009820-4

J. RANADE • *DOS to OS/2: Conversion, Migration, and Application Design*, 0-07-051264-7

K. BRATHWAITE • *Relational Databases: Concepts, Design, and Administration*, 0-07-007252-3

B. JOHNSON AND D. JOHNSON • *DASD IBM's Direct Access Storage Devices*, 0-07-032674-6

M. MARX AND P. DAVIS • *MVS Power Programming*, 0-07-040763-0

G. HOUTEKAMER AND P. ARTIS • *MVS I/O Subsystem: Configuration Management and Performance Analysis*, 0-07-002553-3

A. KAPOOR • *SNA: Architecture, Protocols, and Implementation*, 0-07-033727-6

D. SILVERBERG • *DB2: Performance, Design, and Implementation*, 0-07-057553-3

R. CROWNHART • *IBM's Workstation CICS*, 0-07-014770-1

C. DANEY • *Programming in REXX*, 0-07-015305-1

G. GOLDBERG AND P. SMITH • *The REXX Handbook*, 0-07-028682-8

A. WERMAN • *DB2 Handbook for DBAs*, 0-07-069460-5

J. KNEILING, R. LEFKON, AND P. SOMERS • *Understanding CICS Internals*, 0-07-037040-0

MVS Power Programming

Mitchell Marx

Penelope Davis

McGraw-Hill, Inc.
New York St. Louis San Francisco Auckland Bogotá
Caracas Lisbon London Madrid Mexico Milan
Montreal New Delhi Paris San Juan São Paulo
Singapore Sydney Tokyo Toronto

Library of Congress Cataloging-in-Publication Data

Marx, Mitchell.
    MVS power programming / Mitchell Marx, Penelope Davis.
        p. cm.

    Includes bibliographical references and index.
    ISBN 0-07-040763-0 :
    1. Systems programming (Computer science)   2. MVS (Computer file)
    I. Davis, Penelope.   II. Title.
    QA76.66.M37   1992
    005.2'25–dc20   91-34724
                                                                      CIP

This book is dedicated to our friend Marc J. Strahl

    2 3 4 5 6 7 8 9 0   DOC/DOC   9 7 6 5 4 3 2

ISBN 0-07-040763-0

1733965   *6-28-94*

*The sponsoring editor for this book was Jerry Papke, the editing
supervisor was Fred Dahl, and the production supervisor was Suzanne
W. Babeuf. It was set in Century Schoolbook by Inkwell Publishing
Services.*

Printed and bound by R. R. Donnelley & Sons Company.

Contents

Preface

WHAT THE BOOK IS ABOUT

This book is for all of you who would like to write code that interfaces with the MVS operating system. It presents a practical approach to MVS internals, with particular emphasis on the ESA enhancements to MVS architecture.

The book is based on a series of New York University lectures on MVS internals for systems professionals interested in learning more about their operating environment. Over the years, this group of "students" has included applications programmers; MVS, VM, VSE, VTAM, CICS, and database system programmers; managers, consultants, software engineers, and technical support personnel. The style and presentation of the material is largely the result of their requests and feedback.

HOW THIS BOOK IS ORGANIZED

The chapters in Part 1 introduce the reader to the overall structure of MVS and to the considerations that apply when writing code that executes as a logical extension of the operating system. These considerations include the concepts of modular design and reentrancy.

Each chapter in Part 2 presents a complete and tested code example that is discussed in the text in the form of a code "walkthrough." The MVS components whose services are needed for the program are discussed in an overview in the beginning of the chapter.

The appendixes include additional programs as well the JCL and control statements to assemble and link edit each code example.

MVS/ESA

Several of the program examples exploit the new facilities introduced in ESA architecture, such as the linkage stack, access registers, dataspaces, hiperspaces, and the stacking PC routine.

PREREQUISITES

Most people who have had at least a year of professional experience and have a working knowledge of 370 assembly language will benefit from this book.

WHAT IS INCLUDED

IBM provides extensive documentation on every aspect of MVS, and this book is best read in conjunction with IBM manuals. The manuals that describe the programming interfaces to MVS services, and the component logic manuals are particularly useful. Appendix E contains a list of useful manuals.

If a topic is completely described in an IBM manual, we have not included it. For the same reason, we have not included the formats of macros that invoke MVS services or the CALL formats to invoke callable services. These programming interfaces are well documented in the appropriate reference manuals.

PROGRAMS IN THE BOOK

All the programs in this book were executed on an IBM 3090/600 running ESA 3.1.0 under PR/SM.

Although many of the programs are designed to take advantage of MVS/ESA features, most of the programs will execute on an MVS/XA or MVS/SP system. The programs that illustrate features that are available only in MVS/ESA, such as dataspaces, are not downwardly compatible.

Some of the programs that use ESA features require slight modifications before they will execute under MVS/XA or MVS/SP. Programs that use the ESA linkage stack or include ESA-only macros (such as STORAGE) fall in this category. How to make the necessary modifications will be clear after you read the chapters in Part 1.

Diskettes containing the source code for all the program macros, and JCL in this book are available on 3½-in. diskettes. Included are instructions for transferring the code to mainframe DASD. To obtain diskettes, send $50 (this includes tax and shipping) to:

Diskette
MD-Paladin, Inc.
Suite 169
163 Amsterdam Ave.
New York, NY 10023

Acknowledgments

First and foremost we would like to thank Marc Strahl for reading the manuscript and reviewing the code. In addition to his profound technical expertise, we are indebted to Marc for his enthusiasm, generosity, and ensurance.

Our thanks to Michael Kaminsky for carefully reading and criticizing the manuscript from an applications viewpoint. Our special thanks to Kathy Martinez for her interest and support during the early, critical stages of this project and to Steve Lieblich for his magnanimous act of friendship.

We gratefully acknowledge our editor, Jay Ranade, for his understanding and support. His gift for communicating is truly extraordinary. Our thanks to Dave Fogarty at McGraw-Hill and Fred Dahl at Inkwell Publishing Services for their cooperation and assistance in producing this book.

Finally, we would like to thank the students at NYU's Information Technologies Institute. Their professional needs and countless suggestions shaped the content and presentation of this book.

ABOUT THE AUTHORS

Mitchell Marx is a principal of MD-Paladin Inc., a consulting firm based in New York. He has been the manager of MVS systems at Morgan Stanley & Co. and a software engineer at !Candle Corp. Mr. Marx is an Associate Professor at New York University's Information Technologies Institute.

Penelope Davis is a principal of MD-Paladin Inc., a consulting firm based in New York. Her experience includes applications analysis and design for The Equitable, ADT, and Xerox Corp.

ABOUT THE SERIES

The J. Ranade Series are among McGraw-Hill's primary vehicles to provide mini and mainframe computing professionals with practical and timely concepts, solutions, and applications. The series covers DEC and IBM environments, communications, and networking.

Jay Ranade, Series Editor in Chief and best-selling computer author, is a Senior Systems Architect and Assistant V.P. at Merrill Lynch.

Invoking MVS Services

1

MVS Services

1.1 THE STRUCTURE OF MVS

For the purposes of this book, an *operating system* is a collection of software programs that manages computer hardware for the benefit of applications programs. The operating system manages real and expanded storage, channel paths to devices, and the I/O devices themselves. MVS also provides services such as dispatching and serializing work on the CPUs, handling error recovery, and managing catalogs and data sets.

A *component* is a group of these services with related functions and control structures. The components themselves have no particular hierarchical relationship to one another—that is, there is no central supervisory structure for them. Rather, they are like a bundle of services, each component calling another for its services. Even as central a part of MVS as the Dispatcher, which selects work and causes it to run on an available CPU, is itself called by other components when they are ready to relinquish control of a CPU.

A *macro* is the instruction level interface to components. MVS components use macros to invoke the services of other components. These system macros are available to your applications as well. In fact, you use many of them already. When you want to execute a program while in a TSO session, for example, you issue the command

```
CALL   'LIBRARY(PROGRAM)'
```

This command causes TSO to issue an ATTACH macro. The ATTACH macro invokes the services of Task Management to build a Task Control Block (TCB). Task Management, in turn, invokes the services of Program Management to load the program into virtual storage with a LOAD macro. As part of loading that program into virtual storage, the Program Management component of MVS makes a request to the Virtual Storage Management (VSM) component to provide storage for the program load module. The request is in the form of a GETMAIN macro instruction. GETMAIN is the standard method that every MVS component uses when it wants to invoke the virtual storage acquisition services of VSM. User-written programs can also issue the GETMAIN macro to acquire virtual storage. In doing so they are using the same interface that MVS uses internally.

Figure 1.1 briefly names and describes the major components of MVS and the macros by which other MVS components and user programs invoke their services. Wherever a macro is listed with an asterisk (*), it includes all macros beginning with the same letters. In the Cross Memory Services macros, for example, ET* means ETCON, ETCRE, ETDEF, ETDES, and ETDIS.

1.2 INTERFACES TO COMPONENT SERVICES

1.2.1 Macros

By far the most common way to invoke a service from an MVS component within MVS code and in user code is with an assembly language macro. The assembler expands macros into machine instructions during the first pass it makes through a source module. During the second and third passes, the assembler processes the generated instructions (along with the other instructions coded in the source) resolving labels, generating the binary values for instructions and their operands, building the External Symbol Directory (ESD) and the Relocation Directory (RLD), and, generally, doing what is necessary to make an object module from the source code.

The rules for coding macros are illustrated in Fig. 1.2.

- As in any line of assembler code, there are five fields:

    1. *Label field:* Begins in column 1 and may contain a user-selected name to be used for branching to the macro.

    2. *Opcode field:* Begins following one or more spaces after the label field and contains the macro name.

Component	Description	Macros
Address Space Services	Creates and destroys address spaces.	ASCRE ASDÉS ASEXT
Allocation	Logically connects files with address spaces	DYNALLOC
Auxiliary Storage Manager (ASM)	Manages page slots; moves data to expanded storage and DASD in page and swap operations	No Macro Interface
Catalog Services	Updates, maintains and queries system catalog	CATALOG LOCATE INDEX CAMLST
Console	Manages messages to and from system consoles	WTO WTOR DOM
Command Processor	Central console command handler; queues commands to tasks	MGCR QEDIT
Cross Memory Services (PCAUTH)	Facilitates inter-address space data movement/program execution	ALESERV PCLINK AT* AX* ET* LX* TESTART*
Data in Virtual (DIV)	Facility for dealing with a dataset as virtual object	DIV
Dump Services	Dumps portions of virtual storage to dump datasets	SDUMP SNAP
Global Resource Serialization (GRS)	Gives a task or address space exclusive control of a resource	ENQ DEQ RESERVE GQSCAN
Input/Output Supervisor (IOS)	Performs all input/output operations to all devices	Access Method Macros (OPEN CLOSE etc.)

Figure 1.1 MVS components.

Component	Description	Macros
Job Entry Sub-system (JES)	Manages the SPOOL, sysout devices, batch jobs	IEFSSREQ
Program Manager (Contents Supervisor)	Brings programs into virtual storage and manages their use	LOAD DELETE LINK SYNCH XCTL IDENTIFY
RASP	Creates and manages dataspaces and hiperspaces.	DSPSERV HSPSERV
Real Storage Manager (RSM)	Keeps track of all real storage frames; satisfies frame requests	PG*
Recovery Termination Manager (RTM)	Normal/abnormal task termination and cleanup; global recovery	ABEND ESTAE ESPIE SETRP SETFRR CALLRTM
Supervisor/ Dispatcher	Various control functions;selects units of work to run on processors, manages MVS locks	SCHEDULE CALLDISP PURGEDQ SUSPEND CIRB RESUME SETLOCK
System Management Facility (SMF)	Collects data on system events; writes event data to MANx files	SMF*
Subsystem Interface	Queues requests to subsystems defined in subsystem name table	IEFSSREQ
System Authorization Facility (SAF)	Central interface to resource security systems (RACF etc.)	RAC* FRACHECK
System Resource Manager (SRM)	Regulates amount of storage and CPU each unit of work gets	SYSEVENT

Figure 1.1 *(Continued).*

Component	Description	Macros
Task Services	Creates dispatchable units of work (tasks); controls task serialization and authority	ATTACH DETACH CHAP WAIT POST EVENTS MODESET EXTRACT
Timer Services	Maintains queues of events scheduled for specific times.	STIMER TTIMER TIMERM
Virtual Lookaside Facility (VLF)	ESA only: Faclility for managing datasets as virtual objects, thus avoiding I/O	COF*
Virtual Storage Manager (VSM)	Allows programs to allocate and free ranges of virtual addresses	GETMAIN FREEMAIN STORAGE CPOOL VSM*

Figure 1.1 *(Continued).*

3. *Operand field:* Begins following one or more spaces after the opcode field and contains the operands of the macro, which are separated by commas.

4. *Comment field:* Begins following one or more spaces after the operand field up to and including column 71 and is for user-supplied documentation.

5. *Continuation field:* Column 72 is the continuation field. Any symbol coded in column 72 will cause the assembler to look for additional operands in column 16 of the following line.

■ Macros contain two types of operands, *positional* operands and *keyword* operands. In Fig. 1.2, the first line contains positional operands. All positional operands are required and must be coded in order. All positional operands must be coded before the first keyword operand. If a positional operand is omitted and other positional operands are coded following the omitted operand, as in the first line of Fig. 1.3, a comma must be coded to indicate the missing operand. If the omitted operands are the last in a series of positional operands, the commas need not be coded. The other operands of the macro in Fig. 1.2 are keyword operands as indicated by an equal sign between the keyword and the operand. Keyword operands may be coded in any order after the positional operands and may be omitted at will. No commas are used when keyword operands are omitted. If keyword or positional

```
0...|....1....|....2....|....3....|....4....|....5....|....6....|....7..
label    MACRO operand1,operand2,      COMMENT                          X
               KEYWORD=operand,        COMMENT                          X
               KEYWORD=(R),            COMMENT                          X
               KEYWORD=(suboperand1,suboperand2),                       X
               KEYWORD=(suboperand1,(R))
```

Figure 1.2 Coding macros.

operands are not coded, the macro expands with default values for the omitted operands.

- Some macro operands, like the fourth and fifth lines in Fig. 1.2, require several values. These suboperands are enclosed in parentheses. As with positional operands, a comma must be coded to indicate the absence of any suboperand that is omitted. If the first suboperand is the only one coded, the parentheses around the suboperands and the commas indicating missing suboperands may be omitted. The fourth line of Fig. 1.3 shows a keyword operand with the first suboperand omitted.

- Operands can be self-defining terms such as constants, reserved words that have meaning for the particular macro being coded, addresses of data areas where operand values reside, or registers containing the operand values. Enclosing an operand or suboperand in parentheses indicates that the operand or suboperand is a register. The third line in Fig. 1.2 shows an example of a register used as an operand. The fourth and fifth lines illustrate keyword operands that expect two suboperands. The fourth line uses constants or data area labels for the suboperands; while the fifth line uses a constant or label for the first suboperand, and a register, as indicated by parentheses, for the second suboperand.

Figure 1.4 illustrates one way of coding a GETMAIN macro. The first line contains a label GET1, which may be used as a branch address

```
0...|....1....|....2....|....3....|....4....|....5....|....6....|....7...
label    MACRO ,operand2,        COMMENT                               X
               KEYWORD=operand,   COMMENT                               X
               KEYWORD=(R),       COMMENT                               X
               KEYWORD=(,suboperand2) COMMENT
```

Figure 1.3 A macro with omitted operands.

```
0...|....1....|....2....|....3....|....4....|....5....|....6....|....7...
GET1    GETMAIN RU,                      COMMENT                        X
            LV=(0),                      COMMENT                        X
            LOC=BELOW,                   COMMENT                        X
            SP=3,                        COMMENT                        X
            MF=(E,(PARMLIST))            COMMENT
```

Figure 1.4 Example of the GETMAIN macro.

elsewhere in the code. Following the macro opcode GETMAIN, the positional operand RU indicates that the GETMAIN is unconditional and returns the acquired virtual storage address in general register 1. By referring to the manual* we can see the other values this positional operand might have (LC, EC, RC, etc.), indicating the other ways that GETMAIN can operate. The line ends with a symbol in column 72, indicating that there are other operands beginning in column 16 on the following line.

On the second line, the parentheses around the value for the LV = keyword operand indicate that the value used for the GETMAIN length can be found in register 0. BELOW, the value for the keyword operand LOC = on the third line, is a reserved word for the GETMAIN macro. It indicates that the acquired storage should have a virtual address below 16 meg. The SP = operand on the fourth line has the value of a constant, 3, indicating a GETMAIN from subpool 3. The keyword operand on the fifth line, MF = , has two suboperands. The first suboperand is a reserved word "E," indicating the *execute* macro format. The second suboperand is the label of a data area elsewhere in the code. In this case it is the address of the parameter list built by the *list* form of the macro. While each operand has been coded on a separate line in the example, doing so was not necessary. The operands could have been coded on the same line and separated and by commas.

1.2.2 Entries to Services—SVC, Branch, and PC Routines

Macros that invoke services from MVS components expand during assembly into

- Parameters detailing what the user is requesting from the service.

- Instructions that transfer control to the service.

Application Development Macro Reference (GC28-1822).

```
116            GETMAIN RU,LV=512,SP=3,LOC=BELOW
117+      CNOP   0,4
118+      B      IHB0005B           BRANCH AROUND DATA
119+IHB0005L DC  A(512)             LENGTH
120+IHB0005F DC  AL1(0)             RESERVED
121+      DC     AL1(0)             RESERVED
122+      DC     AL1(3)             SUBPOOL
123+      DC     BL1'00010010'      MODE BYTE
124+IHB0005B L   0,IHB0005L         LOAD LENGTH
125+      L      15,IHB0005F        LOAD GETMAIN PARMS
126+      SR     1,1                ZERO RESERVED REG 1
127+      SVC    120                ISSUE GETMAIN SVC
```

Figure 1.5 SVC entry to GETMAIN.

An *SVC* transfer of control is illustrated in the assembler output shown in Fig. 1.5. A user makes a request for 512 bytes of below-the-line storage in subpool 3 from Virtual Storage Manager by coding the GETMAIN macro on line 116. The assembler has expanded the macro into lines 117 through 127 as indicated by the plus sign (+) following the statement numbers.

The operands coded on GETMAIN expand into the parameters on lines 119 through 123. Lines 124 and 125 load these parameters into registers 0 and 15 in preparation for the transfer of control to the VSM service. The transfer of control is accomplished with the SVC 120 instruction on line 127. When this instruction is executed, an SVC interrupt occurs on the processor on which the code is executing. VSM's GETMAIN service executes as a logical extension of the MVS routines that receive control as a result of the interrupt.

Branch entries are used in situations in which you cannot transfer control to a component's service routine with an SVC, such as

- When your code is running under an SRB rather than a TCB.

  A unit of work gets control when the Dispatcher component of MVS selects it to run on an available processor. There are two types of control blocks that the Dispatcher scans to select the next unit of work for dispatch: Service Request Blocks (SRBs) and Task Control Blocks (TCBs). All code runs under one of these control blocks.

  SRBs are used primarily when a task in one address space wants a routine to execute in another address space. SRB routines cannot take SVC interrupts. (See Chap. 9 for more about SRBs.)

- When your code is using Dual Address Space (DAS).

  The Dual Address Space feature allows code to fetch data from and store data into address spaces other than the one in which the code is executing. Code using DAS cannot issue SVCs. (See Chap. 7 for more about cross memory services.)

In Fig. 1.6, the GETMAIN on line 116 is coded with BRANCH = YES. This causes GETMAIN to expand into instructions that fetch the address of the Communication Vector Table (CVT) on line 127, find the address of the GETMAIN routine in the CVT on line 128, and branch directly into the routine on line 129. Since this type of GETMAIN does not cause an SVC interrupt, it can be used in an SRB routine or cross memory code using DAS.

The *program call (PC) entry* is used by those macros that invoke component services that are new in MVS/ESA, such as DSPSERV, and by older macros that have been enhanced so that they can execute in access register addressing mode or from within another PC routine. PC routines under ESA can use the linkage stack to save the caller's environment. They provide a method of synchronously invoking routines that reside in the private area of specialized address spaces. PC routines do not incur the delay of SVC interrupts or the overhead of interrupt handler routines.

STORAGE in Fig. 1.7 is an example of an MVS/ESA macro that expands into a call to a PC routine. While it will produce the same result as the GETMAINs in Figs. 1.5 and 1.6, (invoking a Virtual Storage Manager service routine to obtain 512 bytes of below-the-line subpool 3 storage and returning the address of the acquired storage in register 1) STORAGE can be executed in access register mode while GETMAIN cannot. The expansion of STORAGE first builds parameters for the service on

```
116          GETMAIN RU,LV=512,SP=3,LOC=BELOW,BRANCH=YES
117+         CNOP  0,4
118+         B     IHB0005B              BRANCH AROUND DATA
119+IHB0005L DC    A(512)               LENGTH
120+IHB0005F DC    AL1(0)               RESERVED
121+         DC    AL1(0)               RESERVED
122+         DC    AL1(3)               SUBPOOL
123+         DC    BL1'00010010'        MODE BYTE
124+IHB0005B L     0,IHB0005L           LOAD LENGTH
125+         L     15,IHB0005F          LOAD GETMAIN PARMS
126+         SR    1,1                  ZERO RESERVED REG 1
127+         L     15,16(0,0)           ADDRESS OF CVT
128+         L     15,504(0,15)         CVTCRMN ENTRY POINT
129+         BALR  14,15                CALL GETMAIN
```

Figure 1.6 Branch entry to GETMAIN.

```
116             STORAGE OBTAIN,COND=NO,LENGTH=512,LOC=BELOW,SP=3,ADDR=(1)
117+            CNOP  0,4
118+            B     IHB0009B            .BRANCH AROUND DATA
119+IHB0009L DC       A(512)             .STORAGE LENGTH
120+IHB0009F DC       AL1(0)             .RESERVED BYTE
121+            DC     AL1(0*16)          .KEY
122+            DC     AL1(3)             .SUBPOOL
123+            DC     BL1'00010010'      .FLAGS
124+IHB0009B DS       0F
125+            L     0,IHB0009L          .STORAGE LENGTH
126+            L     15,IHB0009F         .CONTROL INFORMATION
127+            L     14,16(0,0)          .CVT ADDRESS
128+            L     14,772(14,0)        .ADDR SYST LINKAGE TABLE
129+            L     14,160(14,0)        .OBTAIN LX/EX FOR OBTAIN
130+            PC    0(14)               .PC TO TO STORAGE RTN
```

Figure 1.7 PC entry to STORAGE.

lines 119 through 123, then loads the parameters into registers 0 and 15 in lines 125 and 126.

PC routines are identified by unique numbers. Lines 127 and 128 locate the address of a table of PC routine numbers specified by an address in the CVT. Every PC routine used by MVS is identified by a unique number in this System Function Table (SFT). The STORAGE macro expands so that L 14,160(14,0) on Line 129 contains the displacement (160) of the PC number for the STORAGE service in the SFT. The PC number is loaded by the instruction on line 129 into register 14, and, when PC 0(14) on line 130 is executed, control is passed to the the routine indicated by the PC number in register 14. PC routines are covered in detail in Chap. 10.

1.2.3 SPLEVEL and SYSSTATE

There are two macros that do not generate executable code but control how other macros in the assembly expand: SPLEVEL and SYSSTATE.

SPLEVEL. By default, macros expand into code that is compatible with the version of MVS under which the assembly program is executing. SPLEVEL can be used to force macro expansions for a different version of the operating system and is especially useful if code must be downwardly compatible. Suppose, for example, that you are writing a module on an ESA system which you will supply to another installation that is XA. Without SPLEVEL, macros in your code will expand for MVS version 3 (ESA). Coding

SPLEVEL SET = 2

forces the macros to expand for MVS/XA. If you are writing a macro that will conditionally expand based on the SPLEVEL, include the GBLC symbol &SYSSPLV and use AIF statements to test its value. A value of '1' is MVS/SP, '2' is MVS/XA, and '3' is MVS/ESA. See the MODULE macro in Appendix A for the use of &SYSSPLV within a macro.

SYSSTATE. By default, macros assembled on an ESA system expand for primary space addressing mode and do generate instructions to extract values from or load values into the access registers. SYSSTATE can be used to cause macros to expand compatibly with access register addressing mode. Coding

SYSSTATE ASCENV = AR

causes macros following SYSTATE to yield expansions that use the access registers.

If you are writing a macro that will conditionally expand based on the SYSSTATE, include the GBLC symbol &SYSASCE and use AIF statements to test its value. A value of '1' means primary space mode; '2' means access register mode.

1.2.4 Nonmacro Interfaces

There are many useful MVS component services for which IBM does not supply a macro interface. Since these services are not all described in one place, they are difficult to find out about, but often are surprisingly easy to use.

The routine in Fig. 1.8 invokes a service from the Program Management component of MVS. It locates the entry point address of a module that you know is on the Link Pack Area Queue (LPAQ). The routine provides greater speed and efficiency than a LOAD macro, which expands into an SVC 8 and searches other queues as as well as the LPAQ.

```
212          L     3,CVTPTR        CVT ADDRESS TO REG 3
213          LA    9,MODNAME       ADDRESS OF MODULE NAME FIELD
214          L     8,CVTQLPAQ      HEAD OF LPAQ TO REG 8
215          L     15,CVTQCDSR     ADDR OF LPAQ SCAN RTN: IEAQCDSR
216          BALR  14,15           INVOKE LPAQ SCAN ROUTINE
217          B     CDEFOUND        CDE FOUND; PROCESS CDE
218 NOTFOUND DS    0H              CDE NOT FOUND
```

Figure 1.8 Invoking an MVS service without using a macro.

The routine that is branch-entered on line 216 searches the LPAQ for the CDE of a module using the module name as a search argument. (This code is used in the ANCHOR program in Chap. 8.)

This particular service is documented in the System Logic Library Program Management volume under the name of the routine, IEAQCDSR, that is invoked on line 216. The documentation describes the inputs and outputs of the routine and the system environment (locks, disablement, etc.) that is necessary to invoke the service. As the code in Fig. 1.8 demonstrates, the call to the service is easily made.

1.3 EXTENSIONS TO COMPONENT SERVICES

Not only can you exploit the power of MVS services in your code, but you can enhance and customize the services themselves. You might want to add an additional function that is not included in the service, such as enhanced console message processing for automated operations, or you might want to include some specialized function that has a more direct relation to your company's business, such as accounting for cost charge-back.

Many products supplied by software vendors include extensions to MVS components. Security packages, such as ACF2 or Top Secret, front-end the IBM-supplied OPEN SVC so that they can check a user's authority to access a data set before it is opened. Common storage monitors, such as CSMON or the CSA function in OMEGAMON, insert their code before GETMAIN.

The two most common ways to enhance an MVS component are in an exit and with a front end or hook.

1.3.1 Exits

Exits are places in MVS or JES code where control is transferred to a user-written program with a specific assigned name. In Fig. 1.9, for example, the MVS module IEFSMFIE transfers control to module IEFUSI. The IEFUSI that is shipped with an MVS system is merely a stub containing instructions to set a return code of 0 and branch back to the caller. By substituting your own IEFUSI module for the stub, you can add function to the component that calls IEFUSI.

IEFUSI is called by System Management Facility (SMF) at the point in batch job processing just before a job step is started in an initiator address space. By substituting your own IEFUSI module, you can modify characteristics of a job step before it is started; you can even set a flag in the parameter list passed to the exit to tell SMF to cancel execution of that job step.

In Fig. 1.9, IEFSMFIE, the caller of IEFUSI, first sets up an ESTAE recovery routine to protect the component in case the exit abends. IEFS-

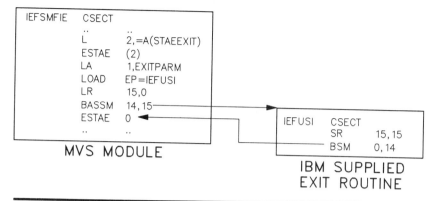

Figure 1.9 An MVS module with an exit.

MFIE then puts the address of a parameter list in register 1 and finds the entry point of the exit. LOAD EP = IEFUSI in Fig. 1.9 is a simplification of the actual way IEFSMFIE finds the address of IEFUSI, but the effect is the same. IEFSMFIE transfers control to IEFUSI with a BASSM and cancels the ESTAE routine when control is returned.

Exits are installed in the Pageable Link Pack Area (PLPA) or the Modified Link Pack Area (MLPA) of common storage by link editing them into one of the libraries named in SYS1.PARMLIB(LPALSTxx) for PLPA or by specifying them in SYS1.PARMLIB(IEALPAxx) for MLPA. See *MVS Initialization and Tuning* (GC28-1828) for more details about these PARMLIB members. Like any PLPA module, an exit must be refreshable (see Chap. 3).

The exit points in various MVS and JES components are documented in *MVS SPL: User Exits* (GC28-1836) and *JES2 User Modifications and Macros* (LT00-3160). The documentation includes the exit name, what the component is doing when it calls the exit, and the parameters provided by the caller for the exit's use.

1.3.2 Hooks

Hooks are another way to enhance a service provided by an MVS component, as illustrated in Fig. 1.10. The left part of the figure shows the table that contains the entry point addresses of all SVC routines in the system. The address of this table is in CVT + X'C8'. The SVC First Level Interrupt Handler (FLIH) uses an SVC number as an index into the SVC table to locate the module that provides the service requested. The instruction SVC 120, for example, will cause SVC FLIH to index 120 entries into the SVC table to locate the entry point for GETMAIN.

The right part of Fig. 1.10 illustrates how a user can save the address of the IBM SVC from the SVC table in a "hook" module and then replace the entry point address in the SVC table with the address of the hook

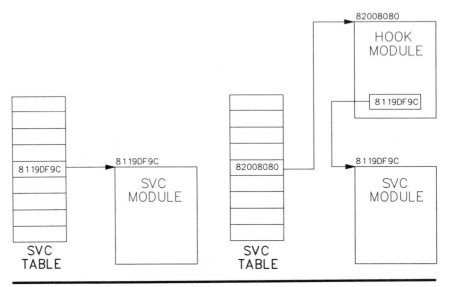

Figure 1.10   Hooking an SVC module.

module. This will cause SVC FLIH to transfer control to the hook module when the SVC is invoked; after it executes its own code, the hook can branch to the module originally specified in the SVC table.

Component services that are invoked by a branch or a PC instruction can be front-ended by replacing the pointer to the service module with a pointer to a user module. The user code will end in a branch to the original service.

Modules

2.1 GOOD SOFTWARE DESIGN

A source module is the basic unit of software. A load module is one or many source modules that have been compiled and linked together by the linkage editor in such a way as to make the source code executable by the operating system. Load modules can be tens of thousands of bytes long. If they were generated from single source modules they would be impossible to debug and modify. Besides simplicity, there are other reasons for dividing source code into smaller units than the load modules they will eventually become:

- Dividing software function into small, discrete, source-code units encourages good design by requiring a more careful and detailed analysis of function before any code is written.

- Small source units become more independent and less reliant on the function of other units. This facilitates making changes to one unit without affecting other units. It also tends to keep problems isolated in single units.

- Small units of code can be tested faster and more completely because the possible states in code increase geometrically, not algebraically, with the number of branches.

- Writing small, discrete units of source code tends to generate "primitives" or base-level functions that can be used in other software.

■ Source code can be worked on by more people at the same time when there are more, less complex, single-function source modules rather than fewer, more complex, multifunction modules.

2.2 STANDARD LINKAGE CONVENTION

When source code consists of several modules there must be a universally agreed-on convention to:

■ Transfer control from one module to another

■ Communicate parameters from one module to another

■ Preserve the state of a module when it transfers control to another module and restore that state when that module receives control back. This allows modules not to be concerned with the internal workings of any modules that they call

The convention for intermodule communication uses the general registers as described in Fig. 2.1. A module that transfers control to another module is described as the *caller*, and the module that receives control is described as the *called* module. Note that the specified registers may be used for other purposes when they are not being used for transferring control between modules.

In an MVS/XA environment, a program can preserve the caller's state by saving and restoring the contents of the general registers. Before it issues any instructions that modify the general register contents, the called module issues STM 14,12,12(13) (or the SAVE macro, which expands into an STM) to save the contents of the registers in the 72-byte area provided by the calling module. The called module restores the

Register	Contents
0	A single parameter supplied by a calling module.
1	A single parameter or, more commonly, the address of a parameter list supplied by a calling module.
13	Address of a 72 byte area of storage to save general registers. Supplied by a calling module for the called module at entry.
14	The address at which a calling module receives control back from any module it calls (the return address).
15	The address at which a called module receives control (the entry point address).

Figure 2.1   General register conventions.

contents of the general registers by issuing LM 14,12,12(13) before returning control to the caller with with BR 14. The RETURN macro, which expands into the same LM and BR instructions, can also be used to return control. An example of the complete series of instructions for saving and restoring the calling module's registers can be found in Fig. 3.4 in Chap. 3.

Since programs that run in an MVS/ESA environment can be called in access register addressing mode as well as in the MVS/XA addressing modes (primary space and secondary space), preserving the state of a calling program involves more than just saving and restoring the contents of the general registers. The contents of the access registers and the addressing mode in the PSW must be preserved as well. This is accomplished by using the ESA linkage stack.

2.3 THE LINKAGE STACK

The linkage stack is a *last-in-first-out* (LIFO) stack containing entries that describe the contents of the general registers, access registers, PSW, and cross-memory information from the control registers. One linkage stack is created for each dispatchable unit of work (TCB or SRB) in the system. Programs "push" or create an entry on the stack by issuing the BAKR or PC (stacking type) instruction, and "pop" or reload the registers and PSW from the stack by issuing the PR instruction. The use of the stack in programs invoked with the PC instruction is covered in Chap. 10.

Figure 2.2 illustrates a dispatchable unit of work, represented by a Task Control Block (TCB), and its associated linkage stack. The stack consists of sections, each beginning with a 128-byte header entry, followed by a variable number of 168-byte state entries, and ending with a 128-byte trailer entry. Control register 15 is the stack pointer and contains the virtual address of the next available state entry.

2.3.1 LSEXPAND

Whenever a program issues a BAKR or PC (stacking PC) instruction, the fields in the stack state entry specified by control register 15 are filled in and the address in control register 15 is incremented to point to the next available slot for a state entry in the current stack section. If there is not enough free space in the current section for a new state entry, bit 32 of the trailer entry is examined. If the bit is on, another stack section exists, and the new entry is created in the next section. If the bit is off, the program issuing the BAKR or PC takes a program check X'0030'.

When a linkage stack is first created for a new task, it contains one section consisting of a header entry, trailer entry, and a default number of 96 state entries. Additional sections with additional slots for state

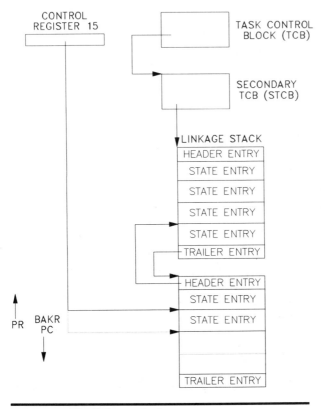

Figure 2.2   The linkage stack.

entries can be allocated by issuing the LSEXPAND macro for up to a maximum of 16,000 state entries. Since the stack pointer in control register 15 is incremented by a BAKR or PC instruction *before* a state entry is filled by a subsequent BAKR or PC, the additional stack sections must be allocated before they are actually used and before a program check X'0030' occurs.

2.3.2 BAKR

The contents of stack state entries formed by the BAKR instruction vary slightly from those formed by the PC instruction. Figure 2.3 illustrates a BAKR-type stack state entry and the ESA instructions that extract or modify fields in the entry.

- Bytes 0 through 63 contain the contents of the general registers at the time the stack state entry was formed in the order: 0, 1,..., 15.

- Bytes 64 through 127 contain the contents of the access registers at the time the stack state entry was formed in the order: 0, 1,..., 15.

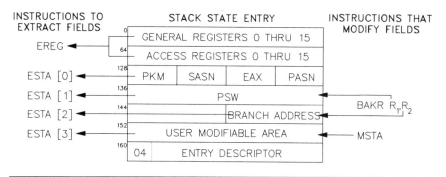

Figure 2.3 BAKR-type stack state entry.

2.3.3 EREG

The EREG instruction can be used to extract general and access register pairs from the stack state entry and load the appropriate registers with their contents.

EREG 5,7

for example, loads general registers 5, 6, and 7 with the three fullwords starting at byte 20 in the stack state entry and access registers 5, 6, and 7 with the three fullwords starting at byte 84. Both the general and access registers are loaded regardless of the current addressing mode. The stack state entry is not changed by the EREG instruction.

- Bytes 128 though 135 in Fig. 2.3 contain four 2-byte fields for the PSW key mask (PKM), the secondary address space number (SASN), the extended authorization index (EAX) and the primary address space number (PASN). These fields, which were extracted from control registers 3, 8, and 4, respectively when the stack state entry was formed, are used to reestablish the cross-memory environment when the stack is popped by the PR instruction.

- Bytes 136 through 143 contain the contents of the PSW when the stack state entry was created. When an entry is formed by the BAKR instruction, the contents of the first register operand of BAKR replace the second word of the PSW in the stack state entry. When a called program issues

BAKR 14,0

to save the state of the caller, the return address in register 14 replaces the address portion of the PSW in the stack state entry. When the called program concludes with a PR instruction, the stack is popped and the updated PSW returns control to the caller. If the first operand of BAKR is 0, no-register is indicated, and the PSW in the stack state entry will contain the address of the instruction following BAKR.

When the stack state entry is formed by a PC instruction (stacking PC) rather than a BAKR, the PSW contains the address of the instruction following the PC.

- Bytes 144 through 147 are not used.
- Bytes 148 through 151 contain the contents of the second register operand of BAKR which is the branch address. When the second operand of BAKR is 0, no-register is indicated. In this case BAKR does not branch, and the address of the instruction following the BAKR is placed in the branch address field in the stack state entry.

   When the stack state entry is formed by a PC instruction rather than a BAKR, bytes 148 through 151 contain the contents of the operand of PC (the PC routine number). (See Chap. 10 for more on PC routines.)

- Bytes 152 through 159 contain an 8-byte field for user data. The MSTA instruction is used to store the contents of an even-odd pair of general registers.

      MSTA 2

   for example, stores the contents of registers 2 and 3 in the user modifiable area.

2.3.4 ESTA

The ESTA instruction can be used to extract fields from the stack state entry into even-odd pairs of general registers. The second register operand of ESTA contains a value of 0, 1, 2, or 3 to indicate which of the stack state entry fields is to be extracted. The values in brackets following each ESTA in Fig. 2.3 are the codes used to extract the indicated fields. ESTA does not change the stack state entry. The following instructions,

      LA   0,0 LOAD ESTA CODE OF 0 INTO R0

      ESTA 2,0 EXTRACT XMS INFO INTO R2 AND R3

load general register 2 with the PKM/SASN and register 3 with the EAX/PASN.

      LA   4,3 LOAD ESTA CODE OF 3 INTO R4

      ESTA 6,4 EXTRACT USER DATA INTO R6 AND R7

load general registers 6 and 7 with the user data previously stored by the MSTA instruction.

- Bytes 160 through 167 are the stack entry descriptor. Every header, trailer, and state entry in the stack contains an entry descriptor. The first byte of this field indicates whether the entry is a header entry, trailer entry, state entry created by BAKR, or a state entry created by PC. X'04' in this byte indicates a state entry created by BAKR while X'05' indicates a state entry created by PC.

ESTA returns a condition code based on the value in this byte and thus can be used to determine which instruction created a state entry. A condition code of 0 after ESTA indicates that the entry was created by BAKR, while 1 indicates that it was created by PC.

Figure 3.5 in Chap. 3 illustrates how a called program can preserve the state of its caller by issuing BAKR 14,0 to create a stack state entry before it issues any instructions that modify the PSW or the contents of the general, access, or control registers.

Note that the SAVE and RETURN macros, since they do not expand into instructions that use the linkage stack, are not as suitable a method of preserving and restoring the state of a calling module in an ESA environment as are BAKR and PR.

2.4 ADDRESSING MODE (AMODE)

Another aspect of module communication that must be considered is a module's AMODE/RMODE. AMODE and RMODE are linkage editor attributes which, when resolved by the linkage editor, are recorded in the PDS directory for a load module.

AMODE determines whether an address is interpreted as 24 bit or 31 bit. As illustrated in Fig. 2.4, when the AMODE bit (bit 32) in the PSW is 0 (AMODE 24), the instruction-fetch hardware interprets only the low-order 24 bits of the PSW address word as the virtual address of the next instruction to be fetched. When the AMODE bit is off, the address will necessarily reside below the 16-meg line, since the highest number addressable in 24 bits is X'00FFFFFF'. When the AMODE bit is on (AMODE 31), the instruction-fetch hardware interprets the PSW as a 31-bit address, which allows addressability both above and below the 16-meg line (up to X'7FFFFFFF').

The following instructions will give different results depending on the condition of the AMODE bit:

```
L    3, = A(X'3B008000')
LA   5,0(0,3)
```

The sum of the displacement, base, and index registers in the second operand of LA 5,0(0,3) is X'3B008000'. If the AMODE bit in the active PSW is 1, X'3B008000' is the virtual address formed by the second oper-

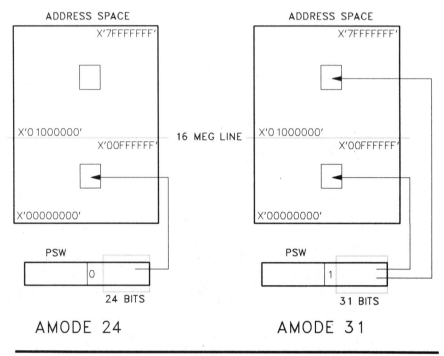

Figure 2.4 Addressing mode (AMODE).

and and the contents in register 5 after completion of the instruction. If bit 32 of the active PSW is off, however, the virtual address formed by the second operand of LA 5,0(0,3) is only the low-order 24 bits of the sum of the displacement, base, and index registers, that is, X'008000'. This will be the contents of register 5 after the instruction is executed with a 24-bit-mode PSW.

There are 2 instructions that can be used to change the AMODE bit in the PSW:

- BSM saves the value of the PSW AMODE bit in the high-order bit of the first register operand and sets the PSW AMODE bit according to the high-order bit in the second register operand. BSM, using the new PSW AMODE bit setting, then causes a branch to the virtual address in the second register operand. For example, if the following instructions were executed with a PSW AMODE bit setting of 0,

```
L    14, = A(X'00000008')
L    15, = A(X'BB008000')
BSM  14,15
```

at the conclusion of the BSM, register 14 would contain X'00000008', the PSW would have an AMODE bit of 1, and a branch would be taken to the instruction at address X'3B008000'.

- BASSM operates the same way as BSM except that, in addition to saving the value of the current PSW AMODE bit in the first register operand, it loads the virtual address of the instruction following BASSM into the low-order 31 bits of the first register operand. For example, if the following instructions were executed with a PSW with an AMODE bit of 1,

```
L        15, = A(X'0B008000')
BASSM    14,15
MVC      ...
```

at the conclusion of the BASSM, register 14 would contain 1 in the high-order bit and the address of the MVC instruction in the low-order 31 bits. The PSW would have an AMODE bit of 0, and a branch would be taken to the instruction at address X'008000'.

2.5 RESIDENCY MODE (RMODE)

RMODE refers to the residency mode of a load module. The options are RMODE 24, specifying that the module will be loaded below the 16-meg line, and RMODE ANY, specifying either above or below the 16-meg line. The linkage editor assigns a default of 24 when the RMODE is not specified by the user. If any CSECT in a load module is AMODE 24, the load module will be resolved as RMODE 24. When the RMODE value is specified in your source code, the value will be found in ESD data.

The Program Management component of MVS invokes the loader service to bring a program from DASD into virtual storage. If the residency mode (RMODE) of the load module is 24, the loader will use storage with addresses below X'00FFFFFF' to contain the module. If the RMODE of a module is ANY, the loader will try to load the module into storage with addresses above X'00FFFFFF'. If the loader is invoked as part of an ATTACH, LINK, or XCTL, control will be transferred to the newly loaded module with a PSW in the AMODE specified by the module.

Problems can arise when load modules with different RMODEs communicate. Assume that the calling program in Fig. 2.5 has an RMODE of ANY and is loaded as part of the ATTACH at the start of a new step in a batch job. The loader loads the calling module into storage with a virtual address greater than X'00FFFFFF' if it is available. Since the module AMODE is 31, ATTACH sets the AMODE bit in the PSW to 1 before transferring control to the module. The calling module issues a LOAD macro which causes the loader to bring the called module into virtual storage. Since the called module has an RMODE of 24, the loader loads the module into virtual storage with an address less than X'00FFFFFF'.

The calling program uses LA 1,PARMLIST to put the virtual address of the parameter list it will pass to the called program into register 1. Since the parameter list resides in the calling module, it has an address

```
|                              CALLING MODULE                              |
|                                                                          |
| MODULE1  CSECT                    CALLING PROGRAM                         |
| MODULE1  AMODE 31                 LOAD WITH 31 BIT ADDRESSING MODE        |
| MODULE1  RMODE ANY                LOAD ABOVE 16 MEG IF POSSIBLE           |
| ..        ..     ..                                                      |
|           LOAD  EP=MODULE2        LOAD PROGRAM TO CALL                    |
|           LR    15,0              ENTRY POINT OF CALLED MODULE TO R15     |
|           LA    1,PARMLIST        ADDRESS OF PARMLIST TO REGISTER 1       |
|           BASSM 14,15             CALL THE PROGRAM                        |
| ..        ..     ..                                                      |
| PARMLIST DS    5A                 PARAMETER LIST                          |
|                                                                          |
|                              CALLED MODULE                               |
|                                                                          |
| MODULE2  CSECT                    CALLED PROGRAM                          |
| MODULE2  AMODE 24                 LOAD WITH 24 BIT ADDRESSING MODE        |
| ..        ..     ..                                                      |
|           L     2,0(1)            LOAD FIRST PARAMETER INTO R2            |
| ..        ..     ..                                                      |
|           BSM   0,14              RETURN TO THE CALLER                    |
```

Figure 2.5 Addressing problem caused by inconsistent AMODEs.

greater than X'00FFFFFF'. The calling module passes control to the called module with BASSM 14,15 causing a branch to the entry point in the called module after setting the AMODE bit in the PSW to 0. When the called module issues L 2,0(1) in an attempt to address the parameter list passed by the caller, the 31-bit address in register 1 will be interpreted as a 24-bit address because the PSW AMODE bit is 0.

It may seem that one solution to the problem of intercommunication between modules of different RMODEs is to have all the modules in a system use the same RMODE. The reason this is not possible is that various MVS component structures themselves have AMODE and RMODE restrictions. A program that does QSAM I/O, for example, must have an AMODE of 24 since the parameter list for OPEN and CLOSE uses the high-order byte of an address word for flags. A program that references fields in the Secondary TCB (STCB), by contrast, must have an AMODE of 31, since the STCB always resides above X'00FFFFFF' in storage. Figure 2.6 illustrates another solution. An AMODE 31 calling program can dynamically acquire 24-bit addressable storage for the parameter list it passes to an AMODE 24 program by specifying LOC = BELOW on the GETMAIN macro.

Another solution to the problem is illustrated in Fig. 2.7. The called module receives control with a 24-bit PSW since the 31-bit caller trans-

```
                          *  CALLING MODULE

MODULE1  CSECT                       CALLING PROGRAM
MODULE1  AMODE 31                    LOAD WITH 31 BIT ADDRESSING MODE
MODULE1  RMODE ANY                   LOAD ABOVE 16 MEG IF POSSIBLE
..       ..    ..
         GETMAIN RU,LV=20,           .. GETMAIN                          X
                 LOC=BELOW           .. BELOW 16 MEG STORAGE FOR PARMLIST
         MVC   (20,1),PARMLIST       MOVE PARMLIST TO GETMAINED STORAGE
         LOAD  EP=MODULE2            LOAD PROGRAM TO CALL
         LR    15,0                  ENTRY POINT OF CALLED MODULE TO R15
         BASSM 14,15                 CALL THE PROGRAM
..       ..    ..
PARMLIST DS    CL(20)                PARAMETER LIST
```

Figure 2.6 31-bit caller providing 24-bit parameter list.

ferred control with a BASSM. Before processing the caller's parameter list, which resides in 31-bit storage, the called module issues O 15, = A(X'80000000') to set the high-order bit in the second register operand of the BSM that follows. The BSM, since the high-order bit of the second operand is on, turns on the AMODE bit in the PSW thus causing the operands of any following instructions to be interpreted as 31-bit addresses. The caller's parameter list can now be addressed when

```
                          CALLED MODULE

MODULE2  CSECT                       CALLED PROGRAM
MODULE2  AMODE 24                    LOAD WITH 24 BIT ADDRESSING MODE
..       ..    ..
         LA    14,BEGIN24            WHERE 24 BIT ADDRESSING RESUMED
         LA    15,BEGIN31            WHERE 31 BIT ADDRESSING BEGINS
         O     15,=A(X'80000000')    SET 31-BIT BEGIN ADDRESS TO 31 BIT TYPE
         BSM   14,15                 GO INTO 31-BIT MODE
BEGIN31  DS    0H                    NOW WE ARE AMODE 31
         L     2,0(1)                LOAD FIRST PARAMETER INTO R2
..       ..    ..
         BSM   0,14                  GO BACK TO 24-BIT MODE
BEGIN24  DS    0H                    NOW WE ARE BACK TO AMODE 24
..       ..    ..
         PR                          RETURN TO THE CALLER
```

Figure 2.7 Accessing above-the-line storage in a 24-bit module.

the second operand of L 2,0(1) is translated. The BSM also saves the current state of the PSW AMODE bit in the high-order bit of the first register operand. After processing the caller's parameter list, the module issues another BSM to reset the PSW AMODE bit to the state it was in before the first BSM was issued.

2.6 PASSING PARAMETERS—THE CALL MACRO

Figure 2.8 illustrates the parameter structures generated by the expansion of the CALL macro. The upper half of the figure is the parameter structure in an XA environment or in an ESA module in primary addressing mode (SYSSTATE ASCENV = P) (see Chap. 1). The lower half of the figure shows the parameter structure generated by the access register mode (SYSSTATE ASCENV = AR) expansion of CALL. In both cases general register 1 contains the address of a list of parameter addresses.

IBM considers this the "standard" parameter format. CALL statements in such high-level languages as COBOL, FORTRAN, PASCAL, and PLI generate parameter structures that look like those in Fig. 2.8.

Most IBM macros that invoke MVS services, by contrast, expand into the parameter structure illustrated in Fig. 2.9. Note that register 1

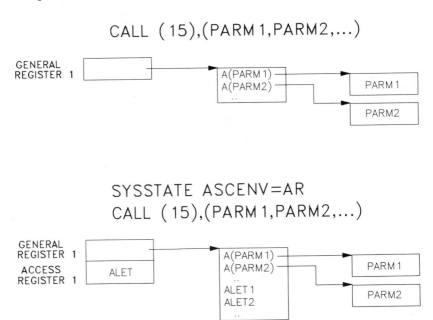

Figure 2.8   The CALL macro.

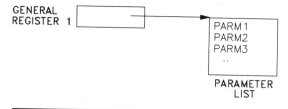

GENERAL
REGISTER 1

PARM1
PARM2
PARM3
..

PARAMETER
LIST

Figure 2.9   IBM macro-generated parameters.

contains the address of the parameter list itself rather than a pointer to a list of parameter addresses.

In order to make some MVS services available to high-level language programs, IBM has packaged these selected services so that they can be invoked with the CALL macro. The Virtual Storage Manager service that gets a cell from a cell pool, for example, would be invoked in an assembly language program with the CPOOL macro

```
CPOOL GET,U,CPID = (5).
```

A high-level language program might invoke the same service by issuing a CALL to CSRPGET, an interface module that transfers control to the same VSM cell pool service.

```
CALL   CSRPGET,(ALET,ANCHOR,CELLADDR,RC).
```

MVS services that can be invoked with CALL are documented in *Callable Services for High Level Languages* (GC28-1843).

A few considerations regarding the use of the CALL macro follow.

- CALL only builds a parameter structure and transfers control to a module. It does not bring a module into virtual storage. If a module is not in virtual storage, issue a LOAD macro for the module before issuing CALL.

```
LOAD   EP = MODULE
LR     15,0
CALL   (15),(parameters...)
```

The expansion of the CALL macro transfers control with BALR rather than BASSM. CALL should not, therefore, be used to transfer control between modules with different AMODEs. This can be a consideration when the CALL statement is used in high-level languages.

- The parameter structure built by CALL in access register mode (the lower half of Fig. 2.8) includes an ALET as well as an address for each parameter. This allows CALL to pass parameters that reside, not only

```
                          CALLING MODULE

MODULE1  CSECT
         ..  ..                ..
         SAC  512              GO INTO ACCESS REGISTER MODE
         SSYSTATE ASCENV=AR    SET ACCESS REGISTER MODE MACRO EXPANSION
         LAE  5,PARM2          PARM2 IS IN ANOTHER ADDRESS SPACE
         CALL MODULE2,(PARM1,(5))
         ..  ..                ..
PARM1    DS   F                1ST PARAMETER
         ..  ..                ..

                          CALLED MODULE

MODULE2  CSECT
..       ..  ..
         LM   3,4,0(1)         PARM ADDRESSES INTO GENERAL REGS 3 AND 4
         LAM  3,4,8(1)         PARM ALETS    INTO ACCESS  REGS 3 AND 4
..       ..  ..
```

Figure 2.10   The CALL macro in access register mode.

in the calling address space, but in any other address space whose ALET is currently in one of the access registers. Fig. 2.10 shows how a module receives control in access register mode, loads the parameter addresses into general registers, and loads the corresponding ALETs for each parameter into access registers. (See Chap. 7 for more on access register addressing mode.)

2.7 COMMUNICATING BETWEEN MODULES IN DIFFERENT LANGUAGES

When software consists of modules written in different source languages, the same intermodule communication considerations apply. Calling modules must pass parameters and transfer control, and called modules must preserve the state of the caller. The COBOL program in Fig. 2.11 builds a parameter list in the working storage section and transfers control to an assembly language program with the COBOL CALL instruction. COBOL, like most high-level languages, compiles into instructions that observe the intermodule communication convention described in the foregoing. When the called module receives control, it can expect register 15 to contain the entry point; register 14, the return address; register 13 to point to an 18 fullword register save area; and register 1 to contain the pointer to the caller-supplied parameter list.

```
                        CALLING MODULE


        IDENTIFICATION DIVISION.
        PROGRAM-ID.  MODULE1.
        ..  ..                    ..
        WORKING-STORAGE SECTION.
        01  CALLERS-PARMLIST.
            03 CBL-PARM1         PIC 9(4) COMP.
            03 CBL-PARM2         PIC X(8).
        ..  ..                    ..
        PROCEDURE DIVISION.
        CALL-MODULE2-ROUTINE.
            CALL 'MODULE2' USING CALLERS-PARMLIST.
        ..  ..                    ..


                        CALLED MODULE

MODULE2  CSECT
..       ..   ..
         BAKR  14,0              PRESERVE CALLER'S STATE ON STACK
..       ..   ..
         L     8,0(1)            ADDRESS OF PARMLIST FROM CALLER
         USING PARMLIST,8        MAP PARMLIST SUPPLIED BY CALLER
         L     5,PARM1           LOAD FIRST PARAMETER INTO R5
..       ..   ..
         PR                      POP LINKAGE STACK AND RETURN TO CALLER
PARMLIST DSECT                   DSECT THAT MAPS PARMLIST FROM CALLER
PARM1    DS    F                 FIRST PARAMETER
PARM2    DS    CL8               SECOND PARAMETER
..       ..    ..
```

Figure 2.11 A COBOL module calling an assembler module.

Note that, instead of writing the COBOL CALL statement,

CALL 'MODULE2' USING CALLERS-PARMLIST.

we could have written

CALL 'MODULE2' USING CBL-PARM1 CBL-PARM2.

The first CALL generates the parameter structure in Fig. 2.12, where register 1 points to the *address* of a parameter list. The second CALL

CALL (15),(PARMLIST)

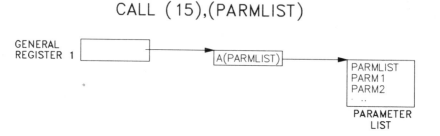

Figure 2.12   Passing a PARMLIST with CALL.

generates a parameter structure similar to Fig. 2.8, where register 1 points to a list of individual parameter addresses. The advantage of using the first type of CALL is that the called module can issue

    L   8,0(1)

to load a register with the address of the caller's parameter list and

    USING PARMLIST,8

to map the caller's parameter list with a DSECT so that it can reference the caller's parameters by labels in the DSECT rather than by explicit base register and displacement. Note how the caller's parameter list in working storage corresponds to the called program's DSECT mapping.

The parameter structure in Fig. 2.12 is similar to the way in which a module receives a parameter string when it is coded in JCL,

    // EXEC   PGM = program,PARM = 'parameter string'

and the way a module receives a parameter string when it is invoked in a TSO session:

    CALL   'library(program)' 'parameter string'

In both cases, the called program receives the address of the address of a parameter list in register 1. The first parameter in the list is a halfword containing the length of the parameter string, and the second parameter is the string itself. Programs that receive parameters from the EXEC card in batch or the parameter field in the TSO CALL command can include instructions similar to the following before processing the parameter string.

    L   1,0(1)   PARMLIST ADDRESS TO REG 1
    LH   2,0(1)   LENGTH OF PARM STRING TO REG 2
    LA   3,2(1)   ADDRESS OF PARM STRING TO REG 3

2.7.1 C Language Considerations

C programs call other programs by naming them as functions. When a C program invokes a function, it copies the function arguments (parameters) into an area of storage allocated for that purpose and loads the address of that area into general register 1. The invoked function receives a copy of the argument values and cannot change the argument variables themselves.

If the calling C program wishes to allow the invoked function to change the value in a variable, it can pass a pointer to that variable. The called program can change the variable because it receives a copy of the pointer which, just like the original pointer, points to the variable itself.

C invokes a function by loading its address into register 15 and transferring control with BALR 14,15. Functions return fixed-point and character values in general register 15 and floating-point values in floating-point registers 0 and 1.

Figure 2.13 illustrates how a C program can call an assembly language module by naming it as a function. Line 22 invokes the function "dynal" to transfer control to the DYNAL module which dynamically allocates a file. The source for DYNAL is in Appendix C.

When it is entered, DYNAL expects register 1 to contain the address of a parameter list address (as in Fig. 2.12.). Line 11 defines the parameter list, and line 12 defines a pointer variable, adparm, that contains the address of the parameter list. When line 22 calls DYNAL with "dynal(adparm)," the pointer variable's address is placed in register 1. Figure 2.14 contains assembly language code that invokes DYNAL in the same way as the C program in Fig. 2.13.

Note that the C program uses a header file, dynprm.h, to map the parmlist for the DYNAL module in much the same way as the assembly language caller uses the DYNPRM DSECT. In both cases the mapping allows the calling module to refer to parameter list fields by name rather than by explicit base and displacement.

The DYNPRM DSECT invoked in Fig. 2.14 appears in Appendix C. The dynprm.h header file appears in Fig. 2.15. Some mainframe C compilers* provide a utility program to convert an assembly language DSECT to a C header file.

When a C program receives control at the default entrypoint of MAIN, it expects register 1 to contain the address of a parameter address in the same format as that generated by // EXEC PGM = program, PARM = 'parameter string'. The C program parses the PARM= string into the argc and *argv[ ] arguments used by function MAIN. This restricts calling programs to passing parameters that can be expressed as character strings.

---

*Like the SAS C compiler which was used to test the examples in this book.

```
/*********************************************************************/   1
/*              Call DYNAL to dynamically allocate a file        */    2
/*********************************************************************/   3
#include <stdio.h>                                                       4
#include <stdlib.h>                                                      5
#include <string.h>                                                      6
#include <dynprm.h>                        /* parmlist mapping      */   7
                                                                         8
void main()                                                             9
{                                                                       10
   struct DYNPRM   parmlist;               /* parmlist for dynal    */  11
   struct DYNPRM   *adparm = &parmlist;    /* pointer to parmlist   */  12
   char space = ' ';                                                    13
                                                                        14
   memset(adparm,space,LDYNPRM);          /* initialize parmlist   */   15
                                                                        16
   strncpy(parmlist.dyfunct,"AL",2) ;      /* allocation            */  17
   strncpy(parmlist.dydisp,"SHR ",4) ;     /* DISP=SHR              */  18
   strncpy(parmlist.dydsn,"TEST.DSN",8);   /* dataset name          */  19
   strncpy(parmlist.dyddname,"TESTDD",6);  /* ddname                */  20
                                                                        21
   dynal(adparm);                          /* call dynal            */  22
```

Figure 2.13 A C module calling DYNAL.

```
            ..       ..
            LA    R5,PARMLIST           DYNAL PARMLIST ADDRESS        52
            ST    R5,ADPARM             SAVE PARMLIST ADDRESS         53
            USING DYNPRM,R5             MAP THE PARMLIST              54
            MVC   DYFUNCT(L'FUNCT),FUNCT    ..MOVE                    55
            MVC   DYDISP(L'DISP),DISP       ..VALUES                  56
            MVC   DYDSN(L'DSN),DSN          ..TO DYNAL                57
            MVC   DYDDNAME(L'DDNAME),DDNAME ..PARMLIST                58
            LA    R1,ADPARM             ADDRESS OF PARMLIST ADDRESS   59
            L     R15,=V(DYNAL)         ADDRESS OF DYNAL SERVICE      60
            BASSM R14,R15               INVOKE THE SERVICE            61
            ..       ..
FUNCT       DC    CL(L'DYFUNCT)'AL'     ALLOCATE                      80
DISP        DC    CL(L'DYDISP)'DISP'    DISP=SHR                      81
DSN         DC    CL(L'DYDSN)'TEST.DSN' DSN=TEST.DSN                  82
DDNAME      DC    CL(L'DYDDNAME)'TESTDD' DDNAME                       83
            ..       ..
ADPARM      DS    F                     ADDRESS OF PARMLIST          128
PARMLIST    DS    CL(LDYNPRM)           PARMLIST FOR DYNAL           129
            ..       ..
            DYNPRM                      DYNAL PARMLIST MAPPING       150
            ..       ..
```

Figure 2.14 An assembler module calling DYNAL.

```
/****************************************************************/  1
/*         Header file that maps parmlist for DYNAL program    */  2
/****************************************************************/  3
struct DYNPRM                                                       4
{                                                                   5
  short dyplen;             /* length of this parmlist      */  6
  short dyreturn;           /* return code                  */  7
  short dyreason;           /* reason code                  */  8
  char  dyfunct[2];         /* function requested           */  9
  char  dyddname[8];        /* ddname                       */  10
  char  dydsn[44];          /* dataset name                 */  11
  char  dydisp[4];          /* disp=(xxx,)                  */  12
  char  dyndisp[6];         /* disp=(,xxx)                  */  13
  char  dycdisp[6];         /* disp=(,,xxx)                 */  14
  char  dyatype[4];         /* allocation type (trk,cyl)    */  15
  int   dyprim;             /* primary allocation           */  16
  int   dysec;              /* secondary allocation         */  17
  int   dydir;              /* directory blocks for dsorg = po */  18
  char  dyrecfm[4];         /* recfm (F, FB, V, VB, FBA, etc.) */  19
  short dylrecl;            /* logical record length        */  20
  short dyblksiz;           /* block size                   */  21
  char  dydsorg[2];         /* dsorg                        */  22
  char  dyunit[8];          /* unit type                    */  23
  char  dyvolser[6];        /* vol=ser=                     */  24
  char  dy99err[4];         /* error data from SVC 99       */  25
  char  _f0[80];            /* filler                       */  26
#define LDYNPRM 200         /* length of this parmlist      */  27
};                                                                  28
                                                                   29
typedef struct DYNPRM DYNPRM;                                      30
int  dynal(DYNPRM *p);      /* function prototype           */  31
```

Figure 2.15   C header file functioning like a DSECT.

register 1 is expected to contain a standard MVS parameter list like that illustrated in Fig. 2.8, consisting of parameter addresses. Figure 2.16 illustrates how an assembly language program can provide a standard MVS parameter list to a C program by invoking the C program at entry-point $MAINC (line 38).

2.8 ASSEMBLY AND LINK EDIT

Figure 2.17 illustrates JCL for a job that compiles a COBOL source module in STEP1, assembles an assembler language source in STEP2, and combines the object modules produced in the first two steps into a load module in STEP3. The flow of the job is illustrated in Fig. 2.18.

The first library in the //SYSLIB concatenation in the assembly step represents libraries that contain user- and installation-written assembly language macros and source code brought into source modules by COPY statements. Libraries that contain macros that set up reentrancy, such as those in Appendix A, and macros that contain DSECTs that map user-created control blocks are placed at this point in the JCL. The other libraries in the SYSLIB concatenation contain IBM-supplied macros that

```
                              CALLING MODULE

          ..      ..
          LA    R15,ARGV1              ..ADDRESS OF 1ST ARGUMENT          30
          ST    R15,PARMLIST           ..TO PARMLIST                     31
          LA    R15,ARGV2               ..ADDRESS OF 2ND ARGUMENT        32
          ST    R15,PARMLIST+4          ..TO PARMLIST                    33
          LA    R15,ARGV3              ..ADDRESS OF 3RD ARGUMENT         34
          ST    R15,PARMLIST+8          ..TO PARMLIST                    35
          OI    PARMLIST+8,X'80'       SET HIGH-ORDER BIT IN LAST PARM   36
          LA    R1,PARMLIST            ADDRESS OF PARMLIST TO R1         37
          L     R15,=V($MAINC)         SPECIAL ENTRYPOINT TO C PROGRAM   38
          BASSM R14,R15                INVOKE THE C PROGRAM              39
          ..      ..
ARGV1     DC    C'123.123'             1ST ARGUMENT                      72
ARGV2     DC    C'456.456'             2ND ARGUMENT                      73
          ..      ..
PARMLIST  DS    3F                     PARMLIST IN WORKING STORAGE       95
ARGV3     DS    CL10                   THIRD ARGUMENT IN WORKIN STORAGE  96
..        ..      ..


                              CALLED MODULE

/*****************************************************************/  1
/* This program receives 2 character format numbers.  It converts the */  2
/*  numbers to floating-point, adds them, and converts the sum back    */  3
/*  to character format in the parameter list supplied by caller.      */  4
/*****************************************************************/  5
#include <stdio.h>                                                  6
#include <stdlib.h>                                                 7
                                                                    8
void main(int argc, char *argv[])                                   9
{                                                                  10
   float f1,f2,f3;                                                 11
                                                                   12
   f1 = atof(argv[1]);              /* convert 1st arg to float */  13
   f2 = atof(argv[2]);              /* convert 2nd arg to float */  14
   f3 = f1 + f2 ;                   /* add the two numbers      */  15
   sprintf(argv[3],"%f",f3);        /* result to third arg      */  16
}                                                                  17
```

Figure 2.16   An assembler program calling a C program.

```
//MAKELOAD JOB ()
//*-------------------------------------------------------------------*
//*        COBOL COMPILE SOURCE MODULE TO PRODUCE AN OBJECT MODULE    *
//*-------------------------------------------------------------------*
//STEP1     EXEC PGM=IKFCBL00,REGION=2048K,PARM='DECK,TERM,NOLOAD,SYST'
//SYSLIB    DD   DISP=SHR,DSN=user.copylib
//SYSPRINT  DD   SYSOUT=*
//SYSTERM   DD   SYSOUT=*
//SYSUT1    DD   UNIT=VIO,SPACE=(CYL,(2,2))
//SYSUT2    DD   UNIT=VIO,SPACE=(CYL,(2,2))
//SYSUT3    DD   UNIT=VIO,SPACE=(CYL,(2,2))
//SYSUT4    DD   UNIT=VIO,SPACE=(CYL,(2,2))
//SYSIN     DD   DISP=SHR,DSN=user.source.library(module1)
//SYSPUNCH  DD   DISP=SHR,DSN=user.object.library(module1)
//*-------------------------------------------------------------------*
//*        ASSEMBLE SOURCE MODULE TO PRODUCE AN OBJECT MODULE     *
//*-------------------------------------------------------------------*
//STEP2     EXEC PGM=IEV90,PARM='LIST,XREF(SHORT),DECK,TERM,TEST'
//SYSLIB    DD   DISP=SHR,DSN=user.maclib
//          DD   DISP=SHR,DSN=SYS1.MACLIB
//          DD   DISP=SHR,DSN=SYS1.AMODGEN
//          DD   DISP=SHR,DSN=SYS1.MODGEN
//SYSPRINT  DD   SYSOUT=*
//SYSTERM   DD   SYSOUT=*
//SYSUT1    DD   SPACE=(CYL,(1,1)),UNIT=VIO
//SYSUT2    DD   SPACE=(CYL,(1,1)),UNIT=VIO
//SYSUT3    DD   SPACE=(CYL,(1,1)),UNIT=VIO
//SYSIN     DD   DISP=SHR,DSN=user.source.library(module2)
//SYSPUNCH  DD   DISP=SHR,DSN=user.object.library(module2)
//*-------------------------------------------------------------------*
//*        LINK THE OBJECT MODULES PRODUCED IN STEPS 1 AND 2          *
//*        WITH A LOAD MODULE TO PRODUCE A COMBINED LOAD MODULE       *
//*-------------------------------------------------------------------*
//STEP3     EXEC PGM=IEWL,PARM='XREF,LIST,CAL'
//SYSLIB    DD   DISP=SHR,DSN=SYS1.COBV2R4.VSCLLIB
//SYSPRINT  DD   SYSOUT=*
//OBJECT    DD   DISP=SHR,DSN=user.object.library
//LOADMODS  DD   DISP=SHR,DSN=load.library1
//SYSLMOD   DD   DISP=SHR,DSN=load.library2
//SYSUT1    DD   UNIT=(3380,SEP=(SYSLMOD,SYSLIN)),SPACE=(1024,(200,20))
//SYSLIN    DD   *
          ENTRY    MODULE1
          INCLUDE  OBJECT(MODULE1,MODULE2)
          INCLUDE  LOADMODS(MODULE3)
          NAME     PROGRAM1(R)
/*
```

Figure 2.17 Assembly and link edit JCL.

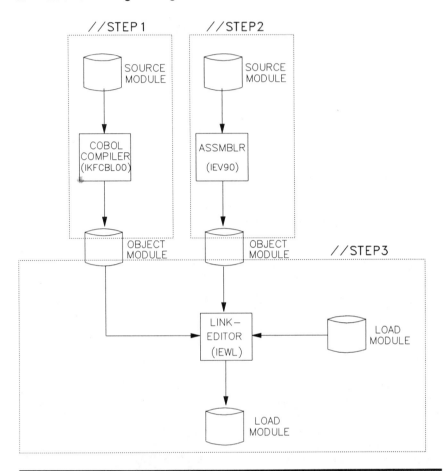

Figure 2.18   Assembly and link edit.

invoke MVS component services and map MVS control blocks. Note that SYS1.MODGEN exists only on MVS/ESA systems.

STEP3 illustrates how the link editor can accept object modules and load modules as input. The link editor attempts to resolve external symbol references in modules by matching them with external symbol definitions in other modules. (See Chap. 8 for a description of external symbols in load modules.) If PARM = CAL is used on the EXEC statement, the link editor searches the libraries named in the //SYSLIB DD concatenation for modules containing external symbols not resolved in modules explicitly named in INCLUDE control statements.

The link edit control statements under the //SYSLIN DD card perform the following functions:

■ ENTRY: names the label on a CSECT, START, or ENTRY statement in any of the modules that are being combined into the new load module that will receive control when a branch is taken to the module. The entry point does not have to be in the first CSECT of the new load module.

■ INCLUDE: specifies object and load modules that are to be included in the resulting load module. The format for INCLUDE is:

DDNAME(member, . . . , member)

where DDNAME refers to a DD card for a load or object library you have added to the link edit JCL.

■ NAME: is the PDS member name of the new load module created in the load library specified by the //SYSLMOD DD card. The member name is what you code on the // EXEC PGM= card to load a module at the beginning of a job step and what you code on the the EP= operand of LOAD, LINK, ATTACH, and XCTL to dynamically load a module in a program. If possible, it is good practice to give the same name to the load module on the NAME card as to the entry point symbol on the ENTRY card since it obviates the need for external documentation relating the entry point name to the module name. The (R) after the module name indicates that the new load module will replace any existing module with that name in the load library.

3

Multiuser Code

3.1 WHY MULTIUSER CODE

Consider the millions of input/output-related operations that are performed on a large production machine every day. If MVS were to load the modules for access methods, I/O drivers, and Input/Output Supervisor (IOS) into storage each time a user wanted to do a read or a write operation, there would be few computer resources left for useful work. Storage would be consumed by the multiple copies of these modules; CPU cycles would by used by the MVS Program Manager to bring the modules into storage, keep track of them once there, and delete them when the users' tasks were completed.

If single copies of each of the most heavily used MVS modules could be loaded into storage at system initialization and if these copies could be used by any task that needed the services that each module provided, the savings in resource utilization would increase geometrically in proportion to the number of users of each module.

Most of MVS's code resides in the MVS Nucleus and in the Pageable Link Pack Area (PLPA) in storage. The modules, loaded into these areas at system initialization, can be used by any process that requires the services these modules provide; multiple users, running on separate CPUs in a multiengine machine, can execute the single copy of a PLPA or Nucleus module at the same time.

Code that you write can also be multiuser. Logical extensions of the operating system such as MVS exits or special-purpose SVC routines, and even heavily used application routines, can take advantage of the same efficiencies that MVS exploits for its own code.

3.2 TYPES OF MODULES

When object modules are link-edited, parameters on the PARM= field are used to assign attributes to the resulting load module. (See Chap. 8 for a full discussion of assembly and link edit parameters.) The link editor writes the attributes describing a module as multiuser into the user-data field in the PDS directory entry for each member of a load library. (You can see the attributes for the modules in SYS1.LPALIB when you browse it under TSO—the fields on the far right of the screen contain RU, RN, and RF, for "reusable," "reentrant," and "refreshable," respectively.)

Modules that are single-user are not marked in the PDS directory, and there is no link editor parameter to describe them. Such modules are called "nonreusable," meaning that a fresh copy must be loaded each time the module is used.

Some modules are multiuser in that a single copy can remain in storage and be reused, but only one user can be active in the code at a time. A module that uses a constant field as a counter but initializes the field to 0 at the beginning of the code might be used by multiple tasks if each task waited until the previous task completed before it performed the initialization. Such modules are marked "serially reusable."

If a module can support multiple users executing a single copy of the module *at the same time*, that module is marked "reentrant."

Refreshable modules, like reentrant modules, can support multiple users executing at the same time. In addition, they can be reloaded while users are actively executing them. A reentrant module that is not refreshable might contain a field that is changed once at load time. If the module were "refreshed" while users were active in it, the one-time change would be lost. Note that modules in PLPA, since they are paged in but never paged out, cannot be changed in any way and must be refreshable even if they are not link-edited with the REFR parameter. All of the program examples in this book are refreshable with the exception of HOOKSVC in Appendix C, which is reentrant.

3.3 HOW MULTIUSER CODE WORKS

Figure 3.1 illustrates single-user modules. Two tasks, represented by TCBs (task control blocks), are active simultaneously in separate address spaces. Code executing in address space 1 issues a LOAD macro for a load module stored on DASD, and the Program Management component of MVS brings the module into storage. Code executing in address space

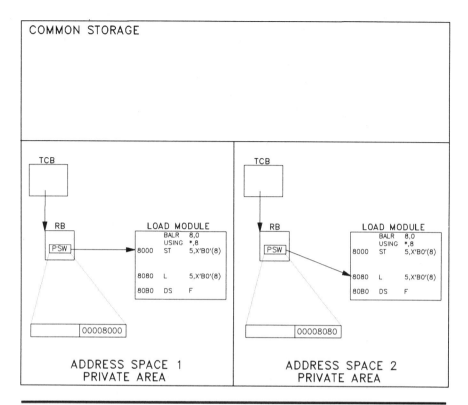

Figure 3.1 Single-user modules.

2 issues a LOAD macro for the same module, and another copy is loaded into address space 2's private area. If both tasks are executing at the same time on different CPUs in a multiprocessor complex (such as a 3090/200, 3090/400, etc.), multiple copies of the same code may exist in real storage and be executing at the same time, but each copy will have only one user.

Figure 3.2 shows two tasks executing the same module at the same time, but since the module has been loaded into a common storage area (CSA, PLPA, MLPA, or the MVS Nucleus), only one copy of the module exists in real storage. This is obviously a more efficient use of resources. The storage requirements for the module are cut in half and, since only one LOAD was issued for the module, the use of Program Management services is reduced, thus saving CPU cycles.

However, code that is shared by multiple tasks must be written in a special way. Simply loading code into common storage does not make it shareable by multiple users. Suppose in Fig. 3.2 that instead of executing two separate copies of the load module, the tasks in address spaces 1 and 2 execute the same physical copy that has been loaded into common storage (note that the addresses are now in the common, rather than the

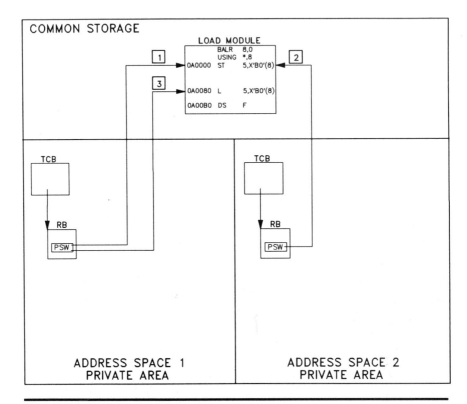

Figure 3.2 Single-user module with multiple users.

private, area of virtual storage.) The following sequence of events might occur:

1. The task in address space 1 is dispatched and executes the ST instruction at address 0A0000, storing the contents of register 5 in the 4 bytes beginning at 0A00B0.

The task in address space 1 takes an I/O interrupt. The PSW, which now points to the instruction after the ST, is saved in the RB by the First Level Interrupt Handler (FLIH).

2. The task in address space 2 is dispatched and executes the ST instruction at 0A0000. This stores the contents of register 5 in the same 4 bytes used by the task in address space 1, thus *overlaying* what the task in address space 1 stored.

3. The task in address space 1 gets redispatched and starts executing instructions from the address in the PSW saved in the RB. When the L instruction at address 0A0080 is executed, instead of loading register 5 with the value that task in address space 1 stored at address 0A00B0, it picks up the value stored there by the task in address space 2.

Figure 3.3 illustrates the solution to the problem of overlay when several users share the same piece of code. The two tasks are still executing under their individual TCBs in separate address spaces. The load module has now been loaded into common storage. But the 4 bytes that are the operand of the ST and the L instructions are no longer part of the module. Each task in each address space has a unique area of working storage associated with it and the 4 bytes exist there. Overlay cannot occur because each task has its own copy of the values that could be changed by another task executing the same code.

But how does each task "know" to use its own working storage? The answer lies in the way MVS handles the registers for a task when it is interrupted. When a task is interrupted, the FLIH saves the values in the CPU's general registers into the executing program's Request Block (RB). When Task Management readies the task to be dispatched again, it moves the register values to the TCB. When the dispatcher activates the task, it loads the CPU's registers from the TCB. If the working storage for a task is addressed by one of the registers reloaded from the TCB, the

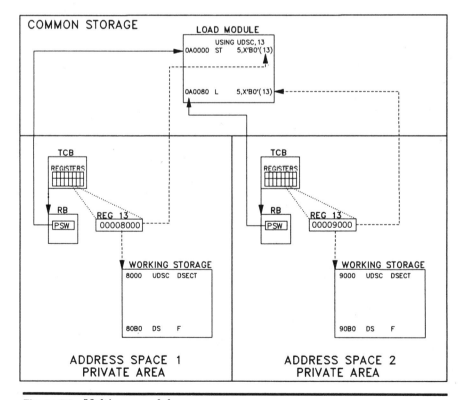

Figure 3.3   Multiuser module.

instruction operands that use that register as a base register will reference the working storage that belongs to that task.

The same sequence of events that causes an overlay when the two tasks execute the same module will now work as follows (refer to Fig. 3.3):

1. The task in address space 1 is dispatched and executes the ST instruction at address 0A0000. Since the target operand of the store has 13 as a base register, and since register 13 contains 8000, this instruction stores the value in register 5 in the 4 bytes at 80B0 in address space 1. Address space 1's page and segment tables are used for the DAT translation of the virtual address 80B0.

The task in address space 1 takes an interrupt. The First Level Interrupt Handler saves the PSW (containing the next instruction address) and the general registers, including register 13, in the RB.

2. The task in address space 2 gets dispatched. The Dispatcher loads the general registers from the TCB and the pointer to address space 2's page and segment tables for address translation. (Where this pointer has been saved and where it is loaded will be covered in Chap. 7.) When the ST at address 0A0000 is executed, the value in register 5 is stored in the 4 bytes beginning at 90B0 in address space 2's private area. The value stored by the task in address space 1 is not overlaid; it has a different address in another address space.

3. The task in address space 1 is redispatched and starts executing instructions from the address in the PSW saved in the RB. When it executes the L instruction at address 0A0080, it uses the value in register 13 restored from the TCB and address space 1's page and segment tables to retrieve the value that it saved at address 80B0 in address space 1.

The task in address space 2, when it is redispatched, will use the value in register 13 from its own TCB and address space 2's page and segment tables to retrieve the value that it saved at address 90B0 in address space 2.

3.4 REENTRANT PROGRAM STUBS

Figures 3.4, 3.5, and 3.6 contain code that can run in common storage and be shared by multiple users. The examples are written in the form of programs stubs that you can use to build reentrant modules. Fig. 3.4 will run in an XA or ESA environment, since it uses only the XA instruction set. Fig. 3.5 will run only in an ESA system and will exploit some of the features of the ESA architecture. (It uses the linkage stack and can be called by access register mode programs—see Chaps. 7 and 10.)

Figure 3.6 uses assembly language macros that will give an XA or ESA expansion depending on the SPLEVEL at assemble time (see Chap. 1). The source code for the macros is given in Appendix A.

```
                TITLE 'MVS/XA FRAME FOR REENTERABLE CODE'                    1
*+-------------------------------------------------------------------+      2
*|                         MAINTENANCE LOG                            |      3
*+----------+--------------------------------------+---------+--------+      4
*| DATE     |      DESCRIPTION                      | CHANGED | REFER  |      5
*+----------+--------------------------------------+---------+--------+      6
*| 01/04/91 | WRITTEN                               | MJM     |        |      7
*+----------+--------------------------------------+---------+--------+      8
*                                                                    |      9
*+-------------------------------------------------------------------+     10
*|  THIS IS A SAMPLE FRAME FOR REENTERABLE CODE UNDER MVS/XA.        |     11
*|  TO USE THIS FRAME:                                               |     12
*|                                                                   |     13
*|  1) PUT DATE WRITTEN AND AUTHOR IN MAINTENANCE LOG.               |     14
*|  2) FILL IN THE INTERNAL DOCUMENTATION IN THE SECTION BELOW.      |     15
*|  3) CHANGE ALL "XAFRAME" TO THE CSECT NAME.                       |     16
*|  4) SET THE AMODE AND RMODE AND THE SUBPOOL FOR                   |     17
*|     "GETMAIN" AND "FREEMAIN" MACROS.                              |     18
*|  5) PUT CODE, CONSTANTS, WORK AREA FIELDS ETC. IN PLACE           |     19
*|     OF THE LINES MARKED "*====>"                                  |     20
*|  6) ASSEMBLE AND LINK-EDIT WITH THE "RENT" PARAMETER.             |     21
*+-------------------------------------------------------------------+     22
*                                                                    |     23
*+-------------------------------------------------------------------+     24
*|  FUNCTION:                                                        |     25
*|                                                                   |     26
*|  INPUTS:                                                          |     27
*|                                                                   |     28
*|  OUTPUTS:                                                         |     29
*|                                                                   |     30
*|  PROGRAM LOGIC:                                                   |     31
*|                                                                   |     32
*|  MODULES CALLED:                                                  |     33
*|                                                                   |     34
*|  DSECTS:                                                          |     35
*|                                                                   |     36
*|  ATTRIBUTES:                                                      |     37
*|                                                                   |     38
*+-------------------------------------------------------------------+     39
XAFRAME  CSECT                                                             40
*        *----------------------------------------*                        41
*        *      SPECIFY AMODE AND RMODE          *                         42
*        *----------------------------------------*                        43
XAFRAME  AMODE 31                                                          44
XAFRAME  RMODE ANY                                                         45
*        *----------------------------------------*                        46
*        *      REGISTER SAVE AREAS              *                         47
*        *----------------------------------------*                        48
WXAFRAME DSECT               USER ACQUIRED STORAGE FOR REENTRABLE          49
GENREGS  DS    18F           GENERAL REGISTER SAVE AREA                    50
FLTREGS  DS    4D            FLOATING POINT REGISTER SAVE AREA             51
XAFRAME  CSECT                                                             52
*        *----------------------------------------*                        53
*        *      REGISTER EQUATES                 *                         54
*        *----------------------------------------*                        55
         PRINT NOGEN                                                       56
         COPY  EQUATES               REGISTER EQUATES                      57
```

Figure 3.4 Reentrant program stub for MVS/XA.

```
          PRINT GEN                                                  58
*         *-------------------------------------*                    59
*         *    ENTRY POINT                      *                    60
*         *-------------------------------------*                    61
          USING XAFRAME,15          ADDRESSING ON ENTRY POINT        62
          B     BEGIN               BRANCH AROUND EYECATCHER         63
          DC    C' XAFRAME '         CSECT NAME                      64
          DC    C' &SYSDATE '        DATE OF ASSEMBLY                65
          DC    C' &SYSTIME '        TIME OF ASSEMBLY                66
BEGIN     DS    0H                                                   67
          STM   14,12,12(13)        SAVE REGISTERS IN CALLER'S SAVEAREA  68
          LR    12,15               LOAD BASE REGISTER WITH ENTRY POINT  69
          DROP  15                  DROP ADDRESSING ON ENTRY POINT   70
          USING XAFRAME,12          SET ADDRESSING ON BASE REGISTER  71
*         *-------------------------------------*                    72
*         *    GET STORAGE FOR WORK AREA        *                    73
*         *-------------------------------------*                    74
          LA    0,LXAFRAME          LENGTH OF STORAGE                75
          GETMAIN RU,               UNCONDITIONAL REGISTER GETMAIN  X 76
                LV=(0),             LENGTH OF STORAGE               X 77
                LOC=BELOW,          BELOW 16M                       X 78
                SP=1                SUBPOOL OF STORAGE                79
          LR    2,13                A(CALLER'S SAVE AREA) => R2      80
          ST    13,4(1)             SAVE A(CALLER'S SAVE AREA)       81
          ST    1,8(13)             A(SAVE AREA) => CALLER'S SAVE AREA  82
          LR    13,1                A(SAVE AREA FOR THIS MODULE) => R13  83
          USING WXAFRAME,13         ADDRESSING FOR SAVE AREA         84
          LM    14,2,12(2)          RESTORE REGS 14 - 2  FROM CALLER'S  85
          STD   0,FLTREGS           ..SAVE                           86
          STD   2,FLTREGS+8         ..FLOATING                       87
          STD   4,FLTREGS+16        ..POINT                          88
          STD   6,FLTREGS+24        ..REGISTERS                      89
*======> ADD EXECUTABLE CODE HERE <===================================  90
          B     EXIT00              BRANCH TO EXIT ROUTINE           91
*-----------------------------------------------------------------*   92
*         EXIT ROUTINES                                           *   93
*-----------------------------------------------------------------*   94
*         *-------------------------------------*                    95
*         *    EXIT WITH RETURN CODE = 0        *                    96
*         *-------------------------------------*                    97
EXIT00    DS    0H                                                   98
          LA    15,X'00'                                             99
          B     EXIT                                                100
*======> ADD ADDITIONAL EXITS WITH RETURN CODES HERE <=================  101
*-----------------------------------------------------------------*  102
*         COMMON EXIT                                             *  103
*-----------------------------------------------------------------*  104
EXIT      DS    0H                                                  105
          LD    0,FLTREGS           ..RESTORE                       106
          LD    2,FLTREGS+8         ..FLOATING                      107
          LD    4,FLTREGS+16        ..POINT                         108
          LD    6,FLTREGS+24        ..REGISTERS                     109
          LA    0,LXAFRAME          LENGTH OF STORAGE               110
          LR    1,13                ADDRESS OF WORK AREA => R1       111
          L     13,GENREGS+4        ADDRESS OF CALLER'S SAVE AREA   112
          ST    15,16(,13)          RETURN CODE TO CALLER'S R15     113
```

Figure 3.4 *(Continued)*

```
*        *------------------------------------*              114
*        *     FREE WORK AREA STORAGE          *              115
*        *------------------------------------*              116
         FREEMAIN RU,                                      X 117
              LV=(0),         LENGTH OF STORAGE            X 118
              A=(1),          ADDRESS OF STORAGE           X 119
              SP=1            SUBPOOL OF STORAGE              120
         LM   14,12,12(13)    RESTORE CALLER'S REGISTERS     121
         BSM  0,14            RESTORE AMODE AND RETURN        122
*        *------------------------------------*              123
*        *     LITERALS                        *              124
*        *------------------------------------*              125
         LTORG                                               126
*---------------------------------------------------------*  127
*        CONSTANTS                                        *  128
*---------------------------------------------------------*  129
*======> PUT CONSTANTS HERE <=============================== 130
*---------------------------------------------------------*  131
*        WORK AREA                                        *  132
*---------------------------------------------------------*  133
WXAFRAME DSECT                                               134
*======> PUT WORK AREA FIELDS HERE <======================== 135
LXAFRAME EQU  *-WXAFRAME                                     136
*---------------------------------------------------------*  137
*        OTHER DSECTS                                     *  138
*---------------------------------------------------------*  139
*======> PUT ADDITIONAL DSECTS HERE <======================= 140
         END                                                141
```

Figure 3.4 *(Continued)*

3.4.1 Reentrant Program Stub for MVS/XA

Lines 1 through 39 in Fig. 3.4 contain documentation for the module. You can look through some of the other program examples in this book to see how the internal documentation sections are used.

It is good practice, from a design and source-code management standpoint, to restrict object modules to single CSECTs and to have each CSECT represent code that has a single function.* If, in the program documentation section, you can describe the module in one simple sentence, your module probably has a single function. Single-function modules can be used as "building blocks" called by any routine that requires that simple, single function. Ideally, programs are built by linking the building blocks together. New programs can be written very quickly when they can call modules that perform discrete services.

The CSECT statement and the AMODE and RMODE statements on lines 40 through 45 begin the module and set the addressing and residency modes.

---

*See Glenford J. Meyers, *Reliable Software through Composite Design*, New York: Van Nostrand Reinhold, Inc., 1975.

Lines 46 through 51 and lines 131 through 136 together constitute the DSECT that maps the working storage that each user acquires. DSECTs do not generate object code. They allow you to use labels, rather than explicit base and displacement notation, to refer to areas for which storage was not obtained at program load time. In this case, each user obtains working storage with the GETMAIN in lines 72 through 79. In line 83 the address of the storage, returned by GETMAIN in register 1, is loaded into register 13. The USING WXAFRAME,13 on line 84 causes the assembler to resolve labels in the DSECT as displacements off register 13.

The CSECT that is interrupted for the beginning of the working storage DSECT is resumed with the CSECT statement on line 52.

Lines 64 through 66 assemble into an "eyecatcher" with the date and time of assembly and the CSECT name. When examining a dump or looking at storage on the live system (with OMEGAMON, RESOLVE, or a similar product), the eyecatcher makes it easy to locate the code and verify the maintenance level. Most IBM modules contain eyecatchers that include CSECT name, date, time of assembly, and the names of PTFs that have been applied.

The execution of this module begins at line 63 with a branch around the eyecatcher. The module assumes that standard register usage conventions have been observed by the caller and that registers 1, 13, 14, and 15 contain parameter list address, caller's save area address, return address, and entry point address respectively. If this module calls another module, that module can make the same assumptions.

Line 68 saves the registers at entry in the caller's save area. Line 69 loads the entry point address into the base register, and the USING on line 61 tells the assembler to use the entry point address as the base for operand displacement resolution. BALR 12,0, USING 12,* is not coded, since this loads the address of the instruction *after* the BALR into the after base register. As a consequence, displacements for operand addresses in the object code will not correspond to the location counter values for the operand labels in the listing. This can be confusing when debugging a module. When the base register contains the same value as the entry point address, the location counter will match up with displacements in operand addresses in the object code.

Lines 76 through 79 invoke the services of Virtual Storage Manager to acquire unique working storage for each caller in his own address space (see Fig. 3.3). The LA 0,LXAFRAME on line 75 loads the length of the working storage DSECT into register 0. The way LXAFRAME on line 136 is coded is a good example of making a program "self-maintaining" by creative use of the assembler. If a field is added to the working storage DSECT, * (the current value of the location counter) in *-WXAFRAME will increase by the length of the field. The subtraction of the two location counter values, * and WXAFRAME, will always equal the length of the DSECT and therefore the amount of storage that is needed for the GET-MAIN.

Note that the total length of the DSECT must not exceed 4096 bytes. The LA instruction on line 75 assembles as a displacement with no base register, and the displacement field in object code is only 12 bits long. If your program needs more than 4K working storage, do GETMAINs and save the addresses of the GETMAINed areas in the working storage. (GETMAIN and FREEMAIN are covered in more detail in Chap. 4.) In this case, GETMAIN returns the address of the obtained storage in register 1.

Line 80 temporarily puts the address of the caller's save area into register 2. This allows the values in registers 0, 1, and 2 (which are destroyed by the GETMAIN and the next four instructions) to be restored from the caller's save area by the LM 14,2,12(2) on line 85. This is necessary since register 1 may contain the address of an input parameter list.

Line 81 saves the address of the caller's save area in the working storage, and line 82 back-chains the address of the save area for this module into the caller's save area. Note that the register save area is the first 18 fullwords of the GETMAINed working storage (line 50). Line 83 loads the address of the save area into register 13. If this module calls another module, that module will receive the address of a save area in register 13.

Each user of this module has obtained a unique working storage area in which he includes a register save area and has loaded its address into register 13. The USING WXAFRAME,13 on line 84 causes labels for fields in the working storage to be resolved using register 13 as the base register.

Lines 86 through 89 save the floating point registers in the work area. Note that the numbers for register operands (e.g., the 2 in STD 2,FLTREGS+8) refer, not to one of the 16 general registers, but to one of the four even-odd pairs of floating point registers. If you do not write code that makes use of the floating point registers, you can omit these lines as well as lines 106 through 109, where the floating point registers are restored, as well as the four doublewords on line 51, where the floating point registers are saved.

Lines 90 and 91 represent the code that you will insert to make this stub into a module that performs a useful function. Lines 95 through 100 contain an exit routine that will cause the module to return X'00' in register 15. Modules should always return a return code, and callers should always check the return code. Any additional exit routines that you may want to add at line 101 should load register 15 with a unique return code. The condition that the return code represents should be documented in the OUTPUTS section of the documentation (after line 29). In addition, exit routines can issue messages with WTO, put reason codes in the caller's registers 0 or 1, or perform other cleanup tasks required by the conditions that caused the program to branch to that exit. Lines 404 through 408 of the program DYNAL in Appendix C use the PERCRC macro in an exit routine to pass the return code from a system service back to the caller as reason codes in registers 0 and 1. The source for PERCRC is in Appendix A.

Setting up exit routines in this manner, rather than loading return codes and performing exit functions in the body of the code, makes it easier to keep track of the various error conditions since they are all together in the source listing. It also makes the logic in the body of the code easier to follow.

All the exit routines end with a branch to one common exit on line 105. After line 111 preserves the address of the working storage in register 1 for the FREEMAIN on lines 114 through 120, line 112 loads the address of the caller's save area into register 13. Line 113 saves the return code into the register 15 slot in the caller's save area so it will be reloaded when the LM on line 121 restores the caller's registers.

FREEMAIN invokes Virtual Storage Management services to release the work area storage. Note that line 122 issues a BSM 0,14 rather than a BR 14 to return to the caller. This allows this module, whatever its AMODE (in line 44), to be called by 24- or 31-bit callers and to return control in the same AMODE.

The LTORG on line 126 causes literals used in the body of the code to assemble within the CSECT. Without LTORG they would assemble in the work area DSECT. Additional DSECTS that map parameter lists and user or system control blocks can be included after the work area DSECT where noted on line 137.

3.4.2 REENTRANT PROGRAM STUB FOR MVS/ESA

The frame for ESA-only code in Fig. 3.5 performs the same function as the XA frame, but it uses the ESA linkage stack rather than the caller's save area to preserve the caller's registers. (Addressing modes, features of ESA architecture, and how to use the ESA features in your code are covered in Chap. 7.) While the XA example in Fig. 3.4 can only be called by callers in primary space addressing mode, this ESA module can be called by programs in any addressing mode. Lines 77 and 117 use the STORAGE macro rather than GETMAIN and FREEMAIN to obtain and release private area storage for the work area. GETMAIN and

```
            TITLE 'MVS/ESA FRAME FOR REENTERABLE CODE'                      1
*+--------------------------------------------------------------------+    2
*|                       MAINTENANCE LOG                              |    3
*+-----------+----------------------------------------+---------+--------+  4
*|  DATE     |           DESCRIPTION                  | CHANGED | REFER  |  5
*+-----------+----------------------------------------+---------+--------+  6
*| 01/04/91  | WRITTEN                                | MJM     |        |  7
*+-----------+----------------------------------------+---------+--------+  8
*                                                                      |    9
*+--------------------------------------------------------------------+   10
*|    THIS IS A SAMPLE FRAME FOR REENTERABLE CODE UNDER MVS/ESA.      |   11
*|    TO USE THIS FRAME:                                              |   12
*|                                                                   |   13
*|    1) PUT DATE WRITTEN AND AUTHOR IN MAINTENANCE LOG.             |   14
*|    2) FILL IN THE INTERNAL DOCUMENTATION IN THE SECTION BELOW.    |   15
*|    4) CHANGE ALL "ESFRAME" TO CSECT NAME.                         |   16
*|    3) SET THE AMODE AND RMODE AND THE SUBPOOL FOR "STORAGE" MACRO.|   17
*|    5) PUT CODE, CONSTANTS, WORK AREA FIELDS ETC. IN PLACE         |   18
*|       OF THE LINES MARKED "*====>"                               |   19
*|    6) ASSEMBLE AND LINK-EDIT WITH THE "RENT" PARAMETER.           |   20
*+--------------------------------------------------------------------+   21
*                                                                      |   22
*+--------------------------------------------------------------------+   23
*|    FUNCTION:                                                       |   24
*|                                                                   |   25
*|    INPUTS:                                                         |   26
*|                                                                   |   27
*|    OUTPUTS:                                                        |   28
*|                                                                   |   29
*|    PROGRAM LOGIC:                                                  |   30
*|                                                                   |   31
*|    MODULES CALLED:                                                 |   32
*|                                                                   |   33
*|    DSECTS:                                                         |   34
*|                                                                   |   35
*|    ATTRIBUTES:                                                     |   36
*|                                                                   |   37
*+--------------------------------------------------------------------+   38
ESFRAME   CSECT                                                            39
*         *------------------------------------------*                     40
*         *     SPECIFY AMODE AND RMODE             *                     41
*         *------------------------------------------*                     42
ESFRAME   AMODE 31                                                         43
ESFRAME   RMODE ANY                                                        44
*         *------------------------------------------*                     45
*         *     REGISTER SAVE AREAS                 *                     46
*         *------------------------------------------*                     47
WESFRAME  DSECT                      USER ACQUIRED STORAGE FOR REENTRABLE   48
GENREGS   DS    18F                  GENERAL REGISTER SAVE AREA            49
FLTREGS   DS    4D                   FLOATING POINT REGISTER SAVE AREA     50
STRGLEN   DS    F                    LENGTH OF STORAGE                     51
ESFRAME   CSECT                                                            52
*         *------------------------------------------*                     53
*         *     REGISTER EQUATES                    *                     54
*         *------------------------------------------*                     55
          PRINT NOGEN                                                      56
          COPY EQUATES               REGISTER EQUATES                      57
```

Figure 3.5 Reentrant program stub for MVS/ESA.

```
            PRINT GEN                                                       58
*           *------------------------------------------*                    59
*           *    ENTRY POINT                     *                          60
*           *------------------------------------------*                    61
            USING ESFRAME,15          ADDRESSING ON ENTRY POINT             62
            B     BEGIN               BRANCH AROUND EYECATCHER              63
            DC    C' ESFRAME '        CSECT NAME                            64
            DC    C' &SYSDATE '       DATE OF ASSEMBLY                      65
            DC    C' &SYSTIME '       TIME OF ASSEMBLY                      66
STACKLIT    DC    C'F1SA'             CALLER'S SAVE AREA ON STACK           67
BEGIN       BAKR  14,0                PUSH REGISTERS AND PSW ONTO STACK     68
            MSTA  0                   INITIALIZE MODIFIED AREA TO REGS 0,1  69
            LAE   12,0(15,0)          LOAD BASE REGISTER WITH ENTRY POINT   70
            DROP  15                  DROP ADDRESSING ON ENTRY POINT        71
            USING ESFRAME,12          SET ADDRESSING ON BASE REGISTER       72
*           *------------------------------------------*                    73
*           *    GET STORAGE FOR WORK AREA        *                         74
*           *------------------------------------------*                    75
            LA    0,LESFRAME          LENGTH OF WORK AREA STORAGE           76
            STORAGE OBTAIN,COND=NO,   OBTAIN WORK AREA STORAGE            X  77
                  LENGTH=(0),         LENGTH OF STORAGE                   X  78
                  SP=1,               STORAGE SUBPOOL                     X  79
                  ADDR=(1)            ADDRESS OF STORAGE OBTAINED            80
            ST    1,8(0,13)           A(SAVE AREA) => CALLER'S SAVE AREA    81
            LAE   13,0(1,0)           A(SAVE AREA THIS CSECT) => R13        82
*                                     INDICATE CALLER'S SAVEAREA ON STACK   83
            MVC   4(L'STACKLIT,13),STACKLIT                                 84
            USING WESFRAME,13         ADDRESSING FOR SAVE AREA              85
            ST    0,STRGLEN           SAVE SUBPOOL AND LENGTH               86
            EREG  14,2                EXTRACT REGS FROM STACK               87
            STD   0,FLTREGS           ..SAVE                                88
            STD   2,FLTREGS+8         ..FLOATING                            89
            STD   4,FLTREGS+16        ..POINT                               90
            STD   6,FLTREGS+24        ..REGISTERS                           91
*======> ADD EXECUTABLE CODE HERE <====================================     92
            B     EXIT00              BRANCH TO EXIT ROUTINE                 93
*-------------------------------------------------------------------*       94
*           EXITS ROUTINES                                          *       95
*-------------------------------------------------------------------*       96
*           *------------------------------------------*                    97
*           *    EXIT WITH RETURN CODE = 0       *                          98
*           *------------------------------------------*                    99
EXIT00      DS    0H                                                       100
            LA    15,X'00'            SET RETURN CODE TO X'00'             101
            B     EXIT                BRANCH TO COMMON EXIT                102
*======> ADD ADDITIONAL EXITS WITH RETURN CODES HERE <==================   103
*-------------------------------------------------------------------*      104
*           COMMON EXIT                                             *      105
*-------------------------------------------------------------------*      106
EXIT        DS    0H                                                       107
            LD    0,FLTREGS           ..RESTORE                            108
            LD    2,FLTREGS+8         ..FLOATING                           109
            LD    4,FLTREGS+16        ..POINT                              110
            LD    6,FLTREGS+24        ..REGISTERS                          111
            LA    0,LESFRAME          LENGTH OF WORK AREA STORAGE          112
            LR    2,15                RETURN CODE => R2                     113
```

Figure 3.5 *(Continued).*

```
*          *----------------------------------------*           114
*          *     RELEASE STORAGE FOR WORK AREA     *           115
*          *----------------------------------------*           116
           STORAGE RELEASE,COND=NO, FREE WORK AREA STORAGE    X 117
                    LENGTH=(0),      LENGTH OF STORAGE         X 118
                    ADDR=(13),       ADDRESS OF STORAGE        X 119
                    SP=1             STORAGE SUBPOOL             120
           LA   0,3                  ..RESTORE REGS 0 AND 1      121
           ESTA 0,0                  ..FROM STACK MODIFIABLE AREA 122
           LR   15,2                 RETURN CODE => R15          123
           PR                        RESTORE REGS AND RETURN     124
*          *----------------------------------------*           125
*          *     LITERALS                          *           126
*          *----------------------------------------*           127
           LTORG                                                128
*          *----------------------------------------*           129
*          *     CONSTANTS                         *           130
*          *----------------------------------------*           131
*======> PUT CONSTANTS HERE <=========================================  132
*----------------------------------------------------------------------* 133
*          WORK AREA                                            * 134
*----------------------------------------------------------------------* 135
WESFRAME DSECT                                                   136
*======> PUT WORK AREA FIELDS HERE <==================================  137
LESFRAME EQU   *-WESFRAME                                        138
*----------------------------------------------------------------------* 139
*          OTHER DSECTS                                         * 140
*----------------------------------------------------------------------* 141
*======> PUT ADDITIONAL DSECTS HERE <=================================  142
           END                                                  143
```

Figure 3.5 *(Continued)*

FREEMAIN cannot obtain and release private area storage while in access register (AR) addressing mode but may still be used in AR mode to obtain and release storage from common area subpools.

The BAKR 14,0 on line 68 does three things:

1. It builds a stack state entry containing the registers, current PSW, and XMS-related status.

2. It updates the linkage stack pointer.

3. It updates the second fullword (the address portion) of the PSW it saved in the stack state entry with the contents of register 14 (the return address).

When the stack is popped with the PR on line 124, the PSW loaded from the stack state entry causes the instruction at the return address to be executed. Control is returned to the caller by replacing the PSW rather than by executing a branch.

Unlike the LM 14,12,12(13) instruction on line 121 of the XA stub, the PR instruction on line 124 does not reload registers 0, 1, and 15 from the linkage stack. In order to make the ESA stub consistent with the XA stub, line 69 issues MSTA 0 to store registers 0 and 1 into the user-modifiable area of the stack state entry built by BAKR. ESTA 0,0 on line 122 restores these registers before PR returns control to the caller. The registers could have been restored from the saved registers with EREG 0,1 as in line 87, but the MSTA/ESTA combination allows exit routines to put a reason code in the modifiable area and have the reason code loaded into register 0 or 1 before returning control to the caller.

While the XA program stub used LR 12,15 to load the base register with the entry point address, line 70 of the ESA stub issues LAE 12,0(15,0) to load both the general register with the entry point virtual address and the access register with 0. Zero in an access register means the current primary address space.

3.4.3 REENTRANT PROGRAM STUB USING MACROS

The program stub in Fig. 3.6 uses the MODULE and ENDMOD macros to establish reentrancy (Appendix A contains source for the macros). These macros will expand into the same instructions as the XA stub in Fig. 3.3 or the ESA stub in Fig. 3.4, depending on the SPLEVEL in effect during the assembly. To produce an XA expansion regardless of the default SPLEVEL, uncomment line 43.

3.5 WRITING REENTRANT CODE

The guidelines for writing reentrant code are simple:

- A user may not change instructions or storage in the code. This prohibits modifying branch addresses, branch conditions, and mask bytes in instructions. It also prohibits modifying in-line parameter lists and constants in program storage.
- A user may change only the values in registers and in his own GET-MAINed working storage (a unique area for each user, addressed by a register).

Figures 3.7 and 3.8 contain snippets of code that perform the same function; they build a parameter list and call an unspecified service routine. Figure 3.7 is nonreusable, while Fig. 3.8 is reentrant.

Both examples use as the first parameter the contents of the PARM= field on the // EXEC card of a batch program. This field is of variable length. The first 2 bytes contain the length of the rest of the field (PARM='1234', for example, would look like X'0004F1F2F3F4' in storage). Fig. 3.7, after loading the address and length of the PARM= field

```
            TITLE   'FRAME FOR REENTERABLE CODE USING MACROS'            1
*+---------------------------------------------------------------------+  2
*|                         MAINTENANCE LOG                              |  3
*+----------+------------------------------------+---------+---------+  4
*| DATE     |         DESCRIPTION                 | CHANGED | REFER   |  5
*+----------+------------------------------------+---------+---------+  6
*| 01/04/91 |   WRITTEN                           | MJM     |         |  7
*+----------+------------------------------------+---------+---------+  8
*                                                                     |  9
*+---------------------------------------------------------------------+ 10
*|  THIS IS A SAMPLE FRAME FOR REENTERABLE CODE UNDER MVS.             | 11
*|  THE MACROS WILL EXPAND XA OR ESA DEPENDING ON THE SYSTEM           | 12
*|  WHERE THIS MODULE IS ASSEMBLED.  TO FORCE AN XA EXPANSION          | 13
*|  WHEN ASSEMBLING ON AN ESA SYSTEM, UNCOMMENT THE LINE CONTAINING    | 14
*|  THE "SPLEVEL" MACRO.  TO USE THIS FRAME:                           | 15
*|                                                                     | 16
*|  1) PUT DATE WRITTEN AND AUTHOR IN MAINTENANCE LOG.                 | 17
*|  2) FILL IN THE INTERNAL DOCUMENTATION IN THE SECTION BELOW.        | 18
*|  3) SET THE CSECT NAME, AMODE, RMODE AND OTHER ATTRIBUTES OF        | 19
*|     THE MODULE WITH OPERANDS ON THE "MODULE" MACRO (SEE APPENDIX).  | 20
*|  4) PUT CODE, CONSTANTS, WORK AREA FIELDS ETC. IN PLACE             | 21
*|     OF THE LINES MARKED "*====>"                                    | 22
*|  5) ASSEMBLE AND LINK-EDIT WITH THE "RENT" PARAMETER.               | 23
*+---------------------------------------------------------------------+ 24
*                                                                     | 25
*+---------------------------------------------------------------------+ 26
*|  FUNCTION:                                                          | 27
*|                                                                     | 28
*|  INPUTS:                                                            | 29
*|                                                                     | 30
*|  OUTPUTS:                                                           | 31
*|                                                                     | 32
*|  PROGRAM LOGIC:                                                     | 33
*|                                                                     | 34
*|  MODULES CALLED:                                                    | 35
*|                                                                     | 36
*|  DSECTS:                                                            | 37
*|                                                                     | 38
*|  ATTRIBUTES:                                                        | 39
*|                                                                     | 40
*+---------------------------------------------------------------------+ 41
*                                                                        42
*         SPLEVEL SET=2      UNCOMMENT THIS LINE TO FORCE XA EXPANSION   43
*                                                                        44
          MODULE MFRAME,BASE=12,LOC=BELOW,AMODE=31,RMODE=ANY,        X  45
                 TEXT='XA OR ESA FRAME FOR REENTERABLE CODE '           46
*======> ADD EXECUTABLE CODE HERE <==================================== 47
          B       EXIT00       BRANCH TO EXIT ROUTINE                   48
*----------------------------------------------------------------------* 49
*         EXIT ROUTINES                                               *  50
*----------------------------------------------------------------------* 51
*         *------------------------------------*                        52
*         *   RETURN CODE 0                    *                        53
*         *------------------------------------*                        54
EXIT00    DS      0H                                                    55
          LA      15,X'00'    SET RETURN CODE TO X'00'                  56
          B       EXIT        BRANCH TO COMMON EXIT                     57
```

Figure 3.6 Reentrant program stub using macros.

```
*======> ADD ADDITIONAL EXITS WITH RETURN CODES HERE <================   58
*-----------------------------------------------------------------*   59
*         COMMON EXIT                                              *   60
*-----------------------------------------------------------------*   61
EXIT    DS    0H                                                       62
        ENDMOD               RESTORE REGISTERS AND RETURN              63
*-----------------------------------------------------------------*   64
*         CONSTANTS                                                *   65
*-----------------------------------------------------------------*   66
*======> PUT CONSTANTS HERE <======================================   67
*-----------------------------------------------------------------*   68
*         WORK AREA                                                *   69
*-----------------------------------------------------------------*   70
WMFRAME DSECT                                                          71
*======> PUT WORK AREA FIELDS HERE <===============================   72
LMFRAME EQU    *-WMFRAME                                               73
*-----------------------------------------------------------------*   74
*         OTHER DSECTS                                             *   75
*-----------------------------------------------------------------*   76
*======> PUT ADDITIONAL DSECTS HERE <==============================   77
        END                                                           78
```

Figure 3.6 *(Continued)*

in registers 1 and 2 (statements 106 and 107), uses the STC instruction on line 109 to change the MVC instruction in statement 110 by overlaying the length field of the instruction with the low-order byte in register 2. This prevents the code from being multiuser, since one task might change the length of the MVC and another task might be dispatched and execute the changed instruction. Note that statement 108 decrements the length by 1, since length fields in object code are always 1 less than the length they act upon [e.g., CLC 2(4,8),0(5) assembles as X'D50380025000'].

Figure 3.8 uses the EX instruction to achieve the same result while preserving reentrancy.

3.5.1 The EX Instruction

EX has 2 operands, a register and an address, and is coded

```
LOC   OBJECT CODE      ADDR1 ADDR2  STMT    SOURCE STATEMENT

000080 5811 0000             00000  106         L    1,0(1)         ADDRESS OF PARM= STRING TO R1
000084 4821 0000             00000  107         LH   2,0(1)         LENGTH OF PARM= STRING
000088 0620                         108         BCTR 2,0            DECREMENT LENGTH FOR MOVE
00008A 4220 A08F             0008F  109         STC  2,MOVE+1       CHANGE LENGTH OF MVC INSTR.
00008E D200 A0A4 1002  000A4 00002  110 MOVE    MVC  INPARM(0),2(1) MOVE PARM= STRING TO PARMLIST
000094 5810 0224             00224  111         L    1,PSAAOLD-PSA  GET ADDRESS CURRENT ASCB
000098 5010 A0A0             000A0  112         ST   1,ASCB         STORE IN PARMLIST
00009C 4510 A0AC             000AC  113         BAL  1,CALLSERV     BRANCH AROUND PARMLIST
0000A0                              114 PARMLIST CNOP 0,4           ALIGN PARMLIST ON HALFWORD
0000A0                              115 ASCB    DS   A              1ST PARM FOR SERVICE ROUTINE
0000A4                              116 INPARM  DS   CL8            2ND PARM FOR SERVICE ROUTINE
0000AC BFFF A120             00120  117 CALLSERV ICM 15,15,=V(SERVICE) ADDRESS OF SERVICE ROUTINE
0000B0 4780 A0BA             000BA  118         BZ   ERROR1         =0; ROUTINE NOT LINKED
0000B4 05EF                         119         BALR 14,15          INVOKE THE ROUTINE
```

Figure 3.7 Nonreentrant code.

```
LOC    OBJECT CODE          ADDR1 ADDR2  STMT    SOURCE STATEMENT

000080 5811 0000                  00000  106         L     1,0(1)              ADDRESS OF PARM= STRING TO R1
000084 4821 0000                  00000  107         LH    2,0(1)              LENGTH OF PARM= STRING
000088 0620                              108         BCTR  2,0                 DECREMENT FOR EXECUTE
00008A 4420 A092                  00092  109         EX    2,MOVE              MOVE PARM= STRING TO PARMLIST
00008E 47F0 A098                  00098  110         B     AROUND              BRANCH AROUND EXECUTED INSTR.
000092 D200 D070 1002 00070 00002 111 MOVE   MVC    INPARM(0),2(1)            *** EXECUTE ONLY ***
000098                                   112 AROUND  DS    0H
000098 5810 0224                  00224  113         L     1,PSAAOLD-PSA       GET ADDRESS CURRENT ASCB
00009C 5010 D06C                  0006C  114         ST    1,ASCB              PUT IN PARMLIST
0000A0 4110 D06C                  0006C  115         LA    1,PARMLIST          ADDRESS OF PARMLIST TO R
0000A4 BFFF A118                  00118  116 CALLSERV ICM  15,15,=V(SERVICE)   ADDRESS OF SERVICE RTN TO R15
0000A8 4780 A0B2                  000B2  117         BZ    ERROR1              =0; ROUTINE NOT LINKED
0000AC 05EF                              118         BALR  14,15               INVOKE THE ROUTINE
...                                      ...         ...
000000                                   180 WORKAREA DSECT                    WORK AREA MAPPING DSECT
...                                      ...         ...
00006C                                   192 PARMLIST DS   0A                  PARMLIST FOR SERVICE ROUTINE
00006C                                   193 ASCB     DS   A                   1ST PARM FOR SERVICE ROUTINE
000070                                   194 INPARM   DS   CL8                 2ND PARM FOR SERVICE ROUTINE
```

Figure 3.8 Reentrant code.

EX   register,address

Hardware causes the following events occur when an EX is executed:

1. The instruction whose address is in the second operand is copied to a storage area associated with the processor on which the code with the EX is running. The exact location of the storage for the copy is not defined in the architecture.*

2. The low-order byte of the register in the first operand is logically ORed with the second byte in the copy. This is why, on line 111 in Fig. 3.8, the instruction was coded: MVC INPARM(0),2(1). If it were coded MVC INPARM,2(1), the instruction would have assembled as X'D207D0701002' (i.e., length CL8, the length of INPARM) instead of X'D200D0701002'. If the low-order byte in the register operand of EX (line 109) were, for example, X'02', the logical OR of that byte and the second byte of the target (X'07') would yield X'07' and cause the MVC under control of EX to move 8 bytes rather than 3 bytes.

3. The processor fetches and executes the copy. The processor updates the PSW to point to the instruction after the EX instruction.

Any instruction, with the exception of another EX instruction, can be the target of an EX (i.e., specified by the second operand). Attempting to EX an EX causes a program check interrupt code 0003 (S0C3).

In Fig. 3.8, statements 106 through 108 load registers 1 and 2 with the address and length of the PARM= field and decrement the length by 1.

---

*See *370 Principles of Operation* (SA22-7200), published by IBM.

The EX instruction on line 109 causes the MVC in line 111 to move the PARM= field to the parameter list for the length of 1 more than the value in the low-order byte of register 2 (the first operand of the EX). Note that the MVC instruction that is the target of EX could have been anywhere in the module. It is good practice, however, to code the EX within a few instructions of its target instruction, even though it requires an extra branch around the target instruction (line 110). This makes for readable and maintainable code.

3.5.2 Execute and List Macro Formats

Figure 3.7 has an in-line parameter list (statements 115 through 116). If multiple tasks were executing the code at the same time, one task could execute the ST instruction on line 112, storing a parameter in the parameter list and another task could execute the BALR on line 119, invoking the service with the first task's parameter. In Fig. 3.8, the parameter list is in each user's working storage (statements 180 through 194). Now, when each user executes the ST instruction on line 114, he stores the parameter in his own GETMAINed working storage. In reentrant code, any parameter list that is changed as the code executes is in working storage.

This is of particular concern when coding IBM macros that invoke MVS services. Most IBM macros expand into a parameter list and a transfer of control to a service routine with a branch, SVC, or call to a PC routine.

Figure 3.9 shows the expansion of an ESTAE macro coded in statement 62. (ESTAE is covered in Chap. 5.) Line 65 loads the address of the parameter list in lines 66 through 75 into register 1 and branches to line 76. The ST 3,IHB0009+20 in line 76 stores the value in register 3 into the

LOC	OBJECT CODE	ADDR1	ADDR2	STMT	SOURCE STATEMENT	
				62	ESTAE (3)	
				63+*	MACDATE	07/01/81
00007A	0700			64+	CNOP 0,4	ESTAB. FULLWORD ALIGNMENT
00007C	4510 A098		00098	65+	BAL 1,*+28	LIST ADDR IN REG1 SKIP LIST
			00080	66+IHB0009	EQU *	
000080	16			67+	DC AL1(22)	..FLAGS FOR TCB,PURGE,
				+*		..ASYNCH AND CANCEL
000081	000000			68+	DC AL3(0)	FIELD NO LONGER USED
000084	00000000			69+	DC A(0)	SPACE FOR PARM LIST ADDR
000088	00000000			70+	DC A(0)	SPACE FOR TCB ADDR
00008C	00			71+	DC AL1(0)	FLAGS FOR TERM AND RECORD
00008D	01			72+	DC AL1(1)	THIRD FLAG BYTE
00008E	0000			73+	DC AL2(0)	RESERVED
000090	00000000			74+	DC A(0)	SPACE FOR TOKEN
000094	00000000			75+	DC AL4(0)	SPACE FOR EXIT ADDR
000098	5030 A094		00094	76+	ST 3,IHB0009+20	PUT EXIT ADDR IN LIST
00009C	4100 0100		00100	77+	LA 0,256(0,0)	CREATE & PARMLST EQ 0
0000A0	4110 1000		00000	78+	LA 1,0(0,1)	MAKE REG1 POS. XCTL=NO
0000A4	0A3C			79+	SVC 60	ISSUE STAE SVC

Figure 3.9   ESTAE macro: standard form.

field of the parameter list on line 75, thus modifying the parameter list and preventing the code from being multiuser.

The *execute* and *list* forms of macros, specified by the MF = operand, allow MVS services to be invoked in reentrant code. This is illustrated in Fig. 3.10. The first ESTAE on line 62 is the execute form as indicated by MF = (E,____). It expands into code that stores values into the fields in the parameter list generated by the second ESTAE on line 157. This ESTAE is in the list form indicated by MF = L. Note that the list form ESTAE is in the working storage DSECT and that even though it expands with constants in DC fields (as in line 160) these fields map storage that has been acquired with a GETMAIN. Virtual Storage Manager initializes storage GETMAINed in the private area to X'00'.

In order for code to be reentrant, execute and list forms of MVS macros should always be used when the standard form generates a parameter list that is modified at run time. If the standard form generates a parameter list that is not modified, such as in the GETMAINs and FREEMAINs in the program stubs in Figs. 3.4 and 3.5, then the standard form may be used.

There is another macro format, the generate format, used for VTAM and VSAM macros. Generate macros build a remote parameter list without the need to code an MF = L macro. A generate-format macro is functionally equivalent to the combination of the execute and list formats.

In summary, reentrant code:

```
LOC   OBJECT CODE    ADDR1 ADDR2  STMT  SOURCE STATEMENT

                                  62         ESTAE (3),MF=(E,ELIST)
                                  63+*   MACDATE   07/01/81
000052 4110 D068           00068  64+       LA    1,ELIST            LOAD PARAMETER REG 1
000056 5031 0014           00014  65+       ST    3,20(1)            STORE USER EXIT ADDRESS
00005A 94BF 1000     00000        66+       NI    0(1),191           TURN OFF FLAG BITS
00005E 9610 1000     00000        67+       OI    0(1),16            ..FLAGS FOR TCB,PURGE,
                                   +*                                ..ASYNCH, AND CANCEL
000062 94F7 1000     00000        68+       NI    0(1),B'11110111'   INIT BIT 5 TO 0
000066 9464 100C     0000C        69+       NI    12(1),B'01100100'  INIT BIT 1,4,5,7,8 TO 0
00006A 9201 100D     0000D        70+       MVI   13(1),1            FLAG FOUR BYTE EXIT ADDR
00006E D701 100E 100E 0000E 0000E 71+       XC    14(2,1),14(1)      INIT RESERVED FLD TO 0
000074 4100 0100           00100  72+       LA    0,256(0,0)         CREATE & PARMLST EQ 0
000078 0A3C                        73+       SVC   60                 ISSUE STAE SVC
...                                ...        ...
000068                             156 WORKAREA DSECT
                                   157 ELIST    ESTAE ,MF=L
                                   158+*   MACDATE   07/01/81
000068                             159+      DS    0F
000068 16                          160+ELIST DC    AL1(22)           FLAGS FOR TCB,PURGE,
                                   +*                                ASYNCH AND CANCEL
000069 000000                      161+      DC    AL3(0)            FIELD NO LONGER USED
00006C 00000000                    162+      DC    A(0)              PARM LIST ADDR. NOT SPECIFIED
000070 00000000                    163+      DC    A(0)              TCB NOT SPECIFIED
000074 00                          164+      DC    AL1(0)            FLAGS
000075 01                          165+      DC    AL1(1)            THIRD FLAG BYTE
000076 0000                        166+      DC    AL2(0)            RESERVED
000078 00000000                    167+      DC    A(0)              TOKEN VALUE AREA
00007C 00000000                    168+      DC    AL4(0)            EXIT ADDRESS
```

Figure 3.10 ESTAE macro: execute and list forms.

■ Uses a GETMAINed work area to contain any field that might be changed by a user executing the code. The save area for the general registers is in this GETMAINed work area.

■ Does not modify any instruction during execution. Code, such as the following sequence that changes a NOP into an unconditional branch, cannot be used in a reentrant module:

```
BRANCH   BC    0,LABEL
         OI    BRANCH + 1,X'F0'
```

■ Uses the EX instruction to cause MVC, CLC, PACK, or other instructions with lengths in their object code to operate as if the object code were changed.

■ Uses the execute and list forms of MVS macros when the standard form expands into code that modifies an in-line parameter at run time.

Part

2

MVS Component Services

4

MVS Storage Managers

4.1 PHYSICAL STORAGE

On IBM mainframes, physical main storage is installed in 32- or 64-Mbyte storage elements. These elements consist of microchips on boards in arrays housed in TCMs. (TCMs are the brass box-like objects you see when you look inside a CPU.) Each byte of physical main storage has a unique address, called its *absolute* address, in the range of 0 to 1 less than the quantity of physical storage installed. The computer in Fig. 4.1 has 64 Mbytes of main storage with absolute addresses in the range of 0 (lower left corner) to X'03FFFFFF' (upper right corner).

Figure 4.1 contains a schematic representation of a 370-type computer with two processors sharing main storage. Actual configurations can have from 1 to 6 processors and can be physically or logically partitioned to share storage among the processors. Note that each processor has a complete set of control, floating point, access, and general registers as well as its own PSW, so that each processor is independently fetching and executing instructions.

The storage in Fig. 4.1 represents the amount of physical storage installed. Physical storage is organized into 4K units called *frames*. There is a 7-bit *storage key* associated with each frame.

■ The first four bits are the *access key*. Any instruction that changes a byte in the frame must execute with a PSW key (bits 8 through 11) that is the same as the access key or is 0 (the master PSW key).

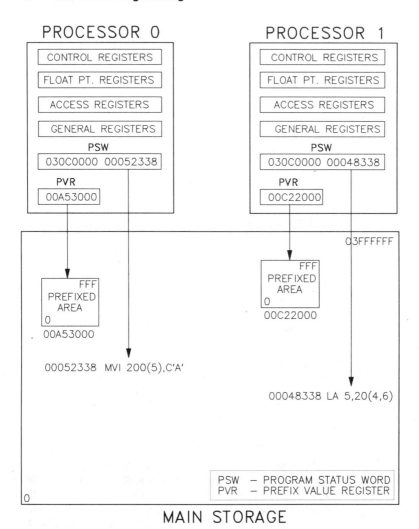

Figure 4.1 Using real addresses.

■ The fifth bit is the *fetch-protect bit*. If this bit is 0 an instruction executing with any PSW key can access (but not change) any byte in the
frame. If the bit is 1, the PSW key must match the access key or be 0 to
access a byte in that frame.

■ The sixth bit is the *reference* bit. Whenever any instruction references
any byte in the frame, storage access microcode sets this bit to 1.
System Resource Manager (SRM) takes periodic samples of a frame's
reference bit. For every sample where the reference bit is 0, SRM
increments the Unreferenced Interval Count (UIC) in the Page Frame
Table Entry (PFTE) for that frame. The PFTE, not to be confused

with the Page Table Entry (PGTE), is the control block RSM uses to keep track of a frame of real storage. The UIC thus represents the demand for the data contained in the frame.

- The seventh bit is the *change* bit. Whenever any instruction changes the contents of any byte in the frame, storage access microcode sets this bit to 1. Real Storage Manager (RSM) only invokes Auxiliary Storage Manager (ASM) to page out data in frames with a change bit of 1 (see Sec. 4.5).

4.2 ABSOLUTE AND REAL ADDRESSES

The *real* address of a byte in storage is the same as its absolute address except for addresses in the low-core range (0 to X'0FFF'). Each processor needs its own area of storage with real addresses in this range to handle interrupts, to store Program Event Recording (PER) data, and for various other operations that are specific to individual processors.

To maintain its own storage with real addresses 0 to X'0FFF', each processor has a Prefix Value Register (PVR) that contains the absolute address of a frame of storage, known as the prefixed area for that processor. Whenever an operation on a processor accesses storage within the range of addresses 0 to X'0FFF', storage access microcode adds the value of the PVR to the address before accessing storage. In Fig. 4.1, for example, if the operand of an instruction executing on processor 0 referred to address X'2B5', storage access microcode would add the value of the PVR, and the instruction would reference the byte at X'00A532B5'. If the same instruction executed on processor 1, the byte at X'00C222B5' in processor 1's prefixed area would be referenced. During system initialization, Nucleus Initialization Program (NIP) reserves a prefixed area for each processor and issues an SPX (set prefix) instruction to load each processor's PVR with the absolute address of its prefixed area.

4.3 VIRTUAL ADDRESSES

Virtual addressing is a feature of 370 architecture designed to make more efficient use of physical storage and to isolate each program's data. A virtual address is an algorithm used by Dynamic Address Translation (DAT) to locate a byte in real storage. Processors can execute programs using either real or virtual addresses depending on the DAT bit (the sixth bit) of the PSW.

In Fig. 4.1, each processor has X'03' in the first byte of its PSW. Since the DAT bit is 0, the processor treats the second word of the PSW as the *real* address of the next instruction it will fetch and execute. Notice how the second word of processor 0's PSW contains X'00052338' and points to the MVI instruction at real address X'00052338'.

In Fig. 4.2, the two processors are executing the same instructions as

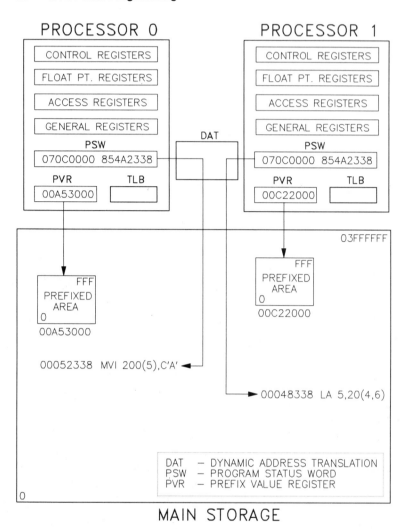

Figure 4.2   Using virtual addresses.

in Fig. 4.1 using *virtual* addresses. Each processor now has X'07' in the first byte of its PSW. Since the DAT bit in the PSW is 1, each processor passes the instruction address to the DAT hardware* before it fetches and executes the instruction. DAT translates the virtual address in each

---

*370 machines have a level of programming, called microcode, that is beneath the instruction level. When an instruction is executed, the programmer can never know which aspects of the instruction's operation are "hard-wired" into the physical hardware or result from microcode software interacting with the hardware. Since instructions produce the same results in a program regardless of the hardware/microcode implementation on a particular machine type or model, the terms *hardware* and *microcode* are used interchangeably throughout this book.

PSW to the real address of the instruction in storage. Note how DAT translates the virtual address, X'054A2338', in the second word of processor 0's PSW to the real address of the MVI instruction, X'00052338'. (The high-order bit in X'854A2338' is not part of the virtual address but indicates an AMODE of 31.)

4.4 DYNAMIC ADDRESS TRANSLATION (DAT)

Figure 4.3 illustrates how DAT translates the virtual address in processor 0's PSW (Fig. 4.2) to an address in real storage:

- DAT uses bits 1 through 11 of the virtual address as an index into a Segment Table whose real address is in control register 1. Each entry in the Segment Table contains the real address of a Page Table. Each Page Table describes a 1-Mbyte range of virtual addresses.

- After locating a Page Table, DAT uses bits 12 through 19 of the virtual address as an index into the Page Table to locate a Page Table Entry (PGTE). The Page Table Entry contains the real address of a frame of

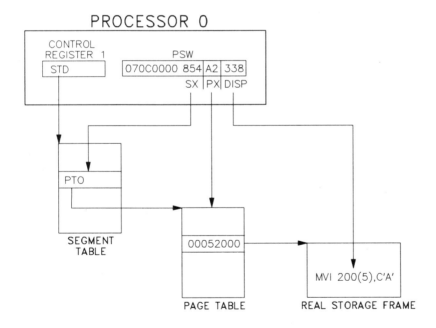

Figure 4.3 Dynamic Address Translation (DAT).

storage. In Fig. 4.3, the page index (PX) portion of the virtual address has indexed to the Page Table Entry that contains the real address (X'00052000') of the frame containing the MVI instruction. [The PGTE also contains bit flags that are used by Virtual Storage Manager (VSM) and Real Storage Manager (RSM) during paging operations.]

- DAT uses bits 20 through 31 of the virtual address to index into the frame to locate a byte. The frame-displacement portion of a virtual address is 12 bits and can thus describe the 4K unique addresses within a frame. In Fig. 4.3 DAT adds the displacement portion of the virtual address (X'338') and the frame address (X'00052000') from the Page Table to reference the MVI instruction at real address X'00052338'.

4.4.1 Segment Table Designator (STD)

Notice in Fig. 4.3 how the whole process of translation depends on the Segment Table Designator (which contains the real address of the Segment Table) in control register 1. Changing the value of the STD so that it specifies a different Segment Table causes an entirely different virtual-address-to-real-address translation since each Segment Table points to a specific set of Page Tables and frames. In Fig. 4.2, processor 0 and processor 1 are both translating the same virtual address (X'054A2338'). But each processor, using the Segment and Page Tables specified by the STD in its own control register 1, is translating this virtual address to a different real address.

4.4.2 Translation Lookaside Buffer (TLB)

Even though it is implemented in microcode, the translation process just described is somewhat time consuming. To make the process more efficient, each CPU has its own Translation Lookaside Buffer (TLB) that contains entries for the frames most recently referenced on that processor.

When DAT receives a virtual address for translation, it simultaneously examines Segment and Page Tables and looks for an entry in the TLB that matches the PX portion of the virtual address. DAT uses the results of whichever method completes first. IBM has estimated that 80 percent of DAT translations are made though the TLB entries.

Since DAT translation depends on the STD, whenever a new STD is loaded into control register 1 on a processor, new TLB entries must be created to reflect the new virtual-to-real correspondence. As part of activating an address space on a processor, the MVS dispatcher issues the Purge TLB (PTLB) instruction to reinitialize that processor's TLB. The processor builds entries in the TLB as Segment Table/Page Table translation locates frames.

4.5 PAGING

Paging refers to moving 4K blocks of data (pages) into and out of real storage frames during the execution of a program. Paging can only occur when a program is using virtual addresses. RSM uses *demand paging* to maximize the use of real storage; System Resource Manager (SRM) uses *swap paging* to regulate the workload level in the system.

MVS does very little with programs that execute using real, rather than virtual, addresses. When a program uses real addresses, the program itself and any data it references must remain in the same real storage frames until the program completes.

Consider the following two instructions that might be part of in a program executing with a DAT-off PSW ('0' in the sixth bit of PSW):

```
LA  5,0(0,4)
ST  3,0(0,5)
```

After the execution of the first instruction, the *real* address of the data at 0(0,4) is in register 5. The data must remain in the same real storage frame for the execution of the ST instruction since the second operand, 0(0,5), references a real address in that frame.

If the same two instructions are executed with a DAT-on PSW (1 in the sixth bit of the PSW), the LA instruction loads a *virtual* address into register 5. MVS can then move the data to a different frame, replacing the frame address in the Page Table Entry with the address of the new frame. The ST instruction, using the same virtual address in register 5, causes DAT to translate the effective address* of 0(0,5) using the new frame address in the Page Table. ST then references the data at its new real address.

4.5.1 A Paging Operation

Figure 4.4 illustrates a paging operation. The top portion of the figure represents a page (4K) of data residing in a real storage frame. The Page Table Entry contains the real address of that frame, the Page Frame Real Address (PFRA). The Page Table Entry also has the GETMAINed bit (bit 31) set indicating that GETMAIN has been issued for storage in this page. The storage key for the frame has the Change (c) bit set, indicating that an instruction has changed storage in the frame.

In the middle portion of Fig. 4.4, the page of data in frame 1 has been paged out to a 4K *slot* in expanded storage. Since the Change bit was set in the storage key, the page of data has been saved. If the Change bit had

---

*The effective address is the sum of the base and index registers and displacement.

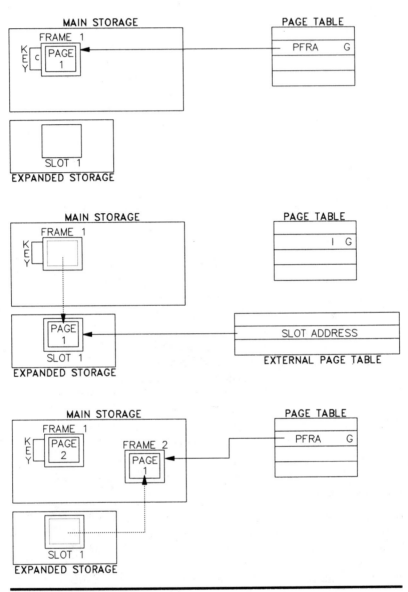

Figure 4.4 Paging.

not been set, the data would not have been paged out, but simply over-
layed when a new page was brought into the frame. Note that RSM has
issued the SSKE instruction to reset the frame's Change bit to 0 after
invoking Auxiliary Storage Manager (ASM) to perform the actual movement of the data.

ASM pages data to and from 4K *slots* in expanded storage or on DASD.
Unlike real storage, where each byte has a unique address, expanded

storage has an address for each slot. Instructions, therefore, cannot use expanded storage to fetch and store individual bytes of data. But since expanded storage is considerably less expensive than real storage and can be accessed much faster than DASD, it makes an ideal auxiliary storage medium.

After the page-out, the address of the data is now in an ASM table, the External Page Table. RSM sets the Invalid (I) bit (bit 5) in the Page Table Entry to 1. This bit indicates that DAT should not use the real address in the Page Table Entry to translate the virtual address, since the frame specified by the real address has been made available to contain other data.

When a program attempts to reference data that has been paged out, a program check type 0011 (page translation exception) occurs when DAT translation encounters the Invalid bit in the Page Table Entry. The program check interrupt handler routine that receives control (see "Interrupts," Chap. 6) then examines the GETMAINed bit in the PGTE. If the bit is 0, GETMAIN was never issued for a virtual address within the page, and the interrupt handler invokes RTM to abend the program with an 0C4 (protection exception). If the GETMAIN bit in the PGTE is 1, the interrupt handler initiates a page-in.

In the bottom portion of Fig. 4.4, a page-in operation has brought the data back into real storage. The original frame (frame 1) now contains other data, so RSM has supplied a new frame (frame 2). After ASM moves the page of data to the new frame, RSM updates the Page Table Entry with the new frame's real address. RSM also issues SSKE to set the Invalid bit to 0. Now when DAT tries again to translate the virtual address, the Page Table Entry will specify the real address of frame 2.

4.5.2 Demand Paging

Demand paging is used to make the most efficient use of real storage. System Resource Manager (SRM) periodically samples the Reference bit in each frame's storage key and maintains an Unreferenced Interval Count (UIC) in each frame's PFTE. As the demand for frames in the system increases, SRM "steals" the less-referenced frames (frames with relatively high UICs) and places them on Real Storage Manager's (RSM's) Available Frame Queue. RSM supplies frames from this "reservoir" to satisfy requests for frames.

When a page that is no longer in real storage is referenced, the "demand" for that page causes RSM and ASM to bring the page into a real storage frame. Demand paging, thus, occurs one page at a time.

You can use the PGSER macro to inform RSM that a page or group of pages is not to be demand-paged. When the following is coded, for example,

PGSER FIX,A = (0),EA = (1)

RSM moves the Page Frame Table Entries for any of the pages described by virtual addresses between the values in register 0 and register 1, from a queue of pageable pages to a queue of nonpageable pages.

4.5.3 Swap Paging

Swap paging, by contrast, is not necessarily driven by demand for real storage but rather to satisfy overall system performance objectives. Swapping involves an entire address space. SRM uses swapping as the way to prevent an address space from using *any* resources. If there is enough real storage but not enough CPU, for example, SRM might swap out one or more address spaces simply to make them nondispatchable and therefore unable to consume CPU cycles.

The SYSEVENT macro can be used to inform SRM that an address space is not eligible to be swapped.

■ SYSEVENT DONTSWAP causes SRM to mark the address space in which it is issued as nonswappable.

■ SYSEVENT TRANSWAP causes SRM to swap out the address space in which it is issued before marking the ASCB as nonswappable. The NSWPRTN program in Chap. 9 contains an example of SYSEVENT TRANSWAP.

Even though an address space is not swappable, its pages will still be demand-paged unless PGSER is issued for those pages.

4.6 MULTIPLE VIRTUAL STORAGE

In Fig. 4.3, the virtual address in the PSW could have been any number from X'00000000' to X'7FFFFFFF'. This 2^{31} range of numbers constitutes an address space. DAT can translate any virtual address in this range to a real address once a Segment and Page Table Entry corresponding to the SX and PX portions of that virtual address have been constructed. An *address space* thus represents all the virtual addresses that a program can potentially reference.

Earlier versions of OS, such as MVT and VS1, were Single Virtual Storage (SVS) systems. There was only one set of Page Tables and therefore a single address space. Ranges of virtual addresses within this address space were assigned to each job for its exclusive use. Individual tasks could only use the virtual addresses within the range that had been assigned to them.

In Multiple Virtual Storage (MVS) systems, each batch job, TSO user, and started task has its own address space and can use the complete range of virtual address from X'00000000' to X'7FFFFFFF'. This is possible because each job, TSO user, or started task has its own Segment

Table and its own Page Tables that define how the virtual addresses in that address space correspond to real storage frames. The MVS Dispatcher activates a particular address space by loading its STD into control register 1. After that, every virtual address in that processor's PSW and every effective address for operands of instructions executed on that processor* will be DAT-translated by that address space's Segment and Page Tables.

4.7 VIRTUAL STORAGE MANAGER

MVS finds it convenient to subdivide an address space into ranges of virtual addresses in order to keep related types of data together (see Fig. 4.5). The line at address X'00FFFFFF' reflects the bimodal addressing that was introduced with 370/XA. Because it is necessary to accommodate both 24- and 31-bit addressing, every area (except PSA and the system area) below the line has a corresponding extension above the line. SQA, for example, is addressable by AMODE 24 and AMODE 31 programs. Extended SQA (ESQA) is addressable only by AMODE 31 programs.

4.7.1 How Virtual Storage Is Organized

Figure 4.5 indicates what control blocks and data are contained in the various regions of virtual storage. The control blocks listed in (E)LSQA, (E)SQA, and the Nucleus are only some of the more significant ones. The description of each control block in *MVS Debugging Handbook* describes where it resides in virtual storage.

Notice on the right-hand side of the figure that these ranges of addresses describe either common storage (shared by all users) or private storage. For all common areas there is one set of Page Tables, the Common Page Tables. The Segment Tables of all address spaces point to the Common Page Tables so that a virtual address within the range of the common areas maps to the same real addresses in every address space.

(E)SQA and the Nucleus contain *control blocks* that must be addressable in any address space. Since many of the most important MVS routines, such as the Dispatcher or Functional Recovery Routines (FRRs), execute in whatever address space happens to be active on the processor, the control blocks used by these routines must be addressable in any address space.

(E)PLPA, (E)FLPA, (E)MLPA, and the Nucleus contain *reentrant modules* that are available to be called by any program in any address

---

*If the PSW is in primary space mode see Chap. 7.

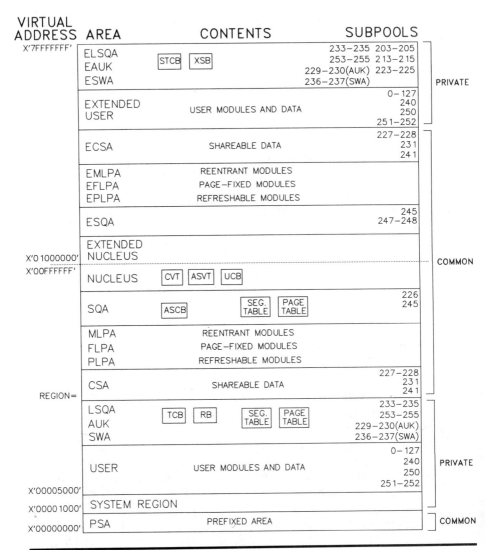

Figure 4.5 An MVS address space.

space. The SVC Second Level Interrupt Handlers, for example, reside in
the Nucleus or in PLPA since they might be executed by a program in
any address space.

(E)CSA contains shareable data that one address space wishes to make
available to other address spaces. VTAM, CICS, JES, and databases are
heavy users of CSA.

The size of common storage is determined at IPL. Nucleus Initialization Program (NIP) adds the size of CSA, SQA, LPA, and the Nucleus
and rounds up to the next megabyte. What is left over is private. The

sizes of CSA and SQA are specified in the IEASYSxx member of SYS1.PARMLIB. The size of the Link Pack Area (LPA) is the sum of the virtual storage occupied by the modules in the LPALIST concatenation and the modules in the PARMLIB members that describe FLPA and MLPA. The size of the Nucleus is determined by the the size of the MVS modules and the user modules linked into the Nucleus (such as CICS SVCs) and, since UCBs reside in the Nucleus, the number of I/O devices defined to the system.

The private areas of storage contain control blocks and data that pertain only to that address space. The control blocks in (E)LSQA describe the virtual storage in use by the address space, the tasks that are executing in that address space, and load modules and data sets in use by those tasks. The data in the user area cannot be addressed by programs in other address spaces unless those programs execute in a cross-memory addressing mode.

4.7.2 Interfaces to VSM

The principal interfaces to VSM services are the GETMAIN, FREE-MAIN, and STORAGE macros. MVS modules and application programs acquire virtual storage by issuing GETMAIN or STORAGE OBTAIN, and release storage by issuing FREEMAIN or STORAGE RELEASE. STORAGE, (available only in MVS/ESA), is more flexible than GET-MAIN and FREEMAIN since it expands into a PC instruction and can be issued in any programming environment.

A program can issue GETMAIN or STORAGE to acquire virtual storage from CSA or SQA in the common area or from LSQA, SWA, or the user area in the private region. The SP= operand indicates in which area VSM should acquire the virtual storage by naming one of the *subpools* within that area. For example:

```
GETMAIN   RU,L=512,SP=239
```

or

```
STORAGE   OBTAIN   LENGTH=512,SP=239
```

will get 512 bytes of storage from SQA by naming subpool 239 on the SP= operand. Fig. 4.4 contains the subpool numbers that describe the storage within each area of an address space.

Many of the areas in an address space are described by more than one subpool. In Fig. 4.5, for example, subpools 228, 229, 231, and 241 all describe CSA. This does not mean that CSA is subdivided into regions with specific sizes for these subpools. Rather, the subpool numbers within a virtual storage area indicate how the storage is managed by VSM,

RSM, and SRM. Virtual storage obtained in CSA subpool 227, for example, is fixed in real storage (the data will not be paged by RSM), while the virtual storage in CSA subpool 241, is pageable.

The attributes that distinguish virtual storage in one subpool from another are listed below. A complete list of all subpools and their attributes appears in *MVS Debugging Handbook Volume I* and in *SLL:VSM logic*.

- *Swappable:* System Resource Manager (SRM) controls the use of the system's resources by regulating the number of address spaces that are in storage at a given time. Storage in LSQA, SWA, and user area subpools is swappable, since these areas are only needed when an address space is in storage.

- *Pageable or fixed:* Real Storage Manager (RSM) pages out the data in lightly referenced pages to expanded storage or DASD. Some programs require storage that is not paged, either for performance reasons or because the program uses real addresses to reference the data. "Fixed" (i.e., nonpageable) storage can be requested by specifying one of the nonpageable subpools on a GETMAIN. The following requests 512 bytes from pageable CSA:

   GETMAIN   RU,L = 512,SP = 241

   while this requests 512 bytes from fixed CSA:

   GETMAIN   RU,L = 512,SP = 228

   When RSM provides real storage frames to contain data in a subpool 227 page, it puts the Page Frame Table Entry representing the frame on a queue of nonpageable frames. SRM will not steal frames if their PFTEs are on this queue.

   Fetch protected: A program might want to GETMAIN storage from a fetch-protected subpool to contain sensitive system or application data. Any program that wishes to access this data will then have to execute with a PSW key that matches the storage key or is 0. The following GETMAIN will get 1024 bytes from fetch-protected CSA:

   GETMAIN   RU,L = 1024,SP = 227

- *Real storage backing:* It usually makes no difference to a program what real storage is specified in the PFRA in the Page Table Entry. Some programs, especially those that use the EXCP access method with format 0 CCWs, require *real* storage whose address is below 16 meg.

Specifying

GETMAIN   RU,L = 1024,SP = 226

will cause VSM to acquire 1024 bytes from an SQA subpool backed by real storage whose address is below 16 meg.

- *Job and step termination:* When an address space or task terminates, Recovery Termination Manager (RTM) performs cleanup by FREEMAINing storage allocated to that task or address space. Depending on the subpool, LSQA storage is freed at task, job step, or address space termination. Storage from CSA or SQA subpools is not automatically FREEMAINed when an address space, job, or task terminates. The following GETMAIN will acquire 1024 bytes of LSQA storage that is freed at task termination whether the task is a job step task or a subtask:

GETMAIN   RU,L = 1024,SP = 233

While this requests 1024 bytes from an LSQA subpool that is FREEMAINed when the job step TCB terminates:

GETMAIN   RU,L = 1024,SP = 235

- *Disabled reference* (ESA only): Since ASM might have to perform I/O to resolve a page fault, programs executing with a disabled PSW cannot use pageable storage. MVS/ESA provides DREF storage, where page faults are resolved by synchronous page movement from expanded storage, as an alternative to using page-fixed real storage.

4.7.3 User Area Subpools

Subpools 0 through 127 are all within the user area of private storage. By default, a GETMAIN issued without the SP = operand acquires storage from subpool zero. Software might GETMAIN storage out of different user area subpools to contain data used for different purposes. Storage used to build on-line screens, for example, might use one user area subpool, while a large in-storage table used by several subtasks might be in another subpool. This allows a program to release all of the storage related to one functional area during abend recovery by issuing a FREEMAIN for the entire subpool. This FREEMAIN, because it does not contain the A = operand, releases all of user area subpool 27:

FREEMAIN RU,SP = 27

If a program requires user area storage in different storage keys, it must GETMAIN storage out of different subpools. The first GETMAIN from a user area subpool sets the storage key to the PSW key. Subsequent GETMAINs from that subpool all obtain storage with that key. By contrast, subpools in CSA and LSQA subpool 230 support multiple keys. The following GETMAIN will obtain 200 bytes from CSA subpool 241 in protect key 5:

```
GETMAIN   RC,SP = 241,LV = 200,KEY = 5
```

There are some areas of virtual storage that have no subpools and from which storage cannot be acquired with a GETMAIN. These areas, which include the MVS Nucleus, FLPA, PLPA, and MLPA, are built at system initialization and are not increased during the life of the IPL.

4.8 NCRYPT WALKTHROUGH

NCRYPT in Fig. 4.6 is a file encryption and deencryption program. NCRYPT uses a character string supplied by the user as the seed for a routine that generates a series of pseudorandom hexidecimal digits. NCRYPT encrypts a file by issuing the XR instruction (line 71) against each byte of the file and a byte consisting of two of the random digits.

4.8.1 The XR Instruction

To deencrypt the file, the user supplies the same character string and executes NCRYPT against the encrypted file. The same string causes NCRYPT to generate the same series of random digits. Because of the way the exclusive OR operation works, XRing each byte of the encrypted file with the same byte that was used to encrypt it, restores each byte to its original, nonencrypted, state.

Encryption of a file:

```
1100 0001    BYTE IN THE FILE (C'A')
1001 1010    BYTE GENERATED BY RANDOM ROUTINE
```
```
0101 1011    RESULT OF THE EXCLUSIVE OR (XR)
```

Deencryption of an encrypted file:

```
0101 1011    BYTE IN THE ENCRYPTED FILE
1001 1010    SAME BYTE GENERATED BY RANDOM ROUTINE
```
```
1100 0001    RESULT OF THE EXCLUSIVE OR (C'A')
```

NCRYPT begins on line 28 with the MODULE macro. Since NCRYPT uses QSAM, which is a 24-bit access method, MODULE includes the operands AMODE = 24 and RMODE = 24. MODULE also includes the

```
*+----------------------------------------------------------------------+  1
*|  FUNCTION:                                                            |  2
*|      ENCRYPTS AND DEENCRYPTS FILES WITH RECFM F, FB, V, VB OR U.      |  3
*|      THE INPUT PARAMETER IS USED AS A KEY TO ENCRYPT A FILE OR        |  4
*|      TO DEENCRYPT A FILE PREVIOUSLY ENCRYPTED WITH THAT KEY.          |  5
*|  INPUTS:                                                              |  6
*|      R1 - ADDRESS OF A PARMLIST. THE 1ST WORD IS THE ADDRESS OF       |  7
*|           A STRING WHOSE LENGTH IS IN THE FIRST HALFWORD.             |  8
*|           THIS IS EQUIVALENT TO  THE JCL // EXEC PARM= STRING         |  9
*|           OR THE PARAMETER SUPPLIED WITH FROM TSO "CALL"              | 10
*|      THE OTHER INPUT IS A FILE TO BE ENCRYPTED OR DEENCRYPTED         | 11
*|      ALLOCATED TO DDNAME "IN" (//IN  DD  DSN=...)                     | 12
*|  OUTPUTS:                                                             | 13
*|      THE INPUT FILE IS ENCRYPTED OR DEENCRYPTED.                      | 14
*|      RETURN CODE IN R15:                                             | 15
*|          0 - FILE HAS BEEN ENCRYPTED OR DEENCRYPTED                   | 16
*|          8 - ENCRYPTION/DEENCRYPTION KEY HAS NOT BEEN SUPPLIED        | 17
*|  LOGIC:                                                               | 18
*|      1) GETMAIN STORAGE FOR REENTRANT WORKAREA                        | 19
*|      2) GET THE ENCRYPTION KEY FROM INPUT PARAMETER                   | 20
*|      3) SET UP INPUT/OUTPUT FILE FOR REENTRANT I/O                    | 21
*|      4) ENCRYPT EACH BYTE OF THE FILE BY XORING IT WITH RANDOM        | 22
*|         DIGIT AND UPDATING THE BYTE IN PLACE                          | 23
*|      5) FREEMAIN STORAGE FOR REENTRANT WORKAREA                       | 24
*|  ATTRIBUTES:                                                          | 25
*|      REENTERABLE, AMODE 24, RMODE  24                                 | 26
*+----------------------------------------------------------------------+ 27
        MODULE NCRYPT,BASE=12,AMODE=24,RMODE=24,FLOATSV=YES,       X 28
              TEXT='BIT-LEVEL FILE ENCRYPTER',LOC=BELOW              29
*         *-----------------------------------------*                30
*         *    GET ENCRYPTION KEY FROM PARM=    *                    31
*         *-----------------------------------------*                32
        L     R1,0(R1)          A(PARM STRING) => R1                 33
        XR    R2,R2             CLEAR REGISTER R2                    34
        ICM   R2,B'0011',0(R1)  LENGTH OF PARM                      35
        BZ    EXIT08            =0; PARM NOT GIVEN                   36
        CH    R2,=H'7'          IS ENCRYPTION KEY LE 7 BYTES?       37
        BNH   USEPRM            YES; DO NOT SET FOR DEFAULT          38
        LH    R2,=H'7'          SET TO TAKE ONLY FIRST 7 BYTES      39
USEPRM  DS    OH                                                    40
        BCTR  R2,0              LESS 1 FOR EXECUTE                   41
        EX    R2,MVIT1          MOVE NAME TO PLIST                   42
        B     MVIT1A                                                 43
MVIT1   MVC   KEYWORK+1(0),2(R1) MOVE KEY TO WORKAREA               44
MVIT1A  DS    OH                                                    45
*         *-----------------------------------------*                46
*         *    MOVE DCB AND OPEN/CLOSE PARMLIST  *                   47
*         *    TO WORKAREA FOR REENTRANCY.       *                   48
*         *-----------------------------------------*                49
        MVC   IN(LINDCB),INDCB     MOVE DCB TO WORKAREA             50
        MVC   OLIST(LOLIST),OLIST1  MOVE OPEN/CLOSE PARMLIST TO WORK 51
*         *-----------------------------------------*                52
*         *    OPEN THE FILE FOR UPDATE          *                   53
*         *-----------------------------------------*                54
        LA    R9,IN                ADDRESS OF THE DCB               55
        OPEN  ((R9),UPDAT),MF=(E,OLIST)                             56
        USING IHADCB,R9            ADDRESSING FOR DCB MAPPING DSECT 57
```

Figure 4.6 NCRYPT.

```
*              *-------------------------------------------*              58
*              *    'XOR' EACH BYTE IN THE FILE       *              59
*              *    WITH A RANDOM BYTE TO ENCRYPT     *              60
*              *    OR DEENCRYPT.                     *              61
*              *-------------------------------------------*              62
               B     M$READIT              INITIAL READ                    63
M$LOOP         DS    0H                                                    64
               BAS   R14,RANDOM            GENERATE 1 RANDOM HEX DIGIT      65
               LR    R2,R1                 PUT IN LOW-ORDER BYTE OF R2      66
               BAS   R14,RANDOM            GENERATE 1 RANDOM HEX DIGIT      67
               SLL   R1,4                  SHIFT HEX DIGIT LEFT 4 BITS      68
               OR    R2,R1                 'OR' RANDOM DIGITS TO MAKE BYTE  69
               IC    R3,0(R4)              .. 'XOR' 1 BYTE FROM INPUT FILE  70
               XR    R3,R2                 .. WITH RANDOM BYTE TO (DE)ENCRYPT 71
               STC   R3,0(R4)              STORE THE BYTE BACK IN FILE BUFFER 72
               LA    R4,1(R4)              POINT AT NEXT INPUT BYTE IN BUFFER 73
M$PUT0         DS    0H                                                    74
               C     R4,ENDREC             END OF INPUT RECORD?             75
               BNE   M$GETI                NO; DO NOT GET INPUT             76
               PUTX  IN                    PUT THE BACK INTO THE FILE       77
M$READIT       DS    0H                                                    78
               GET   IN                    READ A RECORD                   79
               LR    R4,R1                 R4 IS POINTER IN INPUT RECORD    80
               TM    DCBRECFM,DCBRECV      IS THE FILE RECFM=V OR RECFM=U ? 81
               BNO   M$VAR1                NO; PROCESS AS RECFM=F           82
               TM    DCBRECFM,DCBRECU      IS THE FILE RECFM=V ?           83
               BO    M$VAR1                NO; PROCESS THE FILE AS RECFM=F  84
               AH    R1,0(R1)              ADDRESS OF RECORD + LRECL FROM RDW 85
               LA    R4,4(R4)              BYPASS RDW                       86
               B     M$VAR2                                                87
M$VAR1         DS    0H                                                    88
               AH    R1,DCBLRECL           ADDRESS OF RECORD + LRECL FOR RECFM=F 89
M$VAR2         DS    0H                                                    90
               ST    R1,ENDREC             ADDRESS OF END OF RECORD BUFFER + 1 91
M$GETI         DS    0H                                                    92
               B     M$LOOP                PROCESS NEXT BYTE IN INPUT FILE  93
*              *-------------------------------------------*              94
*              *    CLOSE THE FILE                    *              95
*              *-------------------------------------------*              96
C$CLOSE        DS    0H                                                    97
               PUTX  IN                    UPDATE RECORD IN PLACE           98
               CLOSE ,MF=(E,OLIST)                                         99
               B     EXIT00                                               100
*-------------------------------------------------------------------------* 101
*              RANDOM - GENERATE 1 RANDOM HEX DIGIT. ALSO GENERATE NEW   * 102
*                       FLOATING POINT NUMBER FOR NEXT ENCRYPTION KEY.   * 103
*                       INPUTS:                                          * 104
*                           NONE                                         * 105
*                       OUTPUTS:                                         * 106
*                           RANDOM LOW-ORDER 4 BITS IN R1.               * 107
*                           NEW ENCRYPTION KEY IN FIELD 'KEYWORK'.       * 108
*-------------------------------------------------------------------------* 109
RANDOM         DS    0H                                                   110
               BAKR  R14,0                 CREATE STACK STATE ENTRY        111
*                                          .. MAKE ENCRYPTION KEY INTO    112
               MVI   KEYWORK,X'40'         .. NORMALIZED FLOATING POINT NUMBER 113
               LD    F0,KEYWORK            KEY TO FLOATING PT.REGS F0 AND F1 114
```

Figure 4.6 *(Continued)*

```
        AD    F0,PI                 ADD PI                                    115
        LDR   F2,F0                 COPY NUMBER INTO F2 AND F3                116
        MDR   F0,F2                 ... CUBE                                  117
        MDR   F0,F2                 ... THE NUMBER                            118
        STD   F0,KEYWORK            PUT NUMBER BACK INTO KEY AREA             119
        LM    R0,R1,KEYWORK         LOAD INTO GENERAL REGS R6 AND R7          120
        SLDL  R0,16                 SHIFT OUT SIGN AND HIGH ORDER BYTE        121
        SRDL  R0,8                  SHIFT SEED NUMBER BACK                    122
        STM   R0,R1,KEYWORK         SAVE SEED FOR NEXT CALL TO ROUTINE        123
        SRL   R0,20                 SHIFT OFF ALL BUT 4 BITS                  124
        LR    R1,R0                 LOAD INTO REGISTER 1                      125
        PR                          POP STACK AND RETRUN                      126
*-------------------------------------------------------------------*        127
*       EXIT ROUTINES                                               *        128
*-------------------------------------------------------------------*        129
EXIT00  DS    0H                    SUCCESSFUL                                130
        LA    R15,X'00'                                                       131
        B     EXIT                                                            132
EXIT08  DS    0H                    ENCRYPT KEY LENGTH = 0                    133
        LA    R15,X'08'                                                       134
        B     EXIT                                                            135
*-------------------------------------------------------------------*        136
*       COMMON EXIT                                                 *        137
*-------------------------------------------------------------------*        138
EXIT    DS    0H                                                              139
        ENDMOD                                                                140
*-------------------------------------------------------------------*        141
*       CONSTANTS                                                   *        142
*-------------------------------------------------------------------*        143
PI      DC    D'3.14159'            PI                                        144
*-------------------------------------------------------------------*        145
*       OPEN LIST AND DCBS                                          *        146
*-------------------------------------------------------------------*        147
OLIST1  OPEN  (,),MF=L              PARMLIST FOR OPEN/CLOSE                   148
LOLIST  EQU   *-OLIST1              LENGTH OF OPEN/CLOSE PARMLIST             149
INDCB   DCB   DDNAME=IN,                                                  X   150
              DSORG=PS,                                                   X   151
              MACRF=(GL,PL),        UPDATE FILES IN I/O BUFFER            X   152
              EODAD=C$CLOSE                                                   153
LINDCB  EQU   *-INDCB               LENGTH OF THE DCB                         154
*-------------------------------------------------------------------*        155
*       WORK AREA                                                   *        156
*-------------------------------------------------------------------*        157
WNCRYPT DSECT                                                                 158
KEYWORK DS    D                     ENCRYPTION KEY                            159
IN      DS    CL(LINDCB)            DCB IN REENTRANT STORAGE                  160
OLIST   DS    0F,CL(LOLIST)         OPEN/CLOSE PARAMETER LIST                 161
ENDREC  DS    F                     ADDRESS OF END OF RECORD + 1              162
LNCRYPT EQU   *-WNCRYPT             LENGTH OF THE WORKAREA                    163
*-------------------------------------------------------------------*        164
*       OTHER DSECTS                                                *        165
*-------------------------------------------------------------------*        166
        DCBD  DSORG=PS              MAPPING FOR THE DCB                       167
        END                                                                  168
```

Figure 4.6 *(Continued)*

operand LOC = BELOW so that the STORAGE (or GETMAIN) inner macro will obtain the user work area from the below-16-meg private area. Since LOC = defaults to the AMODE of the module in which it is invoked, it is not necessary to code this explicitly. Because NCRYPT uses the floating point registers to generate random numbers, MODULE also includes the FLOATSV = YES operand to save the values in the floating point registers at entry. The ENDMOD macro on line 140 restores the floating point register values before returning control to the caller.

A user invoking NCRYPT supplies an encryption key in the PARM = field on the // EXEC card when executing NCRYPT as a batch job, or in the parameter of the CALL command when executing under TSO:

```
CALL   'library(NCRYPT)'  'string'
```

In either case, the Task Management component of MVS issues GET-MAIN to obtain virtual storage in the private area of NCRYPT's address space. Task Manager then builds a parameter list in this virtual storage consisting of a halfword containing the length of the PARM = string followed by a copy of the string itself. Task Manager then puts the address of this parameter list in a 4-byte area of the storage and stores the address of this 4-byte area in the register 1 field of the Program Request Block (PRB) under which NCRYPT will execute. NCRYPT receives control with this value in register 1.

When NCRYPT receives control, line 33 loads the address of the parameter list into register 1, and lines 34 and 35 insert the first halfword (the length of the string) into register 2. Line 36 tests the condition code set by ICM if a zero-length string was supplied and exits in that case. Lines 37 through 39 test the length of the string and, if it is longer than 7 bytes, set the length in register 2 to 7 so that only the first 7 bytes will be used. Lines 41 and 42 decrement the length by 1 and issue EX to move the bytes of this encryption key to the doubleword KEYWORK on line 159.

As a part of the OPEN service invoked by line 56, Input/Output Supervisor moves DCB information from the data set label (the DSCB for a DASD data set or the tape label for a data set on tape) into fields in the program's DCB. If NCRYPT is to be reentrant, each user must make a copy of the DCB on his own storage so that OPEN can modify it based on the particular characteristics of the file being opened. Lines 46 through 51 copy the DCB and the parameter list used by OPEN and CLOSE from where they are defined in lines 145 through 154 to lines 160 and 161 in the user's work area. Note that lines 53 through 56 use the MF = E form of OPEN against the MF = L form of the parameter list copied to the user's work area.

The USING on line 57 maps the DCB with the IHADCB DSECT. This DSECT, which results from the expansion of the DCBD macro on line

167, allows lines 81, 83, and 89 to refer to DCB fields by labels rather than by explicit displacements.

4.8.2 QSAM I/O in a Reentrant Program

The loop in lines 58 through 93 is entered by a branch to line 78, which issues the QSAM access method GET macro. QSAM invokes the services of Input/Output Supervisor (IOS) to read a *physical* record of the file from a device into a record buffer that OPEN has obtained by issuing GETMAIN for storage in the programs's private area. QSAM moves through the physical record that IOS has read into the record buffer and presents the program with a *logical* record. A file's BLKSIZE corresponds to the size of the physical record on a device; the file's LRECL is the size of the logical record.

Since NCRYPT specified the DCB MACRF = (GL operand on line 152, GET returns the address of the record in the record buffer in register 1. If the DCB had been defined with MACRF = (GM, QSAM would have moved the logical record from the record buffer to a user-supplied work area. MACRF = (GL,PL) allows NCRYPT to process the file directly in the record buffers.

After GETting the address of a logical record, lines 81 through 84 test the RECFM bits in the DCB to determine whether the file contains fixed- or variable-length records. If the RECFM bits indicate that the file to be encrypted has fixed-length records, line 82 branches to line 89 where the address of the last byte of the record plus 1 is calculated by adding the LRECL from the DCB to the address of the record. If the RECFM bits indicate that the file has variable-length records, line 85 determines the address of the last byte plus 1 by adding the record length contained in the 4-byte Record Descriptor Word (RDW) that precedes each variable-length record in storage.

After Lines 65 through 72 encrypt a byte in the record buffer, lines 73 through 76 point at the next byte in the buffer and compare its address with the address of the end of the record. If the end of the record has been reached, line 77 issues PUTX. PUTX causes QSAM to test whether this record is the last one in a block (based on the BLKSIZE in the DCB). If this is the end of a block, PUTX causes QSAM to write a physical record back to its original location on a DASD track. ENCRYPT uses PUTX to update a record in place for two reasons:

1. Encrypted bytes physically overlay the original, nonencrypted, data. If the original data were left on DASD tracks, even though they were not part of a file, the EXCP access method could be used to read the tracks, and the nonencrypted data could be recovered.

2. Because an encrypted byte takes the place of a nonencrypted byte, there is no possibility of causing an out-of-space condition in a file or on a disk.

The last physical record in every DSORG = PS file (as well as the last record in a PDS member) is a device-specific end-of-file indicator. When QSAM reads this record, it branches to the EODAD address in the DCB. In NCRYPT, the EODAD= operand on the DCB (line 153) causes a branch to the PUTX on line 98 where the final, probably incomplete, block is written to the file. This last PUT or PUTX is necessary when MACRF = PL is used, but unnecessary with MACRF = PM. The CLOSE on line 99 uses the same parameter list as OPEN on line 56.

4.8.3 The RANDOM Subroutine

In the encryption loop in lines 64 through 93, lines 65 through 69 generate a random byte by making two calls to the RANDOM subroutine (lines 101 through 126). Each call to RANDOM generates 4 random bits which line 69 ORs together to form a byte. Lines 70 through 72 retrieve a byte from the record buffer, XR it with the random byte, and store it back into the record buffer.

Note that lines 65 and 67 issue the BAS instruction rather than BAL to call the RANDOM subroutine. This is necessary because when BAL is issued in an AMODE 24 program, the Instruction Length Code (ILC), program mask, and condition code from the PSW are placed in the high-order byte of the link register, whereas with BAS, the high order byte contains X'00' (BAS sets the high-order bit to the current AMODE):

| | CONTENTS OF REGISTER 14 |
INSTRUCTION	AFTER EXECUTION
BAL R14,RANDOM	BF006458
BAS R14,RANDOM	00006458

When RANDOM issues BAKR R14,0 on line 111, the entire contents of register 14 are placed in the second doubleword of the PSW in the stack state entry that BAKR creates. When RANDOM returns control with the PR instruction on line 126, the PSW in the stack state entry becomes the active PSW. If, as in the foregoing example, the high-order bit in register 14 was 1, the new PSW will be AMODE 31 and will use all 31 low-order bits of the instruction address. In the example, BAL would have resulted in PR loading a PSW that would attempt to execute the instruction at address X'3F006458' rather than the instruction at X'00006458'!

Note also that the inclusion of BAKR and PR instructions means that the program must be executed on a computer that uses the ESA instruction set. This limitation can be avoided by replacing lines in NCRYPT with the corresponding lines in Fig. 4.7. The GBLC instruction before the MODULE macro in line 28 allows the symbol "&SYSSPLV" to be used

```
         GBLC  &SYSSPLV              TO TEST &SYSSPLV IN OPEN CODE      28
         MODULE NCRYPT,BASE=12,AMODE=24,RMODE=24,FLOATSV=YES,        X 28
         ..
         AIF   ('&SYSSPLV' LE '2').RAND1   IS THIS XA OR SP ?        111
         BAKR  R14,0                 CREATE STACK STATE ENTRY        111
         AGO   .RAND1A                                               111
.RAND1   ANOP                                                        111
         STM   R2,R14,SAVE1          SAVE REGISTERS IN WORK AREA     111
.RAND1A  ANOP                                                        111
         ..
         AIF   ('&SYSSPLV' LE '2').RAND2   IS THIS XA OR SP ?        126
         PR                          POP STACK AND RETURN            126
         AGO   .RAND2A                                               126
.RAND2   ANOP                                                        126
         LM    R2,R14,SAVE1          LOAD REGISTERS FROM WORK AREA   126
         BR    14                                                    126
.RAND2A  ANOP                                                        126
         ..
WNCRYPT  DSECT                                                       158
         AIF   ('&SYSSPLV' GT '2').SAVE1   IS THIS ESA ?             158
SAVE1    DS    13F                   SAVE AREA FOR REIGISTERS 2-14   158
.SAVE1   ANOP                                                        158
```

Figure 4.7 Saving and restoring registers based on SPLEVEL.

outside of macros in same way it is used within the MODULE and ENDMOD macros. Depending on the SPLEVEL in effect at the time of assembly, the AIF instructions that replace lines 111, 126, and 158 will cause XA or ESA code to be generated.

4.8.4 Floating Point Numbers

The RANDOM subroutine uses floating point arithmetic. Floating point numbers have two principal uses:

1. They can contain very large or very small numbers. A floating point number can be as small as 5.4×10^{-79} or as large as 7.2×10^{75}.

2. They can contain fractions. Unlike fixed point or packed numbers, there is no need to multiply and divide a floating point number by a power of the base to force the fractional part to the left of the radix point. Line 144 of NCRYPT, for example, represents PI as 3.14159 rather than as 314159 (and divide by 100,000).

Floating point numbers are similar to the fraction-and-exponent format used in "scientific notation." The number 12.3, for example, can be represented:

12.3×10^0

1.23×10^1

$.123 \times 10^2$

The last form, in which the first nonzero digit is just to the right of the decimal point, is considered "normalized."

Numbers used in computers, which are base 2 (but represented as base 16) can be expressed in a similar fraction-and-exponent format. The number X'0000B328', for example, could be written:

$.B328 \times 16^4$

Floating point numbers in floating point registers or in storage have the format (single floating point):

EEFFFFFF

where EE represents the exponent (power of 16) and FFFFFF represents the fractional portion. The exponent byte is always 64 greater than its true value. This allows a floating point number to represent numbers with negative exponents (i.e., fractions). For example, if the first byte of a floating point number is X'40' it means 16^0; if the first byte is X'3F', it means 16^{-1}. Thus the number X'0000B328' would be represented in a floating point register in normalized form as

44B32800

The first bit in a floating point number is not part of the exponent. Rather, it indicates whether the number as a whole is positive or negative. The floating point representation of $-$X'0000B328' is, therefore

C4B32800

The RANDOM subroutine first turns the encryption key moved into KEYWORK by line 44 into a normalized floating point number by moving X'40' into the first byte (line 113). RANDOM uses the double form of floating point numbers in which an even-odd pair of floating point registers is used to contain a single number. (There are two other floating point formats: single, a 4-byte format; and extended, a 16-byte format.)*

Principles of Operation contains a complete description of all floating point formats as well as samples of code for converting positive and negative fixed point numbers into floating point format.

After line 114 loads the floating point number into a pair of floating point registers, lines 115 through 118 add PI to the number and cube it. This generates a pseudorandom number. Lines 199 and 120 move the result from the floating point registers 0 and 1 to general registers 0 and 1 where lines 121 and 122 shift off the sign, exponent, and high-order factional byte.

Line 123 then stores the digits that remain into KEYWORK so that the next call to RANDOM will use the new value when it generates the next pseudorandom number. Lines 124 and 125 shift off all but 4 bits of the value in register 0 and load these 4 bits into register 1 where the caller expects to find this value.

5

Task Management and Recovery

5.1 TASKS

Before there was MVS there were tasks. Tasks and the structures that define them have remained substantially unchanged since the days of the Single Virtual Storage (SVS) operating systems like MVT and VS1 that evolved into OS/MVS (Multiple Virtual Storage). Tasks, defined to MVS by Task Control Blocks (TCBs), have three functional roles.

5.1.1 Dispatching

All units of work are defined to MVS either as a task, with a TCB, or as a service request, with a Service Request Block (SRB). The MVS Dispatcher selects units of work to execute on available processors from queues of TCBs and SRBs. SRBs (see Chap. 9) are quite limited in the types of work that can execute under them and are used almost exclusively as a way for a task in one address space schedule work to execute in another address space. All other work executes under TCBs.

5.1.2 Resource Control

As illustrated in Fig. 5.1, the TCB anchors queues of control blocks that describe individual resource elements owned by the unit of work the TCB represents. Resources in the following areas are owned by tasks:

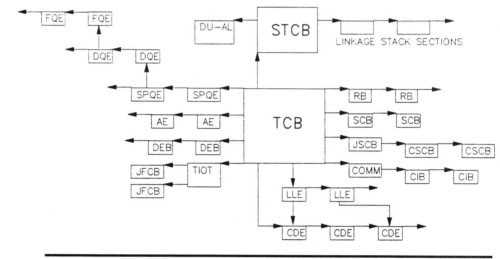

Figure 5.1 TCB control block queues.

- *Virtual storage:* Subpool Queue Elements (SPQEs) describe the private area subpools either owned by the task or shared with other tasks. SPQEs, in turn, anchor chains of Descriptor Queue Elements (DQEs) and Free Queue Elements (FQEs) that describe the allocated virtual storage within each subpool. Allocated Elements (AEs) describe LSQA storage owned by the task.

- *Load modules:* Contents Directory Entries (CDEs) describe program load modules in virtual storage owned by the task. The chain of CDEs off the TCB is known as the Job Pack Area Queue (JPAQ). Load List Elements (LLEs) maintain a count of the number of times the LOAD and DELETE macros were issued by any program executing under that TCB for individual modules.

- *Input/output:* The Task Input Output Table (TIOT) contains an entry for each data set allocated to the current task. Each entry in the TIOT points to a Job File Control Block (JFCB) where the data set is described in detail. After any work under the current TCB OPENs a data set on a DASD volume, the Data Extent Block (DEB) contains the physical address of the data on the volume and points to the program's Data Control Block (DCB).

5.1.3 Interface to MVS Components

Some of the control block queues in Fig. 5.1 allow a unit of work to communicate with MVS components or request special processing from an MVS component under certain circumstances.

- *CONSOLE:* Each Command Scheduling Control Block (CSCB) chained from the TCB through the Job Step Control Block (JSCB) represents an MVS console command issued with the MGCR macro from any program executing under the TCB. The CONSOLE address space dequeues a CSCB when it executes the command.

  Each Command Information Block (CIB) chained from the TCB through the Console Communication Area (COMM), represents a START, STOP, MODIFY, or MOUNT command directed at this unit of work from an MVS console. A program can dequeue a CIB with the QEDIT macro after processing the command.

- *Cross Memory Services (XMS):* The TCB through the Secondary TCB (STCB) points to the Dispatchable Unit Access List (DU-AL). The DU-AL contains entries for every address space to which programs under the TCB can establish access register mode addressability. This facility exists only in MVS/ESA.

- *Linkage stack (ESA only):* The sections of the linkage stack are chained from the TCB through the STCB. State entries are created in linkage stack sections by the BAKR and PC (stacking-type) instructions.

- *Task Manager and Dispatcher:* The queue of Request Blocks (RBs) from the TCB represents subunits of work that execute serially. When the MVS Dispatcher selects a task to execute on a processor, it transfers control to the first RB on the queue.

- *Recovery Termination Manager (RTM):* Each STAE Control Block (SCB) represents an ESTAE recovery routine that can receive control from RTM2 when a program check occurs in a program executing under the TCB.

The TCB and its related control blocks are all located in LSQA and ELSQA.

5.2 MULTIPLE TASKS IN AN ADDRESS SPACE

TCBs and the units of work they represent can be in one of three states.

- *Active:* An active task is currently executing on a processor.

- *Ready:* A ready task can be dispatched when the MVS Dispatcher selects it as the highest priority work.

- *Nondispatchable:* A nondispatchable task cannot be selected by the Dispatcher until some event occurs to make the task *ready*. The most common reason a task is nondispatchable is because a WAIT macro has been issued by a program executing under the TCB. When another program issues POST against the Event Control Block (ECB) for the WAIT, Task Manager changes the task status to *ready*.

Some applications and subsystems take advantage of the fact that they might execute on a multiengine machine. They create multiple ready tasks within their address space in the expectation that several of the tasks will be dispatched and execute on different processors at the same time. In these applications, multitasking can provide a performance advantage, but often it creates the need for additional and complex intertask communication and serialization mechanisms.

Other applications use multitasking for asynchronous processes, typically for I/O. In this type of application, a processing task will ship an I/O request to one or more I/O subtasks. The subtask will go into wait state until the I/O operation completes, while the processing task is free to do other work. Again, multitasking in such an application usually creates the need for intertask communication and serialization.

Most applications do not multitask. Yet, the dump of a typical batch address space executing an application program shows five TCBs. Four of the TCBs are in wait state and are nondispatchable; the application program executes under the fifth TCB. This raises the question of why there is not just one TCB in the address space. If all the operations within the address space occur serially, why not just queue them on the RB chain off a single TCB? The answer is recovery.

Consider the following scenario:

> You are logged on to TSO and issue a command to invoke a user-written program:
>
> CALL   'MYID.LIBRARY(PROGRAM)'.
>
> When the program you CALL begins to execute, your TSO session goes into a wait state. The CALLed program contains an error. Your TSO session becomes active again, issues message IEA995I containing the system completion code, and resumes in the same state as before the CALL.

What has happened is that the TSO CALL command actually generated an ATTACH so that your program executed under is own TCB. When the error in the program was encountered, the program check interrupt passed control to Recovery Termination Manager (RTM). RTM2, the subcomponent of RTM that deals with task recovery, released the resources associated with the abending TCB and issued DETACH for it. The fact that the abending work was its own task allowed RTM to handle it as a separate unit. The TSO task that issued the ATTACH was not affected by the abend in the subtask and merely reported it with the IEA995I message.

The facilities that RTM2 provides to recover from errors on a task level and to terminate tasks without affecting the other tasks in address spaces is the primary reason multitasking is used in MVS.

5.3 MVS TASK MANAGER

Task Management is the MVS component that is responsible for:

- Creating and initializing tasks in response to an ATTACH macro
- Managing the Request Block queue
- Removing tasks in response to the DETACH macro
- Performing various services related to the TCB including those invoked by the EXTRACT, CHAP, WAIT, POST, and TESTAUTH macros. These services are discussed in the chapters where the macros are used in programs.

5.3.1 Creating Tasks

Figure 5.2 illustrates the creation of a new task with the ATTACH macro. The ATTACH service

- Initializes a new TCB.
- Updates the address pointers that describe the relationship of the new TCB to other TCBs in the address space. Each TCB contains the address of the TCB that ATTACHed it, called its "mother" task, the TCB it last ATTACHed, called its "daughter" task, and the TCB last ATTACHed by its mother TCB, called its "sister" task. Taken together, these pointers describe each TCB's location in a tree structure that includes all the TCBs in the address space.
- Builds control blocks on the queues illustrated in Fig. 5.1 for the new TCB. The ATTACH in Fig. 5.2, for example, includes the GSPV = operand to create an SPQE for subpool 5, ESTAI = to build an SCB for the ESTAE routine whose address is in register 2 and EP = to build an RB and a CDE for the first program to execute under the new TCB.

In Fig. 5.2, note how the SF = (E and SF = L forms of ATTACH are used to achieve reentrancy. The MF = operand, which is used in other macros for that purpose, contains the address of a user parameter list. The first program that executes under the new task receives the address of the user parameter list in register 1. Note also how ATTACH returns the new task's TCB address which is saved for later use by DETACH.

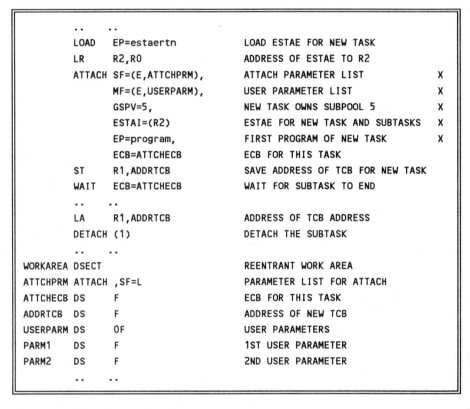

```
          ..      ..
          LOAD    EP=estaertn              LOAD ESTAE FOR NEW TASK
          LR      R2,R0                    ADDRESS OF ESTAE TO R2
          ATTACH  SF=(E,ATTCHPRM),         ATTACH PARAMETER LIST            X
                  MF=(E,USERPARM),         USER PARAMETER LIST              X
                  GSPV=5,                  NEW TASK OWNS SUBPOOL 5          X
                  ESTAI=(R2)               ESTAE FOR NEW TASK AND SUBTASKS  X
                  EP=program,              FIRST PROGRAM OF NEW TASK        X
                  ECB=ATTCHECB             ECB FOR THIS TASK
          ST      R1,ADDRTCB               SAVE ADDRESS OF TCB FOR NEW TASK
          WAIT    ECB=ATTCHECB             WAIT FOR SUBTASK TO END
          ..      ..
          LA      R1,ADDRTCB               ADDRESS OF TCB ADDRESS
          DETACH  (1)                      DETACH THE SUBTASK
          ..      ..
WORKAREA  DSECT                            REENTRANT WORK AREA
ATTCHPRM  ATTACH  ,SF=L                    PARAMETER LIST FOR ATTACH
ATTCHECB  DS      F                        ECB FOR THIS TASK
ADDRTCB   DS      F                        ADDRESS OF NEW TCB
USERPARM  DS      0F                       USER PARAMETERS
PARM1     DS      F                        1ST USER PARAMETER
PARM2     DS      F                        2ND USER PARAMETER
          ..      ..
```

Figure 5.2   Creating a subtask.

5.3.2 Managing the Request Block Queue

An RB describes the state a processor must be in when it executes the program associated with that RB. Each RB, as illustrated in Fig. 5.3, contains a Program Status Word (PSW) and slots for the 16 general registers. In addition, each RB points to a Extended Status Block (XSB), not illustrated in Fig. 5.3, which contains slots for the control register values that describe a cross-memory environment and slots for the 16 ESA access registers.

A TCB with two queued RBs is illustrated in the first line of Fig. 5.3. When Task Manager put the first RB at the head of the queue, it copied the register values from the RB to the TCB. If this were an ESA system, Task Manager would also have copied the access register values from the XSB to an ESA extension of the TCB, the Secondary TCB (STCB), which is chained off the TCB.

When the MVS Dispatcher selects the TCB to execute on a processor, it loads the processor's general registers from the TCB, the access registers (ESA only) from the STCB, and the appropriate control registers

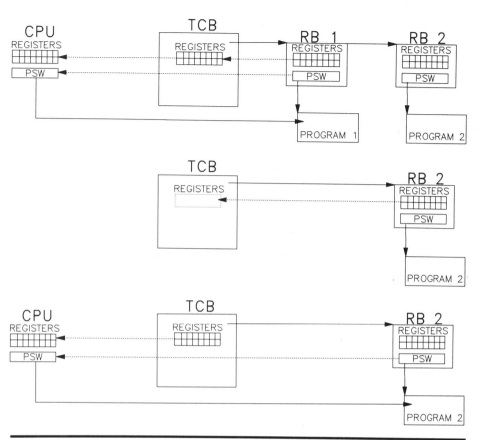

Figure 5.3 Request blocks.

from the first XSB. The Dispatcher then issues a LPSW (load PSW) instruction against the PSW in the first RB. Since this PSW contains the address of an instruction in the module (program 1) associated with the RB, the module begins to execute on the processor.

When the program executing under the first RB ends with a BR 14 or PR instruction, it executes an SVC 3 instruction whose address was placed in the register 14 slot of the RB when it was created. SVC 3 invokes Task Manager's EXIT routine which dequeues the RB for the completed program and copies the general registers from the next RB on the queue into the TCB. This is illustrated in the second line of Fig. 5.3.

The third line in the figure illustrates what happens when the TCB is dispatched again. The MVS Dispatcher loads the processor's general and control registers from the TCB and the first XSB and issues an LPSW instruction against the PSW in the first RB on the queue. Since RB 2 is now at the head of the queue, the PSW contains the address of the next instruction in program 2, which begins to execute on the processor.

Several MVS services can build RBs and chain them onto the queue. The LINK service, whether invoked with the LINK macro or called by the ATTACH service, adds Program Request Blocks (PRBs); the SVC First Level Interrupt Handler adds SVC Request Blocks (SVRBs), the SCHEDXIT service adds Interrupt Request Blocks (IRBs). As shown in Chap. 6, RBs allow a program to be interrupted, another program to execute, and the original program to be resumed at the point of interruption.

5.3.3 Removing Tasks

A task is removed when

- The program executing under the only RB on the queue completes. When the EXIT routine receives control to dequeue that RB, it detects that there are no more RBs and starts the termination process.

- A program executing under an RB on the TCB's RB queue abends and RTM is unable to recover.

- The program that ATTACHed the task issues DETACH for the task.

However the termination process is begun, removing a task involves reversing the actions taken when the task was created.

- Resources owned by the task, represented by control blocks on the queues from the TCB, must be released. This is the responsibility of RTM2 rather than the Task Management DETACH service.

- The pointers in the other TCBs in the address space that describe the "family" relationship to this TCB are changed by DETACH to reflect the removal of this task.

- The TCB itself is released. DETACH invokes Virtual Storage Manager (VSM) with a FREEMAIN for the LSQA storage that contains the TCB. If the task that ATTACHed this task is waiting for this task to complete, as in Fig. 5.2, DETACH issues POST against the WAITing task's ECB.

5.4 RTM2: TASK RECOVERY AND TERMINATION

RTM2 is the subcomponent of RTM that is responsible for task-level recovery and termination.

RTM1, the other major subcomponent of RTM, is responsible for recovery when an error is not associated with an individual task in a specific address space. Many MVS component routines establish RTM1 recovery with Functional Recovery Routines (FRRs), since they deal with global (system-wide) control blocks. SRB routines also employ RTM1 recovery because they involve more than a single address space. (See Chap. 9 for more on RTM1, FRRs, and SRBs.)

5.4.1 SVC 13: The ABEND Macro

SVC 13, generated by the ABEND macro, is the only interface to RTM2. SVC 13 is issued as part of normal task termination by the Task Manager EXIT routine and in abnormal termination by RTM1 or user programs. RTM2 itself issues SVC 13 to terminate the subtasks of a task it is in the process of terminating. RTM2 performs the following functions:

- During abnormal termination, RTM2 calls ESTAE routines to analyze and recover from the error.

- During both normal and abnormal termination, RTM2 calls resource manager routines to clean up the control blocks that relate the task to other MVS components. Resource manager routines are named in the CSECT IEAVTRML in the MVS Nucleus and are called by RTM2 in the order named.

Some applications own resources that are not cleaned up by the IBM-supplied resource managers. A table in common storage used by several applications, for example, might be serialized by the presence of a token in one of the table's fields. When an application uses the table it puts a certain value in the token field; other applications test the field and do not access the table if they see that value. This type of "nonstandard ENQ" should be released if a task terminates while owning it. A resource manager routine that will be called by RTM2 during termination can be installed by adding its name to IEAVTRML with the AMASPZAP utility or by writing a program that uses the RESMGR macro to define the routine "on the fly."

5.4.2 ESTAE Routines

ESTAE is an abbreviation for Extended Specify Task Abnormal Exit and, as the name implies, ESTAE routines are exit routines for RTM2.

In Fig. 5.4, the executing module in the lower left establishes an ESTAE routine for the current task by issuing

```
LOAD    EP = newestae
LR      3,0
ESTAE   (3)
```

Once LOAD has invoked Program Management to bring the ESTAE module into storage, ESTAE causes the RTM2 to take the following actions:

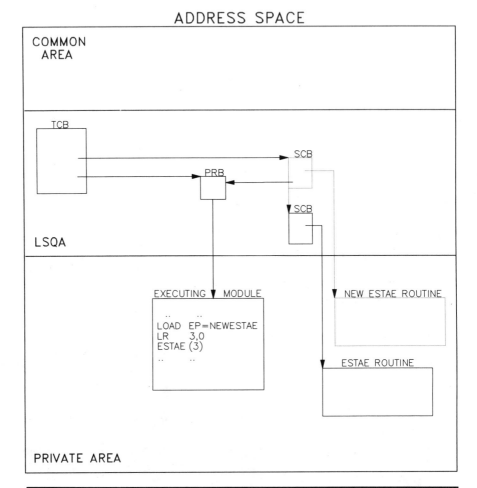

Figure 5.4 Establishing an ESTAE routine.

- RTM builds a STAE Control Block (SCB). The SCB contains the virtual address of the ESTAE routine as well as the address of the parameter list for the ESTAE routine if PARAM = was coded as an operand on the ESTAE macro. The SCB also contains the address of the issuer's Request Block. Since ESTAE can be issued in a LINKed program, in a type 2, 3, or 4 SVC routine, or in an asynchronous exit routine, the SCB can specify a PRB, SVRB, or IRB.

The SCB contains the address of another control block not shown in Fig. 5.4, the SCB Extension (SCBX). The SCBX contains the addressing environment in effect when ESTAE was issued and, on an ESA system, the current linkage stack pointer.

- RTM adds the new SCB to the head of the SCB queue off the current TCB. The SCB queue, therefore, represents all the currently defined ESTAE routines for this task in the reverse order from that in which they were defined.

When the ABEND SVC is issued for a task, RTM2 receives control under an SVRB as illustrated in Fig. 5.5. After RTM2 builds the RTM2 Work Area (RTM2WA) to track and control its own processing, RTM2 examines register 1, which was set by the issuer of ABEND, to see whether the request for processing was for normal task termination or for an error condition. If it is normal termination, RTM2 proceeds to

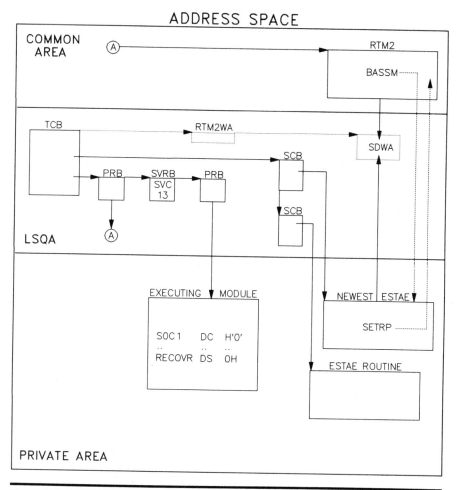

Figure 5.5 ESTAE recovery.

release the resources represented by the control blocks queued off the TCB.

However, if RTM2 was called as the result of an error condition, it examines the SCB queue and, if it finds an SCB, issues the SYNCH macro to create a PRB under which the ESTAE routine will execute. (This is the PRB at the head of the RB queue in Fig. 5.5.) RTM2 then builds a System Diagnostic Work Area (SDWA) to pass information about the abend to the ESTAE routine, and puts the address of the SDWA into register 1 before it branches to the ESTAE routine. The ESTAE routine can modify fields in the SDWA before returning control to RTM2. A new SDWA is built every time RTM2 calls an ESTAE routine.

Before RTM2 transfers control to the ESTAE routine, it restores as much of the environment as it can from the SCB so that the ESTAE routine is entered with the same addressing mode, PASN, SASN, and (ESA) linkage stack pointer that existed when the ESTAE routine was established. When the ESTAE routine receives control, it can obtain information about the abend from fields in the SDWA as well as the address of the user parameter list identified by the PARAM = operand of ESTAE macro.

ESTAE routines end with the SETRP macro. SETRP expands into instructions that modify fields in the SDWA, load a return code into register 15 and branch to RTM2. The return code, set with the RC = operand on SETRP, tells RTM2 what action to take when it receives control back from the ESTAE exit.

■ RC = 4 tells RTM2 to stop processing the abend and cause a retry routine, specified by the SETRP RETADDR = operand, to receive control. Usually this "routine" is nothing more than an address in the program that issued ESTAE where control should be returned in the event of an error. The retry address is commonly passed to the ESTAE routine in the ESTAE PARAM = parameter list.

To accomplish retry, RTM2 locates the RB whose address is in the ESTAE routine's SCB, changes the PSW in that RB so that the address portion contains the retry address, dequeues any RBs in front of the RB it has located, and invokes EXIT so that Task Manager dequeues the ABEND SVRB itself. This puts the RB associated with the ESTAE routine at the head of the RB queue. When the TCB is dispatched again and the PSW from the first RB on the queue is loaded, the instruction at the retry address receives control.

■ RC = 0 tells RTM2 to continue terminating the task. If there is another SCB on the queue, RTM2 will again go through the process of calling the ESTAE routine it specifies. That routine, in turn, can tell RTM2 to retry or continue with termination. If none of the ESTAE routines causes retry, RTM2 will invoke every ESTAE routine in the SCB queue before it finally terminates the task. This process of calling each ESTAE routine in turn up through the SCB chain is called "percolation." When an ESTAE routine ends with RC = 0, telling RTM2 to continue task termination, it is said to "percolate."

5.4.3 Additional Macros

In addition to ESTAE, the following macros also establish RTM2 task recovery routines:

- STAE is virtually identical to ESTAE.

- FESTAE causes a fast-path branch entry to the ESTAE service. It is only used by type 2, 3, or 4 SVC routines in PSW key 0.

- The STAI = or ESTAI = parameter on the ATTACH macro establishes the first ESTAE routine for the new task created by the ATTACH service. This ESTAE will also be established as the first ESTAE for any subtask ATTACHed by the new task. STAI = does not save as much of the addressing environment as ESTAI =, especially in MVS/ESA, and ESTAI = is preferred.

- ESTAEX (ESA only) causes a PC entry, rather than an SVC or branch entry, to the ESTAE service. Since ESTAEX establishes an ESTAE routine that can operate in access register addressing mode as well as in primary space mode (see Chap. 10) and creates an ALET qualified parameter list, it is the preferred MVS/ESA interface. ESTAEX routines, in contrast to other ESTAE-type routines that execute in the AMODE of the ESTAE issuer, all execute with AMODE 31.

- The ARR = parameter on the ETDEF macro establishes the recovery routine for a PC routine. ETDEF ARR = does not create an SCB and will never be entered through RTM2 percolation. (See Chap. 10 for more on PC routines and ARRs.)

5.5 EDEBUG WALKTHROUGH

The EDEBUG program in Fig. 5.6 is a skeleton for an interactive debugging utility that runs under TSO. It illustrates how RTM2 transfers control to an ESTAE routine when a program check occurs and how the ESTAE routine directs RTM2 either to retry or to percolate the abend based on the contents of fields in the SDWA.

Any program can establish EDEBUG as its ESTAE routine by including the code in Fig. 5.7. The LOAD macro brings the EDEBUG module into virtual storage and returns its entry point and AMODE in register 0. (See Chap. 8 for more on LOAD.) After issuing LR to transfer the entry point to one of the registers 2 through 12, the program issues ESTAE,

```
*+------------------------------------------------------------+  1
*|   FUNCTION:                                                |  2
*|      SKELETON FOR INTERACTIVE DEBUGGER THAT RUNS AS AN ESTAE UNDER  3
*|      TSO.  (ACKNOWLEDGMENTS TO DAVID B. COLE)              |  4
*|   LOGIC:                                                   |  5
*|      1) CHECK FOR SDWA.  IF NO SDWA, PERCOLATE THE ABEND.  |  6
*|      2) USE TPUT TO OUTPUT ENTRYPOINT ADDRESS, ABEND PSW, AND  7
*|         ABEND CODE.                                        |  8
*|      3) CHECK WHETHER THE ABEND WAS CAUSED BY AN IMPLANTED |  9
*|         @DB@ BREAKPOINT. IF YES, PROMPT FOR RETRY.         | 10
*|      4) ISSUE SETRP RC=4 TO RETRY INTO THE ABENDING CODE OR | 11
*|         SETRP RC=0 TO PERCOLATE THE ABEND                  | 12
*|   INPUTS:                                                  | 13
*|      R1 - ADDRESS OF SDWA SUPPLIED BY RTM2.                | 14
*|   OUTPUTS:                                                 | 15
*|      MESSAGES ON TSO TERMINAL.                             | 16
*|      MODIFICATIONS TO SDWA.                                | 17
*|   ATTRIBUTES:                                              | 18
*|      AMODE 31, RMODE 24, REENTERABLE                       | 19
*+------------------------------------------------------------+ 20
EDEBUG   CSECT                                                  21
EDEBUG   AMODE 31                                               22
EDEBUG   RMODE 24                                               23
         USING EDEBUG,R15         SET ADDRESSING ON ENTRYPOINT  24
         B     BEGIN              BRANCH AROUND DOCUMENTATION    25
         DC    C' EDEBUG '        CSECT NAME                     26
         DC    C' &SYSDATE '      DATE OF ASSEMBLY               27
         DC    C' &SYSTIME '      TIME OF ASSEMBLY               28
BEGIN    DS    0H                                                29
         PRINT NOGEN                                             30
         COPY  EQUATES                                           31
         PRINT GEN                                               32
*        *----------------------------------------*             33
*        *    TEST WHETHER THERE IS AN SDWA     *               34
*        *----------------------------------------*             35
         CH    R0,=H'12'          WAS AN SDWA OBTAINED ?         36
         BNE   Y$SDWA             YES; CONTINUE                  37
         LA    R15,0              SET FOR PERCOLATION            38
         BR    R14                RETURN TO RTM2                 39
Y$SDWA   DS    0H                                                40
         DROP  R15                DROP ADDRESSING ON ENTRYPOINT  41
         STM   R14,R12,12(R13)    SAVE REGS IN RTM2'S SAVEAREA   42
         LR    R12,R15            LOAD ENTRYPOINT INTO BASE REG  43
         USING EDEBUG,R12         SET ADDRESSING ON BASE REGISTER 44
         GETMAIN RU,LV=LEDEBUG,   ..GET < 16M STORAGE FOR      X 45
               LOC=BELOW          ..REENTERABLE WORK AREA        46
         LR    R2,R13             ADDRESS OF CALLER'S SAVE AREA  47
         ST    R13,4(R1)          SAVE CALLER'S SAVE AREA ADDRESS 48
         ST    R1,8(R13)          ADDRESS OF OUR SAVEAREA TO CALLR 49
         LR    R13,R1             ADDRESS OF WORKAREA TO R13     50
         USING WEDEBUG,R13        MAP WORK AREA                  51
         LM    R14,R2,12(R2)      RESTORE REGS FROM CALLERS SAVEA 52
         LR    R3,R1              ADDRESS OF SDWA                53
         USING SDWA,R3            MAP SDWA                       54
```

Figure 5.6 EDEBUG.

```
*         *------------------------------------------*              55
*         *      UNCOMMENT THE FOLLOWING 2 LINES  *              56
*         *      TO TEST FOR RECURSIVE ENTRY.     *              57
*         *------------------------------------------*              58
*         TM    SDWAERRD,SDWASTAE     RECURSIVE ENTRY ?            59
*         BO    EXIT00                YES; PERCOLATE THE ABEND     60
*         *------------------------------------------*              61
*         *      OUTPUT ENTRY POINT ADDRESS        *              62
*         *------------------------------------------*              63
          MVC   PUTGET(L'MSG1),MSG1   MOVE MESSAGE TO OUTPUT AREA  64
          XTOC  PLIST=XTOCLIST,       ..CHANGE                  X  65
                ADIN=SDWAEPA,         ..HEX VALUE               X  66
                LIN=L'SDWAEPA,        ..OF SDWA FIELD           X  67
                ADOUT=PUTGET+L'MSG1,  ..TO PRINTABLE            X  68
                LOUT=L'SDWAEPA*2      ..CHARACTERS                 69
          LA    R0,L'MSG1+L'SDWAEPA*2 LENGTH OF OUTPUT FIELD FOR TPUT 70
          LA    R1,PUTGET             ADDRESS OF OUTPUT AREA       71
          TPUT  (R1),(R0),R           SEND MESSAGE TO TERMINAL     72
*         *------------------------------------------*              73
*         *      OUTPUT ABEND PSW                  *              74
*         *------------------------------------------*              75
          MVC   PUTGET(L'MSG2),MSG2   MOVE MESSAGE TO OUTPUT AREA  76
          XTOC  PLIST=XTOCLIST,       ..CHANGE                  X  77
                ADIN=SDWAEC1,         ..HEX VALUE               X  78
                LIN=L'SDWAEC1,        ..OF SDWA FIELD           X  79
                ADOUT=PUTGET+L'MSG2,  ..TO PRINTABLE            X  80
                LOUT=L'SDWAEC1*2      ..CHARACTERS                 81
          LA    R0,L'MSG2+L'SDWAEC1*2 LENGTH OF OUTPUT FIELD FOR TPUT 82
          LA    R1,PUTGET             ADDRESS OF OUTPUT AREA       83
          TPUT  (R1),(R0),R           SEND MESSAGE TO TERMINAL     84
*         *------------------------------------------*              85
*         *      OUTPUT ABEND CODE                 *              86
*         *------------------------------------------*              87
          MVC   PUTGET(L'MSG3),MSG3   MOVE MESSAGE TO OUTPUT AREA  88
          XTOC  PLIST=XTOCLIST,       ..CHANGE                  X  89
                ADIN=SDWAABCC,        ..HEX VALUE               X  90
                LIN=L'SDWAABCC,       ..OF SDWA FIELD           X  91
                ADOUT=PUTGET+L'MSG3,  ..TO PRINTABLE            X  92
                LOUT=L'SDWAABCC*2     ..CHARACTERS                 93
          LA    R0,L'MSG3+L'SDWAABCC*2 LENGTH OF OUTPUT FIELD FOR TPUT 94
          LA    R1,PUTGET             ADDRESS OF OUTPUT AREA       95
          TPUT  (R1),(R0),R           SEND MESSAGE TO TERMINAL     96
*         *------------------------------------------*              97
*         *      IF ABEND 0C1 CAUSED BY A @DB@      *              98
*         *      TRAP, PROMPT FOR CONTINUATION.     *              99
*         *      OTHERWISE PERCOLATE THE ABEND.     *             100
*         *------------------------------------------*             101
          XR    R1,R1                 CLEAR REGISTER              102
          ICM   R1,B'0011',SDWACMPC   SYSTEM COMPLETION CODE      103
          SRL   R1,4                  RIGHT JUSTIFY               104
          C     R1,S0C1               IS IT 0C1 ?                 105
          BNE   EXIT00                NO; PERCOLATE ABEND         106
          L     R1,SDWANXT1           A(NEXT INSTRUCTION) FROM PSW 107
          CLC   0(L'EDB,R1),EDB       IS IT OUR EDB TRAP ?        108
          BNE   EXIT00                NO; PERCOLATE ABEND         109
          LA    R0,L'PROMPT           LENGTH OF PROMPT LITERAL    110
          LA    R1,PROMPT             ADDRESS OF PROMPT LITERAL   111
```

Figure 5.6   *(Continued)*

```
                  TPUT  (R1),(R0),R             TPUT PROMPT MESSAGE              112
                  LA    R0,L'PUTGET             LENGTH OF TPUT/TGET BUFFER      113
                  LA    R1,PUTGET               ADDRESS OF TPUT/TGET BUFFER     114
                  ICM   R1,B'1000',GETFLAGS     SET FLAG FOR TGET               115
                  TGET  (R1),(R0),R             GET TERMINAL RESPONSE INTO BUF  116
                  OC    PUTGET(L'GO),FOLD       CHANGE RESPONSE TO UPPER CASE   117
                  CLC   PUTGET(L'GO),GO         IS IT "GO" ?                    118
                  BE    EXIT04                  YES; RETRY INTO CODE            119
                  B     EXIT00                  PERCOLATE THE ABEND             120
*----------------------------------------------------------------------*       121
*         PERCOLATE THE ABEND                                           *       122
*----------------------------------------------------------------------*       123
EXIT00    DS    0H                                                              124
          LR    R2,R13                  A(SAVE AREA) => R2                      125
          L     R13,SAVEGEN+4           RESTORE A(CALLER'S SAVE AREA)           126
          FREEMAIN RU,LV=LEDEBUG,A=(2)  FREE WORK AREA STORAGE                  127
          LR    R1,R3                   SDWA ADDRESS TO R1                      128
          SETRP RC=0,REGS=(14,12),DUMP=NO                                      129
*----------------------------------------------------------------------*       130
*         RETRY                                                         *       131
*----------------------------------------------------------------------*       132
EXIT04    DS    0H                                                              133
          LR    R2,R13                  A(SAVE AREA) => R2                      134
          L     R13,SAVEGEN+4           RESTORE A(CALLER'S SAVE AREA)           135
          FREEMAIN RU,LV=LEDEBUG,A=(2)  FREE WORK AREA STORAGE                  136
          L     R15,SDWANXT1            A(NEXT INSTRUCTION) FROM PSW            137
          LA    R15,L'EDB(R15)          BUMP FOR LENGTH OF EDB TRAP             138
          LR    R1,R3                   SDWA ADDRESS TO R1                      139
          SETRP RC=4,RETREGS=YES,RETADDR=(15),FRESDWA=YES,              X      140
                REGS=(14,12),DUMP=NO                                           141
*----------------------------------------------------------------------*       142
*         CONSTANTS                                                     *       143
*----------------------------------------------------------------------*       144
SOC1      DC    A(X'000000C1')          SOC1 COMPARE VALUE                      145
EDB       DC    C'aDBa'                 EDB TRAP COMPARE VALUE                  146
GETFLAGS  DC    B'10000000'             FLAGS FOR TGET                          147
MSG1      DC    C'ENTRY POINT ADDRESS ... '                                    148
MSG2      DC    C'PSW AT ABEND .......... '                                    149
MSG3      DC    C'ABEND CODE ............ '                                    150
PROMPT    DC    C'ENTER GO TO CONTINUE'                                         151
GO        DC    C'GO'                                                           152
FOLD      DC    (L'PUTGET)B'01000000'   UPPERCASE MASK                          153
          LTORG                                                                 154
*----------------------------------------------------------------------*       155
*         MAP WORK AREA                                                 *       156
*----------------------------------------------------------------------*       157
WEDEBUG   DSECT                         USER ACQUIRED REENTRABLE STORAGE        158
SAVEGEN   DS    18F                     GENERAL REGISTER SAVE AREA              159
XTOCLIST  DS    4F                      PLIST FOR XTOC                          160
PUTGET    DS    CL256                   TPUT/TGET BUFFER                        161
LEDEBUG   EQU   *-WEDEBUG                                                       162
*----------------------------------------------------------------------*       163
*         OTHER DSECTS                                                  *       164
*----------------------------------------------------------------------*       165
          IHASDWA DSECT=YES       MAP SDWA                                      166
          END                                                                  167
```

Figure 5.6 (*Continued*)

```
        ..      ..
        LOAD  EP=EDEBUG            LOAD INTERACTIVE DEBUGGER MODULE
        LR    R3,R0                ADDRESS OF MODULE TO R3
        ESTAE (R3),MF=(E,ELIST)    SET EDEBUG AS AN ESTAE
        ..      ..
        DC    H'0',C'@DB@'         ** Break Point **
        ..      ..
        DC    H'0',C'@DB@'         ** Break Point **
        ..      ..
WORKAREA DSECT                     REENTRANT WORK AREA
ELIST   ESTAE ,MF=L               PARAMETER LIST FOR ESTAE
        ..      ..
```

Figure 5.7 Establishing EDEBUG as an ESTAE.

using that register as the first operand. Note that the second positional operand of ESTAE is omitted and defaults to CT (create). The list and execute forms of the ESTAE macro are coded to preserve reentrancy.

5.5.1 Breakpoints

Once ESTAE has been issued, the recovery environment is established for any module executing under the current RB, and RTM2 will transfer control to EDEBUG when any program check occurs. In order to insure that EDEBUG receives control at specific points in the program, the user sets breakpoints in the code. Figure 5.7 contains two breakpoints. EDEBUG distinguishes program checks caused by breakpoints from program checks caused by errors with two tests:

1. Is the program check an operation exception (S0C1)?
2. Do the 4 bytes following the abending instruction contain the literal '@DB@'?

EDEBUG interprets the two lines with DC H'0',C'@DB@' as implanted breakpoints because

1. H'0' causes a S0C1.
2. The high-order 2 bits of an instruction's opcode are the Instruction Length Code (ILC). Microcode uses the ILC to update the PSW after an instruction is executed so that it points to the next instruction. H'0', even though it is not a valid instruction, has an ILC of 2 and causes the

PSW to be updated.* The address of the next instruction, therefore, is the '@DB@' literal. This satisfies the second test.

After the user includes the ESTAE for EDEBUG and sets breakpoints in the program, he reassembles the program and CALLs it from a TSO session.

When the first breakpoint is encountered and EDEBUG receives control from RTM2, it first determines whether RTM2 has provided the address of an SDWA in register 1. When RTM2 cannot build an SDWA, it puts a value of 12 in register 0, which EDEBUG tests on line 36. Without an SDWA from which EDEBUG can get abend information, there is nothing for it to do. Line 38 loads '0' into register 15 to tell RTM2 to percolate the abend, and line 39 returns to RTM2 with BR 14. The most frequent reason why RTM2 does not provide an SDWA is that RTM's GETMAIN for LSQA storage for the SDWA has failed. This can happen if an ESTAE retries and is entered recursively without freeing the SDWA, or if the abend itself is related to GETMAIN.

In lines 42 through 52, EDEBUG stores registers into a save area provided by RTM2 and sets up reentrancy. Lines 53 and 54 load the SDWA into register 3 and set up addressing so that the labels in the IHASDWA macro on line 166 can be used to refer to SDWA fields by name.

5.5.2 Preventing Recursive Retry

The commented lines 55 though 60 are included to illustrate how an ESTAE routine can test the SDWA flag byte SDWAERRD for recursive entry. Some ESTAE routines can set a retry address that is before the the error in the program that established them. These ESTAEs recover; the program encounters the error again; and, unless the ESTAEs test for recursion, they repeat the process forever. Since EDEBUG sets the retry address by incrementing the address of the abending instruction, it will never recover to an address before the error.

 Lines 61 through 72 build a message containing the entry point of the abending module. Line 64 moves the first part of the message to a formatting buffer in the user's work area. The XTOC macro, whose source appears in Appendix B, builds a parameter list and calls the HEXPRT module, also in Appendix B, to put into the message buffer printable characters that correspond to the hexidecimal value in the SDWA field SDWAEPA. XTOC illustrates how a macro can be used to generate a

---

*Instruction execution microcode adds the ILC to the address in the PSW for some types of instruction abends but not for other types. This means that the address in the SDWA PSW might be of the instruction following the one that abended or, if the PSW is not incremented, to the abending instruction itself. See the sections "Types of Instruction Ending" and "Interruption Action" in *Principles of Operation* for a full discussion.

calling sequence for frequently called modules. The TPUT on line 72 invokes a TSO/VTAM service that writes the message to the user's terminal:

ENTRY POINT ADDRESS..000065B8

In similar fashion lines 73 through 84 write the message

PSW AT ABEND.........070C1000000065E2

and lines 85 through 96 output:

ABEND CODE...........00C1

Lines 102 through 109 compare the completion code in the SDWA to '0C1' and the 4 bytes following the abending instruction to '@DB@'. If either test fails, it means that the abend was caused by a genuine error and not by an implanted breakpoint. A branch is taken to EXIT00 on line 124 where, after issuing FREEMAIN to release the virtual storage for the work area, EDEBUG loads the address of the SDWA into register 1 and issues SETRP RC = 0 to return to RTM2 with a request to terminate the task.

Otherwise, EDEBUG issues TPUT on line 112 to send:

ENTER GO TO CONTINUE

to the user's terminal. Since the register (,R) forms of TPUT and TGET both expand merely into an SVC 93 instruction, line 115 inserts the flag values that indicate a TGET into the high-order byte of the first operand. This leaves only the three low-order bytes of the first operand for the address of the area where TGET on line 116 will return the user's response. The LOC = BELOW operand of GETMAIN on line 46 assures that this area is in below-16-meg storage and has a virtual address that is three rather than four bytes.

After TGET invokes the TSO/VTAM service to receive the user's response, OC on line 117 changes any lowercase characters in the response to uppercase in preparation for comparing the response to GO on line 118. If the response is not GO, EDEBUG branches to EXIT00 and returns to RTM2 with SETRP RC = 0.

If the user has responded GO, lines 137 and 138 calculate a retry address for RTM2. For most abends including 0C1, the abend PSW in the SDWA contains the address of the instruction following the abending instruction, in this case to the '@DB@' following H'0'. Adding the length of the '@DB@' literal to the instruction address in the abend PSW, therefore, generates the address of the instruction following the implanted breakpoint. The SETRP macro on lines 140 and 141 stores this retry address into the SDWA and branches back to RTM2 with a return code of '4' in register 15.

SETRP uses the RETADDR= operand to specify the retry address and FRESDWA=YES to tell RTM2 to FREEMAIN the SDWA storage. Since RTM2 provides a new SDWA for each entry to an ESTAE routine, each time EDEBUG is entered a new SDWA is created. It is the responsibility of the ESTAE routine to tell RTM2 to free the SDWA or of the retry routine to issue its own FREEMAIN.

When RTM2 receives control again, it ceases terminating the task and adjusts the RB queue so that the RB associated with the program containing the retry address is first. Since RTM2 also puts the retry address into the PSW in that RB,the next dispatch of the task on a processor will cause the task to begin execution at the retry address.

6

Interrupts

6.1 INTERRUPTS

The 370 system architects designed the interrupt mechanism so that hardware could talk to software. For example, when hardware clocks determine that the time for some scheduled process has arrived, control must be transferred to the code for that process. Or, when hardware parity checking detects that a byte of storage is corrupt, Recovery Termination Manager (RTM) routines in MVS must receive control to terminate the unit of work that is accessing the corrupt storage. When the computer hardware detects one of the events to be handled by the operating system, it sends a signal to a processor that causes an interrupt.

6.2 TYPES OF INTERRUPTS

Hardware events cause one of the five types of interrupts listed below:

- *Program check:* The failure of an instruction to complete successfully causes a program check interrupt on the processor where the instruction is executing.

- *Input/output:* The subchannel system notifies a processor that an I/O operation is complete by causing an input/output interrupt on that processor.

- *Machine check:* When the hardware detects that it is not operating correctly and cannot correct the problem, it initiates a machine check interrupt.

- *External interrupt:* When the value in the Time of Day (TOD) clock exceeds the value in a CPU's Clock Comparator, that CPU experiences an external interrupt. System components and user programs issue the STIMER and STIMERM macros to establish time values that will be loaded into a CPU's Clock Comparator.

  A program executing on one of the processors in a multiengine machine (such as an IBM 3090/200, 400, or 600) issues the SIGP instruction to cause an external interrupt on one of the other processors. At system initialization, for example, the processor that bootstraps MVS issues SIGPs to activate the other processors in the machine.

- *Restart:* An operator takes a CPU out of stop state by keying selections on the processor controller (3092) console, or by pressing the Start key on the keyboard. These actions generate restart interrupts.

There is a sixth type of interrupt that is not caused by an event in hardware but is initiated by programs to transfer control to other programs.

- *SVC:* When a program issues the SVC (Supervisor Call) instruction, an interrupt occurs on the processor where the code is executing. Application programs and operating system routines use the SVC instruction to invoke MVS component service routines.

6.3 OLD AND NEW PSWs

As illustrated in Fig. 6.1, an interrupt on a processor causes the following two events to occur:

1. The Program Status Word (PSW) currently active on that processor is stored at a specific location in that processor's low-address storage. Since the PSW describes the state of the program that is active on the processor, saving the PSW preserves that state so that the program can be resumed later.

   Each type of interrupt stores the current PSW in its own unique Old PSW field in low-address storage. An I/O interrupt, for example, causes the current PSW to be stored in the I/O Old PSW field located at address X'38'.

2. A new PSW is loaded onto the processor from a specific location in the processor's low-address storage. There are six New PSW fields corresponding to the six interrupt types. The address portion of a New

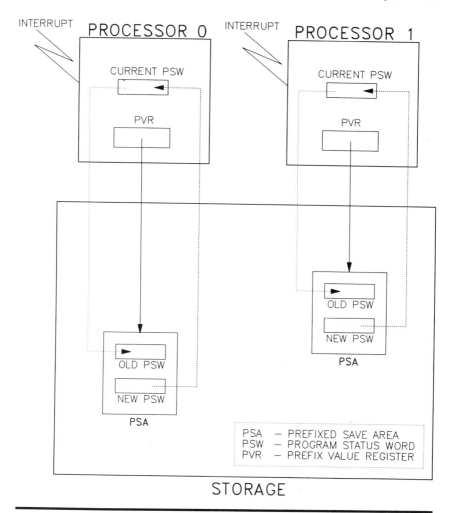

Figure 6.1 Interrupts on two processors.

PSW points to the MVS First Level Interrupt Handler (FLIH) routine for that type of interrupt. The machine check New PSW at address X'70', for example, contains the address of the machine check FLIH in its low-order four bytes.

As illustrated in Fig. 6.1, each processor in a multiengine machine can take interrupts and will save its current PSW at the appropriate Old PSW address for the interrupt type. Each processor has its own area of low-address storage (addresses 0 through 4095) whose absolute address is in its Prefix Value Register.

6.3.1 Interrupt Mask Bits in the PSW

There are three bits in the PSW that enable and disable a processor for interrupts:

■ When PSW bit 6 is 0, the processor will not accept an I/O interrupt.

■ When PSW bit 7 is 0, the processor will not accept an external interrupt.

■ When PSW bit 13 is 0, the processor will not accept a machine check interrupt.

The instructions STOSM and STNSM can be used to change the I/O and external mask bits. The machine check mask bit can only be changed when a new PSW is loaded with an LPSW instruction. Since there are no mask bits for program check, restart, and SVC interrupts, a processor is always physically enabled for these types of interrupts.

The interrupt mask bits in the PSW prevent the possibility that a second interrupt of the same type could overlay the Old PSW from a previous interrupt. When an I/O interrupt is taken, for example, the I/O New PSW that is loaded has an I/O interrupt mask of 0, and that processor is disabled for I/O interrupts. If all the processors in a machine are disabled for I/O interrupts, completed I/Os will queue up in the subchannel system until one of the processors becomes enabled to accept an I/O interrupt by having an active PSW with 1 in the I/O interrupt mask bit.

6.3.2 First Level Interrupt Handlers

All New PSWs contain the addresses of their respective FLIH routines and have interrupt mask bits of 0 to disable the processor for further interrupts while the FLIH routines are executing. FLIH routines

■ Save the registers at interrupt into an MVS control block, the Logical Communications Control Area (LCCA). There is one LCCA for each processor in a multiengine machine.

■ Copy the Old PSW from low storage, where it was saved by the hardware, to a control block related to the type of interrupt.

■ Route control to Second Level Interrupt Handler (SLIH) routines that complete the processing of the interrupt.

Once the FLIH has copied the Old PSW into a control block, it is safe for another interrupt to overlay the Old PSW in low core. This means that a Second Level Interrupt Handler (SLIH) routine can operate with the PSW enabled for interrupts. Later, after the interrupt has been processed, an LPSW instruction will be issued against the Old PSW that was saved in the control block to resume the original program at the point it was interrupted.

6.4 SVC FIRST LEVEL INTERRUPT HANDLER

When a program executes an SVC instruction to request a service from an MVS component, and SVC FLIH receives control:

- FLIH checks to make sure the caller is executing under a TCB and not an SRB, is in primary space addressing mode, and holds no locks. If any of these conditions is not true, SVC FLIH invokes Recovery Termination Manager (RTM) to abend the issuing task.

- FLIH copies the SVC Old PSW to the Request Block (RB) for the interrupted unit of work. After the interrupt is processed, the original unit of work will resume when the RB is dispatched.

- FLIH uses the SVC number, which was saved at low-storage address X'8B' as part of the operation of the SVC instruction, to index into a table that contains an 8-byte entry for every routine that can be invoked with an SVC instruction.

6.4.1 SVC Table Entries

Each SVC Table entry contains the address of an SVC routine and a fullword with bit flags indicating what type of additional processing FLIH will do before either transferring control to the SVC routine or branching to the MVS Dispatcher. The SVC routines themselves are the Second Level Interrupt Handlers. The DSECT in lines 305 through 325 of the SVCLIST program in this chapter describes the complete format of an SVC table entry.

When SVC FLIH locates the SVC Table entry for a routine, it examines the APF bit in the bit flags portion of the entry. If this bit is on, the program that issued the SVC must be executing under an APF authorized TCB. If the JSCBAUTH bit in the TCB's Job Step Control Block (JSCB) is 0, the task is not APF authorized, and SVC FLIH invokes RTM to abend the task that issued the SVC.

The caller of an SVC routine cannot hold locks. SVC FLIH issues the SETLOCK TEST macro and abends the routine if any locks are held. Locks required by an SVC routine must be obtained by SVC FLIH or by the SVC routine itself.

SVC FLIH then examines the SVC-routine-type flags in the SVC Table entry. The type attribute assigned to an SVC routine determines how it will receive control. There are five types of SVC routines (type 5 is not used in MVS/XA and MVS/ESA).

6.4.2 Type 2, 3, and 4 SVC Routines

Types 2, 3, and 4 SVC routines, like ordinary programs that receive control through the LINK macro, execute under control of a Request

Block (RB). Like ordinary programs, type 2, 3, or 4 SVC routines can issue SVCs and establish task-level recovery with ESTAE. When a type 2, 3, or 4 SVC routine issues an SVC, FLIH saves the PSW in the current RB (which happens to be an SVRB) and builds another SVRB for the new SVC routine.

Because SVC routines execute under SVRBs and are interruptible, SVC FLIH will only obtain suspend-type locks (LOCAL lock or CMS lock) for these SVC routine types. If SVC FLIH obtains a lock for the SVC routine, the routine cannot issue the SVC instruction until it releases the lock.

Figure 6.2 illustrates how SVC FLIH adds an SVRB onto the RB queue for a type 2, 3, or 4 SVC routine.

ADDRESS SPACE

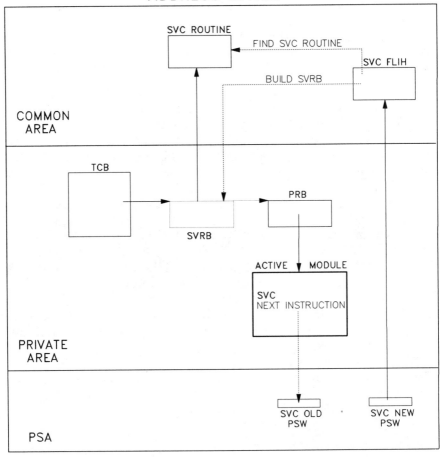

Figure 6.2 Type 2, 3 or 4 SVC routine.

6.4.3 Type 1 and Type 6 SVC Routines

In contrast to type 2, 3, or 4 SVC routines, type 1 and 6 SVC routines are not interruptible. These SVC routine types do not execute under an SVRB, but rather, in the case of a type 1 routine, directly under the SVC issuer's TCB or, in the case of a type 6 routine, as a logical extension of the SVC FLIH.

Since they are not interruptible, the SVC FLIH will obtain spin-type locks, as well as suspend-type locks, on behalf of these routines. Bit flags in the SVC Table entry indicate to SVC FLIH which locks it should obtain before transferring control to the SVC routine.

Type 1 routines execute enabled, unless they request a spin-type lock. SVC FLIH always obtains the LOCAL lock for a type 1 routine.

Type 6 routines execute under control of SVC FLIH itself and, like FLIH, execute disabled. Since the processor cannot accept another interrupt while a type 6 routine is executing, a type 6 routine should be of short duration.

6.4.4 Transferring Control to the SVC Routine

After determining the SVC routine type and building an SVRB if necessary, SVC FLIH:

- Examines the lock bits in the SVC Table entry and issues SETLOCK to acquire the indicated MVS locks. (See Chap. 8 for more on MVS locks.)

- For type 2, 3, and 4 routines, SVC FLIH builds a key zero (bits 8 through 11 are 0), supervisor-state (bit 15 is 0) PSW, using the SVC routine address and AMODE from the SVC Table entry. FLIH puts this PSW into the SVRB along with the contents that the general registers will have when the SVC routine is entered (Fig. 6.3). The PSW and registers will be loaded from the SVRB when it is dispatched.

  Note that register 14 in the SVRB contains the address of the Task Manager EXIT PROLOG routine that frees any locks obtained by FLIH and releases the SVRB storage. If the *nonpreemptive* bit in the SVC Table entry is set, indicating that the interrupted unit of work will be resumed after the interrupt is processed, EXIT PROLOG dispatches the previous RB. If the nonpreemptive bit is not set, the EXIT PROLOG calls the MVS Dispatcher.

- For type 1 and 6 routines, FLIH loads the registers (Fig. 6.3) and transfers control to the routine at the address in the SVC Table entry. For a type 1 routine, this is done by loading an enabled, supervisor-state, key-zero PSW with the routine address.

Register	Contents
0-1	Same contents as when SVC was issued.
	Can be used to pass parameters to the SVC routine.
3	Address of the Communications Vector Table (CVT).
4	Address of the SVC issuer's Task Control Block (TCB).
5	Type 2, 3, or 4 SVC routines: Address of the current SVRB.
	Type 1 and 6 SVC routines: Address of the current RB.
6	SVC routine entry point. Can be used as base register.
7	Address of the SVC issuer's Address Space Control Block (ASCB).
8-12	Unpredictable.
13	Same contents as when SVC was issued.
	Issuer might not have provided a register save area for SAVE.
14	Address of an EXIT PROLOG routine provided by SVC FLIH.
15	Same contents as when SVC was issued.
	Can be used to pass parameters to the SVC routine.

Figure 6.3 Registers at entry to an SVC routine.

After SVC FLIH has finished processing the interrupt, it calls the MVS Dispatcher.

6.5 SVC ROUTINES VS. PC ROUTINES

The main function of an SVC routine is to allow a program to transfer control to a service that has more PSW authority than itself. SVC routines are entered in supervisor state and key zero. Since the issuer's Old PSW is loaded from the PRB after the SVC routine has completed, control is returned to the issuing program in the original PSW state and key. An SVC routine may be appropriate if you want to provide a service requiring a supervisor state or key zero PSW to problem-state, TCB-key programs.

Since PC routines (see Chap. 10) also allow programs to transfer control to services with more authority and to receive control in their original state, they can provide an alternative to SVC routines. Many of the new services in MVS/ESA, such as DSPSERV, ALESERV, and STORAGE, are invoked with macros that expand into PC routine calls rather the more traditional SVCs. IBM has enhanced some of the older services, such as POST, to provide an optional PC routine interface that is invoked by the LINKAGE = SYSTEM parameter on these macros.

6.6 WRITING, TESTING, AND INSTALLING
SVC ROUTINES

If you are writing and installing an SVC routine:

- Determine whether the SVC routine must complete without being interrupted. If this is the case, make the SVC routine a type 1 or type 6. Otherwise make it a type 3, which executes enabled, can issue other SVCs, and can use ESTAE recovery routines. Type 1 and 6 SVC routines must use Functional Recovery Routines (FRRs) (see Chap. 9).

  If the SVC is going to change MVS control blocks or read MVS control blocks that are changed frequently by other components, consider having the SVC routine itself obtain the MVS locks that serialize those control blocks rather than having SVC FLIH obtain the locks for the routine. Obtaining locks yourself allows you to hold them only while you require them. (See Chap. 8 for MVS locks and the SETLOCK macro.)

- Since a single copy of an SVC routine could have more than one user at a time, it must be reentrant. If the module is to reside in the Pageable Link Pack Area (PLPA), it must also be refreshable, since PLPA modules are paged in but changed pages of PLPA modules are not paged out. If the module is not refreshable, install it in the Modified Link Pack Area, where changed pages are paged out, or define the routine as type 2 and link edit it into the MVS Nucleus.

- Test the SVC routine by dynamically loading it (on a test system, of course) with the REPMOD program in Appendix C or a similar utility (OMEGAMON or LOOK). Use the SVCUPDTE macro to dynamically define the routine in the SVC Table as one of the user SVCs (SVC number in the range 200 to 255).

  Examples of the use of SVCUPDTE are in the programs HOOKDRV and HOOKIN in Appendix C. These programs use SVCUPDTE to dynamically install HOOKSVC, another program in Appendix C, as a front end for an existing SVC routine. Figure 1.10 in Chap. 1 illustrates the way an SVC front end works.

6.7 SVCLIST WALKTHROUGH

The program SVCLIST in Fig. 6.4 prints the contents of the in-storage SVC Table.

6.7.1 QSAM I/O in AMODE 31 Programs

The MODULE macro on line 21 establishes reentrancy for SVCLIST. It assigns an AMODE of 31 because the program addresses fields in the

```
*+----------------------------------------------------------------+  1
*|   FUNCTION:                                                     |  2
*|      PRINT SVC ROUTINE ADDRESSES AND ATTRIBUTES.               |  3
*|   INPUTS:                                                       |  4
*|      NONE                                                       |  5
*|   OUTPUTS:                                                      |  6
*|      PRINTED LIST OF SVC TO FILE WITH DDNAME=PRINT             |  7
*|   PROGRAM LOGIC:                                                |  8
*|      1) SET UP REENTRANT QSAM I/O; OPEN OUTPUT FILE.           |  9
*|      2) USE NUCLKUP TO FIND ADDRESS OF IGCERROR (UNUSED SVC ENTRY). | 10
*|      3) LOCATE THE SVCTABLE.                                   | 11
*|      4) LOOP THROUGH SVC TABLE ENTRIES, PRINTING ENTRY POINTS | 12
*|         AND ROUTINE ATTRIBUTES.                                | 13
*|      5) PRINT THE ADDRESS OF IGCERROR.                        | 14
*|      6) CLOSE OUTPUT FILE.                                    | 15
*|   MODULES CALLED:                                              | 16
*|      NONE                                                      | 17
*|   ATTRIBUTES:                                                  | 18
*|      AMODE 31, RMODE 24, REENTRANT, USES ESA-ONLY INSTRUCTIONS. | 19
*+----------------------------------------------------------------+ 20
           MODULE SVCLIST,BASE=12,LOC=BELOW,AMODE=31,RMODE=24,      X 21
                  TEXT='PRINT SVC TABLE'                             22
*          *-------------------------------------------*            23
*          *    SET UP OUTPUT FILE AND OPEN            *            24
*          *-------------------------------------------*            25
           MVC    PRINT(LPRINT),MPRINT    COPY DCB TO REENTRANT AREA 26
           MVC    OLIST(LOLIST),MOLIST    COPY OPEN LIST TO REENTRANT AREA 27
           OPEN   (PRINT,OUTPUT),MF=(E,OLIST)   OPEN PRINT FILE      28
           MVI    OUTLINE,X'40'           ..INITIALIZE PRINT LINE   29
           MVC    OUTLINE+1(L'OUTLINE-1),OUTLINE   ..TO SPACES      30
           ZAP    SVCCNTR,=P'0'           INITIALIZE SVC COUNTER    31
           ZAP    LINECNT,=P'99'          INITIALIZE LINE COUNTER   32
*          *-------------------------------------------*            33
*          *    GET ADDRESS OF UNUSED SVC              *            34
*          *    ENTRY POINT IN MVS NUCLEUS             *            35
*          *-------------------------------------------*            36
           NUCLKUP BYNAME,NAME=NUCMOD,ADDR=(0)                       37
           N      R0,HIGHOFF              TURN OFF HIGH ORDER BIT    38
           ST     R0,NULL                 SAVE THE ADDRESS          39
*          *-------------------------------------------*            40
*          *    LOCATE THE SVC TABLE                   *            41
*          *-------------------------------------------*            42
           L      R3,CVTPTR               ADDRESS OF THE CVT        43
           L      R3,CVTABEND-CVT(R3)     ADDRESS OF THE SCVT       44
           L      R3,SCVTSVCT-SCVTSECT(R3)  ADDRESS OF THE SVC TABLE 45
           USING SVC,R3                   MAP THE SVC TABLE         46
*----------------------------------------------------------------*  47
*          LOOP THRU SVC TABLE FORMATTING AND PRINTING          *  48
*----------------------------------------------------------------*  49
           LA     R4,256                  NUMBER SVCTABLE ENTRIES   50
MAINLOOP   DS     0H                                                51
           CP     LINECNT,PAGEMAX         END OF PAGE ?             52
           BL     NOHEAD                  NO; CONTINUE              53
           BAS    R14,HEADRTN             CALL HEADING RTN          54
           ZAP    LINECNT,=P'0'           ZERO LINE COUNTER         55
NOHEAD     DS     0H                                                56
           ICM    R1,B'1111',SVCEP        ENTRY POINT FROM TABLE    57
```

Figure 6.4 SVCLIST.

```
          N     R1,HIGHOFF             TURN OFF HIGH ORDER BIT          58
          CL    R1,NULL                NO SVC ?                         59
          BNE   ISOKSVC                NO; PROCESS TABLE ENTRY          60
*                                      MOVE "UNUSED" TO ADDRESS         61
          MVC   OUTADDR+1(L'UNUSED),UNUSED                              62
          B     CKTYPE                 ADD REST OF ENTRY                63
ISOKSVC   DS    0H                                                      64
          ICM   R0,15,SVCEP            ROUTINE ADDRESS IN TABLE         65
          LA    R1,OUTADDR             ADDRESS OF PRINTING AREA         66
          BAS   R14,HEXOUT             CONVERT TO PRINTING CHARS        67
CKTYPE    DS    0H                                                      68
*         *---------------------------------------*                     69
*         *     DETERMINE SVC TYPE                 *                     70
*         *---------------------------------------*                     71
          MVC   TESTBYTE,SVCTYP        TYPE BITS TO WORK AREA           72
          NI    TESTBYTE,X'F0'         MASK OFF ALL BUT TYPE BITS       73
          CLI   TESTBYTE,SVCTP1        TYPE1 ?                          74
          BNE   NTYP1                  NO; TEST OTHER TYPES             75
          MVI   OUTTYPE+1,C'1'         MOVE TYPE TO OUTPUT LINE         76
          B     ENDTYPE                CHECK OTHER ATTRIBUTES           77
NTYP1     DS    0H                                                      78
          CLI   TESTBYTE,SVCTP2        TYPE2 ?                          79
          BNE   NTYP2                  NO; TEST OTHER TYPES             80
          MVI   OUTTYPE+1,C'2'         MOVE TYPE TO OUTPUT LINE         81
          B     ENDTYPE                CHECK OTHER ATTRIBUTES           82
NTYP2     DS    0H                                                      83
          CLI   TESTBYTE,SVCTP34       TYPE3 OR TYPE 4 ?                84
          BNE   NTP34                  NO; TEST OTHER TYPES             85
          MVC   OUTTYPE+1(L'TP34),TP34 MOVE TYPE TO OUTPUT LINE         86
          B     ENDTYPE                CHECK OTHER ATTRIBUTES           87
NTP34     DS    0H                                                      88
          CLI   TESTBYTE,SVCTP6        TYPE6 ?                          89
          BNE   NTYP6                  NO; TEST OTHER TYPES             90
          MVI   OUTTYPE+1,C'6'         MOVE TYPE TO OUTPUT LINE         91
          B     ENDTYPE                CHECK OTHER ATTRIBUTES           92
NTYP6     DS    0H                                                      93
          MVI   OUTTYPE+1,C'U'         UNKNOWN TYPE                     94
ENDTYPE   DS    0H                                                      95
*         *---------------------------------------*                     96
*         *     DETERMINE OTHER ATTRIBUTES         *                     97
*         *---------------------------------------*                     98
          TM    SVCTYP,SVCAPF          APF AUTHORIZATION REQUIRED ?     99
          BZ    NAPF                   NO; DO NOT INDICATE             100
          MVI   OUTAPF+1,C'X'          INDICATE                        101
NAPF      DS    0H                                                     102
          TM    SVCTYP,SVCESR          ESR ?                           103
          BZ    NESR                   NO; DO NOT INDICATE             104
          MVI   OUTESR+1,C'X'          INDICATE                        105
NESR      DS    0H                                                     106
          TM    SVCTYP,SVCNP           NON PRE-EMPTIVE SVC ?           107
          BZ    NNP                    NO; DO NOT INDICATE             108
          MVI   OUTNP+1,C'X'           INDICATE                        109
NNP       DS    0H                                                     110
          TM    SVCTYP,SVCASF          CAN BE ASSISTED ?               111
          BZ    NASF                   NO; DO NOT INDICATE             112
          MVI   OUTASF+1,C'X'          INDICATE                        113
NASF      DS    0H                                                     114
```

Figure 6.4 *(Continued)*

```
*           *--------------------------------------------*        115
*           *       DETERMINE OBTAINED LOCKS       *              116
*           *--------------------------------------------*        117
            TM    SVCLOCKS,SVCLL          LOCAL LOCK ?             118
            BZ    NLL                     NO; DO NOT INDICATE      119
            MVI   OUTLL+1,C'X'            INDICATE                 120
NLL         DS    0H                                              121
            TM    SVCLOCKS,SVCCMS         CMS LOCK ?               122
            BZ    NCMS                    NO; DO NOT INDICATE      123
            MVI   OUTCMS+1,C'X'           INDICATE                 124
NCMS        DS    0H                                              125
            TM    SVCLOCKS,SVCOPT         OPT LOCK ?               126
            BZ    NOPT                    NO; DO NOT INDICATE      127
            MVI   OUTOPT+1,C'X'           INDICATE                 128
NOPT        DS    0H                                              129
            TM    SVCLOCKS,SVCALLOC       ALLOC LOCK ?             130
            BZ    NALLOC                  NO; DO NOT INDICATE      131
            MVI   OUTALLOC+1,C'X'         INDICATE                 132
NALLOC      DS    0H                                              133
            TM    SVCLOCKS,SVCDISP        DISP LOCK ?              134
            BZ    NDISP                   NO; DO NOT INDICATE      135
            MVI   OUTDISP+1,C'X'          INDICATE                 136
NDISP       DS    0H                                              137
            MVC   OUTCNT(L'PATTERN),PATTERN  ..MOVE EDIT PATTERN TO  138
            ED    OUTCNT(L'PATTERN),SVCCNTR  ..OUTPUT AND EDIT SVC NUMBER  139
            BAS   R14,PRINTIT             PRINT THE LINE           140
            LA    R3,SVCLENT(R3)          POINT AT NEXT SVCTABLE ENTRY  141
            AP    SVCCNTR,=P'1'           ADD 1 TO SVC NUMBER      142
            AP    LINECNT,=P'1'           ADD 1 TO LINE COUNTER    143
            BCT   R4,MAINLOOP             PROCESS NEXT SVC TABLE ENTRY  144
*--------------------------------------------------------------------*  145
*           END OF LOOP THROUGH SVC TABLE ENTRIES              *        146
*--------------------------------------------------------------------*  147
*           *------------------------------------------*          148
*           *    PRINT ADDRESS OF IGCERROR     *                  149
*           *------------------------------------------*          150
            MVI   CONTROL,TRIPLE          TRIPLE SPACE             151
            MVC   OUTADDR(L'IGCER),IGCER  MOVE LITERAL TO OUTPUT LINE  152
            ICM   R0,15,NULL              ADDRESS OF IGCERROR      153
            LA    R1,OUTADDR+L'IGCER      ADDRESS OF PRINTING AREA  154
            BAS   R14,HEXOUT              MAKE INTO DISPLAY FORMAT  155
            BAS   R14,PRINTIT             PRINT THE LINE           156
*           *------------------------------------------*          157
*           *    CLOSE PRINT FILE              *                  158
*           *------------------------------------------*          159
            CLOSE ,MF=(E,OLIST)           CLOSE THE FILE           160
            B     EXIT00                                          161
*--------------------------------------------------------------------*  162
*           HEXOUT - CONVERT HEX FULLWORD TO 8 BYTES CHARACTER HEX  *    163
*                    INPUT:  R0 - 4 BYTES OF HEX               *        164
*                            R1 - ADDRESS OF 8 BYTE OUTPUT FIELD  *     165
*                    OUTPUT: CHARACTER FORMAT AT ADDRESS IN R1  *       166
*--------------------------------------------------------------------*  167
HEXOUT      DS    0H                                              168
            BAKR  R14,0                   PUSH ENVIRNONMENT ONTO STACK  169
            LA    R1,8(R1)                ADDRESS LAST BYTE + 1 OF OUTPUT  170
            LA    R2,8                    LENGTH OF OUTPUT FIELD   171
```

Figure 6.4 *(Continued)*

```
ADDRLOOP DS    0H                                                            172
         BCTR  R1,0                    POINT AT PREVIOUS BYTE                 173
         STC   R0,0(R1)                LAST BYTE OF INPUT FIELD               174
         NI    0(R1),X'0F'             MASK OFF HIGH ORDER BITS               175
         SRL   R0,4                    SHIFT OFF LOW ORDER BITS               176
         BCT   R2,ADDRLOOP             BRANCH TO PUT IN OUTPUT                177
         TR    0(8,R1),=C'0123456789ABCDEF'   TRANSLATE OUTPUT               178
         PR                            POP STACK AND RETURN TO CALLER         179
*-----------------------------------------------------------------------*    180
*        HEADRTN - PRINT HEADINGS                                        *    181
*-----------------------------------------------------------------------*    182
HEADRTN  DS    0H                                                            183
         BAKR  R14,0                   PUSH ENVIRNONMENT ONTO STACK           184
         MVI   CONTROL,NEWPAGE         SET NEW PAGE                           185
         MVC   OUTLINE+55(L'HD1),HD1   MOVE PAGE HEADING                      186
         BAS   R14,PRINTIT             PRINT PAGE HEADING                     187
         MVI   CONTROL,DOUBLE          DOUBLE SPACE                           188
         MVC   OUTCNT(L'LCNT),LCNT     ... MOVE COLUMN HEADINGS               189
         MVC   OUTADDR(L'LADDR),LADDR  ...                                    190
         MVC   OUTTYPE(L'LTYPE),LTYPE  ...                                    191
         MVC   OUTAPF(L'LAPF),LAPF     ...                                    192
         MVC   OUTESR(L'LESR),LESR     ...                                    193
         MVC   OUTNP(L'LNP),LNP        ...                                    194
         MVC   OUTASF(L'LASF),LASF     ...                                    195
         MVC   OUTLL(L'LLL),LLL        ...                                    196
         MVC   OUTCMS(L'LCMS),LCMS     ...                                    197
         MVC   OUTOPT(L'LOPT),LOPT     ...                                    198
         MVC   OUTALLOC(L'LALLOC),LALLOC  ...                                 199
         MVC   OUTDISP(L'LDISP),LDISP  ... MOVE COLUMN HEADINGS               200
         BAS   R14,PRINTIT             PRINT COLUMN HEADINGS                  201
         MVC   OUTCNT(L'OUTCNT),DASH   ... MOVE DASHES OVER COLUMN            202
         MVC   OUTADDR(L'OUTADDR),DASH ...                                    203
         MVC   OUTTYPE(L'OUTTYPE),DASH ...                                    204
         MVC   OUTAPF(L'OUTAPF),DASH   ...                                    205
         MVC   OUTESR(L'OUTESR),DASH   ...                                    206
         MVC   OUTNP(L'OUTNP),DASH     ...                                    207
         MVC   OUTASF(L'OUTASF),DASH   ...                                    208
         MVC   OUTLL(L'OUTLL),DASH     ...                                    209
         MVC   OUTCMS(L'OUTCMS),DASH   ...                                    210
         MVC   OUTOPT(L'OUTOPT),DASH   ...                                    211
         MVC   OUTALLOC(L'OUTALLOC),DASH  ...                                 212
         MVC   OUTDISP(L'OUTDISP),DASH ... MOVE DASHES OVER COLUMN            213
         BAS   R14,PRINTIT             PRINT DASHES                           214
         MVI   CONTROL,DOUBLE          SET DOUBLE SPACE                       215
         PR                            POP STACK AND RETURN TO CALLER         216
*-----------------------------------------------------------------------*    217
*        PRINTIT - PRINT AN OUTPUT LINE                                  *    218
*-----------------------------------------------------------------------*    219
PRINTIT  DS    0H                                                            220
         BAKR  R14,0                   PUSH ENVIRNONMENT ONTO STACK           221
         PUT24 PRINT,OUTLINE,REG=3     PRINT THE OUTPUT LINE                  222
         MVI   OUTLINE,X'40'                    ..INITIALIZE PRINT LINE       223
         MVC   OUTLINE+1(L'OUTLINE-1),OUTLINE   ..TO SPACES                   224
         PR                            POP STACK AND RETURN TO CALLER         225
*-----------------------------------------------------------------------*    226
*        EXIT ROUTINES                                                   *    227
*-----------------------------------------------------------------------*    228
```

Figure 6.4 *(Continued)*

```
EXIT00   DS    0H              SUCCESSFUL COMPLETION         229
         LA    R15,X'00'                                     230
         B     EXIT                                          231
*------------------------------------------------------------*  232
*        COMMON EXIT                                       *  233
*------------------------------------------------------------*  234
EXIT     DS    0H                                            235
         ENDMOD                                              236
*------------------------------------------------------------*  237
*        CONSTANTS                                         *  238
*------------------------------------------------------------*  239
HIGHOFF  DC    A(X'7FFFFFFF')  TURN OFF HIGH ORDER BIT  MASK 240
NUCMOD   DC    CL8'IGCERROR'   MODULE NAME FOR NUCLEUS LOOKUP 241
UNUSED   DC    C'UNUSED'       LITERAL FOR UNUSED SVC        242
PAGEMAX  DC    PL2'50'         MAXIMUM LINES/PAGE            243
PATTERN  DC    X'40202120'     EDIT PATTERN FOR SVC NUMBER   244
HD1      DC    C'DUMP OF SVC TABLE'  HEADING                 245
DASH     DC    C'--------------------------'               246
LCNT     DC    C'SVC #'        ...FIELDS USED IN PAGE HEADERS 247
LADDR    DC    C'ADDRESS'      ...                           248
LTYPE    DC    C'TYPE'         ...                           249
LAPF     DC    C'APF'          ...                           250
LESR     DC    C'ESR'          ...                           251
LNP      DC    C'NP'           ...                           252
LASF     DC    C'ASF'          ...                           253
LLL      DC    C'LCL'          ...                           254
LCMS     DC    C'CMS'          ...                           255
LOPT     DC    C'OPT'          ...                           256
LALLOC   DC    C'ALLC'         ...                           257
LDISP    DC    C'DISP'         ...                           258
TP34     DC    C'3 OR 4'       TYPE 3 OR 4 LITERAL           259
IGCER    DC    C'ADDRESS OF IGCERROR (UNUSED SVC) = '        260
*------------------------------------------------------------*  261
*        DCB AND OPEN/CLOSE PARAMETER LIST MODELS          *  262
*------------------------------------------------------------*  263
         PRINT NOGEN                                         264
MPRINT   DCB   DDNAME=PRINT,DSORG=PS,LRECL=133,RECFM=FBA,MACRF=PM 265
LPRINT   EQU   *-MPRINT        LENGTH OF THE DCB             266
         PRINT GEN                                           267
MOLIST   OPEN  (,),MF=L        OPEN/CLOSE PARMLIST           268
LOLIST   EQU   *-MOLIST        LENGTH OF OPEN/CLOSE PARMLIST 269
*------------------------------------------------------------*  270
*        WORK AREA                                         *  271
*------------------------------------------------------------*  272
WSVCLIST DSECT                                               273
NULL     DS    F               A(UNUSED SVC)                 274
PRINT    DS    CL(LPRINT)      PRINT                         275
OLIST    DS    CL(LOLIST)      LIST FOR OPEN                 276
TESTBYTE DS    X               WORK BYTE                     277
SVCCNTR  DS    PL2             SVC NUMBER COUNTER            278
LINECNT  DS    PL2             LINE COUNTER                  279
OUTLINE  DS    CL133           OUTPUT LINE                   280
CONTROL  EQU   OUTLINE,1       PRINT CONTROL CHARACTER       281
NEWPAGE  EQU   C'1'            ANSI PRINT CNTL - NEW PAGE    282
SINGLE   EQU   X'40'           ANSI PRINT CNTL - SINGLE SPACE 283
DOUBLE   EQU   C'0'            ANSI PRINT CNTL - DOUBLE SPACE 284
TRIPLE   EQU   C'-'            ANSI PRINT CNTL - TRIPLE SPACE 285
```

Figure 6.4 *(Continued)*

```
*          *-------------------------------------------*          286
*          *      PRINT LINE FORMAT              *          287
*          *-------------------------------------------*          288
OUTCNT   EQU    OUTLINE+7,8          SVC NUMBER              289
OUTADDR  EQU    OUTLINE+20,8         ADDRESS SVC ROUTINE     290
OUTTYPE  EQU    OUTLINE+30,8         TYPE SVC ROUTINE        291
OUTAPF   EQU    OUTLINE+43,4         ...ATTRIBUTES OF SVC ROUTINE  292
OUTESR   EQU    OUTLINE+48,4         ...                     293
OUTNP    EQU    OUTLINE+53,4         ...                     294
OUTASF   EQU    OUTLINE+58,4         ...                     295
OUTLL    EQU    OUTLINE+73,4         ...                     296
OUTCMS   EQU    OUTLINE+78,4         ...                     297
OUTOPT   EQU    OUTLINE+83,4         ...                     298
OUTALLOC EQU    OUTLINE+88,4         ...                     299
OUTDISP  EQU    OUTLINE+93,4         ...                     300
LSVCLIST EQU    *-WSVCLIST           LENGTH OF THE WORK AREA 301
*-------------------------------------------------------------------*  302
*          MAP SVCTABLE ENTRY                                *  303
*-------------------------------------------------------------------*  304
SVC      DSECT                                                  305
SVCENTRY EQU    *                                               306
SVCEP    DS     AL4                  ENTRY POINT OF SVC ROUTINE  307
SVCATTR1 DS     0XL2                 ATTRIBUTE BYTES         308
SVCTYP   DS     X                    SVC TYPE                309
SVCTP1   EQU    B'00000000'          TYPE 1                  310
SVCTP2   EQU    B'10000000'          TYPE 2                  311
SVCTP34  EQU    B'11000000'          TYPE 3 OR 4             312
SVCTP6   EQU    B'00100000'          TYPE 6                  313
SVCAPF   EQU    B'00001000'          REQUIRES APF AUTHORIZATION  314
SVCESR   EQU    B'00000100'          ESR                     315
SVCNP    EQU    B'00000010'          NON-PREEMPTIBLE         316
SVCASF   EQU    B'00000001'          ASF                     317
SVCRESV1 DS     X                    RESERVED                318
SVCLOCKS DS     XL2                  LOCKS                   319
SVCLL    EQU    B'10000000'          LOCAL LOCK              320
SVCCMS   EQU    B'01000000'          CMS LOCK                321
SVCOPT   EQU    B'00100000'                                  322
SVCALLOC EQU    B'00010000'          SALLOC  LOCK            323
SVCDISP  EQU    B'00001000'          DISP LOCK               324
SVCLENT  EQU    *-SVC                LENGTH OF AN SVCTABLE ENTRY  325
*-------------------------------------------------------------------*  326
*          OTHER DSECTS                                      *  327
*-------------------------------------------------------------------*  328
         PRINT NOGEN                                            329
         CVT DSECT=YES,LIST=NO                                  330
         IHASCVT                                                331
         END                                                    332
```

Figure 6.4 *(Continued)*

SVC Table, which resides above the 16-meg line. When the program produces output, however, it uses the Queued Sequential Access Method (QSAM). Like many older access methods, QSAM uses 24-bit addresses and requires that callers be AMODE 24. When performing I/O, SVCLIST first switches the PSW to AMODE 24, invokes QSAM, then switches the PSW back to AMODE 31 so that the SVC Table is again addressable.

RMODE = 24 is coded on the MODULE macro to insure that the program load module itself is loaded below the 16-meg line. If the program were loaded above the 16-meg line, the instruction following the call to QSAM could not be fetched, since, at that point, the PSW is AMODE 24. Note that when SVCLIST switches to an AMODE 24 PSW, it must be able to address the work area (specifically the DCB for QSAM PUT) acquired by the STORAGE macro embedded in the MODULE macro. Since, by default, the STORAGE macro acquires virtual storage in the same RMODE as its caller, the LOC = BELOW on the MODULE macro is not really necessary.

The two MVC instructions on lines 26 and 27 copy the DCB and the OPEN/CLOSE parameter list to the reentrant work area since fields in the DCB are changed by OPEN. Note that the OPEN on line 28 is issued while the program is still AMODE 31. Although QSAM is a 24-bit access method, OPEN and CLOSE (line 160) can be issued with a 31-bit PSW.

6.7.2 NUCLKUP Macro

After initializing the output line and counters on lines 29 through 32, SVCLIST issues the NUCLKUP macro to get the virtual address of the CSECT IGCERROR in the MVS Nucleus. The address of this routine is in the entry point portion of every SVC Table entry for which no routine has been defined. When a caller issues an SVC with an invalid number, IGCERROR gets control and causes RTM to abend the caller with an SFxx. In order to find the SVCs for which no routine has been defined, SVCLIST compares the entry points in SVC Table entries with the address of IGCERROR returned by NUCLKUP in register 0. Since the AMODE of IGCERROR returned by NUCLKUP in bit 0 of register 0 is not always the same as the AMODE in the SVC Table entry, an N instruction is used on line 38 to unconditionally turn the AMODE bit off. Before the entry point in each SVC Table entry is compared with the address of IGCERROR on line 59, another N instruction is used on line 58 to turn off the AMODE bit from the SVC Table entry.

Lines 43 through 45 follow the chain from the Communications Vector Table (CVT) to the Secondary CVT (SCVT) to the SVC Table. Since IBM does not supply a mapping DSECT for an SVC Table entry in all levels of MVS, SVCLIST contains its own DSECT on lines 305 through 325. The

USING on line 46 allows SVCLIST to reference fields in an SVC Table entry by names in the DSECT.

6.7.3 Processing SVC Table Entries

Lines 47 through 147 constitute a loop that examines each SVC Table entry and formats output describing the entry point address and the flag bits. Note that BAS is used to call the heading, hex-format, and print subroutines on lines 54, 67, and 140 (see program NCRYPT in Chap. 4). These subroutines, which begin on lines 162, 180, and 217 respectively, use BAKR to push the registers onto the linkage stack and PR to pop the stack and return to their caller. Using the linkage stack frees the programmer from providing register save areas for subroutines and from being concerned with how many levels "deep" a subroutine can be called. Note that the print routine is called, not only in the mainline logic, but also from within the heading subroutine on lines 187, 201, and 214. This contributes to modular design within a program.

When the loop through the SVC Table is complete and a line has been printed for each entry in the table, SVCLIST prints a final line containing the address of IGCERROR (lines 149 through 156), and closes the output file (line 160). Note that the execute form of the CLOSE macro uses the same parameter list as the execute form of OPEN on line 28.

It is in the PRINTIT routine on lines 217 through 225 that SVCLIST changes from AMODE 31 to AMODE 24 to perform QSAM I/O. This is accomplished by the PUT24 macro. (The source for PUT24 and a corresponding GET24 macro are in Appendix B.) PUT24 expands as if the following were coded:

```
          LA       3,AFTER
          LA       15,BEFORE
          BSM      3,15
BEFORE    DS 0H
          PUT PRINT,OUTLINE
          BSM 0,3
AFTER     DS 0H
```

The first LA instruction loads the address where AMODE 24 starts and the second LA, where AMODE 31 resumes. LA always sets the high-order bit in the register operand to 0 so that when the first BSM branches to the address in register 15, it turns the AMODE bit in the PSW off. (Since the program is RMODE 24 the address must be 24 bits.) The first BSM also sets the high-order bit in register 3, which contains the address of the first AMODE 31 instruction, to the current AMODE value in the PSW, in this case to AMODE 31. The BSM after PUT branches to AF-

TER and, since the high-order bit in register 3 has been set by the first BSM, changes the PSW back to AMODE 31.

Note that 0 in the first operand of BSM 0,3 does not mean register 0 but that the operand is omitted. The description of every instruction in *Principles of Operation* states whether the instruction uses 0 in a register operand to indicate "register 0" or "omitted operand."

Cross-Memory Services

7.1 CROSS-MEMORY SERVICES (XMS)

There are many circumstances in which a program executing in one address space needs to access data in the private area of another address space.

7.1.1 Asynchronous Cross-Memory Facilities

Asynchronous cross-memory facilities, SRBs, and the Subsystem Interface, are part of MVS software. They both work by executing parts of a cross-memory operation serially in different address spaces. Moving data cross-memory with an SRB routine, for example, requires the Dispatcher to be called three times. A task in one address space is dispatched, SCHEDULEs an SRB to a second address space, and enters a wait state. The second address space is dispatched, and the code under the SRB executes, moving data to common storage and POSTing the WAIT in the first address space. The task in the first address space accesses the data in common storage only when it is dispatched again. Since the code is always executing in the same address space as the data, using the right Segment and Page Tables to address the data in each address space is not an issue.

7.1.2 Synchronous Cross-Memory Facilities

Synchronous cross-memory methods, by contrast, use features of 370 architecture, rather than operating system software, to allow programs to access more than one address space at the same time. Both Dual Address Space (DAS) and Access Register (AR) mode may be described as synchronous because inter–address space communication is accomplished with *instructions* that are executed without causing a program to be interrupted.

7.2 ADDRESSING MODES

Chapter 4 discussed how Dynamic Address Translation (DAT) uses Segment and Page Tables to translate a virtual address to a real address. The Segment Table Designator (STD) DAT uses for the translation determines the address space in which storage is referenced.

The STD that DAT uses depends on the *addressing mode* bits in the PSW (bits 16 and 17). Figure 7.1 lists the addressing modes and the STD location for each mode.

7.2.1 Primary Space Mode

When PSW bits 16 and 17 are 00, the CPU is in primary space mode. DAT translates the operands of instructions that reference storage with Segment and Page Tables whose STD is in control register 1. All data movement is within the primary address space. The instruction

        SAC   0

sets the PSW addressing mode bits to primary space mode.

PSW Bits 16 and 17	Addressing Mode Name	Segment Table Designator Location	Available in 370/XA
00	Primary Space Mode	Control Register 1	Yes
01	Secondary Space Mode	Control Register 7	Yes
10	Access Register Mode	ASTE pointed to by an Access List Entry	No
11	Home Mode	Control Register 13	No

Figure 7.1 Addressing modes.

7.2.2 Secondary Space Mode

When PSW bits 16 and 17 are 01, the CPU is in secondary space mode. DAT translates the operands of instructions that reference storage with the Segment and Page Tables whose STD is in control register 7.

If control register 7 contains the same STD as control register 1, which is the case when an address space is first dispatched, secondary space mode will cause instructions to fetch and store data from the primary address space.

The SSAR instruction changes the STD in control register 7 so that it points to an address space different from the one specified by the primary STD in control register 1. The SSAR instruction contains the Address Space Number (ASN) of the target address space in its only operand. When SAC 256 is issued, establishing secondary space mode, the PSW bits are set to 01, and the effective addresses of all instruction operands will be translated using the STD in control register 7.

When a CPU is in primary space mode, *all* storage references are in the primary address space. When the CPU is in secondary space mode, *all* storage references are in the secondary address space. To move data cross-memory, there are two special instructions, MVCP and MVCS, that address both the primary and secondary address spaces. For each of these instructions, microcode translates the first operand using the primary STD and translates the second operand using the secondary STD.

- MVCP moves data from the secondary address space to the primary address space.

- MVCS moves data from the primary address space to the secondary address space.

The way MVCP and MVCS operate is not affected by the PSW addressing mode bits. After SSAR establishes a secondary space, it is not necessary to issue SAC 0 or SAC 256 before issuing MVCP or MVCS.

7.2.3 Access Register (AR) Addressing Mode

AR mode uses 16 access registers, built into the 3090 and later 370 architecture machines, to locate the STD for an address space. Programs can address up to 15 address spaces simultaneously by loading access registers 1 through 15 with pointers to address spaces (access register 0 cannot be used).

Since Page Tables reside in LSQA, address spaces involved in cross-memory data movement must be in storage (i.e., neither address space can be swapped out). If an address space is a nonswappable address space, such as JES, this is not a problem. Otherwise, cross-memory code can either schedule an SRB to make the other address space nonswappable or can issue the SETLOCK macro to obtain the CML lock for the target address space, making that address space nonswappable while the lock is held. This applies when using MVCP or MVCS as well.

Code running in secondary space mode or AR mode cannot issue SVCs except ABEND. You can use only MVS services that are invoked with a branch or program call (PC instruction) and are explicitly documented as available to cross-memory callers (such as ATTACHX and STORAGE for AR mode).

7.2.4 Home Mode

A program can transfer control to another program in a different address space by issuing a space-switching PC instruction (see Chap. 10). This changes the primary STD, making the original address space's control blocks in LSQA unaddressable. After a program issues

```
SAC   768
```

all storage operands are translated by the STD for the original, *home* address space. The STD for the home address space is in control register 13.

7.3 THE ASTE—A VIRTUAL STORAGE CONTROL STRUCTURE

The ASTE (Fig. 7.2) contains the essential control information describing a virtual storage space. The fields in the ASTE are pointers to structures that define an address space, dataspace, or hiperspace, and describe its relationship to other virtual storage spaces. Notice in Fig. 7.2 how the ASTE indirectly points to ASTEs for other address spaces.

In pre-ESA versions of the architecture, the only way to find an ASTE was to use the Address Space Number (ASN) as an index into two tables, the ASN First Table (AFT), and the ASN Second Table (AST). ASTE is, in fact, an acronym for ASN Second Table Entry. As part of the execution of the SSAR and the PC instructions, ASN Translation locates the ASTE by indexing into the AFT and AST.

In ESA the ASTE is no longer limited by the architecture of the Address Space Number. By making the ASTE logically independent of ASN First and Second Tables, it can function as a descriptor for virtual spaces that are not address spaces, such as dataspaces and hiperspaces.

The ASTE has been expanded from 4 fullwords to 16 fullwords in ESA. The Address Space Function (ASF) bit (bit 15 of control register 0) determines whether a CPU is operating in non-ESA or ESA mode and whether a 4- or 16- word ASTE is used. Some ESA-only instructions will cause program checks if the ASF bit is not set.

The fields in the ASTE follow.

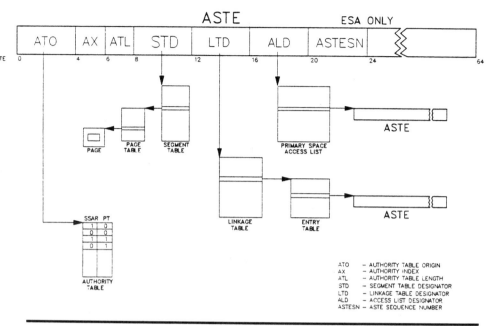

Figure 7.2   The ASTE.

7.3.1 Authority Table Origin (ATO)

The Authority Table origin (ATO) and the Authority Table length (ATL) together specify the real address and length of a table that an address space uses to restrict other address spaces from making it the target of an XMS operation. An address space's Authority Table is checked when:

- A program in another address space issues SSAR to establish the address space as a secondary space.

- A program in another address space issues the ALESERV macro to build an access list entry for the address space but does not use the CHKEAX = NO operand on ALESERV.

- A program executing in AR mode in another address space accesses data through an access list entry created with the ACCESS = PRIVATE operand on the ALESERV.

7.3.2 Authority Index (AX)

When an address space is dispatched, its AX is loaded from the ASTE into control register 4. During the execution of an SSAR instruction, the AX is used as an index into the the target address space's Authority Table. The AX is not used in XMS operations under ESA.

7.3.3 Segment Table Designator (STD)

The STD contains the real address and length of the Segment Table used for DAT translation. Once the Segment Table for an address space has been located, any byte in the address space is accessible by its virtual address.

7.3.4 Linkage Table Designator (LTD)

The LTD describes the real address and length of the PC Linkage Table for an address space. Programs executing in one address space can branch to programs residing in another address space with the PC instruction. The PC Linkage Table points to Entry Tables. PC routines are identified by unique numbers which are indexes into the Linkage and Entry Tables. (See Chap. 10 for PC routines.)

Notice that each entry in the Entry Table points to the ASTE for the address space where the PC routine represented by the Entry Table Entry resides. When MVS dispatches an address space and the ASF bit is 0, the LTD is loaded into the high-order bits of control register 5. When the ASF bit is 1 (ESA), control register 5 contains the address of the ASTE. The linkage table as well as the Primary Space Access List are located through the ASTE rather than by an address in a control register.

7.3.5 ESA Extension to the ASTE

The following fields exist only when the ASF bit in control register 0 is 1.

- The Primary Space Access List Designator (ALD): In access register mode, programs locate the ASTEs for other address spaces by indexing into a table called an access list. While there are access lists associated with each TCB or SRB in the address space (Dispatchable Unit Access Lists—DU-ALs), there is only one access list associated with the address space as a whole. This is the Primary Space Access List (PS-AL). Notice in Fig. 7.2 how the PS-AL points to ASTEs for other address spaces.

- The ASTE sequence number (ASTESN): Since the entries in access lists can be reused, there must be a mechanism for verifying that an access list entry points to the same ASTE that it did when it was created. The ASTESN in the ASTE is compared with an ASTESN in the access list entry in the process of access register translation. If the ASTESNs do not match a program check, 002C occurs.

7.4 USING ACCESS REGISTER MODE

Figure 7.3 illustrates establishing access register communication with an address space using the ALESERV macro.

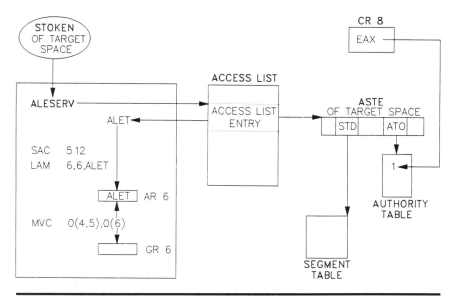

Figure 7.3   ALESERV.

A program issues an ALESERV macro using the STOKEN of the target address space as input. If the CHKEAX = YES operand is used, ALESERV uses the Extended Authorization Index (EAX) in control register 8 to index into the target address space's Authority Table. If the SSAR bit in the target's Authority Table is 1, ALESERV builds an access list entry that points to the ASTE for the target address space. If CHKEAX = NO, EAX checking does not take place.

ALESERV builds an entry on the access list and returns an Access List Entry Token (ALET) in the ALESERV parameter list. The ALET contains an index pointing to the new access list entry.

7.4.1 STOKEN vs. ASN

During address space creation, MVS assigns an address space number to a new address space. This number is the same as the address space's index into MVS's Address Space Vector Table (ASVT). Address space creation stores the ASN in the ASCB and builds the ASTE.

STOKENs are identifiers used by PCAUTH and RASP to keep track of each address space, dataspace, or hiperspace in the system. Unlike address space numbers, which are used by the architecture in ASN translation, STOKENs exist only in MVS/ESA software. They allow MVS to keep track of virtual storages without tying them to ASN First and Second Tables, which means that MVS can create and destroy virtual storages that do not have address space numbers (dataspaces and hiperspaces).

7.4.2 Access Lists

ALESERV can create an access list entry on one of two access lists, the Primary Space Access List (PS-AL) or the Dispatchable Unit Access List (DU-AL). Entries in the PS-AL are available to any task in the address space, while entries in the DU-AL are available only to code running under the TCB or SRB where the ALESERV was issued, or code running under a subtask ATTACHed with the ALCOPY = YES operand on ATTACH. By using the DU-AL, access lists can be associated with units of work (TCBs or SRBs) regardless of the address space in which the code is currently executing. This allows programs to branch into code in other address spaces using the PC instruction while maintaining the same cross-memory addressability as when they were in their home address space. When coding ALESERV specify AL = WORKUNIT to create a DU-AL entry or AL = PASN to create a PS-AL entry.

7.4.3 Access List Entry Token (ALET)

The ALET (Fig. 7.3) returned by ALESERV when the access list entry was created is loaded into access register 6 with the LAM 6,6,ALET instruction. Bit 7 of the ALET is 1 for access list entries in the PS-AL and 0 for access list entries in DU-AL. The last 2 bytes of the ALET are an index into the access list.

7.4.4 Access Registers

In access register mode, base registers in operand addresses refer not only to general registers but to access registers as well. In MVC 0(4,5),0(6), the 5 in the first operand causes access register 5 to be used for Access Register Translation (ART) and general register 5 in forming the virtual address for DAT. Similarly, the 6 in the second operand refers to an access register–general register pair.

Note that access registers are only paired with general registers that function as base registers in instruction operands that reference storage. Index registers do not refer to corresponding access registers. The operands of the LA instruction, for example, are in the form: LA R1,D2(X2,B2). If LA 4,0(5,6) is executed in access register mode, only the 6 refers to an access register-general register pair. The virtual address of the second operand is still formed by adding the displacement to the values in the base and index registers, but the address space where the virtual address is translated by DAT comes from access register translation of the value in access register 6 only. LA 4,0(5,6) would not load access register 4, since 4 is not a base register in a storage operand.

The only way to change values in access registers is with the ESA-only instructions: LAE, CPYA, LAM, EREG, and SAR. Note that the same restriction regarding a base register in a storage operand applies. LAE 4,0(0,6) will cause access register 4 to be loaded with the value in access register 6 since 6 is a base register (LAE R1,D2(X2,B2).) LAE 4,0(5,0), on the other hand, will not cause access register 4 to be loaded since the 5 in the second operand refers to an index, not a base, register (the 0 for a base register in the LAE instruction means no register, not register 0).

7.4.5 AR Mode Cross-Memory Move

The SAC 512 instruction sets bits 16 and 17 of the PSW to 10 to initiate access register addressing mode. From this point, any instruction that has a virtual address as an operand, such as the MVC 0(4,5),0(6), will perform access register translation (ART) in addition to DAT translation.

Figure 7.4 illustrates cross-memory data movement in AR mode. The execution of the MVC instruction initiates AR translation based on the ALET in access register 5, for the first operand; and access register 6, for the second operand. Since access register 5 contains X'00000000', AR translation uses the primary STD.

Since the ALET in access register 6 has bit 7 off, ART locates the access list entry in the DU-AL specified by the Dispatchable Unit Control Table (DUCT) anchored off control register 2. Whenever a TCB or SRB is dispatched on this processor, the dispatcher loads the new work unit's DU-AL address into the DUCT. If ALET bit 7 had been 1, ART would have indexed into the PS-AL.

ART locates the correct access list entry by using the last two bytes of the ALET as an index into the access list. The Access List Entry Sequ-

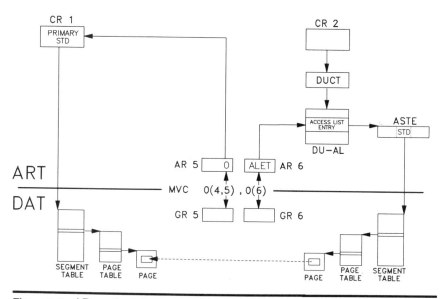

Figure 7.4 AR mode data movement.

ence Number (ALESN) in the ALET is compared with the ALESN in the access list entry to verify that the access list entry is still valid. If the ALSESNs do not match, a program check 002A occurs. Otherwise, the address of the ASTE for the target address space is obtained from the access list entry. ART locates the STD for the target address space in the ASTE and hands it to DAT for virtual address translation. When ART and DAT have successfully completed for the two operands of the MVC 0(4,5),0(6), the real addresses of the two operands have been found and the move operation takes place.

There are two points to note regarding access register translation:

- Just as DAT maintains a lookaside list (the TLB) for the most recently referenced virtual addresses, ART maintains its own lookaside list, the Access Lookaside Buffer (ALB), for the most recently located ASTEs. Like DAT, ART performs translation in parallel with a check for the ASTE in the ALB.

- When an access register contains a value of X'00000000', ART gives DAT the primary space STD. An access register value of X'00000000' always refers to the primary address space. When an access register contains the value of X'00000001', ART gives the STD from control register 7 (the secondary space STD) to DAT. An access register value of X'00000001' causes access register mode to perform like secondary space mode in that the operands are fetched from, and stored to, the secondary address space. An access register value of X'00000002' causes AR mode to perform like home mode.

7.5 PROGRAMS IN THIS CHAPTER

The two examples of code in this chapter both perform the same function. While executing in one address space, a program establishes addressability to another address space, chains through the TCBs and CDEs in the second address space, and moves the names of the modules from the CDEs to the first address space. The program in the first address space then prints the names of the modules. (CDEs and other Program Management control blocks will be discussed in Chap. 8.)

ESAMOVE, illustrated in Fig. 7.11, uses AR mode which is available only in MVS/ESA. XAMOVE, illustrated in Fig. 7.12, uses secondary space mode which is available in MVS/SP, MVS/XA, and MVS/ESA.

7.6 ESAMOVE WALKTHROUGH

In Fig. 7.6 ESAMOVE receives the name of the target address space from PARM= on the JCL EXEC card. Lines 35 through 53 store the target address space name and length into a parameter list that will be

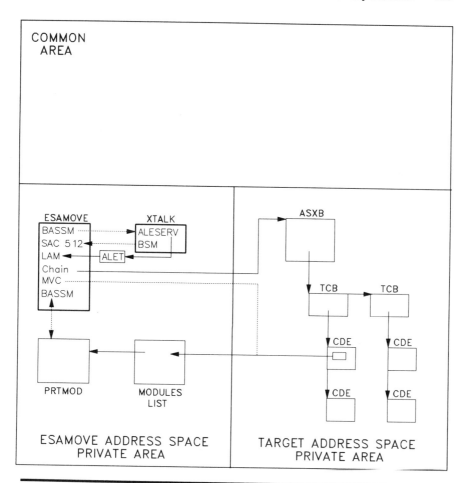

Figure 7.5 ESAMOVE and XTALK.

input to the XTALK module. XTALK will build the access list entry for
the target address space and return the ALET in the parameter list.

Line 156 defines the parameter list in ESAMOVE's work area. The
USING statement on line 40 allows ESAMOVE to reference fields in the
parameter list by the names in the XMSESA DSECT (line 164). Fig. 7.7
contains the XMSESA DSECT itself.

Note that line 40 uses LAE rather than LA to load the parameter list
address into register 3. When LAE is issued in primary space mode,
X'00000000' is loaded into the access register for the first operand. When
lines 74 through 107 execute in AR mode and access fields in the parameter list, X'00000000' in the access register assures that ART will locate
the parameter list fields in the primary address space.

```
*+-------------------------------------------------------------------+    1
*|  FUNCTION:                                                        |    2
*|    PRINTS NAMES OF ALL MODULES LOADED IN ANOTHER ADDRESS SPACE.   |    3
*|  INPUTS:                                                          |    4
*|    ADDRESS SPACE NAME FROM PARM= ON // EXEC CARD.                 |    5
*|  OUTPUTS:                                                         |    6
*|    MODULE NAME LIST TO OUTPUT FILE.                               |    7
*|    ACCESS LIST ENTRY FOR TARGET ADDRESS SPACE.                    |    8
*|      (THIS CAN BE DELETED WITH ALESERV DELETE.)                   |    9
*|    R15 - RETURN CODE                                              |   10
*|        0 - MODULE NAMES WRITTEN TO OUTPUT FILE.                   |   11
*|        8 - TARGET ADDRESS SPACE NAME NOT IN PARMLIST.             |   12
*|       12 - XTALK ROUTINE NOT LINK-EDITED.                         |   13
*|       16 - XTALK ROUTINE ERROR. OTHER REGISTERS CONTAIN:          |   14
*|            0 - RETURN CODE FROM XTALK.                            |   15
*|            1 - REASON CODE FROM XTALK.                            |   16
*|       20 - PRINT ROUTINE NOT LINK-EDITED.                         |   17
*|       24 - PRINT ROUTINE ERROR.                                   |   18
*|  PROGRAM LOGIC:                                                   |   19
*|    1) PUT ADDRESS SPACE NAME FROM // EXEC PARM= INTO PARMLIST.     |   20
*|    2) CALL XTALK TO SET UP ACCESS LIST ENTRY AND RETURN ALET.     |   21
*|    3) GO INTO ACCESS REGISTER MODE.                               |   22
*|    4) CHAIN THROUGH TCBS IN TARGET ADDRESS SPACE, MOVING          |   23
*|       MODULE NAMES FROM CDES FOR EACH TASK TO LIST IN THIS        |   24
*|       ADDRESS SPACE.                                              |   25
*|    5) GO INTO PRIMARY SPACE MODE.                                 |   26
*|    6) INVOKE PRINT TO PRINT MODULE NAME LIST.                     |   27
*|  MODULES CALLED:                                                  |   28
*|    XTALK, PRINT                                                   |   29
*|  ATTRIBUTES:                                                      |   30
*|    REENTERABLE, AMODE=31, RMODE=24, APF AUTHORIZED                |   31
*+-------------------------------------------------------------------+   32
            MODULE ESAMOVE,BASE=12,LOC=BELOW,AMODE=31,RMODE=24,       X   33
                 TEXT='MODULE NAMES IN ANOTHER ADDRESS SPACE'            34
*         *-------------------------------------------------*             35
*         *     GET ADDRESS SPACE NAME AND LENGTH *                      36
*         *     FROM PARM= ON // EXEC CARD.       *                      37
*         *-------------------------------------------------*             38
            LAE  R3,PARMLIST            ADDRESS OF PARMLIST => R3         39
            USING XMSESA,R3             MAP PARMLIST                      40
            MVI  XMNAME,X'40'               ..SET MODULE NAME            41
            MVC  XMNAME+1(L'XMNAME-1),XMNAME   ..IN PARMLIST TO SPACES   42
            L    R1,0(R1)               ADDRESS OF PARM STRING => R1      43
            XR   R2,R2                  CLEAR R2                          44
            ICM  R2,B'0011',0(R1)       LENGTH OF PARM                   45
            BZ   EXIT08                 =0; PROGRAM NAME NOT GIVEN        46
            ST   R2,XMNAMEL             SAVE IN PARMLIST                  47
            BCTR R2,0                   LESS 1 FOR EXECUTE                48
            EX   R2,MVIT1               MOVE NAME TO PLIST                '9
            B    MVIT1A                 BRANCH AROUND EXECUTED INSTR
MVIT1    MVC  XMNAME(0),2(R1)         ** EXECUTE ONLY **                  !
MVIT1A   DS   0H                                                         2
            MVC  MODLIST(L'XMNAME),XMNAME  MOVE ASCB NAME TO MODNAME LIST  53
*         *-------------------------------------------------*             54
*         *     CALL ROUTINE TO BUILD               *                    55
*         *     ACCESS LIST ENTRY                   *                    56
*         *-------------------------------------------------*             57
```

Figure 7.6 ESAMOVE.

```
         MODESET MODE=SUP              GET A SUPERVISOR STATE PSW        58
         LAE   R1,PARMLIST             PARMLIST FOR XTALK ROUTINE        59
         ICM   R15,15,=V(XTALK)        ADDRESS OF ROUTINE TO R15         60
         BZ    EXITOC                                                    61
         O     R15,=A(X'80000000')     SET FOR 31 BIT MODE               62
         BASSM R14,R15                 INVOKE ROUTINE                    63
         LTR   R15,R15                 RC = 0 ?                          64
         BNZ   EXIT10                  NO; EXIT RC=8                     65
         MODESET MODE=PROB             GET A SUPERVISOR STATE PSW        66
*        *-------------------------------------*                        67
*        *    GO INTO ACCESS REGISTER MODE     *                        68
*        *-------------------------------------*                        69
         SAC   512                     GO INTO AR ASC MODE               70
         LAE   R12,0(R12,0)            LOAD BASE AR WITH X'00'           71
         CPYA  A13,A12                 LOAD WORK AREA AR WITH X'00'      72
         SYSSTATE ASCENV=AR            SET FOR AR MACRO EXPANSIONS       73
*---------------------------------------------------------------------* 74
*************    THE FOLLOWING CODE RUNS IN ACCESS REGISTER MODE  ****** 75
*---------------------------------------------------------------------* 76
*        *-------------------------------------*                        77
*        *    CHAIN THRU TCBS IN TARGET ADDRESS *                       78
*        *    SPACE, WRITING MODULE NAMES TO    *                       79
*        *    LIST IN THIS ADDRESS SPACE        *                       80
*        *-------------------------------------*                        81
         LAE   R7,MODNAMES             ADDRESS OF TABLE OF MODULES       82
         LAM   A6,A6,XMALET            LOAD ACCESS REGISTER W ALET       83
         L     R6,XMASCB               ADDR ASCB FROM PARMLIST           84
         L     R6,ASCBASXB-ASCB(,R6)   ADDR ASXB FROM PARMLIST           85
         L     R6,ASXBFTCB-ASXB(,R6)   ADDR FIRST TCB                    86
         USING TCB,R6                  MAP TCB                           87
*                                      ..COPY ALET FOR TARGET ADDRESS    88
         CPYA  A8,A6                   ..SPACE INTO ACCESS REGISTER A8    89
         XR    R9,R9                   CLEAR COUNTER                     90
T$CBLOOP DS    OH                                                        91
         USING CDENTRY,R8              MAP CDE                           92
         ICM   R8,15,TCBJPQ            ADDRESS OF JOB-PACK-AREA QUEUE     93
         BZ    N$EXTCB                 =0; NO MODULES FOR THIS TCB        94
C$DELOOP DS    OH                                                        95
         MVC   O(L'CDNAME,R7),CDNAME   MOVE CDE MODULE NAME TO LIST       96
         LA    R9,1(R9,0)              INCREMENT COUNTER                 97
         LAE   R7,L'CDNAME(,R7)        POINT AT NEXT ENTRY IN LIST       98
         ICM   R8,15,CDCHAIN           ADDRESS OF NEXT CDE ON JPAQ       99
         BNZ   C$DELOOP                ^=0; PROCESS NEXT CDE            100
N$EXTCB  DS    OH                                                      101
         ICM   R6,15,TCBTCB            ADDRESS IF NEXT TCB ON TCB QUEUE 102
         BNZ   T$CBLOOP                ^=0; POINT AT NEXT TCB          103
         ST    R9,MODCOUNT             SAVE NUMBER OF MODULES IN LIST   104
*---------------------------------------------------------------------* 105
*************    END OF ACCESS REGISTER MODE CODE *********************** 106
*---------------------------------------------------------------------* 107
*        *-------------------------------------*                       108
*        *    GO INTO PRIMARY SPACE MODE        *                      109
*        *-------------------------------------*                       110
         SAC   0                       GO INTO PRIMARY ASC             111
         SYSSTATE ASCENV=P             SET FOR PRIMARY MACRO EXPANSIONS 112
```

Figure 7.6 *(Continued)*

```
*       *----------------------------------------*                                113
*       *      PRINT LIST OF MODULE NAMES      *                                  114
*       *----------------------------------------*                                115
        LA    R1,MODLIST            LIST OF MODULE NAMES                          116
        ICM   R15,15,=V(PRTMOD)     ADDR PRINT MODULE TO R15                      117
        BZ    EXIT14                =0; NOT LINK-EDITED                           118
        BASSM R14,R15               INVOKE ROUTINE                                119
        LTR   R15,R15               RC = 0 ?                                      120
        BNZ   EXIT08                NO; EXIT RC=8                                 121
        B     EXIT00                                                             122
*-------------------------------------------------------------------*            123
*       EXIT ROUTINES                                               *            124
*-------------------------------------------------------------------*            125
EXIT00  DS    0H                    SUCCESSFUL                                    126
        LA    R15,X'00'                                                          127
        B     EXIT                                                               128
EXIT08  DS    0H                    TARGET ADDRESS SPACE NAME                     129
        LA    R15,X'08'             NOT IN PARMLIST                               130
        B     EXIT                                                               131
EXIT0C  DS    0H                    XMSESA ROUTINE NOT LINK EDITED                132
        LA    R15,X'0C'                                                          133
        B     EXIT                                                               134
EXIT10  DS    0H                    PERCOLATE RETURN AND REASON                   135
        PERCRC RC=X'10'             CODE FROM XMSESA ROUTINE                      136
        B     EXIT                                                               137
EXIT14  DS    0H                    PRINT ROUTINE NOT LINK EDITED                 138
        LA    R15,X'14'                                                          139
        B     EXIT                                                               140
EXIT18  DS    0H                    ERROR IN PRINT ROUTINE                        141
        LA    R15,X'18'                                                          142
        B     EXIT                                                               143
*-------------------------------------------------------------------*            144
*       COMMON EXIT                                                 *            145
*-------------------------------------------------------------------*            146
EXIT    LR    R2,R15                PRESERVE REGISTER 15                          147
        MODESET MODE=PROB           GET A PROBLEM STATE PSW                       148
        LR    R15,R2                RESTORE  REGISTER 15                          149
        ENDMOD                                                                   150
*-------------------------------------------------------------------*            151
*       WORK AREA                                                   *            152
*-------------------------------------------------------------------*            153
WESAMOVE DSECT                                                                    154
MODMAX   EQU   500                  MAXIMUM ENTRIES IN MODULE LIST               155
PARMLIST DS    0F,CL(XMSESAL)       PARMLIST FOR XMSESA                          156
MODLIST  DS    CL8,F,CL(MODMAX)     LIST OF MODULE NAMES                         157
MODCOUNT EQU   MODLIST+8,4          COUNT OF MODULE NAMES IN LIST                158
MODNAMES EQU   MODLIST+12,8         FIRST MODULE NAME IN LIST                    159
LESAMOVE EQU   *-WESAMOVE                                                        160
*-------------------------------------------------------------------*            161
*       OTHER DSECTS                                                *            162
*-------------------------------------------------------------------*            163
        XMSESA                      MAP USER PARMLIST                             164
        IHAASCB                     ADDRESS SPACE CONTROL BLOCK (ASCB)            165
        IHAASXB                     ADDRESS SPACE EXTENSION BLOCK (ASXB)          166
        IKJTCB                      TASK CONTROL BLOCK (TCB)                      167
        IHACDE                      CONTENTS DIRECTORY ENTRY (CDE)                168
        END                                                                      169
```

Figure 7.6 *(Continued)*

```
          MACRO                    PARMLIST FOR XTALK SERVICE        1
          XMSESA                                                     2
.*+----------------------------------------------------------------+ 3
.*|     PARMLIST FOR XTALK                                          | 4
.*|     THIS PARMLIST CAN ALSO BE USED FOR CALLS TO GETASCB         | 5
.*+----------------------------------------------------------------+ 6
XMSESA    DSECT                                                       7
XMNAMEL   DS     F             LENGTH OF ADDRESS SPACE NAME           8
XMNAME    DS     CL8           ADDRESS SPACE NAME                     9
XMASCB    DS     F             ASCB                                  10
XMSTOKEN  DS     CL8           STOKEN                                11
XMALET    DS     F             ALET                                  12
XMSESAL   EQU    *-XMSESA      LENGTH OF PARMLIST                    13
          MEND                                                       14
```

Figure 7.7 XMSESA DSECT.

7.6.1 The MODESET macro

Some instructions can be issued only when the PSW is in supervisor state
(i.e., PSW bit 15 is 0). Before ESAMOVE calls XTALK (which contains
the SPKA instruction) line 58 issues the MODESET macro with the
MODE = SUP operand to change the PSW bit.

In addition to changing the PSW problem-state bit, a program can
issue MODESET with the KEY = ZERO operand to change the PSW
storage key (bits 8 through 11) so that it contains 0. A program executing
with a key-zero PSW can access data in any real storage frame regardless
of the storage key for that frame.*

Since a program executing with a supervisor-state, key-zero, PSW can
change any storage or issue any privileged instruction, the use of the
MODESET macro must be regulated.

MODESET expands into an SVC 107 instruction. As part of processing
the SVC interrupt, SVC First Level Interrupt Handler (FLIH) locates
the SVC Table Entry for SVC 107, and examines the Authorized Program Facility (APF) bit in that entry (see Chap. 6). If the bit is 1, SVC
FLIH tests the JSCBAUTH bit in the Job Step Control Block (JSCB)
whose address is in the TCB for the executing task. If the JSCBAUTH
bit is 1, FLIH continues processing the interrupt. If the bit is 0, FLIH
abends the task that issued MODESET.

---

*There are two other mechanisms that limit access to frames: (1) *Low Address Protection
(LASP):* This protects storage with addresses 0–511 in the prefixed frame. It is controlled
by bit 3 of control register 0. MVS/XA provides the PROTPSA macro to override LASP. In
MVS/ESA, the LCTL instruction must be used to load a new value in control register 0. (2)
Page Protection: If bit 22 of a Page Table Entry is 1, any instruction that attempts to
change data in the frame, regardless of PSW key, will experience a protection exception
(0C4). The page-protect bit can be changed to 0 by finding the real address of a Page Table
Entry (use the virtual address to index into the Segment and Page Tables with the
DATOFF INDMVCL0 macro) and issue the DATOFF INDXC0 macro to change the bit.

A task's JSCBAUTH bit is set to 1 whenever the loader loads a program into storage that was link edited with PARM = 'AC = 1' from an APF authorized library. (A library is defined as APF authorized by including it in SYS1.PARMLIB member IEAAPFxx or specifying LINKAUTH = LNKLST in the SYS1.PARMLIB member IEASYSxx.)

The whole process of restricting the use of the MODESET macro depends on the restrictions placed on access to APF authorized libraries. Most installations protect access to these libraries with vendor-supplied security packages such as RACF, Top Secret, or ACF2.

Lines 59 through 66 in ESAMOVE load the address of the XMSESA parameter list address into register 1 (line 59) and calls module XTALK to build an access list entry on the DU-AL for the target address space.

7.6.2 XTALK

When XTALK (Fig. 7.8) receives control, lines 30 through 38 examine the CVT prefix to determine whether the operating system is SP3 or greater (ESA).

Lines 39 through 48 call the GETASCB module to search the ASVT for the target address space's ASCB. The source for GETASCB is in Appendix B. GETASCB returns the ASCB address in field XMASCB in the XMSESA parameter list. Lines 53 through 56 find the Address Space Second Block (ASSB) of the target address space by locating its address in the ASCB. Line 58 copies the STOKEN, which will be input to the ALESERV macro on line 63, from the ASSB to field XMSTOKEN in the XMSESA parameter list.

ALESERV (lines 63 through 69), using the STOKEN as input, builds an access list entry and returns an ALET into field XMALET. Note that because we are using the CHKEAX = NO parameter for ALESERV (line 66), the EAX is not used to check the SSAR bit in the target address space's Authority Table when the access list entry is created. CHKEAX = NO requires a supervisor-state or key-zero PSW. The latter is set by the SPKA 0 on line 59. When the ENDMOD macro on line 95 issues PR, it pops the original PSW with its original key.

Note also that the ALESERV operand ACCESS = PUBLIC is allowed to default. If we had coded ACCESS = PRIVATE, bit 7 in the access list entry would have been 1 when the entry was created and every storage access to that address space would cause EAX checking.

7.6.3 AR Mode Move

When control is returned to ESAMOVE, line 70 issues SAC 512 to change the addressing mode bits in the PSW to AR mode. The LAE 12,0(12,0) and CPYA 13,12 on lines 71 and 72 make sure that the access registers corresponding to the base register for the code (register 12) and the addressing register for the work area (register 13) contain

```
*+-------------------------------------------------------------------------+    1
*|  FUNCTION:                                                              |    2
*|    ESTABLISH ACCESS REGISTER COMMUNICATION WITH ANY FULL FUNCTION       |    3
*|    (I.E. NOT DATASPACE OR HIPERSPACE) ADDRESS SPACE                     |    4
*|  INPUTS:                                                                |    5
*|    R1 - ADDRESS OF PARMLIST SUPPLIED BY CALLER MAPPED BY XMSESA         |    6
*|  OUTPUTS:                                                               |    7
*|    ACCESS LIST ENTRY FOR TARGET ADDRESS SPACE ON DU-AL                  |    8
*|    (DISPATCHABLE UNIT-ACCESS LIST).                                     |    9
*|    ALET FOR ACCESS LIST ENTRY IN XMSESA PARMLIST.                       |   10
*|  R15 RETURN CODE:                                                       |   11
*|     0 - ACCESS LIST ENTRY CREATED FOR ADDRESS SPACE                     |   12
*|     8 - OPERATING SYSTEM IS NOT SP3 OR ABOVE (ESA).                     |   13
*|    12 - GETASCB SCAN ROUTINE IS NOT LINKEDITED                          |   14
*|    16 - GETASCB SCAN ROUTINE DID NOT FIND TARGET ADDRESS SPACE          |   15
*|    20 - ALESERV FAILED. RETURN CODE IN R0, REASON CODE IN R1.           |   16
*|  LOGIC:                                                                 |   17
*|    1) CHECK OPERATING SYSTEM LEVEL FOR MVS/ESA                          |   18
*|    2) CALL GETASCB SCAN ROUTINE TO GET A(ASCB) OF TARGET ADDRESS        |   19
*|       SPACE                                                            |   20
*|    3) GET STOKEN OF TARGET ADDRESS SPACE FROM ASSB. (ASCB=>ASSB)        |   21
*|    4) USE STOKEN AS INPUT TO ALESERV TO MAKE ACCESS LIST ENTRY.         |   22
*|  ATTRIBUTES:                                                            |   23
*|    AMODE=31, RMODE=ANY, REENTRANT, APF AUTHORIZED                       |   24
*+-------------------------------------------------------------------------+   25
          MODULE XTALK,BASE=12,LOC=BELOW,AMODE=31,RMODE=ANY,            X   26
                 TEXT='BUILD ACCESS LIST ENTRY ANY ADDRESS SPACE'           27
          LR    R3,R1              PARMLIST                                  28
          USING XMSESA,R3          MAP PARMLIST                              29
*         *-------------------------------------------*                      30
*         *   CHECK IF MVS SP3 OR ABOVE (MVSESA)  *                          31
*         *-------------------------------------------*                      32
          L     R4,CVTPTR          A(CVT)                                    33
          S     R4,=A(CVTMAP-CVTFIX)  BACKUP FOR LENGTH OF CVT PREFIX        34
          USING CVTFIX,R4          MAP CVT BEGINNING AT PREFIX               35
          LA    R4,CVTPRODN-CVTFIX(R4)  POINT TO MVS VERSION                 36
          CLC   0(L'SP3,R4),SP3    IS THIS SP3 OR ABOVE                      37
          BL    EXIT08             NO; EXIT WITH RC-8 ERROR                  38
*         *-------------------------------------------*                      39
*         *   CALL SCAN OF ASVT TO OBTAIN A(ASCB) *                          40
*         *-------------------------------------------*                      41
          LR    R1,R3              PARMLIST                                  42
          ICM   R15,15,=V(GETASCB) A(ROUTINE TO R R15)                       43
          BZ    EXIT0C             GETASCB NOT LINKEDITED                    44
          O     R15,=A(X'80000000')  SET FOR 31 BIT                         45
          BASSM R14,R15            INVOKE ROUTINE                            46
          LTR   R15,R15            WAS ASCB FOUND                           47
          BNZ   EXIT10             NO; EXIT WITH RC=16                       48
*         *-------------------------------------------*                      49
*         *   GET STOKEN OF TARGET ADDRESS SPACE  *                          50
*         *-------------------------------------------*                      51
          DROP  R4                 DROP R4 ADDRESSABILITY                    52
          L     R4,XMASCB          A(ASCB) OF TARGET ADDRESS SPACE           53
          USING ASCB,R4            MAP ASCB                                  54
          L     R5,ASCBASSB        A(ASSB) OF TARGET ADDRESS SPACE           55
          USING ASSB,R5            MAP ASSB                                  56
*                                  MOVE STOKEN OF TARGET TO PARMS            57
```

Figure 7.8　XTALK.

```
          MVC   XMSTOKEN(L'XMSTOKEN),ASSBSTKN                              58
          SPKA  0                          GET A KEY ZERO PSW               59
*         *-----------------------------------------*                       60
*         *   CREATE ENTRY IN ACCESS LIST      *                            61
*         *-----------------------------------------*                       62
          ALESERV ADD,                                               X      63
                STOKEN=XMSTOKEN,        STOKEN FROM ASSB OF TARGET    X      64
                ALET=XMALET,            ALET RETURNED BY ALESERV      X      65
                CHKEAX=NO,              DO NOT CHECK EAX              X      66
                AL=WORKUNIT,            USE THIS TCB'S ACCESS LIST    X      67
                ACCESS=PUBLIC,          CREATE PUBLIC ACCESS LIST ENTRY X   68
                MF=(E,ALELIST)                                              69
          LTR   R15,R15                  RETURN CODE = 0                    70
          BNZ   EXIT14                   NO, EXIT RC=20.                    71
          B     EXIT00                                                      72
*-----------------------------------------------------------------------*   73
*         EXIT ROUTINES                                             *        74
*-----------------------------------------------------------------------*   75
EXIT00    DS    0H                       SUCCESSFUL                         76
          LA    R15,X'00'                                                   77
          B     EXIT                                                        78
EXIT08    DS    0H                       NOT EXECUTING ON ESA SYSTEM        79
          LA    R15,X'08'                                                   80
          B     EXIT                                                        81
EXIT0C    DS    0H                       ASVT SCAN ROUTINE NOT LINKED       82
          LA    R15,X'0C'                                                   83
          B     EXIT                                                        84
EXIT10    DS    0H                       TARGET ASCB NOT FOUND BY SCAN      85
          LA    R15,X'10'                                                   86
          B     EXIT                                                        87
EXIT14    DS    0H                       ALESERV FAILED                     88
          PERCRC RC=X'14'                                                   89
          B     EXIT                                                        90
*-----------------------------------------------------------------------*   91
*         COMMON EXIT                                               *        92
*-----------------------------------------------------------------------*   93
EXIT      DS    0H                                                          94
          ENDMOD                                                            95
*-----------------------------------------------------------------------*   96
*         CONSTANTS                                                 *        97
*-----------------------------------------------------------------------*   98
SP3       DC    C'SP3'    MVS/ESA                                           99
*-----------------------------------------------------------------------*  100
*         WORK AREA                                                 *       101
*-----------------------------------------------------------------------*  102
WXTALK    DSECT                                                            103
ALELIST   ALESERV MF=L                PARMLIST FOR ALESERV                 104
LXTALK    EQU   *-WXTALK                                                   105
*-----------------------------------------------------------------------*  106
*         OTHER DSECTS                                              *       107
*-----------------------------------------------------------------------*  108
          XMSESA                        MAP PARMLIST FOR GETASCB           109
          CVT     DSECT=YES,PREFIX=YES,LIST=YES     MAP CVT                110
          IHAASCB DSECT=YES,LIST=YES                MAP ASCB               111
          IHAASSB LIST=YES                          MAP ASSB              112
          END                                                             113
```

Figure 7.8 *(Continued)*

X'00000000'. The SYSSTATE ASCENV = AR macro on line 73 sets a global SETC symbol for the assembler and causes any macros that follow to yield an expansion compatible with access register mode. The SYS-STATE ASCENV = P (line 112) directly after the SAC 0 that returns to primary space mode, resets macro expansion to nonaccess register mode. Although there happen to be no macros between the two SSYSTATEs, setting the macro expansion mode is good practice, making the code more maintainable.

Now that ESAMOVE is in AR mode, whenever an access register contains the ALET for the target address space *and* the general register with the same number contains a virtual address that is valid in the target address space, the operands of ordinary instructions will reference storage in the target address space. Line 83 issues LAM 6,6,ALET to load access register 6 with the ALET returned by XTALK, and the instructions on lines 84 through 87 use general register 6 to contain the virtual addresses that chain to the first TCB in the target address space. Similarly, CPYA 8,6 (line 89) copies the ALET for the target address space into access register 8, and the instructions on lines 90 through 100 run the CDE chains, using general register 8 for the virtual addresses that are the chain pointers.

Line 82 issues LAE 7,MODNAMES to load the virtual address of the table of module names (line 157) and an ALET of X'00000000' into general/access register 7. While in access register mode, always use LAE instead of LA to load an address since LAE loads the access register as well as the general register. The second operand of the MVC on line 96 refers to an address in a CDE in the target address space. The USING CDENTRY,8 (line 92) causes this operand to assemble as a displacement off general register 8. The CPYA on line 89 has loaded access register 8 with the ALET for the target address space. The actual cross-memory move is accomplished with an ordinary MVC (line 96).

ESAMOVE returns to primary space mode by issuing SAC 0 (line 111), resets macro expansions to non-ESA mode (line 112), and calls PRTMOD (Fig. 7.9) to print the list of module names (lines 113 through 121).

7.7 SECONDARY SPACE MODE CROSS-MEMORY MOVE

Figure 7.10 illustrates a cross-memory move using the MVCP instruction. The register operand of the SSAR contains the ASN for the secondary address space (SASN). When the SSAR is executed, ASN Translation uses this ASN as an index into the ASN First Table and the ASN Second Table, anchored off control register 14, to locate an ASTE. SSAR uses the AX in control register 4 as an index into the Authority Table

```
*+----------------------------------------------------------------+     1
*|   FUNCTION:                                                     |     2
*|      PRINT ROUTINE FOR XMS MODULE NAME PROGRAMS.                |     3
*|   INPUTS:                                                       |     4
*|      R1 - ADDRESS OF MODULE NAME LIST.  FIRST FULLWORD          |     5
*|         WORD IS THE NUMBER OF ENTRIES IN THE LIST.              |     6
*|   OUTPUTS:                                                      |     7
*|      R15 - RETURN CODE                                          |     8
*|         00 - FOUND                                              |     9
*|   PROGRAM LOGIC:                                                |    10
*|      1) LOOP THROUGH MODULE LIST TABLE, PRINTING EACH ENTRY.    |    11
*|   ATTRIBUTES:                                                   |    12
*|      REENTERABLE, AMODE=24, RMODE=24                            |    13
*+----------------------------------------------------------------+    14
          MODULE PRTMOD,BASE=12,LOC=BELOW,AMODE=24,RMODE=24,      X    15
                 TEXT='PRINT MODULE NAME LIST'                         16
          LA    R3,0(R1)               ASCB NAME                       17
          L     R9,8(R1)               NUMBER OF MODULES IN LIST       18
          LA    R7,12(R1)              POINT TO FIRST ENTRY IN LIST    19
          MVC   PRINT(L'PRINT),MPRINT  COPY DCB TO WORK AREA           20
          MVC   OLIST(L'OLIST),MOLIST  COPY OPEN/CLOSE LIST TO WORK    21
          OPEN  (PRINT,OUTPUT),MF=(E,OLIST) OPEN PRINT LIST            22
          MVI   OUTLINE,X'40'          MOVE A SPACE TO OUTLINE         23
          MVC   OUTLINE+1(L'OUTLINE-1),OUTLINE  PROPAGATE SPACES       24
          MVC   MPRT1(L'H1),H1         MOVE FIRST HEADING TO PRINT     25
          MVC   MPRT1+L'H1-8(8),0(R3)  MOVE ASCB NAME TO PRINT LINE    26
          PUT   PRINT,OUTLINE          WRITE FIRST RECORD              27
PRLOOP    DS    0H                                                     28
          MVI   OUTLINE,X'40'          MOVE A SPACE TO OUTLINE         29
          MVC   OUTLINE+1(L'OUTLINE-1),OUTLINE  PROPAGATE SPACES       30
          MVC   MPRT1(L'MPRT1),0(R7)   MOVE MODULE TO PRINT            31
          PUT   PRINT,OUTLINE          WRITE MODULE NAME               32
          LA    R7,8(R7)               POINT TO NEXT MODNAME IN LIST   33
          BCT   R9,PRLOOP              LOOP THRU NAMES                 34
          CLOSE MF=(E,OLIST)           CLOSE THE PRINT FILE            35
*----------------------------------------------------------------*    36
*         EXIT ROUTINES                                          *    37
*----------------------------------------------------------------*    38
EXIT00    DS    0H                     SUCCESSFUL                      39
          LA    R15,X'00'                                              40
          B     EXIT                                                   41
*----------------------------------------------------------------*    42
*         COMMON EXIT                                            *    43
*----------------------------------------------------------------*    44
EXIT      DS    0H                                                     45
          ENDMOD                                                       46
*----------------------------------------------------------------*    47
*         CONSTANTS                                              *    48
*----------------------------------------------------------------*    49
H1        DC    C'MODULES IN ADDRESS SPACE        '                   50
*----------------------------------------------------------------*    51
*         DCB AND OPEN/CLOSE PARMLIST                            *    52
*----------------------------------------------------------------*    53
LRECL     EQU   133                                                    54
BLKSIZE   EQU   LRECL*10                                               55
MPRINT    DCB   DDNAME=PRINT,DSORG=PS,MACRF=PM,RECFM=FBA,LRECL=LRECL, X 56
                BLKSIZE=BLKSIZE                                        57
```

Figure 7.9 PRTMOD.

```
LPRINT   EQU    *-MPRINT                                                  58
MOLIST   OPEN   (,),MF=L                                                  59
LOLIST   EQU    *-MOLIST                                                  60
*--------------------------------------------------------------*         61
*        WORK AREA                                             *          62
*--------------------------------------------------------------*         63
WPRTMOD  DSECT                                                            64
MODMAX   EQU    500              MAXIMUM ENTRIES IN MODULE LIST           65
PRINT    DS     CL(LPRINT)       PRINT DCB                                66
OLIST    DS     CL(LOLIST)       LIST FOR OPEN                            67
OUTLINE  DS     CL(LRECL)        OUTPUT LINE                              68
MPRT1    EQU    OUTLINE+5,8      FIRST OUTPUT FIELD                       69
LPRTMOD  EQU    *-WPRTMOD                                                 70
         END                                                             71
```

Figure 7.9 *(Continued).*

specified by the ASTE, and the SSAR bit in the Authority Table is checked for a value of 1. If the bit is 0, a program check 0025 occurs. Otherwise, the STD for the secondary address space is loaded from the ASTE into control register 7, and the SASN is loaded into the low-order bytes of control register 3.

The first operand of the MVCP instruction contains a virtual address that DAT translates according to the Segment and Page Tables specified by the STD in control register 1; the second operand contains a virtual address translated by the Segment and Page Tables specified by the STD in control register 7.

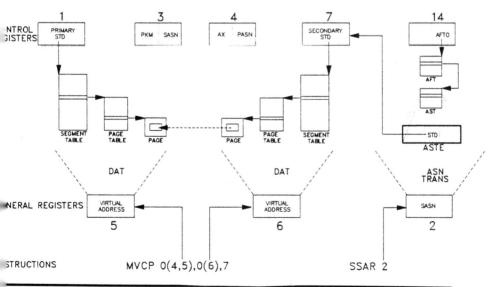

Figure 7.10 Cross-memory move using MVCP.

7.8 XAMOVE WALKTHROUGH

Figure 7.11 illustrates the way XAMOVE and XASAC use secondary space mode to chain through the TCBs and CDEs in a target address space. XASAC issues MVCP to move the module names in the CDEs to the primary space.

XAMOVE (Fig. 7.12) receives the name of a target address space from PARM= on the JCL EXEC card (lines 34 through 52) and calls module GETASCB (in Appendix B) to search the ASVT for the ASCB corresponding to that address space (lines 53 through 62.)

In 370/XA, code that runs in secondary space mode must reside in common storage because the instruction fetch microcode does not know whether to fetch instructions from the primary or secondary address

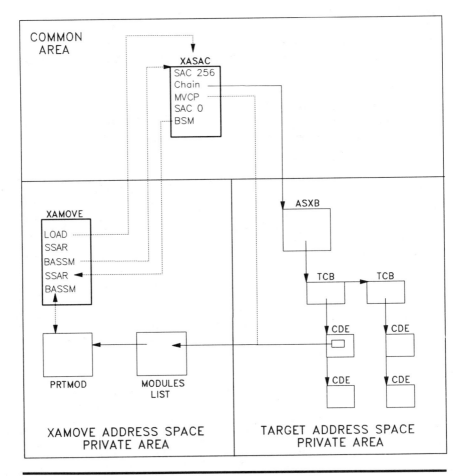

Figure 7.11 XAMOVE and XASAC.

```
*+----------------------------------------------------------------------+   1
* | FUNCTION:                                                            |   2
* |     PRINTS NAMES OF ALL MODULES LOADED IN ANOTHER ADDRESS SPACE      |   3
* | INPUTS:                                                              |   4
* |     NAME OF AN ADDRESS SPACE ON   // EXEC  PARM=                     |   5
* | OUTPUTS:                                                             |   6
* |     MODULE NAME LIST TO OUTPUT FILE.                                 |   7
* |     R15 - RETURN CODE                                                |   8
* |          0 - MODULE NAMES WRITTEN TO OUTPUT FILE.                    |   9
* |          8 - TARGET ADDRESS SPACE NAME NOT ON PARM= .                |  10
* |         12 - GETASCB ROUTINE NOT LINK-EDITED.                        |  11
* |         16 - GETASCB ROUTINE ERROR.                                  |  12
* |         20 - ERROR IN LOAD OF SECONDARY SPACE ROUTINE.               |  13
* |         24 - ERROR IN SECONDARY SPACE ROUTINE.                       |  14
* |         28 - PRINT ROUTINE NOT LINK-EDITED.                          |  15
* |         28 - ERROR IN PRINT ROUTINE                                  |  16
* | PROGRAM LOGIC:                                                       |  17
* |     1) PUT ADDRESS SPACE NAME FROM // EXEC PARM= INTO PARMLIST.      |  18
* |     2) CALL GETASCB TO SCAN ASVT FOR ADDRESS OF TARGET ASCB.         |  19
* |     3) LOAD SECONDARY SPACE MODULE INTO PAGEABLE CSA.                |  20
* |     4) USING ASN FROM TARGET ASCB, SET TARGET AS SECONDARY SPACE.    |  21
* |     5) BRANCH INTO MODULE LOADED INTO CSA IN STEP 3 .                |  22
* |        THIS CODE MOVES THE NAMES OF MODULES IN THE TARGET            |  23
* |        ADDRESS SPACE TO A LIST IN THIS ADDRESS SPACE.                |  24
* |     6) RESTORE ORIGINAL SASN AND AX.                                 |  25
* |     7) INVOKE MODULE TO PRINT MODULE NAME LIST.                      |  26
* | MODULES INVOKED:                                                     |  27
* |     GETASCB, XASAC, PRTMOD                                           |  28
* | ATTRIBUTES:                                                          |  29
* |     REENTERABLE, AMODE=31, RMODE=24, APF-AUTHORIZED                  |  30
*+----------------------------------------------------------------------+  31
          MODULE XAMOVE,BASE=12,LOC=BELOW,AMODE=31,RMODE=ANY,        X  32
                 TEXT='MODULE NAMES FROM ANOTHER ADDRESS SPACE'         33
*         *-----------------------------------------*                   34
*         *  GET ADDRESS SPACE NAME AND LENGTH   *                      35
*         *  FROM PARM= ON THE // EXEC CARD      *                      36
*         *-----------------------------------------*                   37
          LA   R3,PARMLIST         ADDRESS OF PARMLIST TO R3            38
          USING XMSXA,R3           MAP PARMLIST                         39
          MVI  XMNAME,X'40'                 ..SET MODULE NAME IN        40
          MVC  XMNAME+1(L'XMNAME-1),XMNAME   ..PARMLIST TO SPACES       41
          L    R1,0(R1)            ADDRESS OF PARM= STRING TO R1        42
          XR   R2,R2                                                    43
          ICM  R2,B'0011',0(R1) LENGTH OF PARM                         44
          BZ   EXIT08              =0; PROGRAM NAME NOT GIVEN           45
          ST   R2,XMNAMEL          SAVE IN PLIST                        46
          BCTR R2,0                LESS 1 FOR EXECUTE                   47
          EX   R2,MVIT1            MOVE NAME TO PLIST                   48
          B    MVIT1A              BRANCH AROUND EXECUTED INSTRUCTION   49
MVIT1     MVC  XMNAME(0),2(R1)     ** EXECUTE ONLY **                   50
MVIT1A    DS   OH                                                       51
          MVC  MODLIST(L'XMNAME),XMNAME  MOVE ASCB NAME TO MODNAME LIST 52
*         *-----------------------------------------*                   53
*         *  CALL SCAN OF ASVT TO OBTAIN A(ASCB) *                      54
*         *-----------------------------------------*                   55
          LR   R1,R3               PARMLIST                             56
          ICM  R15,15,=V(GETASCB)    MODULE ADDRESS TO REG 15           57
```

Figure 7.12 XAMOVE.

```
        BZ    EXITOC              =0; ROUTINE NOT LINKED          58
        O     R15,=A(X'80000000')  SET FOR ENTRY AMODE 31         59
        BASSM R14,R15             INVOKE THE ROUTINE.             60
        LTR   R15,R15             WAS ADDRESS SPACE FOUND?        61
        BNZ   EXIT10              NO; EXIT                        62
*       *------------------------------------------*             63
*       *    LOAD MODULE THAT WILL RUN IN          *             64
*       *    SECONDARY SPACE MODE INTO CSA         *             65
*       *------------------------------------------*             66
        MODESET MODE=SUP          GET SUPERVISOR STATE PSW        67
        LOAD  EP=XASAC,                                         X 68
              GLOBAL=(YES,P),     LOAD INTO PAGEABLE CSA         X 69
              ERRET=EXIT14,       ERROR ROUTINE                  X 70
              EOM=NO              DELETE MODULE AT END-OF-TASK     71
        ST    RO,ADDRCSA          SAVE ADDRESS OF ROUTINE         72
*       *------------------------------------------*             73
*       *    SET SECONDARY ASN TO TARGET           *             74
*       *    ADDRESS SPACE                         *             75
*       *------------------------------------------*             76
        LA    RO,1                .. GET AX                       77
        AXSET AX=(RO)             .. OF 1                         78
        ST    RO,XMAXOL           SAVE THE OLD AX                 79
        MODESET MODE=PROB         RETURN TO PROBLEM STATE         80
        ESAR  R2                  EXTRACT SASN                    81
        ST    R2,XMSASNOL         SAVE THE OLD SASN               82
        L     R2,XMASCB           ASCB OF TARGET ADDRESS SPACE    83
*                                 GET ADDRESS SPACE NUMBER FROM ASCB  84
        LH    R2,ASCBASID-ASCB(R2)                                85
        SSAR  R2                  SET AS SECONDARY ADDRESS SPACE  86
*       *------------------------------------------*             87
*       *    INVOKE TCB SCAN ROUTINE THAT          *             88
*       *    RUNS IN SECONDARY SPACE MODE          *             89
*       *------------------------------------------*             90
        L     R15,ADDRCSA         ENTRY POINT OF ROUTINE TO R15   91
        LA    R1,MODLIST          ..ADDRESS OF MODULES LIST       92
        ST    R1,XMMODS           ..TO PARMLIST                   93
        LA    R1,PARMLIST         ADDRESS OF PARMLIST TO R1       94
        BASSM R14,R15             INVOKE THE ROUTINE              95
        LTR   R15,R15             RC = 0 ?                        96
        BNZ   EXIT18              NO; EXIT WITH ERROR             97
*       *------------------------------------------*             98
*       *    RESTORE ORIGINAL SASN AND AX          *             99
*       *------------------------------------------*            100
        L     R2,XMSASNOL         .. RESTORE                     101
        SSAR  R2                  .. ORIGINAL SASN               102
        MODESET MODE=SUP          GET A SUPERVISOR STATE PSW     103
        L     RO,XMAXOL           .. RESTORE                     104
        AXSET AX=(RO)             .. OLD AX                       105
        MODESET MODE=PROB         RETURN TO PROBLEM STATE        106
        DELETE EP=XASAC           DELETE THE ROUTINE FROM CSA    107
*       *------------------------------------------*            108
*       *    PRINT LIST OF MODULE NAMES            *            109
*       *------------------------------------------*            110
        LA    R1,MODLIST          LIST OF MODULE NAMES           111
        ICM   R15,15,=V(PRTMOD)   ADDRESS OF PRINT MODULE        112
        BZ    EXIT1C              =0? ; EXIT                     113
        BASSM R14,R15             INVOKE ROUTINE                 114
```

Figure 7.12 *(Continued)*

```
              LTR    R15,R15             RC = 0 ?                        115
              BNZ    EXIT20              NO; EXIT                        116
              B      EXIT00                                             117
*-----------------------------------------------------------------*    118
*             EXIT ROUTINES                                        *    119
*-----------------------------------------------------------------*    120
EXIT00        DS     0H                  SUCCESSFUL                     121
              LA     R15,X'00'                                          122
              B      EXIT                                               123
EXIT08        DS     0H      ADDRESS SPACE NAME NOT IN PARM=            124
              LA     R15,X'08'                                          125
              B      EXIT                                               126
EXIT0C        DS     0H                  GET ASCB ROUTINE NOT LINKED    127
              LA     R15,X'0C'                                          128
              B      EXIT                                               129
EXIT10        DS     0H                  GETASCB DID NOT FIND TARGET ASID 130
              LA     R15,X'10'                                          131
              B      EXIT                                               132
EXIT14        DS     0H                  ERROR IN LOAD OF MODULE TO CSA 133
              PERCRC RC=X'14'                                           134
              B      EXIT                                               135
EXIT18        DS     0H                  ERROR IN SECONDARY SPACE RTN   136
              PERCRC RC=X'18'                                           137
              B      EXIT                                               138
EXIT1C        DS     0H                  PRINT ROUTINE NOT LINK EDITED  139
              LA     R15,X'1C'                                          140
              B      EXIT                                               141
EXIT20        DS     0H                  ERROR IN PRINT ROUTINE         142
              LA     R15,X'20'                                          143
              B      EXIT                                               144
*-----------------------------------------------------------------*    145
*             COMMON EXIT                                          *    146
*-----------------------------------------------------------------*    147
EXIT          DS     0H                                                 148
              MODESET MODE=PROB          RETURN TO PROBLEM STATE        149
              ENDMOD                                                    150
*-----------------------------------------------------------------*    151
*             WORK AREA                                            *    152
*-----------------------------------------------------------------*    153
WXAMOVE       DSECT                                                     154
ADDRCSA       DS     F                   ADDRESS OF SS MODE ROUTINE     155
MODMAX        EQU    500                 MAXIMUM ENTRIES IN MODULE LIST 156
PARMLIST      DS     0F,CL(XMSXAL)       PARMLIST FOR XMSXA             157
MODLIST       DS     CL8,F,CL(MODMAX)    LIST OF MODULE NAMES           158
MODCOUNT      EQU    MODLIST+8,4         COUNT OF MODULE NAMES IN LIST  159
MODNAMES      EQU    MODLIST+12,8        FIRST MODULE NAME IN LIST      160
LXAMOVE       EQU    *-WXAMOVE                                          161
*-----------------------------------------------------------------*    162
*             OTHER DSECTS                                         *    163
*-----------------------------------------------------------------*    164
              XMSXA                      MAP USER PARMLIST              165
              IHAASCB LIST=NO            ADDRESS SPACE CONTROL BLOCK (ASCB) 166
              END                                                      167
```

Figure 7.12 *(Continued)*.

space. (This "feature" has been corrected in 370/ESA.) For this reason lines 63 though 72 load the module that will execute in secondary space mode, XASAC, into pageable CSA.

Line 78 then issues the AXSET macro to set the AX in control register 4 to 1. An AX of 1 is the master AX and allows the subsequent SSAR to establish any address space as a secondary space. Line 86 issues an SSAR after line 83 has loaded SSAR's register operand with the ASN from the target address space's ASCB. Line 94 loads the address of the XMSXA parameter list (line 157) into register 1 before transferring control to the XASAC module in CSA with the BASSM on line 95. Fig. 7.13 contains the DSECT that maps the parameter list.

7.8.1 XASAC

XASAC (Fig. 7.14) issues the SAC 256 on line 31 to set the PSW addressing mode bits for secondary space mode. Lines 32 through 65 chain through the TCBs and CDEs in the secondary address space. XASAC must be in secondary space mode to run the control blocks since the chain fields contain virtual addresses in the secondary address space.

The MVCP on line 55 is issued while XASAC is in problem state. While the PSW key limits access to storage in the primary address space, the PSW key mask (PKM) in the high-order bytes of control register 3 limits storage access to the secondary space. The PKM consists of 16 bits, each of which represents one of the storage keys 0 through 15. When an MVCP is issued in problem state, the low-order byte of the third operand is inspected. If a bit in the PKM corresponding to the storage key in the third operand is 1, access to the storage in the secondary address space is allowed; otherwise, a program check 0002 occurs. The third operand of MVCP is given a value of X'0080' in line 42 since the ninth bit of the PKM is on. (All address spaces including the primary space are initially dispatched with a default PKM allowing PSW key 8.) If MVCP had been

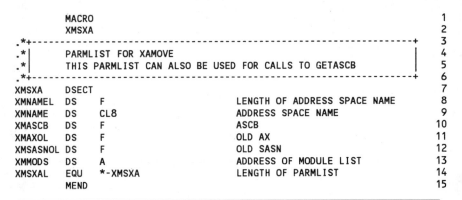

```
            MACRO                                                      1
            XMSXA                                                      2
 .*+-----------------------------------------------------------+       3
 .*|     PARMLIST FOR XAMOVE                                    |       4
 .*|     THIS PARMLIST CAN ALSO BE USED FOR CALLS TO GETASCB    |       5
 .*+-----------------------------------------------------------+       6
XMSXA       DSECT                                                      7
XMNAMEL     DS    F                 LENGTH OF ADDRESS SPACE NAME        8
XMNAME      DS    CL8               ADDRESS SPACE NAME                  9
XMASCB      DS    F                 ASCB                               10
XMAXOL      DS    F                 OLD AX                             11
XMSASNOL    DS    F                 OLD SASN                           12
XMMODS      DS    A                 ADDRESS OF MODULE LIST             13
XMSXAL      EQU   *-XMSXA           LENGTH OF PARMLIST                 14
            MEND                                                       15
```

Figure 7.13   XMSXA DSECT.

```
*+--------------------------------------------------------------------+    1
*|  FUNCTION:                                                          |    2
*|      CHAINS THROUGH TCBS AND CDES IN ANOTHER ADDRESS SPACE,         |    3
*|      MOVING MODULE NAMES TO A LIST IN CALLER'S ADDRESS SPACE.       |    4
*|  INPUTS:                                                            |    5
*|      R1 - PARMLIST MAPPED BY XMSXA MACRO.                           |    6
*|           CALLER HAS SET SECONDARY ADDRESS SPACE.                   |    7
*|  OUTPUTS:                                                           |    8
*|      MODULE NAMES INTO LIST SUPPLIED BY CALLER.                     |    9
*|      R15 - RETURN CODE                                             |   10
*|           0 - MODULE NAMES MOVED TO LIST                            |   11
*|  LOGIC:                                                             |   12
*|      1) GO INTO SECONDARY SPACE MODE.                               |   13
*|      2) CHAIN THRU TCBS AND CDES IN TARGET ADDRESS SPACE, WRITING   |   14
*|         MODULE NAMES TO LIST IN THIS ADDRESS SPACE.                 |   15
*|      3) GO BACK TO PRIMARY SPACE MODE.                              |   16
*|                                                                    |   17
*|  ATTRIBUTES:                                                        |   18
*|      REENTERABLE, AMODE=31, RMODE=ANY, RUNS IN COMMON STORAGE       |   19
*+--------------------------------------------------------------------+   20
             MODULE XASAC,BASE=12,LOC=BELOW,AMODE=31,RMODE=ANY,WORK=NO,  X  21
                    TEXT='MOVE MODULE NAMES USING DAS'                     22
             LR    R3,R1                   ADDRESS OF PARMLIST TO R3       23
             USING XMSXA,R3                MAP PARMLIST                    24
             L     R7,XMMODS               ADDRESS OF TABLE OF MODULES     25
             LA    R7,12(R7)               POINT AT FIRST ENTRY            26
             L     R6,XMASCB               ADDRESS OF ASCB FROM PARMLIST   27
*            *------------------------------------------*                  28
*            *    GO INTO SECONDARY SPACE MODE       *                     29
*            *------------------------------------------*                  30
             SAC   256                     GO INTO SECONDARY SPACE MODE    31
*------------------------------------------------------------------------* 32
************ THE FOLLOWING CODE RUNS IN SECONDARY SPACE MODE  ********* 33
*------------------------------------------------------------------------* 34
*            *------------------------------------------*                  35
*            *    CHAIN THRU TCBS IN TARGET ADDRESS *                      36
*            *    SPACE, WRITING MODULE NAMES TO    *                      37
*            *    TABLE IN PRIMARY ADDRESS SPACE    *                      38
*            *------------------------------------------*                  39
             XR    R9,R9                   CLEAR COUNTER                   40
*                                          ..IN PROBLEM STATE SO SET 3RD   41
             ICM   R4,B'0001',=X'80'       ..OPERAND TO MATCH PSW KEY MASK. 42
             L     R6,ASCBASXB-ASCB(,R6)   ADDR OF ASXB IN SECONDARY ASN   43
             L     R6,ASXBFTCB-ASXB(,R6)   ADDR OF 1ST TCB IN SECONDARY ASN 44
             USING TCB,R6                  MAP TCB                         45
T$CBLOOP DS  0H                                                            46
             ICM   R8,15,TCBJPQ            ADDRESS OF JOB-PACK-AREA QUEUE   47
             BZ    N$EXTCB                 =0; NO MODULES FOR THIS TCB      48
             USING CDENTRY,R8              MAP CDE                         49
C$DELOOP DS  0H                                                            50
             LA    R5,L'CDNAME             LENGTH OF MODULE NAME FOR MVCP   51
*                                          ..MOVE MODULE NAME FROM CDE      52
*                                          ..IN PRIMARAY ADDRESS SPACE TO   53
*                                          ..LIST IN SECONDARY ADDRESS SPC  54
             MVCP  0(R5,R7),CDNAME,R4                                       55
             LA    R9,1(R9)                INCREMENT COUNTER                56
             LA    R7,L'CDNAME(,R7)        POINT AT NEXT ENTRY IN LIST      57
```

Figure 7.14 XASAC.

```
          ICM   R8,15,CDCHAIN          ADDRESS OF NEXT CDE ON JPAQ     58
          BNZ   C$DELOOP               ^=0; PROCESS NEXT CDE           59
N$EXTCB   DS    0H                                                     60
          ICM   R6,15,TCBTCB           ADDRESS IF NEXT TCB ON TCB QUEUE 61
          BNZ   T$CBLOOP               ^=0; POINT AT NEXT TCB          62
*-----------------------------------------------------------------*   63
************ END OF SECONDARY SPACE MODE CODE ********************     64
*-----------------------------------------------------------------*   65
*         *----------------------------------------------*            66
*         *    GO INTO PRIMARY SPACE MODE       *                     67
*         *----------------------------------------------*            68
          SAC   0                      GO INTO PRIMARY    SPACE MODE   69
          L     R7,XMMODS              ..STORE NUMBER OF MODULE NAMES  70
          ST    R9,8(R7)               ..IN MODULE NAME LIST           71
          B     EXIT00                                                 72
*-----------------------------------------------------------------*   73
*         EXIT ROUTINES                                          *    74
*-----------------------------------------------------------------*   75
EXIT00    DS    0H                     SUCCESSFUL                      76
          LA    R15,X'00'                                              77
          B     EXIT                                                   78
*-----------------------------------------------------------------*   79
*         COMMON EXIT                                            *    80
*-----------------------------------------------------------------*   81
EXIT      DS    0H                                                     82
          ENDMOD                                                       83
*-----------------------------------------------------------------*   84
*         WORK AREA                                              *    85
*-----------------------------------------------------------------*   86
WXASAC    DSECT                                                        87
LXASAC    EQU   *-WXASAC                                               88
*-----------------------------------------------------------------*   89
*         OTHER DSECTS                                           *    90
*-----------------------------------------------------------------*   91
          XMSXA                        USER PARMLIST                   92
          PRINT NOGEN                                                  93
          IHAASCB                      ADDRESS SPACE CONTROL BLOCK     94
          IHAASXB                      ADDRESS SPACE EXTENSION BLOCK   95
          IKJTCB                       TASK CONTROL BLOCK              96
          IHACDE                       CONTENTS DIRECTORY ENTRY        97
          END                                                         98
```

Figure 7.14 *(Continued)*

issued while the module were in supervisor state, the third operand of MVCP and the PKM would not have been inspected.

After MVCP has moved all the module names to the primary address space, XASAC returns to primary space mode by issuing SAC 0 (line 69) and returns to the main module with a BSM in the expansion of the ENDMOD macro (line 83).

When control returns to XAMOVE, line 102 issues SSAR to restore the original SASN. This is necessary since some MVS services cannot be called when the PASN and the SASN are different. Line 105 resets the AX to its original value and line 107 deletes the XASAC module from CSA before lines 108 through 116 invoking the PRTMOD routine to print the list of module names.

Program Management

8.1 LOAD MODULES

All software in an MVS environment exists as load modules, which are the objects on which the Program Management component of MVS operates. Load modules are members of RECFM = U partitioned data sets (PDSs) and consist of records of different types as indicated by the first byte of each record. A formatted listing of the records in a load module can be produced by running the AMBLIST utility (Fig. 8.1). The three most important types of records in load modules are:

8.1.1 External Symbol Directory (ESD)

The ESD allows object and load modules to be independent of their source modules so that they do not have to be recompiled before being combined with other modules. Language compilers, including the assembler, generate entries in the ESD when source-code statements refer to symbols that are defined in other modules. ESD entries are also created when source-code statements define symbols that other modules can reference.

Figure 8.2 contains the types of entries in ESD records, the assembly language statements that generate the entries, and the usage of each symbol type.

8.1.2 Text Records

Text records contain the machine instructions that are fetched and executed when the module receives control.

```
//AMBLIST  JOB ()
//*------------------------------------------------------------------*
//* AMBLIST WILL FORMAT THE ATTRIBUTES AND RECORDS IN A LOAD MODULE   *
//*------------------------------------------------------------------*
//LIST     EXEC PGM=AMBLIST,REGION=300K
//SYSLIB   DD DISP=SHR,DSN=load.library
//SYSPRINT DD SYSOUT=*
//SYSIN    DD *
 LISTLOAD OUTPUT=BOTH,DDN=SYSLIB,MEMBER=member
 /*
```

Figure 8.1 JCL for AMBLIST.

Symb. Type	Definition	Assembly Language Statement	Meaning
SD	Section Definition	CSECT or START	Name, length, AMODE and location of a control section.
LR	Entry Symbol	ENTRY	Location of an additional entry point.
PC	Private Code	none	Length and location of an unnamed control section. Typically created when "CSECT" is not coded.
ER	External Symbol	EXTRN or V()	Reference to a CSECT or ENTRY symbol in another module. If unresolved, link-edit return code is 4 (NCAL) or 8 (CAL).
WX	Weak External Symbol	WXTRN	Reference to a CSECT or ENTRY symbol in another module. If unresolved, link-edit return code is 0.
CM	Common blank CSECT	COM	Name, length and location of the part of a COM CSECT that is defined in this module. Link editor combines COM CSECTS with the same name into one CSECT.
PR	Pseudo Register	Q()	Name and location of a symbol in a common external DSECT.

Figure 8.2 ESD symbol types.

8.1.3 Relocation Directory (RLD)

When Program Manager invokes the loader to bring a module from DASD into virtual storage, it does not have to use a pre-defined storage address but can locate the module anywhere.

This is possible because the assembler resolves labels in instruction operands as displacements off a base register specified in a USING statement. When the module is loaded into virtual storage, receives control, and executes

```
LR base,15
```

or

```
BALR base,0
```

it loads the base register with a virtual address. Thereafter, all operand addresses become displacements off that specific virtual address.

Address constants, by contrast, assemble into numerical values that represent their offsets into the object module and not into displacements off a base register. When the loader brings a module into virtual storage, it adds the offset value in each RLD entry to the virtual address of the first byte of the module. This gives each address constant a specific virtual address based on where the module was loaded.

A-type address constants contain offsets after assembly. The other three types of address constants, V-type, Q-type and CXD are assigned offset values after their external symbol references are resolved by the link editor. The assembler makes a Relocation Directory entry for each address constant in the source-code.

8.1.4 Other Types of Load Module Records

There are optional record types that may be produced in load modules:

- *SYM records.* These records are produced in a load module when it has been assembled and link edited with PARM = 'TEST'. The SYM records allow you to use the symbols in the source-code, rather than numerical displacements into the load module, to set breakpoints and to reference data when using TSO TEST to interactively debug the module.

- *IDR Records.* These records contain the history of the load module. IDR records include the date when the module was created by the link editor and any changes that have been made to the module by zapping it with the AMASPZAP utility. Since a fixed number of IDR records is built when a load module is created, applying many zaps can use up all of the available space, causing AMASPZAP to fail. PARM = IGNRIDRFL on the EXEC statement for AMASPZAP allows you to zap a module even when there is no space in the IDR records to record the zap.

8.1.5 Constructing Load Modules

Figure 8.3 illustrates how the link editor combines object modules into a load module. The external symbols from all the input object and load modules are resolved into a Combined External Symbol Directory (CESD). RLD records from one module and ESD records from the following module are combined, where possible, into a single record. Note

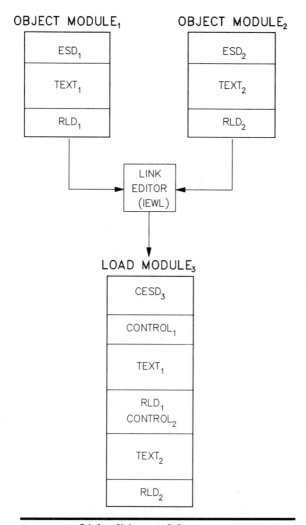

Figure 8.3 Link editing modules.

that the resulting load module can, itself, be link edited with other load modules or object modules and a new CESD will be created that will contain all the external symbols from all the constituent modules.

8.2 MVS PROGRAM MANAGER

Program Management, also known as Contents Supervision, is the MVS component responsible for locating load modules in load libraries on DASD, bringing the modules into virtual storage, and controlling the modules once they are in virtual storage. Whenever possible, Program Management avoids the overhead of loading a module from DASD and satisfies requests for that module with a copy that is already in storage.

Whether Program Management can use an existing copy of a module depends on the way the module was written and what attributes were assigned to it when it was link-edited. Chap. 3 describes how to write programs so that they can be multiuser.

8.2.1 The Contents Directory Entry (CDE)

Attributes are assigned to a module with PARM = on the EXEC statement in the link editor JCL. When the link editor builds a load module in a load library, it stores the attributes in the PDS directory entry for that module. Program Manager, in response to a LOAD, LINK, SYNCH, XCTL, or ATTACH macro, reads the PDS directory entry and sets attribute bits in the Contents Directory Entry (CDE) control block it builds to keep track of the module once it has been brought into storage. When another request is made for the module, Program Manager locates the CDE and, based on the attribute flags, determines if the in-storage copy can be used to satisfy the request.

The CDE attribute bits describe a module as one of four types:

1. *Nonreusable:* If none of the attribute bits is set, the in-storage copy of the module will be used only once. Every request for the module will cause Program Manager to load a fresh copy from DASD.

2. *Serially reusable:* If the REUS bit is set, the single in-storage copy of the module can satisfy multiple requests as long as only one user is active in the module at a time. A serially reusable module might contain storage areas that change during program execution but are reinitialized at the beginning of the code by each user. If requests are made for serially reusable modules with LINK, SYNCH, XCTL, or ATTACH, Program Manager allows only one user in the code at a time and forms a queue of waiting users. If serially reusable modules are LOADed and branch-entered, Program Manager cannot serialize their use.

3. *Reentrant:* The RENT bit in the CDE indicates that multiple users can be active simultaneously in the code. It does not indicate that the storage that contains the module is never modified. A reentrant module might, for example, contain an address pointer that is initialized when the module is loaded. HOOKSVC in Appendix C is an example of reentrant code that is modified when it is loaded.

4. *Refreshable:* The REFR bit in the CDE indicates that not only can multiple users be active simultaneously in the code, but that the storage that contains the module is never modified. Refreshable modules can be reloaded during error recovery even if there are users active in the code. All modules in the Pageable Link Pack Area (PLPA) must be refreshable since fresh copies of these modules can be paged in at any time. All programs in this book are refreshable except for HOOKSVC in Appendix C.

There is no reason ever to write nonreusable or serially reusable code. Writing reentrant and refreshable code takes slightly more effort, but the measurable benefits in terms of reduced program load overhead and module serialization delay are well worth it. Even when you write a program that will execute as a batch job (and will, therefore, be deleted after its only execution when the jobstep TCB is DETACHed), adhering to the reentrant/refreshable standard has advantages. You never know when you might want to call a module that is already written to provide a service in a new piece of software. If a module is reentrant or refreshable, it is much easier to treat it as a function that can be invoked in any execution environment.

8.2.2 Order of Search

When a task issues a LINK, XCTL, SYNCH, LOAD, or ATTACH macro, Program Manager:

1. Searches the CDEs on the Job Pack Area Queue (JPAQ), illustrated in Fig. 8.4, for an in-storage copy of the module. These CDEs represent all the modules brought into storage by programs executing under the Jobstep TCB or any of its subtasks. Task Manager creates a Jobstep TCB when the ATTACH macro is issued with the JSTCB = YES operand. The Initiator task in a batch address space, for example, ATTACHes a new Jobstep task for each //EXEC statement in the JCL.

2. If the module is not found on the JPAQ, Program Manager searches the load libraries named in the //JOBLIB DD or //STEPLIB DD concatenations. Program Manager then issues GETMAINs to acquire virtual storage for a CDE, an Extent List (XL), and the module itself. Program Manager builds the CDE and the XL (which describes the

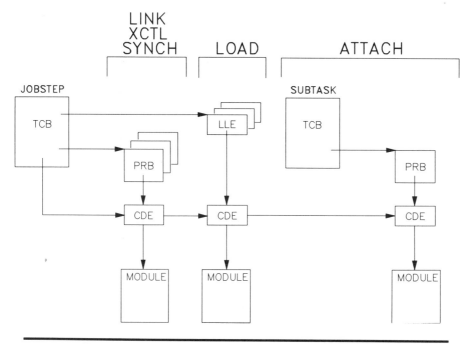

Figure 8.4 Program management macros.

storage occupied by the module) and chains the CDE onto the JPAQ. Program Manager uses a special access method, Program Fetch, to read the module into virtual storage.

If you suspect that a module is being loaded frequently from DASD into virtual storage, either by different tasks or multiple times for the same task, there are two facilities MVS provides to reduce the I/O:

- *Virtual Fetch* employs Virtual Input/Output (VIO) to *page* modules into real storage from DASD or expanded storage rather than to *read* them into storage with the the Program Fetch access method. Since paging from expanded storage does not involve I/O and paging from DASD is more efficient that other types of I/O, Virtual Fetch can reduce both the number of I/Os and I/O response time.

  Note that VIO can have a performance impact on demand paging if Directed VIO (DVIO) is not specified when page data sets are defined. Otherwise, VIO will compete with demand paging for access to the same data sets. The IBM Manual, *SPL: System Modifications* (GC28-1831), describes how to use Virtual Fetch.

- *Virtual Lookaside Facility (VLF)*, available only in MVS/ESA, is a variation on the concept of VIO in that modules can be defined as virtual objects that are paged into real storage rather than read into storage by program fetch. Although VLF can be used for load modules, it is more appropriate for CLISTs and frequently used data files.

An alternative to using either Virtual Fetch or VLF is to determine why Program Manager is repeatedly fetching a module from DASD rather than using a copy of the module that is already in storage. If the module is marked nonreusable, Program Manager is loading a fresh copy to satisfy each request. For assembly language programs, changing the code so that it is serially reusable or reentrant can significantly improve performance. For programs written in high-level languages such as COBOL, specifying the correct compiler options will generate reusable or reentrant code.

If a module is being fetched often for different tasks, consider making the module refreshable and installing it in PLPA. Like Virtual Fetch, this causes the paging routines to keep the module in real storage based on the demand for that module. But, unlike Virtual Fetch, it does not require starting a separate address space or using directed VIO.

3. If Program Manager still has not located the module, it searches the Link Pack Area Queue (LPAQ). This queue contains CDEs for all *active* modules in the Fixed Link Pack Area (FLPA), the Modified Link Pack Area (MLPA) and the Pageable Link Pack Area (PLPA). The ANCHOR program in this chapter adds a CDE for a user control block to the LPAQ.

4. If a CDE for the module is not found on the LPAQ, Program Manager searches the queue of Link Pack Directory Entries (LPDEs) on the Pageable Link Pack Area Queue (PLPAQ) which describe modules in PLPA. If Program Manager finds an LPDE for the module, it uses it to build a CDE on the LPAQ. The PLPAQ, unlike the LPAQ, is not rebuilt when MVS is initialized unless the operator specifies the Construct Link Pack Area (CLPA) parameter at IPL.

5. Finally, Program Manager searches for the module in the libraries named in the LNKLSTxx member of SYS1.PARMLIB. To avoid having to read the PDS directory for each of the libraries in the *system linklist*, as this concatenation of libraries is known, Program Manager invokes Library Lookaside (LLA) to do a hashed search of an in-storage list containing all the members in all the libraries.

8.2.3 Interfaces to Program Manager

Once a CDE for the module has been located, Program Manager builds an additional control block, depending on which macro invoked its services (see Fig. 8.4).

- For LINK, XCTL, and SYNCH, Program Manager builds a Program Request Block (PRB) chained from the current TCB. For ATTACH, Program Manager invokes Task Manager to create a new TCB and builds the first PRB on the RB queue of the new TCB. Request Blocks represent units of work that are executed serially for the current task. PRBs and their extensions, XSBs, contain the registers, PSW, and cross-memory environment that are loaded on a processor when the unit of work is dispatched.

  Invoking XCTL causes Program Manager to build a new PRB and invokes Task Manager to dequeue the RB under which XCTL was issued. In this way, when the code under the XCTL-created PRB completes, the code under the RB previous on the RB queue to the XCTL issuer receives control.

  SYNCH builds a PRB that contains a PSW with a supervisor/problem state and key that may be different from the issuing program. It also builds an XSB that may contain a cross-memory environment different from the issuer. When a module executing under a SYNCH-created PRB completes and is dequeued, the original PSW and cross-memory values from the SYNCH-issuer's RB and XSB are loaded on the processor.

  SYNCH allows a program in supervisor state, for example, to create a PRB with a problem-state PSW. This has the effect of a supervisor-state program transferring control to a problem-state program and receiving control again in supervisor state. RTM2, which executes in supervisor state, uses SYNCH to transfer control to ESTAE routines that can execute in problem-state.

- When a program issues the first LOAD macro under a TCB for a module, Program Manager creates a Load List Element (LLE) on the LLE queue of that TCB. The LLE contains a field called the responsibility count, which represents the sum of all the outstanding LOADs issued for that module under that TCB. Each time LOAD is issued, the responsibility count is incremented. Each time DELETE is issued, the responsibility count is decremented.

8.2.4 CDE Use Count

The CDE also contains a count field called the use count, which is incremented whenever a LINK, XCTL, SYNCH, ATTACH, or LOAD is issued against the module it represents. When a PRB created by LINK, XCTL, SYNCH, or ATTACH is dequeued or when DELETE is issued against the module, the count is decremented. When the count reaches 0, the CDE is dequeued and the module is FREEMAINed.

When Task Manager is DETACHing a TCB, it subtracts the responsibility count in each LLE from the use-count field in the CDE specified by that LLE. This adjusts the use-count field in the CDE for any LOADs for which no DELETEs were issued by the terminating task.

8.3 SERIALIZATION WITH MVS LOCKS

Locks serialize the use of MVS control blocks. *Serialization* means only one user at a time. Serialization with locks is not automatic. Rather, it is an "honor system" that depends on all programs in the system adhering to the following rules:

■ No program will change the contents of a control block, including the fields that chain it to other control blocks, unless it holds the lock for that control block.

■ A program can assume that changes are not being made to a control block only if it holds the lock for that control block.

8.3.1 Why Locks are Necessary

Figure 8.5 illustrates what can happen if programs do not abide by the honor system and make changes to control blocks, or assume changes are not being made, without first obtaining a lock.

The first line of Fig. 8.5 shows a typical queue, or chain, of control blocks. There is a field in each control block, labeled "chain," which contains the address of the next control block in the queue. The last control block contains X'00000000' in its chain field. These control blocks might be Address Space Control Blocks (ASCBs) on the True Dispatch List or CDEs on the Job Pack Area Queue; most MVS components utilize such queues.

Suppose two programs, executing under separate TCBs, attempt to modify the queue. One program wants to add block D to the end of the queue, while the other program wants to remove block C from the queue. The first program might contain the instructions in Fig. 8.6 to locate the control block that is at the end of the queue and to chain the new control block onto the queue. Assume the first program executes and reaches the instruction labeled CHAINIT when it is interrupted. At that point register 6 contains the address of the new control block (block D); and register 5, the address of the control block that is last-in-queue (block C).

If the second program now becomes active, it will unchain block C, and the queue will look like the second line in Fig. 8.5. When the first program becomes active again and executes the ST instruction at CHAINIT, register 5 still contains the address of block C. The ST results in a queue that looks like the third line in the Fig. 8.5 and block D will not have been added to the queue.

If either program had waited for the other to complete, the queue would look like the fourth line in the figure with block D added to the queue and block C removed.

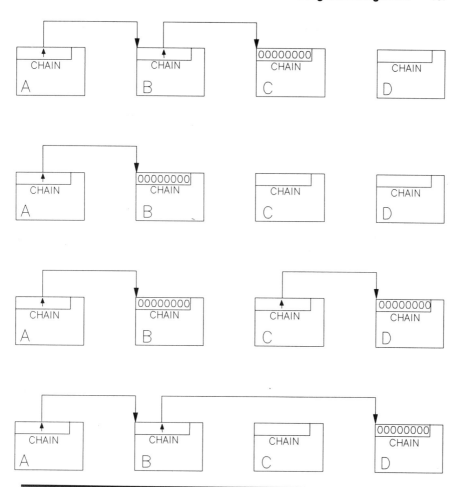

Figure 8.5 Changing control block queues.

8.3.2 MVS Lock Manager

Each lock regulates a specific group of MVS control blocks. Any MVS component or user program that wishes to use one of the control blocks in the group can issue the SETLOCK macro to call MVS Lock Manager who obtains, tests, and releases all locks.

For every lock there is a fullword in storage, known as a lockword, that contains a value describing the holder of the lock or X'00000000' if the lock is free. The issuer of SETLOCK identifies the lockword, either by naming a lock whose address Lock Manager knows, or by supplying the address of the lockword on the ADDR= parameter on SETLOCK.

If the lock is free, Lock Manager obtains it for the caller by putting a caller-identifying value in the lockword. If the lock is not free, Lock Manager uses one of two mechanisms to cause the caller to wait until the

```
          USING BLOCK,5          MAP THE CONTROL BLOCK
          LA    5,BLOCKA         ADDRESS FIRST CONTROL BLOCK ON QUEUE
NEXTBLOK  CLC   CHAIN,=F'0'      IS ADDRESS OF NEXT BLOCK X'00'?
          BE    ENDOFQ           YES; THIS IS THE LAST BLOCK ON QUEUE
          L     5,CHAIN          LOAD ADDRESS OF NEXT BLOCK ON QUEUE
          B     NEXTBLOK         CHECK IF NEXT BLOCK IS END OF QUEUE
ENDOFQ    LA    6,BLOCKD         ..PUT ADDRESS OF NEW BLOCK
CHAINIT   ST    6,CHAIN          ..IN CHAIN FIELD OF PREVIOUS BLOCK
          LR    5,6              LOAD ADDRESS OF NEW END-OF-CHAIN
          MVC   CHAIN,F'0'       X'00' IN CHAIN FIELD OF LAST BLOCK
..        ..    ..
BLOCK     DSECT
CHAIN     DS    A                NEXT CONTROL BLOCK
..        ..    ..
```

Figure 8.6 Adding a control block to a queue.

lock is free. Locks are characterized by the way a requestor waits for the lock if it is held:

8.3.3 Spin Locks

A program that requests a spin lock that is not available, *remains active on the processor on which it is executing* and enters a loop in Lock Manager code that repeatedly tests the lockword against F'0' with the CS (Compare and Swap) instruction. If the lockword contains another value, the lock is not free and the loop continues. If the lock is free, the CS instruction stores a value in the lockword. Lock Manager uses the CS instruction instead of ST because CS and CDS (the doubleword version of CS) are the only two instructions that prevent different processors from simultaneously updating the same bytes in storage.

Spin Locks serialize the control blocks used by components whose functions are critical for continued functioning of the system. If these components were interrupted while holding a lock, very little could get done until they were reactivated. In fact, the components whose control blocks are serialized by spin locks execute with a PSW disabled for I/O and external interrupts so that they can complete their functions without interruption. Whenever an enabled program requests a spin lock, Lock Manager disables the PSW when it obtains the lock.

Since one or more processors can be executing the loop in Lock Manager code and consuming CPU cycles while they are waiting for a spin lock (this is called "spinning on the lock"), code that executes while holding a spin lock must have the shortest possible path-length.

8.3.4 Suspend Locks

When a program requests a suspend lock that is not available, *Lock Manager puts the requestor on a queue and calls the Dispatcher so that* other work can execute on the processor. On which queue the requestor is placed depends on the particular lock and whether the caller is executing under a TCB or an SRB.* When a program calls Lock Manager to release a suspend lock, Lock Manager removes the first suspended unit of work from the queue and makes it dispatchable.

Suspend locks allow programs to execute PSW enabled and to be interrupted while holding the lock. Since the requestor of a suspend lock might be waiting for a comparatively long period of time, suspend locks are for functions that are less critical for overall system operation. For example, there is no work that can be done within an individual address space that is important enough to monopolize the processor on which it is executing. The LOCAL lock, which serializes the control blocks of an individual address space, therefore, is a suspend lock.

8.3.5 Obtaining a Lock

Whenever you are writing code that accesses an MVS control block, determine whether there is a lock that serializes that control block by examining its description in *MVS Debugging Handbook*. Always get the lock if your code *changes* the control block. Since the ANCHOR program in this chapter changes the queue of LPAQ CDEs that are serialized by the CMS lock, it issues SETLOCK to obtain that lock.

If your code uses data in an MVS control block but does not change it, obtaining the lock is probably unnecessary. However, your code may have to account for the possibility that an MVS component executing on another processor can change the control block while your code is extracting data from it. For example, you might include an ESTAE routine to recover from any S0C4s that result when chaining through Address Space Control Block (ASCB) queues while the MVS Dispatcher, running on another processor, is simultaneously reordering that queue.

If you determine that it is appropriate to obtain a lock, examine the description of that lock in *MVS Debugging Handbook Vol. I* to determine whether it is an individual or class lock.

- Individual locks: Some control blocks exist only once in the system while others exist on several queues. There is only one Address Space Vector Table (ASVT) so there is only one lock, the DISP lock, that serializes it. This is an example of an individual lock.
- Class locks: By contrast, there are as many Unit Control Blocks (UCBs) as there are defined I/O devices, and there is a separate IOSUCB lock to serialize each UCB and its subsidiary control blocks. This is known as a "class" of locks.

---

*A program executing under a TCB that requests an unavailable LOCAL lock is not actually placed on a queue. But, since the local dispatcher will not dispatch any task until after it dispatches the TCB or SRB that holds the LOCAL lock, it is implicitly queued (see Chap. 9).

To obtain a class lock, load the address of the lockword into register 11 and specify the ADDR = (11) parameter on the SETLOCK macro. For the Cross-Memory Local (CML) lock, which is really the LOCAL lock of another address space, load the address of the target address space's ASCB into register 11 and issue SETLOCK with the ASCB = (11) parameter. *MVS Debugging Handbook Vol. I* and *MVS Diagnostic Techniques* contain the locations of lockwords. Figure 8.7 illustrates how to supply the address of the lockword for SETLOCK when obtaining a class lock.

A program might perform operations on different control blocks serialized by different locks in the same section of code. In that case, it will need to obtain more than one lock. In order to avoid interlock, where each of two tasks is waiting for a lock held by the other task, locks are arranged in a hierarchy. If a task requests two locks, Lock Manager requires that the lock lower in the hierarchy be obtained first. If a program requests a lock lower in the hierarchy than a lock it already holds, Lock Manager abends the requestor for an unconditional SETLOCK request and returns a bad return code for a conditional SETLOCK request.

This hierarchical arrangement of locks prevents interlock because programs always wait for an unavailable lower-level lock before obtaining a higher-level lock. That is, after they obtain the higher-level lock, they always hold *both* locks. *MVS Debugging Handbook Vol. I* lists locks in hierarchical order.

Be aware of the following considerations when obtaining locks:

- SVC FLIH will abend any program that issues an SVC while it holds a lock. If you need a lock in an SVC routine, SVC FLIH can obtain the lock before it transfers control to the routine based on the lock flags in the SVC Table entry (see Chap. 6). Alternatively, the SVC routine itself can obtain the locks by issuing SETLOCK.

- Programs cannot take page faults while they hold a spin lock. A demand paging operation begins with a page or segment program check interrupt. Program check FLIH abends a disabled program that takes one of these interrupts. Use the PGSER macro to fix program and data storage before obtaining a spin lock.

8.4 THE ANCHOR PROGRAM

Suppose you are designing a set of programs that execute in different address spaces, and you want them to be able to share data in storage. One of the programs can issue GETMAIN or STORAGE to obtain CSA or SQA, but where can that program save the address of the storage so that the programs in the other address spaces can locate it? Three of the most common places used to "anchor" an area of common storage are:

```
          ..        ..              ..
          L      3,CVTPTR           COMMUNICATION VECTOR TABLE ADDRESS
          L      3,CVTRCEP-CVT(3)   ADDRESS OF RSM CONTROL & ENUM. AREA
          LA     4,LRCE(3)          ADDRESS OF RSM INTERFACE TABLE
          USING  RIT,4              MAP RIT
          LA     11,RITGLLK         ADDRESS OF RSMGL LOCKWORD IN RIT
          SETLOCK OBTAIN,MODE=UNCOND  ..UNCONDITIONALLY OBTAIN THE        X
                  TYPE=RSMGL,ADDR=(11)  ..THE RSMGL LOCK                  X
                  RELATED=COMMENT    REQUIRED OPERAND
          ..        ..              ..
          CVT    DSECT=YES,LIST=NO  MAPPING MACRO FOR CVT
          IARRCE                    MAPPING MACRO FOR RCE
          IARRIT                    MAPPING MACRO FOR RIT
          IHAPSA DSECT=YES,LIST=NO  MAPPING FOR PSA; USED BY SETLOCK
  ..        ..        ..            ..
```

Figure 8.7 Obtaining a class lock.

- In the field reserved for users in the CVT (CVTUSER): Using this field and similar fields in other control blocks (e.g., TCBUSER in the TCB) is asking for trouble. Software from a vendor or another program written at your installation might put a value in these fields.

- In a Subsystem Control Table (SSCT). SSCTs, each of which represents a defined subsystem, are queued from the CVT through the JESCT (JES Control Table). Many vendor products anchor common storage areas in SSCTs which they build, either at system initialization, or dynamically.

- In a CDE on the LPAQ: This method for anchoring common storage, illustrated in Fig. 8.8, allows any program to locate the storage by searching the LPAQ CDE chain, by invoking the Program Management routine IEAQCDSR that performs the LPAQ search, or by issuing the LOAD macro. Program Management treats the CDE just like any other CDE—LOAD returns the address and length of the storage in registers 0 and 1, respectively.

The ANCHOR program in Fig. 8.9 obtains a block of storage in CSA or SQA and saves the storage address in a CDE which it builds on the LPAQ. Several other programs in this book use ANCHOR to obtain an easily addressable control block.

- Chapter 10: PCSET calls ANCHOR to obtain a data area into which it puts PC numbers for user-defined PC routines. The CALLPC macro, also in Chap. 10, expands into instructions that call IEAQCDSR, locate

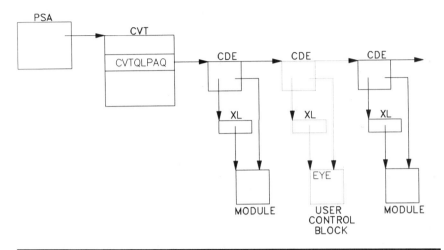

Figure 8.8   The ANCHOR program.

the appropriate PC number in the data area, and issue the PC instruction.

- Chapter 11: DSPACE calls ANCHOR to obtain a control block which itself is an anchor for a queue of control blocks describing user-created dataspaces. The DSPFIND routine, also in Chap. 11, invokes IEAQCDSR to locate the CDE that DSPACE creates.

Two programs in Appendix C are related to ANCHOR:

- UNANCH reverses the actions of ANCHOR, removing the CDE and FREEMAINing the storage obtained for the user control block in common storage.
- REPMOD calls ANCHOR when it replaces or adds a *module* whose CDE is on the LPAQ. Calling REPMOD is equivalent to adding or replacing a member in SYS1.LPALIB without waiting for the next IPL of the system.

8.5 ANCHOR WALKTHROUGH

ANCHOR includes USING statements on lines 28 through 34 for the DSECTs that map the control blocks and parameter lists used in the rest of the program. Placing USING statements together at the beginning of a program rather than at the various points where the USING registers are loaded (lines 48, 67, 72, etc.) helps to document the module and reduces the need for a "register usage" section in the block comments at the beginning of the module.

Lines 219 through 225 contain the macros that generate the DSECTs

```
*+----------------------------------------------------------------+     1
*|   FUNCTION:                                                     |     2
*|      GET STORAGE FOR A CONTROL BLOCK AND ANCHOR IT IN AN LPAQ CDE.|   3
*|   LOGIC:                                                        |     4
*|      1)  SEARCH CDE'S ON LPAQ FOR CONTROL BLOCK CDE.            |     5
*|      2)  IF FOUND; VERIFY THAT EYECATCHER IS FIRST 4 BYTES.     |     6
*|      3)  IF CDE DOES NOT EXIST; GET SQA FOR CDE AND EXTENT LIST.|     7
*|          BUILD CDE AND EXTENT LIST.                            |     8
*|      4)  GET CSA FOR CONTROL BLOCK.                            |     9
*|      5)  GET THE LOCAL AND CMS LOCKS TO SERIALIZE LPAQ.        |    10
*|      6)  PUT ADDRESS OF CONTROL BLOCK IN CDE AND EXTENT LIST.  |    11
*|      7)  IF CDE IS CREATED; CHAIN IT ONTO THE LPAQ.           |    12
*|      8)  RELEASE ALL LOCKS.                                    |    13
*|   INPUTS:                                                       |    14
*|      R1 - PARMLIST MAPPED BY ANKPRM MACRO.                     |    15
*|   OUTPUTS:                                                      |    16
*|      ADDRESS OF THE CONTROL BLOCK IN ANKEP FIELD OF PARMLIST.  |    17
*|      R15- RETURN CODE:                                         |    18
*|          0 = NEW CONTROL BLOCK HAS BEEN BUILT AND ANCHORED.    |    19
*|          4 = CONTROL BLOCK ALREADY EXISTS AND IS ANCHORED.     |    20
*|          8 = GETMAIN FAILED FOR CDE AND EXTENT LIST.           |    21
*|         12 = GETMAIN FAILED FOR CONTROL BLOCK.                 |    22
*|   ATTRIBUTES:                                                   |    23
*|      AMODE 31, RMODE ANY, REFRESHABLE, REQUIRES APF AUTHORIZATION|   24
*+----------------------------------------------------------------+    25
          MODULE ANCHOR,BASE=12,LOC=BELOW,AMODE=31,RMODE=ANY,      X    26
                 TEXT='ANCHOR CONTROL BLOCK ON LPAQ'                    27
*         *----------------------------------------*                    28
*         *    MAP CONTROL BLOCKS USED            *                    29
*         *----------------------------------------*                    30
          USING CVT,R3                 COMMUNICATIONS VECTOR TABLE      31
          USING CDENTRY,R4             CONTENTS DIRECTORY ENTRY         32
          USING XTLST,R6               EXTENT LIST                      33
          USING ANKPRM,R10             USER PARMLIST                    34
          LR    R10,R1                 ADDRESS OF PARMLIST TO R10       35
*----------------------------------------------------------------*      36
*         INVOKE IBM'S IEAQCDSR SERVICE TO SCAN FOR OUR CDE ON LPAQ. *   37
*            INPUTS TO IEAQCDSR SERVICE:                          *      38
*               R8 - HEAD OF LPAQ IN CVT                          *      39
*               R9 - ADDRESS OF 8 BYTE FIELD WITH NAME OF CDE TO FIND * 40
*            OUTPUTS:                                             *      41
*               IF CDE FOUND;                                    *      42
*                  INSTRUCTION AFTER BALR GETS CONTROL           *      43
*                  CDE ADDRESS IS IN R11                         *      44
*               IF CDE NOT FOUND;                                *      45
*                  INSTRUCTION 4 BYTES AFTER BALR GETS CONTROL   *      46
*----------------------------------------------------------------*      47
          L     R3,CVTPTR             A(CVT) => R3                      48
          LA    R9,ANKNAME            A(CONTROL BLOCK NAME) => R9       49
          L     R8,CVTQLPAQ           HEAD OF LPAQ => R8                50
          L     R15,CVTQCDSR          A(LPAQ SCAN ROUTINE)             51
          BALR  R14,R15               INVOKE LPAQ SCAN ROUTINE          52
          B     FNDCDE                CDE FOUND; PROCESS CDE            53
          B     GETSTOR               NOT FOUND; GET STORAGE FOR CDE    54
*----------------------------------------------------------------*      55
*         GET STORAGE FOR LPAQ CDE AND INITIALIZE CDE            *      56
*----------------------------------------------------------------*      57
```

Figure 8.9 ANCHOR.

```
GETSTOR   DS    OH                                                            58
                MODESET MODE=SUP,KEY=ZERO     GET A SUPERVISOR / KEY 0 PSW     59
          LA    R0,LCDE+LXTNT                 LENGTH OF CDE + EXTENT LIST      60
          GETMAIN RC,                         GET SQA STORAGE FOR CDE AND XL X 61
                LV=(R0),                       LENGTH                        X 62
                SP=245,                        SUBPOOL                       X 63
                LOC=BELOW                                                      64
          LTR   R15,R15                        GETMAIN OK ?                    65
          BNZ   EXIT08                         NO; EXIT RC = 8                 66
          LR    R4,R1                          ADDRESS OF CDE => R4            67
          XC    O(LCDE+LXTNT,R4),O(R4)         INITIALIZE STORAGE TO X'00'     68
*         *------------------------------------------*                        69
*         *     INITIALIZE CDE                       *                        70
*         *------------------------------------------*                        71
          LA    R6,LCDE(R4)                    A(EXTENT LIST)                  72
          ST    R6,CDXLMJP                     PUT A(EXTENT LIST) INTO CDE     73
          MVC   CDNAME,ANKNAME                 PUT CONTROL BLOCK NAME IN CDE   74
          OI    CDATTR,CDNIP+CDREN+CDSER+CDNLR .. SET                         75
          OI    CDATTR2,CDXLE                  .. CDE FLAGS                    76
*         *------------------------------------------*                        77
*         *     INITIALIZE XTENT LIST                *                        78
*         *------------------------------------------*                        79
          LA    R5,16                          .. LENGTH OF EXTENT LIST ENTRY  80
          ST    R5,XTLLNTH                     .. INTO EXTENT LIST             81
          LA    R5,1                           .. RELOCATION FACTORS           82
          ST    R5,XTLNRFAC                    .. INTO EXTENT LIST             83
          MVI   XTLMSBLA,X'80'                                                 84
          MODESET MODE=PROB,KEY=NZERO          GET A PROBLEM STATE PSW         85
          OI    SW1,@NOCDE                     SET SWITCH THERE IS NO CDE      86
          B     GETBLOCK                       BRANCH TO OBTAIN CSA FOR BLOCK  87
*----------------------------------------------------------------------*      88
*         IF CDE FOUND, CHECK STORAGE IT POINTS TO FOR EYECATCHER        *     89
*----------------------------------------------------------------------*      90
FNDCDE    DS    OH                                                            91
          LR    R4,R11                         A( CDE ) FROM CVTQCDSR ROUTINE  92
          L     R5,CDENTPT                     ENTRY POINT FROM CDE => R5      93
          CLC   O(L'ANKEYE,R5),ANKEYE          IS EYCATCHER FIRST BYTES?       94
          BNE   GETBLOCK                       NO; AQUIRE STORAGE FOR BLOCK    95
          ST    R5,ANKEP                       PUT ADDRESS IN PARMLIST         96
          B     EXIT04                         EXIT; CONTROL BLOCK EXISTS      97
*----------------------------------------------------------------------*      98
*         GET STORAGE FOR CONTROL BLOCK AND INITIALIZE STORAGE           *     99
*----------------------------------------------------------------------*     100
GETBLOCK  DS    OH                                                           101
          XR    R15,R15                        SET REGISTER TO X'00'          102
          CLI   ANKSP,X'00'                    IS PARMLIST SUBPOOL X'00' ?     103
          BNE   NSPDFLT                        NO; DO NOT SET FOR DEFAULT      104
          MVI   ANKSP,@ANKSP                   SET DEFAULT IN PARMLIST         105
NSPDFLT   DS    OH                                                           106
          ICM   R15,B'0001',ANKSP              SET SUBPOOL FROM PARMLIST       107
          L     R0,ANKLEN                      LENGTH OF ANCHORED DATA AREA    108
          TM    ANKFLAG1,@ANKBEL               BELOW THE LINE STORAGE?         109
          BO    GBELOW                         YES; GETMAIN BELOW 16MEG        110
          GETMAIN RC,                          GET STORAGE FOR CONTROL BLOCK X 111
                LV=(0),                                                      X 112
                SP=(15),                                                    X 113
                LOC=(ANY,ANY)                                                 114
```

Figure 8.9 *(Continued)*

```
        LTR   R15,R15                      GETMAIN OK ?                        115
        BNZ   EXITOC                       NO; EXIT RC= 12                     116
        B     AGET1                        BRANCH AROUND LOC=BELOW GETMAIN     117
GBELOW  DS    OH                                                               118
        GETMAIN RC,                        GET STORAGE FOR CONTROL BLOCK   X  119
              LV=(0),                                                      X  120
              SP=(15),                                                     X  121
              LOC=BELOW                                                        122
        LTR   R15,R15                      GETMAIN OK ?                        123
        BNZ   EXITOC                       NO; EXIT RC= 12                     124
AGET1   DS    OH                                                               125
        ST    R1,ADTBL                     SAVE ADDRESS OF CONTROL BLOCK       126
        LR    R6,R1                        .. INITIALIZE                       127
        LR    R7,R0                        .. AQUIRED                          128
        XR    R8,R8                        .. STORAGE                          129
        XR    R9,R9                        .. TO                               130
        MVCL  R6,R8                        .. X'00'                            131
        MVC   0(L'ANKEYE,R1),ANKEYE        PUT EYECATCHER IN CONTROL BLOCK     132
        ST    R0,L'ANKEYE(R1)              PUT LENGTH OF BLOCK IN CNTL BLK     133
        MODESET MODE=SUP,KEY=ZERO          GET A SUPERVISOR STATE PSW          134
*       *----------------------------------------------*                      135
*       *      GET THE LOCAL LOCK                       *                      136
*       *----------------------------------------------*                      137
        SETLOCK OBTAIN,                    .. HOLDING                      X  138
              MODE=UNCOND,                 .. THE LOCAL LOCK               X  139
              TYPE=LOCAL,                  .. IS REQUIRED BEFORE           X  140
              REGS=USE,                    .. GETTING THE CMS LOCK         X  141
              RELATED=REQUIRED                                                142
*       *----------------------------------------------*                      143
*       *      GET CMS LOCK                             *                      144
*       *----------------------------------------------*                      145
        SETLOCK OBTAIN,                                                    X  146
              MODE=UNCOND,                 .. GET                          X  147
              TYPE=CMS,                    .. THE CMS LOCK                 X  148
              REGS=USE,                    .. TO SERIALIZE                 X  149
              RELATED=REQUIRED             .. LPAQ                             150
        TM    SW1,@NOCDE                   WAS CDE ABSENT ?                    151
        BNO   YESCDE                       NO; DO NOT CHAIN IN                 152
*       *----------------------------------------------*                      153
*       *      CHAIN CDE ONTO LPAQ                      *                      154
*       *----------------------------------------------*                      155
        L     R8,CVTQLPAQ                  HEAD OF LPAQ => R8                  156
        L     R5,CDCHAIN-CDENTRY(R8)       CHAIN FIELD IN FIRST CDE            157
        ST    R4,CDCHAIN-CDENTRY(R8)       A(NEW CDE) INTO CHAIN OF 1ST CDE    158
        ST    R5,CDCHAIN                   A(NEXT CDE) INTO NEW CHAIN          159
YESCDE  DS    OH                                                               160
*       *----------------------------------------------*                      161
*       *      PUT CONTROL BLOCK ADDRESS AND       *                          162
*       *      LENGTH INTO CDE AND EXTENT LIST      *                          163
*       *----------------------------------------------*                      164
        L     R6,CDXLMJP                   A(XTENT LIST)                       165
        L     R1,ADTBL                     SAVE ADDRESS OF CONTROL BLOCK       166
        ST    R1,XTLMSBAD                  PUT A(BLOCK) IN EXTENT LIST         167
        TM    ANKFLAG1,@ANKBEL             BELOW THE LINE STORAGE?             168
        BZ    SET31                        YES; DO NOT SET AMODE BIT IN CDE    169
        TM    ANKFLAG1,@ANK31              SET  BIT ENTRY POINT  ?             170
        BZ    GBELOW1                      NO;DO NOT SET 31BIT ENTRY IN CDE    171
```

Figure 8.9 *(Continued)*

```
SET31    DS    0H                                                       172
         O     R1,=A(X'80000000')  MAKE ENTRYPOINT ADDRESS 31 BIT       173
GBELOW1  DS    0H                                                       174
         ST    R1,CDENTPT          PUT A(CONTROL BLOCK) INTO CDE        175
         ST    R1,ANKEP            PUT ADDRESS IN PARMLIST              176
         L     R1,ANKLEN           LENGTH OF CONTROL BLOCK              177
         STCM  R1,B'0111',XTLMSBLN PUT IN EXTENT LIST                   178
*        *----------------------------------------*                     179
*        *     RELEASE ALL LOCKS                 *                      180
*        *----------------------------------------*                     181
         SETLOCK RELEASE,          .. RELEASE                        X  182
               TYPE=ALL,           .. LOCAL                          X  183
               REGS=USE,           .. AND CMS                        X  184
               RELATED=REQUIRED    .. LOCKS                             185
         MODESET MODE=PROB,KEY=NZERO                                    186
         B     EXIT00                                                   187
*--------------------------------------------------------------*        188
*        EXIT ROUTINES                                         *        189
*--------------------------------------------------------------*        190
EXIT00   DS    0H                  NEW CONTROL BLOCK CREATED            191
         LA    15,X'00'                                                 192
         B     EXIT                                                     193
EXIT04   DS    0H                  CONTROL BLOCK EXISTS AND IS OK       194
         LA    15,X'04'                                                 195
         B     EXIT                                                     196
EXIT08   DS    0H                  GETMAIN FAILED FOR CDE AND XL        197
         LA    15,X'08'                                                 198
         B     EXIT                                                     199
EXIT0C   DS    0H                                                       200
         LA    15,X'0C'            GETMAIN FAILED FOR CONTROL BLOCK     201
         B     EXIT                                                     202
*--------------------------------------------------------------*        203
*        COMMON EXIT                                           *        204
*--------------------------------------------------------------*        205
EXIT     DS    0H                                                       206
         ENDMOD                                                         207
*--------------------------------------------------------------*        208
*        WORK AREA                                             *        209
*--------------------------------------------------------------*        210
WANCHOR  DSECT                                                          211
ADTBL    DS    A                   ADDRESS OF CONTROL BLOCK             212
SW1      DS    X                   SWITCH                               213
@NOCDE   EQU   B'10000000'         CDE DOES NOT EXIST                   214
LANCHOR  EQU   *-WANCHOR                                                215
*--------------------------------------------------------------*        216
*        OTHER DSECTS                                          *        217
*--------------------------------------------------------------*        218
         ANKPRM                    MAP ANCHOR PARMLIST                  219
         IHACDE                    MAP CDE                              220
LCDE     EQU   *-CDENTRY           LENGTH OF CDE                        221
         IHAXTLST                  MAP EXTENT LIST                      222
LXTNT    EQU   *-XTLST             LENGTH OF EXTENT LIST                223
         CVT   DSECT=YES,LIST=YES  MAP CVT                             224
         IHAPSA DSECT=YES,LIST=YES MAP PSA FOR SETLOCK                  225
         END                                                           226
```

Figure 8.9 *(Continued)*

referenced by the USING statements. Note the EQU statements for the lengths of the CDE and XL on lines 221 and 223, respectively. These statements are included since the IBM-supplied macros IHACDE and IHAXTLST do not contain EQU symbols for the length of the DSECT. Line 225 contains the mapping macro for the PSA since the expansions of SETLOCK on lines 138, 146, and 182 reference symbols in the PSA.

8.5.1 LPAQ Search

Lines 36 through 52 call the Program Management module IEAQCDSR to scan the LPAQ for an existing CDE with the same name as the one ANCHOR wishes to create. IEAQCDSR is an example of an MVS component service that you can call in your own programs but which is not documented in *Application Development Macro Reference* or a similar manual for programmers, since it has no macro interface. The system logic manual for Contents Supervision, however, contains a clear description of what the module does, the inputs it expects, and the outputs it produces.

After line 48 loads the address of the CVT into register 3 to correspond to the USING on line 31, lines 49 and 50 load registers 9 and 8 with the two input parameters that IEAQCDSR expects to be in those registers. Line 49 loads the address of an 8-byte field containing the name of the CDE we are looking for. This field is supplied by the caller in the input parameter list. Line 50 loads the address of the first CDE on the LPAQ from the CVT. After retrieving the address of the IEAQCDSR routine from the CVT in line 51, line 52 invokes the routine with a BALR.

If IEAQCDSR has found the CDE on the LPAQ, it returns control to ANCHOR at line 53. If the CDE was not found, control is returned to line 54. (Returning control to a caller at different points rather than always returning to the same point with a return code is an unconventional programming practice, but that is how IEAQCDSR works.)

8.5.2 Building a CDE

If the CDE was not found on the LPAQ, lines 55 through 87 GETMAIN storage for the CDE and XL and build those control blocks "from scratch." Since LPAQ CDEs and XLs reside in SQA, ANCHOR will GETMAIN storage from an SQA subpool. Line 59 issues MODESET because a key-zero PSU will be needed to alter the SQA storage. Line 60 loads the sum of the symbols that represent the lengths of the CDE and the XL, defined on lines 221 and 223, into register 0 which GETMAIN specifies in the LV= operand (line 62) for the amount of storage to acquire. The SP=245 operand on line 63 causes a GETMAIN from SQA.

Since the conditional format of GETMAIN was specified with RC on line 61, lines 65 and 66 can test the GETMAIN return code and exit if it is not 0, rather than abending. GETMAIN returns the address of the storage it obtains in register 1. Line 67 loads that address into register 4 to correspond with the USING for the CDE on line 32. Since GETMAIN does not initialize storage from CSA and SQA subpools to X'00' as it does for private area subpools, line 68 issues XC to do that.

After line 72 loads the address where the XL will be built into register 6 to correspond with the USING on line 33 and line 73 stores the XL address in the CDE, lines 74 through 84 build the CDE and XL.

If the IEAQCDSR routine on line 52 *was* able to find a CDE for the control block specified in the input parameter list, ANCHOR branches to line 91 and, in lines 93 and 94, compares a 4-byte "eyecatcher" in the parameter list with the first 4 bytes of the storage specified by the CDE. If they are the same, ANCHOR assumes that the control block is already allocated and does not GETMAIN storage for it. Line 96 stores the address of the control block into the caller's parameter list and exits with a return code of 4.

If ANCHOR does not find the CDE for the control block or it finds a CDE that contains the address of storage without the eyecatcher in the first 4 bytes, control is transferred to line 101 where ANCHOR prepares to GETMAIN storage for the control block. Line 103 tests whether the caller has supplied a subpool number in the parameter list. If none is supplied, line 105 moves the default subpool from the EQU on line 15 in the ANKPRM parameter list (Fig. 8.10).

By default, ANCHOR obtains above-16-meg storage for the control block it creates. If any of the programs that access that control block are AMODE 24, however, the control block must reside in below-16-meg storage. The caller can tell ANCHOR to acquire 24-bit storage for the control block by setting the flag @ANKBEL in the parameter list. Line 109 tests for this value and line 110 branches to a LOC = BELOW GETMAIN on line 118 if it is specified. Note that at this point in the program the PSW key is 8, and, if the parameter list specifies a CSA subpool (228, 229, 231, or 241) with the ANKSP parameter, GETMAIN will obtain storage with a protect key of 8. This allows non-APF-authorized applications to modify the user control block since they execute with a key-8 PSW.

After obtaining the control block storage in lines 111 through 122 and initializing it to X'00' in lines 127 through 131, line 132 puts the eyecatcher supplied in the parameter list into the first 4 bytes of the control block storage. Since a subsequent execution of ANCHOR will test for the presence of the eyecatcher to determine whether the control block has already been allocated, any program that accesses the control block must be careful about overwriting these bytes.

```
             MACRO                    MAP PARMLIST FOR ANCHOR        1
             ANKPRM                                                  2
.*+----------------------------------------------------------------+ 3
.*|                      MAINTENANCE LOG                            | 4
.*+--------------+-------------------------------+---------+--------+ 5
.*| DATE         |       DESCRIPTION             | CHANGED | REFER  | 6
.*+--------------+-------------------------------+---------+--------+ 7
.*| 10/11/88     | WRITTEN                       | MJM     |        | 8
.*+--------------+-------------------------------+---------+--------+ 9
.*         THIS PARMLIST IS ALSO USED BY UNANCH                      10
.*                                                                   11
ANKPRM   DSECT                                                       12
ANKLEN   DS    F             CONTROL BLOCK LENGTH                     13
ANKEP    DS    A             ENTRY POINT OF CONTROL BLOCK             14
ANKSP    DS    X             SUBPOOL FOR CONTROL BLOCK                15
@ANKSP   EQU   228           DEFAULT SUBPOOL                          16
ANKFLAG1 DS    X             FLAGS                                    17
@ANKVFY  EQU   B'10000000'   VERIFY EYCATCHER FOR UNANCH              18
*                            (EYECATCHER MUST BE SUPPLIED)            19
@ANKFREE EQU   B'01000000'   FREEMAIN TABLE AND CDE ON UNANCH         20
*                            (SUBPOOL MUST BE SUPPLIED)               21
@ANKBEL  EQU   B'00100000'   ANCHOR REQUIRES LOC=BELOW                22
@ANK31   EQU   B'00010000'   AMODE 31 IN CDE ENTRY POINT              23
*                            (ONLY CHECKED IF @ANKBEL SET)            24
         DS    XL2           UNUSED                                   25
ANKNAME  DS    CL8           CONTROL BLOCK NAME                       26
ANKEYE   DS    CL4           EYCATCHER IN MODULE                      27
LANKPRM  EQU   *-ANKPRM      LENGTH OF PARMLIST                       28
         MEND                                                         29
```

Figure 8.10   ANKPRM parmlist.

8.5.3 SETLOCK

Before adding the CDE built in lines 55 through 76 to the LPAQ, ANCHOR issues SETLOCK to obtain the Cross Memory Services (CMS) lock that serializes the LPAQ. Lock Manager requires that a program requesting the CMS lock be in supervisor state and hold the LOCAL lock for the address space in which it is executing. The latter requirement prevents interlocks that could be caused by an address space holding the CMS lock while its own LOCAL lock was being held by another address space. [An address space can hold the LOCAL lock for another address space by obtaining that address space's Cross Memory Local (CML) lock.]

After obtaining the CMS lock on line 146, line 152 tests the switch that was set on line 86 if a new CDE was built. If there is a new CDE, lines 156 through 158 obtain the address of the chain field in the first CDE and store the address of the new CDE into it. Line 159 changes the chain field in the new CDE to point to the CDE that was originally second on the LPAQ (see Fig. 8.8).

Lines 161 through 178 update the CDE and XL with information about the user control block. Line 165 loads the address of the XL from the CDE (line 73 stored it there) to correspond with the USING for the XL on line 33. Line 167 stores the address of the control block into the XL. Lines 168 and 170 test two flags in the parameter list to determine whether the entry point address in the CDE will be a 31-bit or 24-bit type. If 0 in the @ANKBEL flag indicates that the control block resides in above-16-meg storage or if the @ANK31 flag is set in the parameter list, line 173 sets the high-order bit of the address of the control block in register 1 to indicate AMODE 31. Lines 175 and 176 store this address into the CDE and into the caller's parameter list. Lines 177 and 178 put the length of the control block into the XL.

Lines 179 through 185 issue SETLOCK RELEASE,TYPE = ALL to free the CMS and LOCAL locks.

At this point, any task in any address space can issue a LOAD macro with the same value in the EP = operand as was specified in the ANKNAME parameter when the control block was built. The Program Management LOAD service will locate the CDE for the user control block and return its address and length in registers 0 and 1, respectively.

9

The MVS Dispatcher

9.1 THE MVS DISPATCHER

The Dispatcher is the component of MVS that selects the highest priority unit of ready work and makes it active on an available processor. A unit of work is defined either as a *task* (TCB) or as a *service request* (SRB). Figure 9.1 summarizes the differences between tasks and service requests.

The result of ATTACHing a task or SCHEDULEing a service request is that the TCB or SRB representing that unit of work is chained onto one of the TCB or SRB queues in Fig. 9.2. The Dispatcher scans the SRB and TCB queues to select the next unit of work to dispatch. Notice that there is a single queue of global SRBs and a single queue of ready Address Space Control Blocks (ASCBs) for the entire system in common storage. Each address space, by contrast, has its own queue of local SRBs anchored from its ASCB and a queue of TCBs in its private area.

Even though the Dispatcher performs the central control function of selecting and activating units of work, its services are invoked in the same way as the services of other components. Any program can invoke the Dispatcher either by branching into Dispatcher routines, which does not preserve the status of an executing program, or by issuing the CALLDISP macro, which does preserve the caller's status. Various MVS components branch-enter the Dispatcher. Task Management, for example, invokes the Dispatcher when it cannot find ready work in an address space.

TASK	SERVICE REQUEST
Created by the ATTACH macro.	Created by the SCHEDULE macro.
Defined by a Task Control Block(TCB). Task Management builds a TCB when a program issues ATTACH.	Defined by a Service Request Block (SRB). A program builds an SRB itself before issuing SCHEDULE.
Executes in the same address space where it was ATTACHed.	Global SRBs execute before any address space is dispatched. Local SRBs execute in the address space identified in the ASCB= operand of SCHEDULE. This may be the same or a different address space from where SCHEDULE was issued.
TCBs reside in LSQA. Load modules that execute under TCBs can reside in private or common storage.	SRBs reside in common storage (usually In SQA). Load modules that execute under an SRB reside in common storage.
Can issue the SVC instruction.	Cannot issue the SVC instruction except for ABEND (SVC 13).
Can receive control in problem or supervisor state.	Always receives control in supervisor state.
Is preemptible - If a task is interrupted, another unit of work can be dispatched before the task receives control again.	Is non-preemptible - If a service request is interrupted, it will be dispatched again before any other unit of work.
Can have ESTAE or FRR recovery.	Can only have FRR recovery.
Each TCB has its own linkage stack in ESA.	Each SRB has its own linkage stack in ESA

Figure 9.1   Comparison of tasks and service requests.

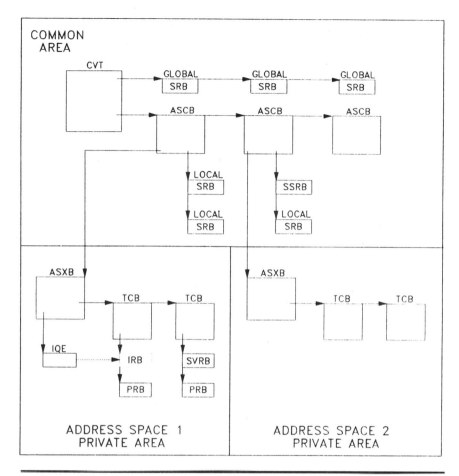

Figure 9.2 Dispatcher queues.

9.2 GLOBAL DISPATCHER

The Global Dispatcher selects Global SRBs and address spaces, represented by ASCBs, for dispatch. The operation of the Global Dispatcher is serialized so that it executes only on a single processor at any one time.

Global Dispatcher exits. When the Global Dispatcher begins execution, it first checks bit flags in the Logical Communications Control Area (LCCA) for the processor on which it is executing to see whether it should execute any special exits. If another processor is in a spin loop, for example, one of the LCCA flags will cause this processor to attempt Alternate CPU Recovery (ACR) on behalf of the looping processor.

Global SRBs.   The Global Dispatcher next dispatches Global SRBs in the order that they are queued. Note that a Global SRB executes "in" the address space that is active on the processor where it is dispatched. Global SRBs are used for high priority work that:

- Operates on objects in common virtual storage or real storage. In this case it does not matter which address space is active on the processor.

- Operates on objects in the private area of a particular address space. In this case, the SRB is SCHEDULEd with CPU affinity. (The SRB field SRBCPAFF specifies a CPU where the address space is active.)

Activating Address Spaces.   The Global Dispatcher next activates the highest-priority ready address space on an available processor. In versions of MVS before 2.0, all were on a single queue. This queue contained ASCBs for dispatchable and nondispatchable address spaces. (An address space is nondispatchable if it is swapped out or all its TCBs are in WAIT state.)

As hardware developed, MVS systems began to support more address spaces. MVS architects noticed that the time it took for the Dispatcher to search a queue of 200 or 300 ASCBs was degrading system performance. In response to this "large-system effect", MVS 2.0 adopted the idea of the true-ready queue from the Virtual Machine (VM) operating system dispatcher.

The ASCB true-ready queue contains ASCBs for address spaces that are immediately dispatchable. This is the ASCB queue represented in Fig. 9.2. The ASCBs on the true-ready queue are sorted in dispatching-priority order so that the Dispatcher merely selects the ASCB that is at the head of the queue.

The true-ready queue itself is not maintained by the Dispatcher but by System Resource Manager (SRM) which, to achieve performance objectives, adjusts address space dispatching priorities and initiates swapping operations.

To activate an address space on a processor, the Dispatcher loads the primary ASN from the ASCB into the processor's control register 4. This initiates ASN translation, which loads the primary STD into control register 1. After this point the Local Dispatcher can execute in the address space, since it will be able to address the control blocks in LSQA.

9.3 LOCAL DISPATCHER

After the Global Dispatcher has activated an address space on a processor, it transfers control to the Local Dispatcher which runs "in" that address space. The Local Dispatcher can execute simultaneously in several address spaces since it only works with control blocks in the private area (LSQA) of the address space in which it is executing.

When the Local Dispatcher receives control, it examines the queues of control blocks chained from the address space's Address Space Extension Block (ASXB) to select the highest-priority unit of work.

9.3.1 Local SRBs

The Local Dispatcher first examines the queue of Local SRBs anchored in ASCB field ASCBSPL. If any SRB holds the LOCAL lock, that SRB is dispatched first. The Dispatcher then dispatches the SRBs in the order they are queued. For each SRB, the Dispatcher constructs a supervisor-state PSW from the SRB fields containing the SRB routine entry point and storage key. The Dispatcher then issues an LPSW instruction to activate the PSW on a processor.

9.3.2 Suspended SRBs

SRBs can issue the SETLOCK macro to obtain locks. If an SRB attempts to obtain a suspend-type lock (LOCAL or CMS lock) and the lock is not available, Lock Manager suspends the SRB. When an SRB is suspended, the Dispatcher moves on to the next SRB on the queue.

Lock Manager suspends an SRB by constructing a control block, a Suspended SRB (SSRB), that represents the status of the SRB when it requested the unavailable lock. Lock Manager adds the SSRB onto a suspend queue for the particular lock requested.

When a suspend lock becomes free, Lock Manager issues SCHEDULE for each SSRB on the suspend queue for that lock. The SCHEDULE service causes the SSRB be added to the ASCB queue where it was queued before it was suspended. The next time the Local Dispatcher examines the queue of local SRBs for the address space, it finds the SSRB and dispatches it. (Notice in Fig. 9.2 that the queue of local SRBs for address space 2 contains an SSRB.)

9.3.3 IQEs

After the Local Dispatcher has processed the Local SRBs, it examines the queue of Interrupt Queue Elements (IQEs) from the ASXB. An IQE contains the address of an Interrupt Request Block (IRB). An IRB is the mechanism by which a TCB or SRB causes a program to execute under a different TCB in the same address space. There are two situations where this is desirable:

- An SRB routine, which cannot issue the SVC instruction, builds an IRB so that a program that contains an SVC executes under one of the TCBs in the same address space.

■ One task in a multitasking application can use an IRB to communicate with another task. Systems that use multithreaded I/O, such a VTAM, use IRBs for intertask communication.

The Local Dispatcher examines each IQE and chains the IRB whose address it contains onto the Request Block (RB) queue for the TCB where it will execute.

Programs BLDIRB and IRBRTN in Appendix C illustrate the process of queueing an IRB to a particular task. The first program, BLDIRB, issues the CIRB macro to create an IRB. BLDIRB then builds an Interrupt Queue Element (IQE) which contains the address of the IRB. BLDIRB then calls the Dispatcher routine (the "stage 2 exit effector") that queues the IQE onto the ASXB of the current address space. Address space 1 in Fig. 9.2 shows an IQE pointing to an IRB queued from the ASXB. The second program in Appendix C, IRBRTN, is an IRB routine. Note that IRBRTN issues WTO, which expands into SVC 34.

9.3.4 TCBs

The Local Dispatcher then examines the queue of TCBs anchored in ASXB field ASXBFTCB.

If any TCB holds the LOCAL lock for the address space, Dispatcher selects it first. If the LOCAL lock is not held, Dispatcher selects the TCB that has the highest priority.

The priority of a TCB is the same as the TCB that ATTACHed it unless:

■ The ATTACHing task used the LPMOD= and DPMOD= operands on the ATTACH macro to set the new TCB's priority lower than itself. A task cannot create a subtask with higher priority than itself.

■ A task issues the CHAP macro to change its own priority or the priority of one of its subtasks. CHAP cannot raise a task's dispatching priority higher than the limit priority set in the ATTACH LPMOD= operand when the task was created.

9.3.5 Request Blocks

Once the Dispatcher selects a TCB, it activates the program described by the first Request Block on that TCB's RB queue. As Fig. 9.2 indicates, this RB could be a Program Request Block (PRB) that describes a LINKed program; an SVC Request Block (SVRB) that describes a type 2, 3, or 4 SVC routine; or an IRB. (Chapter 5 describes the processes of activating an RB on a processor and dequeueing the RB once the program it specifies has completed.)

9.4 RECOVERY TERMINATION MANAGER (RTM1)

When a program is executing and an instruction fails to complete success-fully, the processor on which the program is executing experiences a program check interrupt. The description of each instruction in *Princi-ples of Operation* describes the conditions under which that instruction can fail.

A program check interrupt on a processor causes the current PSW to be saved as the program check Old PSW in that processor's PSA and the program check New PSW to become the active PSW. The program check New PSW contains the address of the MVS program check First Level Interrupt Handler which, in turn, transfers control to RTM1, the part of Recovery Termination Manager responsible for global recovery.

When RTM1 receives control, it first checks whether any Functional Recovery Routines (FRRs) are defined. RTM1 uses FRRs in global re-covery to diagnose errors and to retry into the failing program at a point past the error, if possible.

This is similar to the way RTM2 uses ESTAE routines in task recov-ery. ESTAE routines are always entered unlocked and enabled for inter-rupts. If all the ESTAE routines defined for a particular task fail to recover, RTM2 terminates the task. Thus, the maximum potential dam-age that an ESTAE routine can prevent is the failure of a single TCB.

9.4.1 Functional Recovery Routines (FRRs)

FRRs, on the other hand, can be entered while the processor is in any state. FRRs can receive control in TCB or SRB mode, with locks held, and enabled or disabled for interrupts. MVS uses FRRs to provide recov-ery for program checks in MVS component code. User-written programs use FRRs for recovery in SRB routines or where the state of the MVS locks and the enablement/disablement of the processor must be main-tained during recovery.

An MVS component or user-written program establishes an FRR by issuing the SETFRR macro. SETFRR invokes the RTM1 service that "pushes" the address of the FRR onto a LIFO stack in the PSA of the processor where the SETFRR issuer is executing. If a program that issued SETFRR is interrupted and then dispatched on another proces-sor, it is no longer protected by the FRR, since the FRR is on the original processor's FRR stack. For this reason, FRRs should be used only for code that cannot be interrupted (is disabled), is holding a spin lock (which causes disablement), or is an SRB routine (which is nonpreemptible).

There are actually several FRR stacks associated with each processor. At any given time, one of these stacks will be the current stack. Various MVS components change the current stack indicator in the PSA in order to protect their own operation. When RTM itself executes, for example, the program check stack is the current stack. SETFRR pushes an FRR onto whatever stack is the current stack.

When RTM1 receives control, it checks the current stack for FRRs. If there is an FRR, RTM1 builds an SDWA and transfers control to the FRR. An FRR, like an ESTAE routine, can request retry or percolation when it returns control to RTM1. If the FRR requests retry, RTM1 transfers control to the retry routine. If the FRR requests percolation, RTM1 "pops" the next FRR from the stack. FRRs are not removed from the stack after they are invoked. It is the responsibility of the program that issued SETFRR A (add) to remove it from the stack with SETFRR D (delete).

9.4.2 How RTM1 Communicates with RTM2

If RTM1 is entered because of a program check in a task (TCB) and if no FRR recovers from the program check, RTM1 SCHEDULEs an SRB to the TCB's address space. RTM2 executes under this SRB to initiate termination for the TCB that experienced the program check. RTM2 queues an RB that points to an SVC 13 (ABEND) instruction on the TCB's RB queue. When the TCB is dispatched again, it will execute the ABEND instruction and RTM2 will initiate task recovery or termination. If the task has any ESTAE routines, RTM2 will give control to them at this time.

After RTM2 has terminated all the TCBs in an address space, either normally or abnormally, it passes control back to RTM1, which is responsible for terminating the address space. RTM1 frees any locks, releases any storage still owned by the address space, and dequeues control blocks related to the address space (ASCB, ASSB, etc.).

9.4.3 CALLRTM

The CALLRTM macro also invokes RTM1 to terminate an address space. If CALLRTM TYPE = ABTERM is issued, RTM1 invokes RTM2 to perform task termination in the target address space before RTM1 terminates the address space. If CALLRTM TYPE = MEMTERM is issued, RTM1 terminates the address space without invoking RTM2 for task termination.

As part of terminating a task, RTM2 invokes resource manager routines to release resources owned by the task (see Chap. 5). Since CALLRTM TYPE = MEMTERM terminates an address space without invoking RTM2, these cleanup routines do not execute, and the address space might terminate without releasing all its resources. The MVS console command CANCEL issues CALLRTM TYPE = ABTERM, while the FORCE command issues CALLRTM TYPE = MEMTERM. CAN-

CEL is preferred to FORCE because it causes RTM2 to release all resources owned by tasks in the target address space.

9.5 PROGRAMS IN THIS CHAPTER

SCHDSRB, illustrated in Fig. 9.3, is an SRB scheduling routine. When a calling program supplies the name of an SRB routine and the name of a target address space, SCHDSRB constructs an SRB control block and SCHEDULEs the SRB to the target address space. When the target address space is dispatched, the SRB routine executes.

NSWPRTN, illustrated in Fig. 9.4, is an SRB routine that can be SCHEDULEd by SCHDSRB. NSWPRTN issues the SYSEVENT macro to invoke the SRM service that makes the target address space nons-

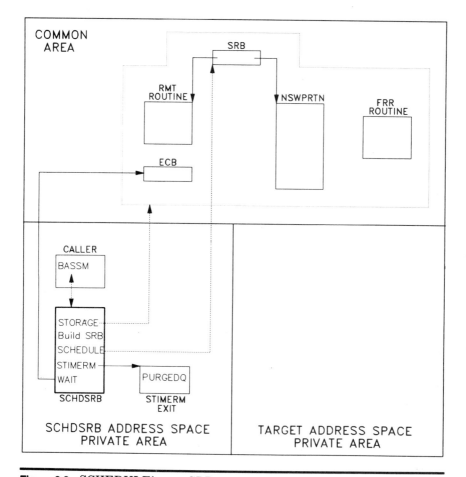

Figure 9.3 SCHEDULEing an SRB.

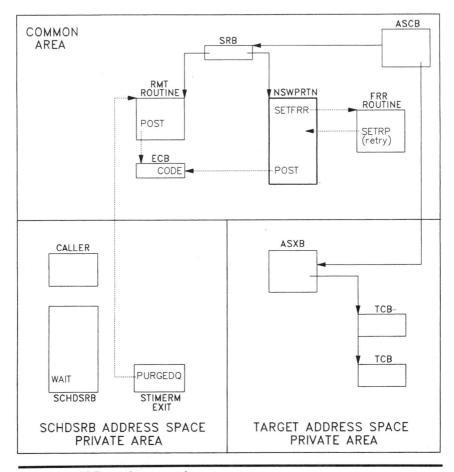

Figure 9.4 SRB routine execution.

wappable. SCHDSRB can thus make any address space nonswappable by SCHEDULEing NSWPRTN to that address space.

Note that the action performed by NSWPRTN must be executed in the target address space. SYSEVENT TRANSWAP cannot be issued by a program in one address space to make another address space nonswappable.

Other MVS services that affect the address space in which they execute are good candidates for SRB routines. For example, a program that wants to be able to establish another address space as its secondary space by issuing the SSAR instruction, can SCHEDULE an SRB routine containing the ATSET macro to that address space. ATSET invokes an XMS service that changes the Authority Table of the address space in which it executes. Like SYSEVENT, it cannot be invoked in one address space to affect another address space.

9.6 SCHDSRB

SCHDSRB is invoked when a calling program includes the lines in Fig. 9.5. The caller supplies the name of a target address space and the name of an SRB routine in the parameter list it passes to SCHDSRB. The parameter list, illustrated in Fig. 9.6, also includes fields for the address and length of a parameter list that will be available to the SRB routine when it executes. Since the SRB routine NSWPRTN requires no input parameters, the caller in Fig. 9.5 sets the length of this parameter list to 0.

When SCHDSRB in Fig. 9.7 receives control, lines 56 through 70 call GETASCB to find the address of the ASCB corresponding to the name of the target address space supplied by the caller. Line 61 copies the name from the caller's parameter list to the parameter list for GETASCB. If GETASCB successfully locates the the target ASCB, its address is returned into field GETADDR in the GETASCB parameter list. When SCHDSRB constructs the SRB control block, line 125 will place this ASCB address into the SRB control block to indicate the target address space for the SCHEDULE service.

9.6.1 Obtaining SQA Storage

As illustrated in Fig. 9.3, SRB control blocks, SRB routines, and their associated RMT routines and FRRs must reside in common storage. To determine how much common storage to obtain, line 75 issues the LOAD

```
          ..          ..                        ..
          LA     R3,PARMLIST                    ADDRESS OF PARMLIST FOR SCHDSRB
          USING  SCHDPRM,R3                     MAP INPUT PARMLIST
          MVC    SCHTASID,=CL8'addrspc'         TARGET ADDRESS SPACE NAME
          MVC    SCHNAME,=CL8'NSWPRTN'          NAME OF SRB ROUTINE
          XC     SCHLPARM,SCHLPARM              INDICATE NO PARMS FOR SRB ROUTINE
          LOAD   EP=SCHDSRB                     LOAD THE SRB SCHEDULING ROUTINE
          LR     R15,R0                         ADDRESS OF THE ROUTINE TO R15
          O      R15,=A(X'80000000')            FORCE 31 BIT ENTRY TO SCHEDULER
          LA     R1,PARMLIST                    ADDRESS OF THE PARMLIST TO R1
          BASSM  R14,R15                        INVOKE THE ROUTINE
          ..          ..                        ..
WORKAREA  DSECT                                 WORK AREA FOR THIS MODULE
PARMLIST  DS     OF,CL(SCHDPRML)                PARMLIST FOR SCHDSRB
          ..          ..                        ..
          SCHDPRM                               MAPPIÏNG MACRO FOR PARMLIST
          ..          ..                        ..
```

Figure 9.5 Calling SCHDSRB.

```
            MACRO                                                      1
            SCHDPRM                                                    2
*----------------------------------------------------------------*    3
*        THIS DSECT MAPS THE PARMLIST FOR THE SCHDSRB ROUTINE   *    4
*----------------------------------------------------------------*    5
SCHDPRM  DSECT                                                         6
SCHAPARM DS     F                   ADDRESS OF PARMLIST FOR SRB RTN    7
SCHLPARM DS     F                   LENGTH  OF PARMLIST FOR SRB RTN    8
SCHTASID DS     CL8                 NAME OF SRB TARGET ADDRESS SPC     9
SCHNAME  DS     CL8                 NAME OF SRB ROUTINE MODULE        10
SCHDPRML EQU    *-SCHDPRM           LENGTH OF THIS PARMLIST           11
            MEND                                                      12
```

Figure 9.6   Parmlist for SCHDSRB.

macro, causing Program Management to bring the SRB routine module (which includes the FRR) into private storage. LOAD returns the length of the module in doublewords in the low-order 3 bytes of register 1. Lines 76 through 78 multiply the number of doublewords by 8 and save the resulting length. Since the SRB routine module is not needed in private area storage, line 79 issues DELETE.

Lines 84 through 86 add the SRB routine module size, the size of the RMT routine, the length of any parameters for the SRB routine, and the size of the DSECT produced by the expansion of the SRBPRM macro on line 288. This macro, illustrated in Fig. 9.8, includes IHASRB, the IBM macro that maps the SRB control block, as well as fields that will be used to communicate between the SRB routine and the SCHEDULEing address space.

Line 89 issues STORAGE to obtain virtual storage in the common area. STORAGE specifies SP = SRBSP, which line 263 equates to SQA subpool 245. This subpool is page-fixed (nonpageable), which is a requirement for the SRB control block. Storage could have been obtained from one of the other page-fixed common storage subpools, 227 or 228 in CSA. Lines 91 through 93 initialize the obtained storage to X'00' since VSM does not clear storage obtained from the common area.

9.6.2 Loading the SRB Routine into SQA

Lines 94 through 107 load the SRB routine (in this case NSWPRTN) into the common storage just obtained. The ADRNAPF = (4) operand for LOAD on line 105 tells Program Manager to load the module beginning at the specific virtual address in register 4. In order to use this operand of LOAD, the load library containing the module must be open. SCHDSRB copies the DCB and OPEN/CLOSE parameter list to the program's work area to preserve reentrancy on lines 98 and 99 and issues OPEN on line 101.

```
*+-------------------------------------------------------------------------+   1
*| FUNCTION:                                                               |   2
*|   THIS PROGRAM SCHEDULES A LOCAL SRB AND WAITS UNTIL THE ROUTINE        |   3
*|   EXECUTING UNDER THAT SRB COMPLETES.                                   |   4
*| INPUTS:                                                                 |   5
*|   R1 - ADDRESS OF A PARMLIST MAPPED BY SCHDPRM DSECT CONTAINING:        |   6
*|        1) THE NAME OF THE SRB ROUTINE LOAD MODULE.                      |   7
*|        2) THE NAME OF THE ADDRESS SPACE WHERE THE SRB ROUTINE           |   8
*|           WILL EXECUTE.                                                 |   9
*|        3) PARAMETERS FOR THE SRB ROUTINE.                               |  10
*| OUTPUTS:                                                                |  11
*|   R15- RETURN CODE.                                                     |  12
*|        0 = THE SRB ROUTINE EXECUTED SUCCESSFULLY.                       |  13
*|        8 = A TARGET ADDRESS SPACE NOT SPECIFIED IN THE PARMLIST.        |  14
*|       12 = THE TARGET ADRESS SPACE WAS NOT FOUND.                       |  15
*|       16 = THE LOAD FOR THE SRB IN PRIVATE STORAGE FAILED:              |  16
*|            R0 CONTAINS THE RETURN CODE FROM LOAD.                       |  17
*|       20 = THE LOAD FOR THE SRB ROUTINE IN SQA FAILED                   |  18
*|            R0 CONTAINS THE RETURN CODE FROM LOAD.                       |  19
*|       24 = THE SRB ROUTINE FAILED.                                      |  20
*|            R0 CONTAINS THE CODE FROM CROSS-MEMORY POST:                 |  21
*|               12 - THE RMT ROUTINE WAS DRIVEN BY PURGEDQ.               |  22
*|               ANY OTHER CODE - ABEND CODE FROM THE FRR SDWA.            |  23
*| LOGIC:                                                                  |  24
*|   1)   CALL GETASCB TO OBTAIN THE TARGET ADDRESS SPACE'S ASCB.          |  25
*|   2)   LOAD THE SRB ROUTINE MODULE INTO PRIVATE STORAGE. OBTAIN         |  26
*|        THE LENGTH OF THE ROUTINE AND DELETE IT.                         |  27
*|   3)   OBTAIN SQA STORAGE FOR:                                          |  28
*|        - THE SRB CONTROL BLOCK (WITH A USER EXTENSION)                  |  29
*|        - THE SRB ROUTINE LOAD MODULE                                    |  30
*|        - PARAMETERS FOR THE SRB ROUTINE                                 |  31
*|   4)   LOAD THE SRB ROUTINE INTO THE OBTAINED SQA STORAGE.              |  32
*|   5)   COPY THE RMT ROUTINE INTO THE OBTAINED SQA STORAGE.              |  33
*|   6)   BUILD THE SRB CONTROL BLOCK.                                     |  34
*|   7)   PUT THE ADDRESS OF THE RMT ROUTINE AND THE PARAMTERS             |  35
*|        FOR THE SRB ROUTINE INTO THE SRB CONTROL BLOCK. COPY             |  36
*|        THE PARAMETERS INTO THE OBTAINED SQA.                            |  37
*|   8)   SCHEDULE THE SRB TO THE TARGET ADDRESS SPACE.                    |  38
*|   9)   SET THE STIMER AND WAIT ON THE ECB.                              |  39
*|        - IF THE SRB ROUTINE COMPLETES BEFORE THE STIMER EXPIRES,        |  40
*|        THE SRB ROUTINE CROSS-MEMORY POSTS THE ECB.  THE SRB             |  41
*|        ROUTINE USE THE POST-CODE AS A RETURN CODE TO THIS ROUTINE.      |  42
*|        - IF STIMER EXPIRES BEFORE THE SRB ROUTINE COMPLETES,            |  43
*|        THE STIMER EXIT ROUTINE RECEIVES CONTROL AND ISSUES PURGEDQ.     |  44
*|        PURGEDQ DRIVES THE RMT ROUTINE IN THE TARGET ADDRESS SPACE       |  45
*|        WHICH POSTS THE ECB.                                             |  46
*|   10)  CANCEL THE STIMER AND FREE THE SQA STORAGE.                      |  47
*| ATTRIBUTES:                                                             |  48
*|   AMODE 31, RMODE ANY, REENTRANT, REQUIRES APF AUTHORIZATION            |  49
*|   ESA DEPENDENCIES (LINKAGE STACK, STORAGE MACRO)                       |  50
*+-------------------------------------------------------------------------+  51
         MODULE SCHDSRB,BASE=12,LOC=BELOW,AMODE=31,RMODE=ANY,          X   52
               TEXT='SCHEDULES AN SRB'                                     53
         LR    R9,R1                 PARMLIST ADDRESS TO R9                 54
         USING SCHDPRM,R9            MAP INPUT PARMLIST                     55
```

Figure 9.7 SCHDSRB.

```
*      *----------------------------------------*      56
*      *    CALL GETASCB TO GET TARGET ASCB   *      57
*      *----------------------------------------*      58
       LA    R3,GETPARMS          PARMS FOR GETASCB ROUTINE          59
       USING GETPRM,R3            MAP GETASCB PARMLIST               60
       MVC   GETNAME,SCHTASID     ADDRESS SPACE NAME TO GETPRM       61
       LA    R1,8                 ..PUT LENGTH OF ADDRESS SPACE      62
       ST    R1,GETNAMEL          ..NAME IN GETASCB PARMLIST         63
       ICM   R15,15,=V(GETASCB)   ADDRESS OF THE GETASCB SERVICE     64
       BZ    EXIT08               =0; NOT LINK-EDITED - EXIT         65
       O     R15,=A(X'80000000')  SET FOR 31 BIT ENTRY               66
       LA    R1,GETPARMS          PARMS FOR GETASCB ROUTINE          67
       BASSM R14,R15              INVOKE THE GETASCB SERVICE         68
       LTR   R15,R15              RC = 0 ?                           69
       BNZ   EXIT0C               NO; EXIT                           70
*      *----------------------------------------*      71
*      *    LOAD THE SRB ROUTINE INTO         *      72
*      *    PRIVATE TO OBTAIN LENGTH          *      73
*      *----------------------------------------*      74
       LOAD  EPLOC=SCHNAME,ERRET=EXIT10                              75
       N     R1,=A(X'00FFFFFF')   TURN OFF NON-LENGTH BITS           76
       SLL   R1,3                 MULTIPLY LENGTH BY 8               77
       ST    R1,LSRBRTN           SAVE LENGTH OF SRB ROUTINE         78
       DELETE EPLOC=SCHNAME       DELETE MODULE FROM PRIVATE         79
*      *----------------------------------------*      80
*      *    GET STORAGE FOR SRB CONTROL BLOCK,*      81
*      *    SRB ROUTINE AND PARMS FOR THE RTN *      82
*      *----------------------------------------*      83
       L     R5,SCHLPARM          ..TOTAL STORAGE = L'SRB PARMS      84
       LA    R5,SRBSIZE1(R1,R5)   ..+ LENGTH OF SRB AND SRB RTN      85
       LA    R5,LSRBRMTM(R5)      ..+ SIZE OF RMT ROUTINE            86
       ST    R5,SRBTSTOR          SAVE AMOUNT TOTAL STORAGE          87
       MODESET MODE=SUP,KEY=ZERO  GET A SUPERVISOR/KEY 0 PSW         88
       STORAGE OBTAIN,LENGTH=(5),ADDR=(4),SP=SRBSP,LOC=BELOW         89
       ST    R4,ADSTOR            SAVE ADDRESS SQA STORAGE           90
       XR    R6,R6                ..INITIALIZE                       91
       XR    R7,R7                ..STORAGE                          92
       MVCL  R4,R6                ..TO X'00'                         93
*      *----------------------------------------*      94
*      *    LOAD THE SRB ROUTINE INTO         *      95
*      *    COMMON STORAGE                    *      96
*      *----------------------------------------*      97
       MVC   LOADLIB(LDCBD),LOADLIBD COPY DCB TO WORK AREA           98
       MVC   OLIST(LOLIST),MOLIST COPY OPEN PARMLIST TO WORK AREA    99
       LA    R6,LOADLIB           ADDRESS OF LOADLIB DCB            100
       OPEN  ((R6),INPUT),MF=(E,OLIST)  OPEN THE LOADLIB           101
       L     R4,ADSTOR            ADDRESS OF SQA STORAGE            102
       LA    R5,SCHNAME           ADDRESS OF SRB MODULE NAME        103
       LOAD  EPLOC=(R5),ERRET=EXIT14,           ..LOAD THE MODULE X 104
             ADRNAPF=(R4),DCB=(R6),SF=(E,LLIST) ..INTO SQA STORAGE 105
       ST    R0,LOADEP            SAVE AMODE/ENTRYPOINT FROM LOAD   106
       CLOSE MF=(E,OLIST)         CLOSE THE LOADLIB                 107
*      *----------------------------------------*      108
*      *    COPY THE RMT ROUTINE TO COMMON    *      109
*      *----------------------------------------*      110
       L     R5,LSRBRTN           LENGTH OF SRB ROUTINE +           111
       LA    R4,0(R4,R5)          ADDR OF SRB RTN = ADDR RMT RTN    112
```

Figure 9.7 *(Continued)*

```
        ST    R4,ADRMTRTN           SAVE THE ADDRESS OF RMT RTN     113
        LA    R5,LSRBRMTM           LENGTH THE THE RMT RTN          114
        LR    R7,R5                 COPY LENGTH TO R7               115
        LA    R6,SRBRMTM            ADDRESS OF RMT RTN IN SCHDSRB   116
        MVCL  R4,R6                 MOVE RMT RTN TO COMMON STORAGE  117
*       *-------------------------------------*                    118
*       *     BUILD THE SRB                   *                    119
*       *-------------------------------------*                    120
        LR    R10,R4                ADDR OF SRB RTN = ADDR SRB      121
        USING SRBSECT,R10           MAP THE SRB                    122
        MVC   SRBID,=CL4'SRB'       MOVE SRB LITERAL TO SRB         123
        L     R4,LOADEP             LOAD AMODE/ENTRYPOINT FROM LOAD 124
        ST    R4,SRBEP              STORE ADDR OF SRB RTN IN SRB    125
        MVC   SRBASCB,GETADDR       ADDRESS OF TARGET ASCB TO SRB   126
        EPAR  R2                    ..THIS ASID                    127
        STCM  R2,B'0011',SRBPASID   ..INTO THE SRB                 128
        L     R2,PSATOLD-PSA        ..ADDRESS OF CURRENT TCB        129
        STCM  R2,15,SRBPTCB         ..INTO THE SRB                 130
        L     R7,ADRMTRTN           ..ADDRESS OF THE RMT RTN        131
        ST    R7,SRBRMTR            ..INTO THE SRB                 132
        ICM   R5,15,SCHLPARM        LENGTH OF PARMS FOR SRB RTN     133
        BZ    NOPARM                =0; DO NOT COPY PARMS TO SQA    134
        LA    R4,SRBEND1            POINT AT PARMS FOR SRB ROUTINE  135
        ST    R4,SRBPARM            SAVE ADDRESS IN SRB             136
        LR    R7,R5                 LENGTH FOR MVCL                 137
        L     R6,SCHAPARM           ADDRESS OF SRB ROUTINE PARMS    138
        MVCL  R4,R6                 COPY PARMS INTO SQA.            139
NOPARM  DS    OH                                                   140
*                                   ..MOVE ADDRESS THIS ASCB TO    141
        MVC   ADASCB,PSAAOLD-PSA    ..COMMON STORAGE FOR XM POST    142
*       *-------------------------------------*                    143
*       *     SCHEDULE THE SRB                *                    144
*       *-------------------------------------*                    145
        SCHEDULE SRB=(R10),SCOPE=LOCAL                             146
*       *-------------------------------------*                    147
*       *     SET THE STIMER. WAIT FOR THE    *                    148
*       *     SRB ROUTINE TO COMPLETE.        *                    149
*       *-------------------------------------*                    150
        ST    R13,ADWORK            ..PASS ADDRESS OF WORKAREA      151
        LA    R5,ADWORK             ..AS PARM TO STIMERM EXIT RTN   152
        LA    R4,SRBTIMM            ADDRESS OF STIMERM EXIT RTN     153
        LA    R1,STIMLIST           STIMERM PARAMETER LIST          154
        STIMERM SET,ID=STIMID,BINTVL=TIMER,EXIT=(R4),PARM=(R5),   X 155
              MF=(E,(1))                                           156
        LA    R1,SRBECB             ..WAIT FOR THE SRB              157
        WAIT  1,ECB=(R1)            ..TO COMPLETE                  158
        XR    R7,R7                 CLEAR R7                       159
        ICM   R7,B'0111',SRBECB+1   PRESERVE THE POST CODE IN R7    160
*       *-------------------------------------*                    161
*       *     FREE SRB AND SRB ROUTINE STORAGE *                   162
*       *-------------------------------------*                    163
        LA    R1,STIMLIST           STIMERM PARAMETER LIST          164
        STIMERM CANCEL,ID=STIMID,MF=(E,(1))    CANCEL THE STIMERM   165
        L     R0,SRBTSTOR           SIZE OF STORAGE IN SQA          166
        L     R1,ADSTOR             ADDRESS OF SQA STORAGE          167
        STORAGE RELEASE,LENGTH=(0),ADDR=(1),SP=SRBSP               168
        MODESET MODE=PROB,KEY=NZERO  GET A PROBLEM STATE/KEY 8 PSW  169
```

Figure 9.7 *(Continued)*

```
             LTR    R15,R7                POST CODE = 0?                     170
             BNZ    EXIT18                NO; EXIT WITH ERROR                171
             B      EXIT00                EXIT                               172
*-----------------------------------------------------------------*         173
*            STIMER EXIT ROUTINE.                                  *         174
*            THIS ROUTINE IS DISPATCHED WHEN THE STIMERM INTERVAL EXPIRES.*  175
*            THE ROUTINE ISSUES THE PURGEDQ MACRO, WHICH CAUSES MVS *         176
*            SUPERVISOR ROUTINES TO:                               *         177
*                1) REMOVE THE SRB ROUTINE FROM ANY DISPATCH QUEUES. *       178
*                2) TRANSFER CONTROL TO THE RMT ROUTINE. THE RMT    *         179
*                   ROUTINE CROSS-MEMORY POSTS THE ECB IN THIS ROUTINE. *    180
*-----------------------------------------------------------------*         181
SRBTIMM DS     0F                                                            182
             BAKR   R14,R0                SAVE ENVIRONMENT ON STACK          183
             LR     R12,R15               ENTRYPOINT TO BASE REGISTER        184
             LA     R2,SRBTIMM-SCHDSRB    ..BACKUP FOR DISPLACEMENT          185
             SLR    R12,R2                ..OF THIS ROUTINE                  186
             L      R13,4(R1)             WORKAREA ADDRESS                   187
             L      R10,ADSTOR            ADDRESS OF SRB                     188
             L      R2,SRBASCB            TARGET ASCB                        189
             LA     R2,ASCBASID-ASCB(R2)  POINT AT ASN OF TARGET ASCB        190
             MVC    PRGFLC(L'SRBFLC),SRBFLC COPY SRBFLC                      191
             NC     PRGFLC(L'SRBCPAFF),=XL2'00' TURN OFF HIGH BYTES          192
             LA     R8,PRGFLC             ASID/TCB FOR PURGEDQ               193
             L      R7,SRBRMTR            ADDRESS OF RMT ROUTINE             194
             LA     R1,PDQLIST            PARMLIST FOR PURGEDQ               195
             PURGEDQ RMTR=(7),ASID=(R2),ASIDTCB=(8),MF=(E,(1))              196
             PR                           RETURN                            197
*-----------------------------------------------------------------*         198
*            RMT ROUTINE.                                          *         199
*            THIS ROUTINE RECEIVES CONTROL WHEN THE STIMERM IN THE  *         200
*            SCHEDULING ADDRESS SPACE EXPIRES AND THE STIMERM EXIT  *         201
*            ROUTINE ISSUES PURGEDQ. THIS ROUTINE CAN FREE RESOURCES *       202
*            SUCH AS LOCKS OR COMMON STORAGE ACQUIRED FOR THE SRB ROUTINE.*  203
*            IN THIS CASE IT POSTS THE ECB FOR THE SCHEDULING TASK. *         204
*-----------------------------------------------------------------*         205
SRBRMTM DS     0F                                                            206
             BAKR   R14,R0                SAVE ENVIRONMENT ON STACK          207
             LR     R9,R15                ENTRYPOINT TO BASE REGISTER        208
             LA     R2,SRBRMTM-SCHDSRB    ..BACK UP FOR DISPLACEMENT         209
             SLR    R9,R2                 ..OF THIS ROUTINE                  210
             LR     R10,R1                ADDRESS OF SRB                     211
             LA     R4,SRBECB             ADDRESS OF SRB ECB                 212
             L      R5,ADASCB             ADDRESS OF SCHEDULER'S ASCB        213
             LA     R6,POSTERR            ERROR ROUTINE FOR POST             214
             LA     R7,12                 POST CODE = 12                     215
             POST   (4),(7),ASCB=(5),ERRET=(6),LINKAGE=BRANCH               216
             PR                           RETURN                            217
*-----------------------------------------------------------------*         218
*            POST ERROR ROUTINE. THIS ROUTINE IS ONLY ENTERED IF THE *       219
*            SCHEDULING ADDRESS SPACE NO LONGER EXISTS             *         220
*-----------------------------------------------------------------*         221
POSTERR DS     0H                                                            222
             PR                           POP THE STACK AND RETURN          223
ESRBRMTM DS    0F                         FORCE FULLWORD ALIGNMENT          224
LSRBRMTM EQU   ESRBRMTM-SRBRMTM           LENGTH OF THE RMT ROUTINE         225
```

Figure 9.7 *(Continued)*

```
*-------------------------------------------------------------*  226
*           EXIT ROUTINES                                     *  227
*-------------------------------------------------------------*  228
EXIT00   DS    OH               SUCCESSFUL COMPLETION           229
         LA    15,X'00'                                          230
         B     EXIT                                              231
EXIT08   DS    OH               LENGTH OF TARGET ADDRES SP=0    232
         LA    15,X'08'                                          233
         B     EXIT                                              234
EXIT0C   DS    OH               TARGET ADDRESS SP NOT FOUND     235
         LA    15,X'0C'                                          236
         B     EXIT                                              237
EXIT10   DS    OH               LOAD OF SRB ROUTINE INTO        238
         PERCRC RC=X'10'        PRIVATE FAILED                  239
         B     EXIT                                              240
EXIT14   DS    OH               LOAD OF SRB ROUTINE INTO        241
         PERCRC RC=X'14'        SQA FAILED                      242
         B     EXIT                                              243
EXIT18   DS    OH               SRB ROUTINE ROUTINE FAILED      244
         PERCRC RC=X'14'                                        245
         B     EXIT                                              246
*-------------------------------------------------------------*  247
*           COMMON EXIT                                       *  248
*-------------------------------------------------------------*  249
EXIT     DS    OH                                                250
         ENDMOD                                                  251
*-------------------------------------------------------------*  252
*           DCB AND OPEN/CLOSE PARMLIST MODELS                *  253
*-------------------------------------------------------------*  254
LOADLIBD DCB   DSORG=PS,MACRF=GL,EODAD=EXIT,LRECL=256,       X  255
               BLKSIZE=256,RECFM=FB,DDNAME=LOADLIB              256
LDCBD    EQU   *-LOADLIBD       LENGTH OF DCB                   257
MOLIST   OPEN  (,),MF=L         OPEN/CLOSE PARMLIST             258
LOLIST   EQU   *-MOLIST         LENGTH OF OPEN/CLOSE PARMLIST   259
*-------------------------------------------------------------*  260
*           CONSTANTS                                         *  261
*-------------------------------------------------------------*  262
SRBSP    EQU   245              SUBPOOL FOR SRB AND ROUTINE STG 263
TIMER    DC    A(10*SECOND)     TIMER VALUE FOR 10 SECONDS      264
SECOND   EQU   100              TIMER VALUE FOR 1 SECOND        265
*-------------------------------------------------------------*  266
*           WORK AREA                                         *  267
*-------------------------------------------------------------*  268
WSCHDSRB DSECT                  WORK AREA FOR SCHDSRB           269
PRGFLC   DS    D                ASID/TCB FOR PURGEDQ            270
LOADEP   DS    A                AMODE/ENTRYPOINT OF SRB ROUTINE 271
LSRBRTN  DS    F                LENGTH OF SRB ROUTINE           272
ADRMTRTN DS    A                ADDRESS IF THE RMT ROUTINE      273
ADWORK   DS    F                ADDRESS OF THIS WORK AREA       274
ADSTOR   DS    A                ADDRESS OF OBTAINED STORAGE     275
STIMID   DS    A                STIMERM ID                      276
SRBTSTOR DS    F                AMOUNT TOTAL STORAGE            277
GETPARMS DS    CL(GETPRML)      PARMS FOR GETASCB               278
STIMLIST STIMERM SET,MF=L       PARMLIST FOR STIMERM            279
PDQLIST  PURGEDQ MF=L           PARMLIST FOR PURGEDQ            280
LOADLIB  DS    OF,CL(LDCBD)     LOADLIB DCB                     281
OLIST    DS    CL(LOLIST)       OPEN/CLOSE PARMLIST             282
```

Figure 9.7 *(Continued)*

```
LLIST     LOAD  ,SF=L              PARMLIST FOR LOAD ADRNPF=           283
LSCHDSRB  EQU   *-WSCHDSRB         LENGTH OF THE WORK AREA            284
*------------------------------------------------------------------* 285
*         OTHER DSECTS                                             * 286
*------------------------------------------------------------------* 287
          SCHDPRM                  MAP PARMLIST FOR THIS ROUTINE     288
          SRBPRM                   MAP SRB AND USER PARMS            289
          GETPRM                   PARMS FOR GETASCB                 290
          IHAASCB                  MAP ASCB                          291
          CVT   DSECT=YES,LIST=NO  MAP CVT                          292
          IHAPSA                   MAP PSA                           293
          END                                                       294
```

Figure 9.7 *(Continued)*

Even though the SRB routine was loaded at a specific virtual address, Line 106 saves the entry point returned by LOAD in register 0, since the LOAD service returns the AMODE of the loaded module in the high-order bit of register 0. Lines 124 and 125 will store this AMODE and address in the SRB control block as the SRB routine entry point.

Lines 108 through 117 copy the RMT routine on lines 198 through 225 to common storage following the SRB routine. The RMT routine will receive control if a PURGEDQ macro is issued to dequeue this SRB routine before it executes. Lines 111 and 112 load the address of the byte following the SRB routine in common storage, and Line 113 saves this address so that lines 131 and 132 can store it in the SRB control block.

Since we know that the RMT routine does not contain any address constants, the MVCL on line 117 can copy it to common storage. This contrasts with the way lines 94 through 107 issued LOAD against the SRB routine, which may or may not contain address constants. As part of LOAD processing, Program Manager adds the module's load point to each address constant in the RLD to calculate its address in virtual storage.

```
          MACRO                                                      1
          SRBPRM                                                     2
*------------------------------------------------------------------* 3
*         DSECT TO MAP SQA STORAGE OBTAINED BY SCHDSRB.  WHEN THE SRB * 4
*         ROUTINE RECEIVES CONTROL, ADDRESS OF THIS STORAGE IS IN R0 * 5
*------------------------------------------------------------------* 6
          IHASRB                   IBM MACRO TO MAP THE SRB           7
ADASCB    DS    A                  SCHEDULING ADDRESS SPACE ASCB     8
SRBECB    DS    A                  ECB FOR SCHEDULER                 9
POSTCC    DS    F                  COMPLETION CODE FOR XM POST       10
FRRFLAG   DS    X                  FRR FLAGS BYTE                    11
@RECUR    EQU   B'10000000'        RECURSIVE FRR ENTRY               12
          DS    3X                 NOT USED                          13
SRBEND1   DS    0F                 PARMS FOR SRB ARE HERE            14
SRBSIZE1  EQU   SRBEND1-SRBSECT    SIZE OF SRB                       15
          MEND                                                       16
```

Figure 9.8 SRBPRM DSECT.

9.6.3 Initializing the SRB Control Block

As a result of the operation of the MVCL on line 117, register 4 contains the address of the byte following the RMT routine in the obtained SQA. Lines 118 through 136 build an SRB control block at this address. Line 121 loads the address of the byte following the SRB routine into register 10. Line 122 issues USING for the SRBSECT DSECT, produced by the expansion of IHASRB in the SRBPRM macro (line 288), so that fields in the SRB can be referenced by name rather than by explicit displacement. Lines 123 through 136 initialize fields in the SRB:

- Lines 124 and 125 retrieve the entry point address of the SRB routine from LOAD on line 104 and store it into the SRB. If the high-order bit of the entry point address is 1, the SRB routine will receive control with an AMODE 31 PSW; if the high-order bit is 0 the routine will receive control with an AMODE 24 PSW.

- Line 126 moves the address of the target address space's ASCB into the SRB control block. This field tells SCHEDULE in which address space the SRB routine will execute. The GETASCB routine on lines 56 through 70 returned this ASCB address into the GETASCB parameter list.

- Line 127 issues EPAR to extract the current primary address space number (PASN) from control register 4; line 128 stores this value into the PURGE ASID field of the SRB control block.

- Line 129 extracts the address of the current TCB from field PSATOLD in the PSA and line 130 stores this address into the the PURGE TCB field of the SRB control block. Note the way line 130 is coded:

```
L    R2,PSATOLD-PSA
```

This assembles as if it were coded

```
L    R2,PSATOLD-PSA(0,0).
```

The displacement portion of the second operand is the difference between two symbols in the PSA mapping DSECT IHAPSA on line 293. To form the virtual address of the second operand, instruction microcode adds this difference to the values in the base and index registers, which, since they are both 0, indicate that no register is used (not register 0). Since there is no base or index register, microcode interprets the displacement portion of the operand as the virtual address. The displacement portion of an instruction operand can contain any number in the range of 0 through 4095. Since the PSA describes storage with virtual addresses in the range of 0 through 4095, the displacement alone can serve as a virtual address in the PSA.

The previous two fields, the PURGE ASID (line 128) and PURGE TCB (line 130), are used to inform RTM which task SCHEDULEd the SRB. If the SRB routine abends, RTM1 transfers control to RTM2 in the SCHEDULEing address space rather than in the address space where the SRB routine is dispatched. RTM2 in the SCHEDULEing address space executes any ESTAE routines associated with the SCHEDULEing task. This is known as SRB-to-task-percolation.

The PURGE ASID/PURGE TCB combination is also checked by the Dispatcher before it gives control to an SRB routine. If the SCHEDULEing task has terminated, the Dispatcher issues PURGEDQ for the SRB routine instead of dispatching it. PURGEDQ drives the Resource Manager Termination (RMT) routine associated with the SRB to free any resources obtained on behalf of the SRB routine. Lines 131 and 132 store the RMT routine address into the SRB control block.

The calling program may have supplied the address and length of parameters for the SRB routine in the SRBPRM parameter list. Line 133 tests the length of the parameters and, if the length is not 0, lines 135 through 139 copy the parameters to common storage following the SRB. Line 135 stores the address of the parameters into the SRBPARM field of the SRB control block. When the SRB routine is dispatched, the contents of this field will be in register 1. In this case, the calling routine in Fig. 9.5 did not supply any parameters for the SRB routine and issued XC to set the parameter length field to 0.

At this point, SCHDSRB has moved all the structures in Fig. 9.3 into common storage and initialized the SRB control block so that it points to the RMT routine, the parameters for the SRB routine, and the SRB routine itself.

Line 142 moves the current ASCB address from the PSA into the obtained common storage. The SRB routine will use this ASCB address to cross-memory POST SCHDSRB when it completes.

9.6.4 SCHEDULEing the SRB

The SCHEDULE macro on line 146 initiates the process of adding the SRB to the appropriate Dispatcher queue. Since line 146 includes the SCOPE = LOCAL operand, the SRB will be added to the queue of local SRBs from the ASCB of the target address space. The SRB routine will actually execute when the Global Dispatcher selects the target address space and the Local Dispatcher selects the SRB from the ASCB queue.

Since the SRB routine executes asynchronously, SCHDSRB issues the WAIT macro on line 158 and itself become nondispatchable until the SRB routine issues POST upon completion.

9.6.5 STIMERM Exit Routine

It is possible, however, that the SRB routine might never POST SCHDSRB. The SRB routine might ABEND and not have an FRR that will POST SCHDSRB. Or the target address space to which the SRB routine was SCHEDULEd might not even exist. The SCHEDULE service does not issue a return code indicating that this is the case.

To prevent this possibility, lines 147 through 156 establish a STIMERM exit routine before line 158 issues WAIT. Even though a task is in a nondispatchable WAIT state, a STIMER or STIMERM exit routine for that task will receive control when the time interval expires.

Note that lines 151 and 152 and the PARM= operand of STIMERM on line 155 pass the address of SCHDSRB's work area to the STIMERM exit routine as a parameter. The STIMERM exit routine on lines 173 through 197 will retrieve the address of the SRB from the work area. Note also that the time interval for the STIMERM, defined on line 264 and referenced by line 155, is 10 seconds of elapsed time, which should be sufficient for any SRB routine to be dispatched and execute. The execute form of STIMERM on lines 155 and 156 and the list form on line 279 are used to preserve reentrancy.

9.6.6 PURGEDQ

If the SRB routine does not POST SCHDSRB within 10 seconds, the STIMERM timer expires, and the exit routine receives control. The STIMERM exit routine on lines 173 through 197 causes the following events to occur:

- Line 196 of the STIMERM exit routine issues the PURGEDQ macro for the SRB.

- PURGEDQ invokes the Dispatcher-related service that removes the SRB from whatever SRB queue it is on. Note that PURGEDQ only affects an SRB if it is still queued. PURGEDQ does not dequeue an SRB that has already been dispatched and is active on a processor.

- PURGEDQ transfers control to the Resource Manager Termination (RMT) routine identified in the PURGEDQ RMTR= operand on line 196. If this operand is not used, no RMT routine receives control.

- The RMT routine on lines 198 through 217 issues POST (line 216) for the ECB that SCHDSRB is WAITing on. After the POST, SCHDSRB is again dispatchable.

The STIMERM exit routine (lines 173 through 197) issues BAKR on line 183 to save the registers on the linkage stack. Since a STIMERM exit routine executes under a Request Block (RB) for the task that issued the STIMERM, BAKR uses the linkage stack associated with the TCB for SCHDSRB. Lines 184 through 186 readjust the base register for the exit routine so that it is the same as the entry point of the module. This makes debugging simpler since displacements from the beginning of the module in a dump will match the location counter in the assembly listing.

Lines 187 and 188 establish addressability to the SRB control block by obtaining its address from SCHDSRB's work area. The address of the work area was passed to the exit routine in the PARM= operand of STIMERM on line 155. Note that there are no USING statements in the exit routine. The registers that are used for addressing—R10 for the SRB, R12 for the module, and R13 for the work area—have all been reloaded with the values corresponding to USING statements that were issued earlier.

Lines 189 through 194 retrieve values from the SRB control block for the the PURGEDQ on line 196. Lines 189 and 190 locate the ASCB for the target address space and load register 2 with the address of the ASCB field that contains the address space number. Lines 191 through 193 copy the contents of SRB field SRBFLC to the program's work area. SRBFLC includes the two SRB fields—the ASN of the SCHEDULEing address (SRBPASID) and the SCHEDULEing TCB's address (SRBPTCB)—that were initialized by lines 127 through 130. Since the high-order two bytes of SRBFLC are not used by PURGEDQ, line 192 sets them to X'00'. After line 194 loads register 7 with the address of the RMT routine from the SRB control block, lines 195 and 196 issue PURGEDQ.

9.6.7 Resource Manager Termination (RMT) Routines

Because PURGEDQ on line 196 includes the RMTR= operand, the PURGEDQ service transfers control to the RMT routine. RMT routines release resources that would have been freed by the SCHEDULEing task or by the SRB routine itself if it had been allowed to execute and had not been dequeued. Many SRB routines, for example, issue FREEMAIN or STORAGE RELEASE for the SRB control block under which they have been dispatched. These SRB routines usually have RMT routines that release the SRB storage. In this case, the RMT routine issues POST on line 216 to take the SCHDSRB task out of WAIT state.

PURGEDQ can be issued in any address space for an SRB directed at any other address space. Since the PURGEDQ service can receive control in any address space, the RMT routine resides in common storage. The RMT routine on lines 198 through 225, for example, might have been driven when Recovery Termination Manager (RTM) issued PURGEDQ in the process of terminating the target address space. RTM retrieves the address of the RMT routine from the SRB control block in a similar fashion to the STIMERM exit routine on lines 173 through 197.

9.6.8 Cross-Memory POST

Since it is uncertain which address space will be dispatched when the RMT routine receives control, POST includes the ASCB= operand so that it can POST SCHDSRB cross-memory. Note that when POST includes the LINKAGE=BRANCH parameter and the LOCAL lock for the address space is not held, POST destroys the values in all registers except 9. When POST includes the ASCB= operand, a POST error routine identified by the ERRET= operand is required. In this case, POST will fail if the SCHDSRB address space has terminated, so the POST error routine on lines 222 through 225 contains only a PR.

9.6.9 Returning Control to SCHDSRB

After the PURGEDQ in the STIMERM exit routine, line 197 "pops" the linkage stack, reloading the registers and causing control to be transferred to the address in register 14. Since the STIMERM exit routine is executing under an RB queued to SCHDSRB's TCB, control is transferred to Task Manager. Task Manager dequeues the STIMERM exit RB and invokes the Dispatcher, which selects the RB now at the head of the RB queue. This is the RB for SCHDSRB. The last instruction that was executed in SCHDSRB was part of the WAIT macro on line 158, so the PSW in SCHDSRB's RB contains the address of the next instruction, the XR on line 159. This is where SCHDSRB resumes execution.

SCHDSRB receives control again at line 159 whether it was POSTed by the SRB completing or by PURGEDQ driving the RMT routine. The SRB routine (NSWPRTN in this case) uses the POST code in the ECB to communicate its completion status to SCHDSRB as does the RMT routine in line 215. Lines 165 through 168 cancel the STIMERM and release the SQA storage obtained by STORAGE OBTAIN on line 89. Note that if SCHDSRB abends before it issues STORAGE RELEASE, the SQA remains allocated even after the address space terminates. SCHDSRB can be enhanced by adding an ESTAE routine to issue STORAGE RELEASE for the OBTAINed SQA.

9.7 NSWPRTN

NSWPRTN in Fig. 9.9 is an example of an SRB routine that could be SCHEDULEd by SCHDSRB. Figure 9.4 illustrates that, as a result of SCHEDULE, NSWPRTN's SRB is on the queue of local SRBs anchored in the target address space's ASCB. When the target address space

```
*+---------------------------------------------------------------+   1
* | FUNCTION:                                                         2
* |   THIS SRB ROUTINE ISSUES SYSEVENT TRANSWAP SO THAT THE ADDRESS   3
* |   SPACE IN WHICH IT EXECUTES BECOMES NON-SWAPPABLE.               4
* | INPUTS:                                                           5
* |   R0 - ADDRESS OF THE SRB CONTROL BLOCK                           6
* |   R1 - ADDRESS OF THE SRB PARM LIST                               7
* | OUTPUTS:                                                          8
* |   THIS ROUTINE INDICATES ITS COMPLETION STATUS TO THE SCHEDULING  9
* |   TASK WITH A POST CODE IN THE SCHEDULER'S ECB.                  10
* | LOGIC:                                                           11
* |   1) ESTABLISH THE FRR RECOVERY ROUTINE                          12
* |   2) ISSUE SYSEVENT TO MAKE THE ADDRESS SPACE NON-SWAPPABLE      13
* |   3) CANCEL THE FRR                                              14
* |   4) CROSS-MEMORY POST THE SCHEDULER'S ECB.                      15
* | ATTRIBUTES:                                                      16
* |   AMODE 31, RMODE ANY, REENTRANT, ESA DEPENDENCIES              17
*+---------------------------------------------------------------+  18
            MODULE NSWPRTN,BASE=9,LOC=BELOW,AMODE=31,RMODE=ANY,   X  19
                ENTRY=SRB,                                        X  20
                TEXT='SRB ROUTINE ISSUE SYSEVENT'                    21
            LR    R10,R0              ADDRESS OF THE SRB             22
            USING SRBSECT,R10         MAP SRB                        23
            XC    POSTCC(L'POSTCC),POSTCC SET POST CODE TO X'00'     24
*           *----------------------------------------*               25
*           *     ESTABLISH FRR RECOVERY             *               26
*           *----------------------------------------*               27
            LA    R2,SRBFRRM          ADDRESS FRR ROUTINE            28
            SETFRR A,FRRAD=(R2),WRKREGS=(R4,R5),PARMAD=(R6)          29
            LA    R1,RETRY            ..PUT RETRY ADDRESS            30
            ST    R1,0(R6)            ..INTO FRR PARAMETER           31
            ST    R10,4(R6)           SRB ADDRESS IN FRR PARMLIST    32
*           *----------------------------------------*               33
*           *     MAKE ADDRESS SPACE NON-SWAPABLE    *               34
*           *----------------------------------------*               35
            LA    R1,TRANSECB         ..MAKE THIS                    36
            SYSEVENT TRANSWAP,ENTRY=BRANCH  ..ADDRESS SPACE NON-SWAP 37
*           *----------------------------------------*               38
*           *     CANCEL THE FRR                     *               39
*           *----------------------------------------*               40
RETRY       DS    0H                  FRR RETRIES TO HERE            41
            SETFRR D,WRKREGS=(R4,R5)  DELETE THE FRR                 42
*           *----------------------------------------*               43
*           *     CROSS-MEMORY POST THE SCHEDULER    *               44
*           *----------------------------------------*               45
            LA    R14,PRADD1          ADDRESS AFTER XMPOST           46
            BAKR  R14,R0              CREATE STACK-STATE ENTRY       47
            LA    R4,SRBECB           ADDRESS OF SRB ECB             48
            L     R5,ADASCB           ADDRESS OF SCHEDULER'S ASCB    49
            LA    R6,POSTERR          ERROR ROUTINE FOR POST         50
            L     R7,POSTCC           POST CODE                      51
            POST  (4),(7),ASCB=(5),ERRET=(6),LINKAGE=BRANCH          52
            PR                        POP THE LINKAGE STACK          53
PRADD1      DS    0H                                                 54
            B     SRBX00              EXIT                           55
```

Figure 9.9 NSWPRTN.

```
*         *----------------------------------------*              56
*         *      POST ERROR ROUTINE. ONLY ENTERED   *             57
*         *      IF SCHEDULING ADDR. SPC. IS GONE    *            58
*         *----------------------------------------*              59
POSTERR  DS    0F                       POP THE STACK AND RETURN  60
         PR                                                       61
*----------------------------------------------------------------* 62
*         FRR ROUTINE.                                          * 63
*         THIS ROUTINE RECEIVES CONTROL IF THERE IS A PROGRAM CHECK * 64
*         IN THE SRB ROUTINE.                                    * 65
*         - IF THE FRR IS NOT ENTERED RECURSIVELY IT ISSUES SETRP RC=4 * 66
*           SO THAT RTM1 TRANSFERS CONTROL TO THE SRB ROUTINE AT THE  * 67
*           RETRY ADDRESS (SUPPLIED IN THE FRR PARAMETER LIST).   * 68
*         - IF THE FRR IS ENTERED RECURSIVELY OR THE FRR ROUTINE  * 69
*           ITSELF ABENDS, RTM1 PERCOLATES THE ABEND TO THE TASK THAT * 70
*           SCHEDULED THE SRB (SRB-TO-TASK PERCOLATION).          * 71
*----------------------------------------------------------------* 72
SRBFRRM  DS    0F                                                 73
         BAKR  R14,R0                    SAVE REGISTERS ON LINKAGE STACK 74
         LR    R9,R15                    ENTRYPOINT TO BASE REGISTER 75
         LA    R2,SRBFRRM-NSWPRTN        ..BACK UP FOR DISPLACEMENT 76
         SLR   R9,R2                     ..OF THIS ROUTINE         77
         LR    R13,R0                    WORK AREA ADDRESS         78
         LR    R3,R1                     SDWA ADDRESS              79
         USING SDWA,R3                   MAP SDWA                  80
         L     R6,SDWAABCC               ABEND CODE FROM SDWA      81
         SLL   R6,8                      CLEAR HIGH-ORDER BYTE     82
         SRL   R6,20                     ABEND CODE IN LOW ORDER BYTES 83
         ST    R6,POSTCC                 SAVE AS POST CODE         84
         L     R4,SDWAPARM               ADDRESS OF PARMLIST IN SDWA 85
         L     R10,4(R4)                 ADDRESS OF SRB            86
         TM    FRRFLAG,@RECUR            RECURSIVE ENTRY ?         87
         BO    FRRABEND                  ABEND                     88
         OI    FRRFLAG,@RECUR            RECURSIVE ENTRY ?         89
         L     R5,0(R4)                  RETRY ADDRESS             90
         LR    R1,R3                     SDWA ADDRESS TO REG 1     91
         SETRP RC=4,RETADDR=(R5),RETREGS=YES,RETRY=FRR            92
         PR                              POP THE STACK AND RETURN TO RTM 93
FRRABEND DS    0H                                                 94
         LR    R1,R3                     SDWA ADDRESS TO REG 1     95
         SETRP RC=0,COMPCOD=(X'200',USER),DUMP=NO                 96
         PR                              POP THE STACK AND RETURN TO RTM 97
*----------------------------------------------------------------* 98
*         EXIT ROUTINES                                          * 99
*----------------------------------------------------------------* 100
SRBX00   DS    0H                        ONLY EXIT FOR SRB ROUTINE 101
         LA    15,X'00'                  ERROR CONDITIONS PASSED THRU 102
         B     SRBEXIT                   POST CODE                 103
*----------------------------------------------------------------* 104
*         COMMON EXIT                                            * 105
*----------------------------------------------------------------* 106
SRBEXIT  DS    0H                                                 107
         ENDMOD                                                   108
*----------------------------------------------------------------* 109
*         WORK AREA                                              * 110
*----------------------------------------------------------------* 111
```

Figure 9.9 *(Continued)*

```
WNSWPRTN DSECT                                                           112
TRANSECB DS     F                      ECB FOR SYSEVENT                  113
LNSWPRTN EQU    *-WNSWPRTN             LENGTH OF THE WORK AREA           114
*----------------------------------------------------------------------* 115
*        OTHER DSECTS                                                  * 116
*----------------------------------------------------------------------* 117
         SRBPRM                        PARMS FOR GETASCB                 118
         IHAFRRS                       MAP FRR                           119
         IHASDWA                       MAP SDWA                          120
         IHAPSA                        MAP PSA                           121
         CVT DSECT=YES,LIST=NO         MAP CVT                           122
         END                                                            123
```

Figure 9.9 *(Continued)*

becomes the highest-priority ready address space, the Global Dispatcher
selects it. The Local Dispatcher, executing in the newly dispatched
address space, examines the queue of local SRBs and dispatches the
NSWPRTN SRB.

NSWPRTN receives control in supervisor state and in the PSW key
specified in the SRBPKF field of the SRB. SCHDSRB left 0 in this field
so NSWPRTN receives control with a key-zero PSW.

MVS/ESA provides a linkage stack for each SRB. The ESA
(SPLEVEL 3) expansion of the MODULE macro on lines 19 through 21
issues BAKR to save the registers on the SRB's linkage stack and issues
the STORAGE macro to obtain work area storage in the private area of
the target address space. The XA (SPLEVEL 2) expansion of the MOD-
ULE macro does not save the caller's registers and uses an area in the
module itself for a work area. The XA expansion, therefore, is not reentrant.

An SRB routine receives control with the address of the SRB control
block in register 0 and the contents of the SRB field SRBPARM in
register 1. Lines 22 and 23 establish addressability to the SRB and the
user fields following it in the SRBPRM DSECT (Fig. 9.8). If the SCHE-
DULEing address space had placed the address of a parameter list in the
SRBPARM field, the SRB routine would process the parameter list at
this point. Line 24 initializes the code that POST on line 52 will use to
communicate its completion status to the SCHEDULEr.

9.7.1 Establishing an FRR

Lines 25 through 32 establish a Functional Recovery Routine (FRR). The
SETFRR macro on line 29 causes RTM1 to put the address of the FRR
on lines 62 through 97 at the top of the FRR normal stack, which is the
current stack. From this point, if RTM1 receives control as the result of a
program check in the SRB routine, RTM1 will transfer control to this
top-of-the-stack FRR. Note that, instead of the SRB routine establishing
an FRR for itself, SCHDSRB could have established the FRR by includ-

ing the address of the FRR in the SRBFRRA field of the SRB and including the FRR = YES operand on the SCHEDULE macro.

The SETFRR on line 29 includes the PARMAD = operand. This causes the SETFRR service to provide an 8-byte parameter area and to place the address of this area into the register operand of PARMAD =. This differs from the PARAM = operand of ESTAE, which specifies the address of a parameter list already obtained by the issuer. Like the ESTAE routine in Chap. 5, NSWPRTN uses the parameter to pass a retry address to the recovery routine. The FRR, like the ESTAE routine, will place the retry address into the SDWA before it returns control to RTM.

As part of dispatching a unit of work (TCB or SRB), the Local Dispatcher loads control register 15 with the virtual address of the next available entry on the linkage stack associated with that unit of work. When the FRR on lines 62 through 97 receives control as the result of a program check in the SRB routine, control register 15 is still pointing at an entry in the SRB routine's linkage stack. BAKR on line 74 creates a stack state entry on this stack.

When the FRR receives control, RTM1 provides the address of a 200-byte area that the FRR can use for working storage in register 0, as well as the address of a Scheduler Diagnostic Work Area (SDWA) in register 1. Line 78 saves the address of the work area and lines 79 and 80 establish addressability to the SDWA (mapped by the IHASDWA DSECT on line 120).

Lines 81 through 83 copy the abend code from the SDWA into a field that line 84 will use as the POST code to communicate the reason for the SRB routine abend to the SCHEDULEing task. Line 85 retrieves the address of the 8-byte parameter that was reserved by the SETFRR PARMAD = on line 29 from the SDWA. The first parameter is the address of the SRB control block and the user fields following it in SQA. Line 23 issued the USING that allows the SRBPRM DSECT on line 118 to map this storage.

9.7.2 FRR Retry

Unlike RTM2, which indicates in the SDWA when task recovery has caused recursive entry into an ESTAE routine, RTM1 does not track FRR recursion. In Lines 87 and 88 the FRR tests a flag bit in one of the user SQA fields and only retries if this is the first entry into the FRR. Line 90 loads the retry address into the register that is indicated by the RETADDR = operand of the SETRP macro on line 92. The FRR returns control to RTM1 in the same way as an ESTAE routine returns control to RTM2, by loading the address of the SDWA into register 1 and issuing SETRP. The RC = 4 operand tells RTM1 to transfer control to the retry address rather than to continue abending the SRB routine. The SETRP macro expands into instructions that store the retry address into the SDWA and the RC= value into register 15. The PR instructions on lines 93 and 97 "pop" the linkage stack (which does not reload registers 0, 1, and 15) and transfer control back to RTM1.

9.7.3 SRB-To-Task Percolation

If this is a recursive entry to the FRR, line 96 issues SETRP RC=0 to tell RTM1 to continue the abend. In this case, RTM1, recognizing that it has been invoked for SRB routine recovery, will invoke RTM2 to abend the *task that issued SCHEDULE* rather than any unit of work in the current address space. If RTM2 detects that the SCHEDULEing task has an ESTAE routine, it will invoke the ESTAE routine. Thus, in what is called SRB-to-task-percolation, an ESTAE routine for a task (TCB) can receive control as the result of an abend in a routine executing under an SRB.

9.7.4 SYSEVENT

After the FRR is established, the SYSEVENT macro on line 37 invokes one of the SRM services that make an address space nonswappable. In contrast to SYSEVENT DONTSWAP, which immediately marks an address space's ASCB as nonswappable, SYSEVENT TRANSWAP causes SRM to swap the address space out of real storage before marking the ASCB. This causes the address space to be swapped back into the "preferred" frames reserved at system initialization for nonswappable users and reduces storage fragmentation. SYSEVENT TRANSWAP should be used for address spaces that will be nonswappable for longer periods of time.

SRB routines cannot issue the SVC instruction, since the SRB control block, unlike the TCBs and RBs for tasks, does not include any fields where the SVC FLIH can save the status of the interrupted unit of work. The SYSEVENT macro on line 37, therefore, includes the ENTRY=BRANCH operand, which causes a branch rather than an SVC entry to the SYSEVENT service.

Whether SYSEVENT has successfully completed or the FRR receives control and retries, the SETFRR D on line 42 receives control and causes RTM1 to remove the FRR from the FRR stack. Like the RMT routine, lines 43 through 61 cross-memory post the SCHDSRB task so that it is again dispatchable. The SRB routine concludes with a PR instruction (in the expansion of the ENDMOD macro) that transfers control to a Dispatcher-related service that dequeues the SRB control block from the ASCB queue and invokes the Local Dispatcher to select the next SRB or TCB for dispatch.

10

Program Call Routines

10.1 PC ROUTINES VS. SVC ROUTINES

In 370/ESA architecture the PC instruction has been enhanced to save the current operating environment on the linkage stack and to take advantage of access register addressing mode. The following discussion applies to the PC instruction in ESA. See Sect. 10.14, "PC Routines in an XA Environment" for a comparison of PC routines in MVS/XA and MVS/ESA.

Programs frequently require actions to be performed on their behalf that they do not have the authority to perform for themselves. For example, when an application program executing with a key 8 PSW issues a LOAD macro, it invokes the Program Management service, which changes control blocks in key 0 storage in LSQA. LOAD acquires more authority than the program that invoked it because it expands into an SVC instruction. The PSW loaded as a result of the SVC interrupt is key 0 and supervisor state.

The operation of the SVC instruction itself is simple. SVC saves the Old PSW and the interrupt code in low-address storage and loads a New PSW. SVC relies on MVS software to save the current operating environment and transfer control to the SVC routine.

Program Call (PC) is the only other instruction besides SVC that allows a program to transfer control to a service with more authority. Like the SVC instruction, PC results in the loading of a new PSW. Unlike SVC, the PC instruction is capable of saving the current operating environment and transferring control to a PC routine on a microcode level. PC does not need to involve operating system software at all.

Figure 10.1 summarizes the relative advantages of PC routines and SVC routines.

10.2 TYPES OF PC ROUTINES

The way a PC routine is defined controls the way the PC instruction operates. A PC routine can be defined as *stacking* or *basic*. For a stacking PC routine, the PC instruction saves the operating environment on the linkage stack before it establishes a new environment. Stacking-type PC routines are only available in ESA. If the PC routine is defined as basic, no linkage stack entry is built. In this case, the caller and the PC routine are responsible for saving the caller's operating environment.

PC routines can also be defined as *space-switching* or *nonspace-switching*. Space-switching PC routines cause the PC instruction to establish a new primary address space before it loads the PSW. Space-switching PC routines, therefore, execute in a different address space from the one where the PC instruction was issued. Nonspace-switching PC routines execute in the same address space where the PC instruction was issued.

Space-switching PC routines allow the routines and data for a logically related group of functions to reside in a single service address space rather than in common storage. Programs executing in other address spaces issue the PC instruction to transfer control cross-memory to the routines in the service address space. The macros that invoke the MVS services to define and install PC routines, for example, all expand into PC calls to the PCAUTH address space. PCAUTH contains all the routines and control blocks for this functional area of MVS. The PCSET routine in this chapter establishes a service address space.

A PC routine can be space-switching and stacking, space-switching and basic, nonspace-switching and stacking, or nonspace-switching and basic.

10.3 THE OPERATING
ENVIRONMENT—CONTROL REGISTERS

The operating environment for a program is the contents of the PSW and the prefix, general, access, floating point, vector, and control registers. This section deals with the contents of control registers. The control registers that can be affected by the operation of the PC instruction are marked with ■. How the PC instruction changes values in the PSW is discussed in Sec. 10.5, "The PC Instruction."

- ■ *Control register 1* contains the primary Segment Table Designator. The primary STD consists of the real address and length of a Segment Table. DAT uses the primary STD for two purposes:

PC Routines	SVC Routines
Can be called in any environment - in SVC routines, SRB routines, other PC routines or in locked or PSW disabled code.	Cannot be invoked in type 1 or 6 SVC routines, SRB routines, PC routines or in locked or disabled code.
Cannot issue SVC instructions except ABEND.	Type 2,3 or 4 SVC routines can issue SVC instructions.
Receives control directly through PC instruction microcode. There is no operating system involvement.	Receives control from the MVS First-Level Interrupt Handler (FLIH).
Can be defined for all address spaces or only for selected address spaces.	Defined for all address spaces.
Can limit callers' access with the PSW Key Mask (PKM).	Can limit callers' access with Authorized Program Facility (APF).
Can receive control in any PSW key in problem or superviser state. Can execute with any PKM or EAX.	Always receives control with PSW key zero and supervisor state. Always executes with caller's PKM and EAX.
Can reside in common storage or in a service address space. The latter provides isolation and common storage constraint relief.	Must reside in common storage.
Can save the caller's operating environment on the linkage stack before receiving control.	MVS FLIH saves registers and the PSW at the time of interrupt in MVS control blocks.
More complex to install.	Easy to write and install.

Figure 10.1 Comparison of PC and SVC routines.

To translate the instruction virtual address in the PSW to a real address. Regardless of the addressing mode, the PSW always fetches instructions using the primary STD.

To translate the storage operands of instructions when in primary space mode. In access register mode, an access register that contains an ALET of X'00000000' causes DAT translation using the primary STD.

Control register 2 contains the address of a pointer to the Dispatchable Unit Access List (DU-AL). The DU-AL contains an entry for every address space with which any program executing under the *currently dispatched TCB or SRB* can communicate in access register addressing mode (see Chap. 7). Since control register 2 is not changed by the PC instruction, space-switching PC routines retain the same DU-AL when they branch to code in other address spaces.

■ *Control register 3* contains two fields:

The PSW key mask (PKM) is an authority mechanism used by some semiprivileged instructions like PC when they execute in problem state.

The secondary address space number (SASN): A change to the SASN initiates Address Space Number Translation. ASN Translation uses the SASN as an index into the ASN First and Second Tables specified by control register 14 to locate the ASN Second Table Entry (ASTE) for that address space. Control register 7 is then loaded with the STD from that ASTE.

■ *Control register 4* contains two fields:

The Authorization Index (AX) is an index into another address space's Authority Table. If a space-switching PC routine is defined with SASN = OLD, it must have AX authority to the caller's address space.

The primary address space number (PASN): A change to the PASN initiates ASN Translation. The STD from the ASTE located by ASN Translation is loaded into control register 1, and the address of that ASTE is loaded into control register 5.

■ *Control register 5* contains the address of the primary space ASTE. The primary space ASTE contains pointers to the Primary Space Access List (PS-AL) and the PC Linkage Table. Control register 5 is modified when a new PASN is loaded into control register 4.

■ *Control register 7* contains the secondary Segment Table Designator. DAT uses the secondary STD to translate the storage operands of instructions when in secondary space mode. In access register mode, an access register that contains an ALET of X'00000001' causes DAT translation using the secondary STD.

■ *Control register 8* contains the Extended Authorization Index (EAX). The EAX is the authorization mechanism for ALESERV when it is issued in problem state.*

---

*ALESERV does not check the EAX when CHKEAX = NO is coded as an operand. CHKEAX = NO can be used only when ALESERV is issued in supervisor state or key zero. When the PRIVATE bit is 1 in an access list entry, every data access causes EAX checking.

Control register 13 contains the home address space STD. A PC routine, like any program, executes under a TCB or an SRB. Since the PC instruction sets a new primary address space when it branches to code in another address space, the current primary address space might not be the same as the address space where the TCB or SRB resides. A program that needs to access its own local control blocks can go into home space mode.

DAT uses the home STD to translate the storage operands of instructions when in home space mode. In access register mode, an access register that contains an ALET of X'00000002' causes DAT translation using the home STD.

Control register 14 contains the address of the ASN First Table (AFT) used by ASN translation. The AFT points to the ASN Second Tables that contain the ASTEs for every active address space in the system.

■ *Control Register 15* points to the next available entry in the active linkage stack (the stack associated with the TCB or SRB under which the code is executing). BAKR and the stacking PC instructions increment this pointer when they create a stack state entry. The PR instruction decrements the pointer when it pops the stack.

10.4 DEFINING A PC ROUTINE—THE ETE

Like SVC routines, PC routines must be defined before they are invoked. An SVC routine is defined to MVS by creating an entry in the SVC Table that contains the routine's address and operating parameters. After the SVC routine has been defined, it is invoked by a unique number:

```
SVC   svcnum
```

SVC FLIH uses "svcnum" as an index into the SVC Table to locate the entry that describes the routine.

In a similar fashion, a PC routine must be predefined by placing an entry in an *Entry Table* as illustrated in Fig. 10.2. The Entry Table Entry (ETE) contains the entry point to the PC routine, as well as the operating environment that will be in effect when the PC routine executes. After the PC routine has been defined, it is available to be called by its unique PC number:

```
L    14, = A(PC number)
PC   0(14)
```

Just as the SVCUPDTE service is available to define an SVC routine, the PCAUTH component of MVS provides services, illustrated in Fig.

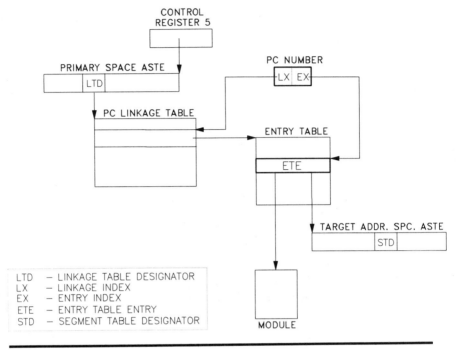

Figure 10.2 Defining a PC routine.

10.3, to build the ETE and install it. The steps in installing a PC routine follow.

10.4.1 ETDEF

Issue the ETDEF macro to build an ETE in user storage. The operands for ETDEF contain the name of the PC routine load module or its address in virtual storage. ETDEF operands also indicate whether the PC routine is stacking or basic, and whether it is space-switching or executes in the same address space where the PC instruction will be issued. Fig. 10.4 illustrates the ETE built by ETDEF.

10.4.2 ETCRE

Issue the ETCRE macro to copy the ETEs from user storage into LSQA (which is nonswappable). Each ETE in the resulting table has an index value corresponding to its location in the table. The first ETE has an Entry Index (EX) of 0, the second ETE has an EX of 1, etc.

10.4.3 LXRES

Issue the LXRES macro to reserve the same slot in every PC Linkage Table of every address space. The index value that corresponds to this

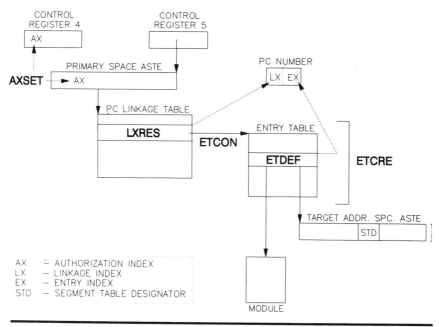

Figure 10.3 PCAUTH macros.

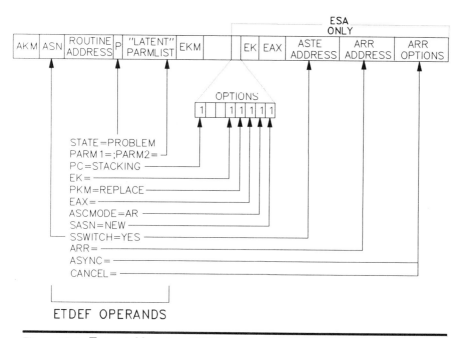

Figure 10.4 Entry table entry (ETE).

slot in every PC Linkage Table is the Linkage Index (LX). The issuer of the LXRES macro provides a parameter list into which LXRES puts the LX it reserves. Because LXRES returns an LX value based on how many LXs have already been reserved system-wide, an individual program can never know what LX value it will receive when it issues LXRES.

The LX reserved by LXRES can be a *system* or *nonsystem* LX as specified by the SYSTEM= operand on the LXRES macro.

10.4.4 ETCON

Issue the ETCON macro to put the real address of the Entry Table into the Linkage Table slot reserved by LXRES. ETCON works differently for system and nonsystem LXs:

- *System LX:* When a program in any address space issues ETCON for a system LX, all address spaces will be connected to that particular Entry Table. The PC Linkage Tables of all address spaces will have the real address of the Entry Table in the slot corresponding to that LX. Any address space can then use PC numbers whose first portion is that LX.

- *Nonsystem LX:* For a nonsystem LX, each address space must issue ETCON individually to connect its Linkage Table with a particular Entry Table. Address spaces that do not issue ETCON for a nonsystem LX will receive a program check S022 when they use any PC number that begins with that LX.

10.4.5 The PC Number

Combine the LX with the EX to form a unique *PC number* and save the PC number in a location from which any program can retrieve it. Notice in the expansion of the STORAGE macro, in Fig. 1.7 in Chap. 1, how STORAGE OBTAIN retrieves its PC number from a known location in the System Function Table (SFT).

10.4.6 Deleting a PC Routine

The following PCAUTH macros reverse the actions of ETCON, LXRES, and ETCRE:

ETDIS disconnects an Entry Table from a Linkage Table.

LXFRE frees a nonsystem LX so that another LXRES request can reserve the slots in PC Linkage Tables corresponding to that LX. System LXs cannot be freed during the life of an IPL.

ETDES disconnects an Entry Table if it is connected to a Linkage Table and releases the LSQA storage it occupies.

10.5 THE PC INSTRUCTION

Each PC routine is assigned a unique number when it is created. This number, a combination of indexes into the PC Linkage Table and Entry Table, is used in the operand of the PC instruction to invoke the PC routine:

```
L     14, = A(PC number)
PC   0(14)
```

PC routines receive control as a direct result of the operation of the PC instruction and without any action by MVS. As illustrated in Fig. 10.2, when the PC instruction is issued, PC instruction microcode locates the Linkage Table from the primary space ASTE, whose address is in control register 5, and uses the PC number to index into the Linkage Table and Entry Tables to locate the Entry Table Entry (ETE) corresponding to the PC number.

The PC instruction is a semiprivileged instruction. When a semiprivileged instruction is issued with a supervisor-state PSW, no further authority checking takes place. When a semipriviledged instruction is issued with a problem-state PSW, one of several mechanisms (depending on the instruction) is used to verify that the caller is authorized to issue that instruction.*

When PC is issued in problem state, The PSW key mask (PKM) in control register 3 is logically ANDed with the authorization key mask (AKM) field in the ETE (See Fig. 10.4). The format of the AKM is the same as the PKM; each bit represents a possible PSW key from 0 to 15. If the AND of the PKM and the AKM is not 0, the PC instruction proceeds. If the AND results in 0, the PC instruction abends with program check 0002.

The contents of the ETE determine the further operations of the PC instruction.

10.6 STACKING PC ROUTINES

If the first bit in the ETE OPTIONS byte is 1 (see Fig. 10.4), this is a stacking PC routine. The PC instruction creates a stack state entry on the linkage stack to save the current operating environment. If the bit is

---

Principles of Operation contains a complete list of authorization mechanisms for semiprivileged instructions.

0, the routine is a basic (not stacking) PC routine, and PC does not create a stack state entry.

10.6.1 PC Stack State Entry

Figure 10.5 illustrates the stack state entry created by the PC instruction. Note that the PC-type stack state entry differs from the stack state entry created by BAKR (illustrated in Fig. 2.3 in Chap. 2) in that bytes 148 through 151 contain the PC number rather than the branch address and byte 160 contains X'05' instead of X'04'. When the ESTA instruction extracts information from the stack state entry, it sets a condition code based on the entry type:

CC = 8 for entries created by BAKR
CC = 4 for entries created by PC

10.6.2 Restoring the Operating Environment

Stacking PC routines end with the PR instruction. PR restores the operating environment that existed when the stack state entry was created. It loads the PSW and the general and access registers of the current processor with the values from the stack state entry. The PSW from the stack state entry contains the address of the instruction after the PC instruction that created that stack state entry.

PR also loads four control register values from the stack state entry into the processor's control registers, restoring the rest of the operating environment as follows.

- The PKM, which controls semiprivileged instruction authority, is loaded into control register 3.

- The EAX, which controls access list entry creation authority, is loaded into control register 8.

- The PASN is loaded into control register 4. Loading the PASN initiates ASN translation, which locates the ASTE corresponding to the

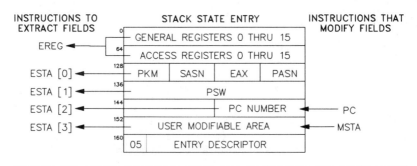

Figure 10.5 PC-type stackstate entry.

PASN. Once the ASTE is located, the STD and the AX are loaded from the ASTE into control registers 1 and 4, respectively, and the address of the ASTE itself is loaded into control register 5.

■ The SASN is loaded into control register 3, initiating ASN Translation. The STD from the ASTE located by this translation is loaded into control register 7.

10.7 SPACE-SWITCHING PC ROUTINES

When the ASN in the ETE contains a value other than 0, this is a space-switching PC routine.

A space-switching PC routine allows the PC instruction to reside in a different address space from the PC routine. That address space must be made the primary address space before the routine address in the ETE (Fig. 10.4) can be DAT translated.

The PC instruction loads the ASN from the ETE into control register 4 as the new PASN. This initiates ASN Translation, locating the ASTE for the new PASN. The real address of this ASTE is also in the ASTE address field in the ETE. It is unpredictable whether the PC microcode locates the ASTE directly from the ETE or by ASN Translation. Once the PC instruction locates the ASTE for the new primary address space, it loads the STD from the ASTE into control register 1.

PC then builds a PSW that contains the address of the PC routine entry point from the ETE. When PC loads this PSW on the processor, the virtual address of the entry point will be translated by DAT according to the Segment and Page Tables whose STD is now in control register 1.

During a space switch, the PC instruction loads the address of the ASTE corresponding to the new PASN into control register 5 so that it becomes the primary space ASTE. Since this new primary space ASTE points to a different PC Linkage Table, the space-switching PC routine itself can issue PC instructions to call routines that might not be defined in the Linkage and Entry Tables of its caller. The space-switch also loads the Authority Index (AX) from the new primary space ASTE into control register 4. This new AX may give the PC routine more SSAR authority than its caller.

Principles of Operation refers to space-switching PC routines with the notation "PC-ss" and to nonspace-switching PC routines with "PC-cp" (Program Call to current primary).

10.8 OTHER ETE FIELDS THAT CHANGE
THE OPERATING ENVIRONMENT

The PC instruction microcode logically ORs the execution key mask (EKM) field in the ETE with the current PKM in control register 3 to form a new PKM that may have more authority.

10.8.1 ETE OPTIONS Byte

If bit 4 in the ETE OPTIONS byte is 1, the PC instruction replaces the PKM with the EKM, rather than ORs it. If bit 5 of the ETE OPTIONS byte is 1 the EAX field in the ETE replaces the EAX in control register 8. (The PKM = REPLACE and EAX = operands on the ETDEF that created this ETE are valid only if this is a stacking PC routine.)

Other fields in the ETE determine how the PC instruction builds the PSW it loads when it transfers control to the PC routine. Bit 63 (labeled "P" in the ETE in Fig. 10.4) indicates whether the PC routine will execute in problem or supervisor state. Bit 3 in the ETE OPTIONS byte determines whether the contents of the entry key (EK) field replaces the current PSW key. Bit 6 in the ETE OPTIONS byte is 1 if the PC routine receives control in access register addressing mode, or 0 if the routine receives control in primary space mode.

Sometimes a space-switching PC routine needs to access storage in the address space where the PC instruction was issued. This is the case, for example, when the PC routine needs to access a parameter list in the caller's address space.

■ If bit 7 of the ETE OPTIONS byte is 0, the SASN in control of register 3 has the value of the caller's PASN. When the PC routine receives control it can go into access register mode and use an ALET of X'00000001' to access data in its secondary address space (which is the caller's primary address space). CKXTALK in this chapter uses this technique to read parameters in the caller's address space.

■ If bit 7 in ETE OPTIONS is 1, the PC routine receives control with the SASN the same as the PASN.

10.8.2 Latent Parameters

The Latent Parmlist field in the ETE contains the address of a parameter list consisting of two fullwords. The PARM1 = and PARM2 = operands on the ETDEF macro define the contents of the parameters. Since ETDEF acquires storage for the parameter list and builds it, the latent parameter values must be known at the time the ETDEF macro is issued. The PC instruction loads the address of the parameter list from the ETE into general register 4 before transferring control to the PC routine. (CKXTALK in this chapter uses a latent parameter.)

10.8.3 Associated Recovery Routines (ARRs)

The ETE can contain the address of an Associated Recovery Routine (ARR) that will receive control if there is a program check in a stacking PC routine. ARRs are written exactly like ESTAE recovery routines but receive control from RTM2 in a different way.

When there is a program check in an ESTAE-protected routine, RTM2 searches a chain of SCBs, which are MVS control blocks, to locate the appropriate ESTAE routine. Since the PC instruction does not involve MVS at all, there are no MVS control blocks for ARRs. RTM2 does not even know that it has received control for a program check in a PC routine until it examines the current linkage stack and sees a PC-type stack state entry. Since the stack state entry contains the PC routine number, RTM2 can locate the ETE and retrieve the ARR address and ARR options from the ETE. RTM2 does not percolate from an ARR to an ESTAE routine.

Note that a PC routine that wishes to pass parameters to an ARR issues the MSTA instruction to store the parameters in the user area of the stack state entry created by PC. See *Extended Addressability* (GC28-1854) for details.

10.9 PC INFORMATION IN A SYSUDUMP

Figure 10.6 illustrates the portion of a SYSUDUMP that contains a description of the ETEs in all the Entry Tables connected to an address space's PC Linkage Table. The PC numbers in the first column are in the format

OLLLEE

where LLL is the LX and EE is the EX. The PC routines numbered 000A00 and 000A01, for example, are the first and second entries in the

PC INFORMATION

PC NUMBER	AUTH KEY MASK	EXEC ASID	ENTRY ADDRESS	EXEC STATE	LATENT PARMS	EXEC KEY MASK	ETE OPTION	ENTRY KEY	EAX	ASTE REAL ADDRESS	ARR ADDRESS	OPTIONS
0000	FF00	0002	83802000	S	00000000 00000000	8000	00	00	0000	0508E080	00000000	
0001	FF00	0002	83802990	S	00000000 00000000	8000	00	00	0000	0508E080	00000000	
..	..	..	..	.	..	..	..	..	..	..	..	
0315	FFFF	0000	811982C8	S	00000000 00000000	0000	00	00	0000	00000000	00000000	
0316	FFFF	0000	8115B9A8	S	00000000 00000000	8000	90	00	0000	00000000	8115BBD4	
..	..	..	..	.	..	..	..	..	..	..	..	
0A00	FFFF	000E	8381A5A8	S	00000000 00000000	FFFF	9A	00	0000	0508E380	8106D1B0	
0A01	FFFF	000E	8380D248	S	00000000 00000000	FFFF	9A	00	0000	0508E380	8106D1B0	
..	..	..	..	.	..	..	..	..	..	..	..	
1404	0100	0000	837AEE90	S	037A7F88 00000000	FFFF	94	70	0000	00000000	00000000	
1405	FFFF	0000	837A9E48	S	037A7F88 00000000	FFFF	94	70	0000	00000000	037AA638	CANCEL=NO
..	..	..	..	.	..	..	..	..	..	..	..	

Figure 10.6 PC information in a SYSUDUMP.

Entry Table whose real address is in the eleventh slot in the PC Linkage Table (the first slot is 0).

The routines numbered 000000, 000001, 000A00, and 000A01 are space-switching, since there are nonzero values in the EXEC ASID fields in the ETEs. The routines numbered 000316, 000A00, 000A01, 001404, and 001405 are stacking since the high-order bit in the ETE OPTIONS byte is 1. These routines also replace the PSW key with the respective values in the entry key field since bit 3 in the OPTIONS byte is 1.

10.10 PROGRAMS IN THIS CHAPTER

Figure 10.7 illustrates how to establish a service address space containing a space-switching PC routine. Fig. 10.8 illustrates how a program in

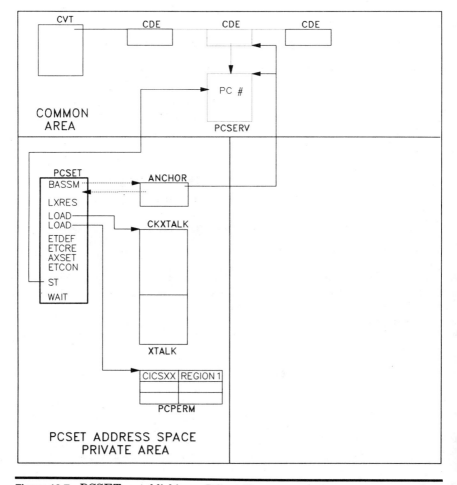

Figure 10.7   PCSET: establishing a PC routine.

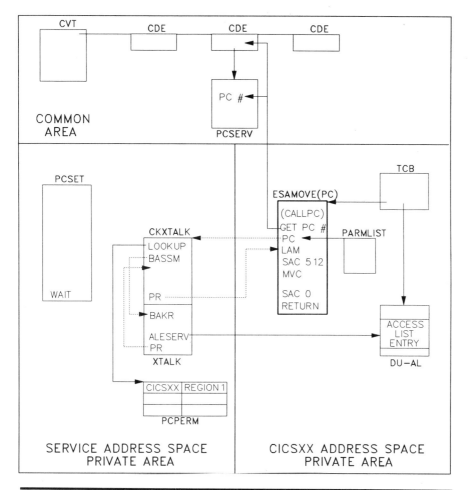

Figure 10.8 ESAMOVE(PC): invoking a PC routine.

another address space can issue the PC instruction to invoke the PC routine in the service address space.

The program ESAMOVE(PC) (Fig. 10.8) in address space CICSXX wishes to access data in another active address space named REGION1. ESAMOVE(PC) issues the CALLPC macro. CALLPC expands into a PC instruction which calls the PC routine CKXTALK in the service address space. CKXTALK does the following:

1. Checks the table PCPERM to see if CICSXX is authorized to communicate with REGION1, and if so:

2. Builds an access list entry for REGION1 on the DU-AL associated with ESAMOVE(PC)'s TCB.

The CALLPC macro returns the ALET for REGION1 to ESA-MOVE(PC). ESAMOVE(PC) loads the ALET into an access register, issues SAC 512, and is now able to access data in REGION1.

The reason for using a PC routine is to provide an authorized service for an unauthorized module. ESAMOVE(PC) performs the same function as ESAMOVE in Chap. 7. However, ESAMOVE requires APF authorization, whereas ESAMOVE(PC) does not. ESAMOVE(PC) cannot call XTALK to build an access list entry because XTALK contains the semi-privileged instruction

SPKA 0

But the PC routine CKXTALK can call XTALK on behalf of ESA-MOVE(PC) because PCSET defined CKXTALK with universal PKM authority on the ETDEF macro. ESAMOVE(PC) is created (Fig. 10.9) by replacing lines 54 through 66 in ESAMOVE (Chap. 7) with the CALLPC macro.

10.11 PCSET—DEFINE A PC ROUTINE

Figure 10.7 illustrates how the PCSET program in Fig. 10.10 establishes CKXTALK as a PC routine. PCSET executes as a started task. Lines 41 through 52 establish addressability to the Console Communications Area and the Command Input Buffer (CIB) chain so that PCSET can process commands issued at the MVS console. (The walkthrough of DSPACE in Chap. 11 explains command processing in a started task.)

10.11.1 A Place to Save the PC Number

Lines 53 through 73 then call the ANCHOR service (see Chap. 8) to obtain common storage for a user control block where PCSET will save the PC number that it will generate. The PCSERV user control block is anchored on the LPAQ so that any program that wishes to call CKXTALK can locate this control block. Once a program locates the PCSERV control block, it can retrieve the PC number and issue a PC instruction using that number to invoke CKXTALK. The USING on line 74 maps the user control block with the PCSERV DSECT in Fig. 10.11. Note that the PCSERV DSECT also contains the parameter lists used by LXRES and ETDEF.

A PC routine cannot be called if the address space in which it resides is swapped out. Lines 75 through 80 issue SYSEVENT to make the PCSET address space nonswappable.

10.11.2 LXRES

Since the LXRES on line 91 uses the SYSTEM = YES operand to obtain a system LX, the LX remains allocated until the next time MVS is

```
                    TO CREATE ESAMOVE(PC):
           REMOVE THE FOLLOWING LINES FROM ESAMOVE
             (WHICH REQUIRE APF AUTHORIZATION):


  *       *  ..                         ..
  *       *-----------------------------------*          54
  *       *     CALL ROUTINE TO BUILD         *          55
  *       *     ACCESS LIST ENTRY             *          56
  *       *-----------------------------------*          57
          MODESET MODE=SUP        GET A SUPERVISOR STATE PSW    58
          LAE   R1,PARMLIST       PARMLIST FOR XTALK ROUTINE    59
          ICM   R15,15,=V(XTALK)  ADDRESS OF ROUTINE TO R15     60
          BZ    EXIT0C                                          61
          O     R15,=A(X'80000000')  SET FOR 31 BIT MODE        62
          BASSM R14,R15           INVOKE ROUTINE                63
          LTR   R15,R15           RC = 0 ?                      64
          BNZ   EXIT10            NO; EXIT RC=8                 65
          MODESET MODE=PROB       GET A SUPERVISOR STATE PSW    66
          ..    ..                       ..


                  REPLACE WITH THESE LINES:
             (WHICH DO NOT REQUIRE APF AUTHORIZATION)


  *       *  ..    ..                  ..
  *       *-----------------------------------*          54
  *       *     CALL CKXTALK IN PCSET ADDRESS *          55
  *       *     SPACE TO BUILD ACCESS LIST ENTRY *       56
  *       *-----------------------------------*          57
          CALLPC PLIST=PARMLIST   CALL PC ROUTINE               58
          LTR   R15,R15           ANY ERRORS                    59
          BNZ   EXIT10            YES; EXIT WITH RC=16          60
          ..    ..                       ..
          PCSERV                                               169
          CVT   DSECT=YES,LIST=NO                              170
```

Figure 10.9 Creating ESAMOVE(PC).

initialized. Before issuing LXRES to obtain an LX, line 87 issues ICM to see whether a previous execution of the PCSET program has obtained an LX and placed its value in the PCSERV control block. If the condition code from ICM indicates a nonzero value for the LX, line 88 branches around the LXRES macro.

If an LX has not been obtained, lines 89 and 90 store a value of 1 into the parameter list for LXRES so that it will obtain one LX, and line 91

```
*+---------------------------------------------------------------------+     1
*|  FUNCTION:                                                          |     2
*|     THIS STARTED TASK DEFINES MODULE CKXTALK AS A PC ROUTINE,       |     3
*|     GENERATES A PC NUMBER FOR THE ROUTINE,  AND SAVES THE PC        |     4
*|     NUMBER IN A USER CONTROL BLOCK ANCHORED OFF A CDE ON THE LPAQ.  |     5
*|  LOGIC:                                                             |     6
*|     1) LOCATE THE CONSOLE COMMUNICATIONS AREA OFF THE CURRENT TCB   |     7
*|        SO THAT THIS PROGRAM CAN PROCESS CONSOLE COMMANDS.           |     8
*|     2) CALL THE ANCHOR SERVICE TO BUILD A TABLE OF PC NUMBERS       |     9
*|        ANCHORED OFF A CDE IN THE LPAQ.  IF THE TABLE ALREADY        |    10
*|        EXISTS, IT IS LOCATED AND REUSED.                            |    11
*|     3) MAKE ADDRESS SPACE NON-SWAPPABLE.                            |    12
*|     4) GET A SYSTEM LX OR, REUSE AN ALREADY OBTAINED SYSTEM LX.     |    13
*|     5) LOAD CKXTALK MODULE.                                         |    14
*|     6) LOAD THE ADDRESS SPACE PERMISSIONS TABLE USED BY CKXTALK.    |    15
*|     7) MODIFY THE ENTRY TABLE ENTRY DEFINITION SO THAT CKXTALK      |    16
*|        IS THE ENTRY POINT ADDRESS AND THE PERMISSIONS TABLE         |    17
*|        ADDRESS IS THE FIRST LATENT PARAMETER.                       |    18
*|     8) CREATE THE ENTRY TABLE.                                      |    19
*|     9) GENERATE A PC NUMBER FROM A COMBINATION OF THE LINKAGE       |    20
*|        INDEX AND ENTRY TABLE ENTRY'S DISPLACEMENT INTO ENTRY TABLE. |    21
*|    10) GET A MASTER AX ("1") SO THAT THE PC ROUTINE HAS SSAR        |    22
*|        AUTHORITY (PC ROUTINE IS DEFINED WITH SASN=OLD).             |    23
*|    11) CONNECT THE ENTRY TABLE TO THE LINKAGE INDEX.                |    24
*|    12) GO INTO A WAIT STATE UNTIL POSTED BY A CONSOLE COMMAND.      |    25
*|        PROCESS ANY "STOP" OR "MODIFY" CONSOLE COMMANDS WHEN POSTED. |    26
*|  INPUTS:                                                            |    27
*|     NONE                                                            |    28
*|  OUTPUTS:                                                           |    29
*|     R15 - RETURN CODE                                               |    30
*|           0 - SUCCESSFUL PC ROUTINE DEFINITION                      |    31
*|          16 - UNSUCCESSFUL                                          |    32
*|               CHECK THE JOB LOG FOR MESSAGE OF LAST OPERATION       |    33
*|               R0 - RETURN CODE OF FAILING OPERATION                 |    34
*|               R1 - REASON CODE OF FAILING OPERATION                 |    35
*|  ATTRIBUTES:                                                        |    36
*|     AMODE 31, RMODE ANY, APF AUTHORIZED, REENTERABLE                |    37
*+---------------------------------------------------------------------+     38
          MODULE PCSET,BASE=12,LOC=BELOW,AMODE=31,RMODE=ANY,          X    39
                 TEXT='ESTABLISH A PC ROUTINE'                             40
*---------------------------------------------------------------------*     41
*        SET UP COMMAND PROCESSING                                    *     42
*---------------------------------------------------------------------*     43
          LA    R1,EXTLIST            PARMLIST FOR EXTRACT                  44
          LA    R3,XTRANSW            ANSWER AREA FOR QEDIT                 45
*                                     GET ADDRESS COMMUNICATION AREA       46
          EXTRACT (R3),'S',FIELDS=(COMM),MF=(E,(1))                        47
          L     R3,XTRANSW            A(COMMUNICATIONS AREA) => R3         48
          USING COMLIST,R3            MAP COMMUNICATIONS AREA              49
          QEDIT ORIGIN=COMCIBPT,CIBCTR=4 SET LIMIT ON QUEUED COMMANDS     50
          L     R4,COMCIBPT           A(COMMAND INPUT BUFFER)             51
          USING CIB,R4                MAP CIB                              52
*---------------------------------------------------------------------*     53
*        CALL ANCHOR SERVICE TO OBTAIN STORAGE FOR THE USER           *     54
*        CONTROL BLOCK AND ANCHOR IT OFF A CDE ON THE LPAQ.           *     55
*---------------------------------------------------------------------*     56
          LA    R5,ANKLIST            A(PARMLIST) => R5                    57
```

Figure 10.10 PCSET.

```
      USING ANKPRM,R5              MAP PARMLIST                          58
      MVC   ANKEYE(L'ANKEYE),EYE   TABLE EYECATCHER TO PARMLIST          59
      MVC   ANKNAME(L'ANKNAME),TBLN TABLE NAME TO PARMLIST               60
      LA    R6,LPCSERV             ..TABLE LENGTH                        61
      ST    R6,ANKLEN              ..TO PARMLIST                         62
      XC    ANKEP(L'ANKEP),ANKEP   INITIALIZE ENTRYPOINT TO X'00'        63
      LOAD  EP=ANCHOR,ERRET=EXIT10 LOAD ANCHOR SERVICE ROUTINE           64
      LR    R2,R0                  ENTRYPOINT TO R15                     65
      WTO   'PCSET: ANCHOR ROUTINE LOADED'                              66
      LR    R15,R2                 ENTRYPOINT TO R15                     67
      LR    R1,R5                  ADDRESS OF PARMLIST => R1             68
      BASSM R14,R15                INVOKE SERVICE                        69
      C     R15,=F'8'              DID ANCHOR SERVICE FAIL ?             70
      BH    EXIT10                 YES; EXIT PERCOLATING RC              71
      WTO   'PCSET: PC NUMBERS TABLE ANCHOR INITIALIZED'                72
      L     R5,ANKEP               TABLE ENTRYPOINT => R5                73
      USING PCSERV,R5              MAP PC SERVICE TABLE BLOCK            74
*     *---------------------------------------*                         75
*     *                                       *                         76
*     *     MAKE THIS ADDRESS SPACE NON-SWAP   *                         76
*     *---------------------------------------*                         77
      MODESET MODE=SUP             GET A SUPERVISOR STATE PSW            78
      LA    R1,TRANSECB            ..MAKE THIS                           79
      SYSEVENT TRANSWAP            ..ADDRESS SPACE NON-SWAPABLE          80
*-------------------------------------------------------------------*   81
*     DEFINE PC ROUTINE. GENERATE PC NUMBER.                       *    82
*-------------------------------------------------------------------*   83
*     *---------------------------------------*                         84
*     *                                       *                         
*     *     GET A SYSTEM LINKAGE INDEX         *                         85
*     *---------------------------------------*                         86
      ICM   R2,B'1111',LXVALUE     HAS LINKAGE INDEX BEEN GOTTEN         87
      BNZ   INDEXIS                YES; DO NOT GET LX                    88
      LA    R2,1                   NUMBER OF LINKAGE INDEXES             89
      ST    R2,LXCOUNT             SAVE IN PC SERVICE BLOCK              90
      LXRES LXLIST=LXL,SYSTEM=YES,MF=(E,LXLIST)                         91
      LTR   R15,R15                RC = 0 ;                              92
      BNZ   EXIT10                 NO; EXIT                              93
      WTO   'PCSET: SYSTEM LINKAGE INDEX OBTAINED'                      94
INDEXIS DS  0H                                                           95
*     *---------------------------------------*                         96
*     *                                       *                         
*     *     LOAD CKXTALK MODULE.               *                         97
*     *---------------------------------------*                         98
      LOAD  EP=CKXTALK,ERRET=EXIT10 LOAD CKXTALK ROUTINE                99
      LR    R2,R0                  ADDRESS OF MODULE => R2              100
      WTO   'PCSET: CKXTALK LOADED'                                    101
*     *---------------------------------------*                        102
*     *                                       *                        
*     *     LOAD TABLE USED BY CXTALK MODULE   *                       103
*     *---------------------------------------*                        104
      LOAD  EP=PCPERM,ERRET=EXIT10 LOAD PERMISSIONS TABLE              105
      LR    R7,R0                  ADDRESS OF MODULE => R7             106
      WTO   'PCSET: PERMISSIONS TABLE LOADED'                          107
*     *---------------------------------------*                        108
*     *                                       *                        
*     *     BUILD HEADER ENTRY                 *                        109
*     *---------------------------------------*                        110
      MVC   ETDESC(LENTABL),MENTBL MOVE ENTRY TABLE TO WORK AREA       111
      LA    R8,ETESNUM             NUMBER OF PC ROUTINES               112
      ETDEF TYPE=SET,HEADER=ETDESC, ADDRESS OF THE HEADER ENTRY      X 113
            NUMETE=(R8)            NUMBER OF PC ROUTINES               114
```

Figure 10.10 *(Continued)*

```
*        *---------------------------------------*              115
*        *     MODIFY THE ENTRY TABLE ENTRY       *              116
*        *---------------------------------------*              117
         ETDEF TYPE=SET,ETEADR=ETD1,  MODIFY ETE IN WORK AREA       X 118
               ROUTINE=(2),           ADDRESS OF THE PC ROUTINE     X 119
               PARM1=(7),             A(PERMIT TABLE) IS 1ST LAT PARM X 120
               PC=STACKING,           STACKING PC ROUTINE           X 121
               SSWITCH=YES,           BRANCH TO ANOTHER ADDRESS SPACE X 122
               ASCMODE=PRIMARY,       RECEIVE CONTROL IN PRIMARY MODE X 123
               SASN=OLD,              OLD PRIMARY IS NEW SECONDARY  X 124
               AKM=(0:15),            CALLER CAN BE IN ANY PSW KEY  X 125
               RAMODE=31,             ENTER IN 31 BIT MODE          X 126
               STATE=PROBLEM,EK=8,    ENTERED IN PROB STATE/TCB KEY X 127
               EKM=(0:15),PKM=OR      AT ENTRY SET NEW PKM 0:15       128
*******  ADD ADDTIONAL "ETDEF TYPE=SET" FOR MORE PC ROUTINES HERE *****  129
*        *---------------------------------------*              130
*        *     CREATE THE ENTRY TABLE.          *              131
*        *---------------------------------------*              132
         ETCRE ENTRIES=ETDESC         CREATE THE ENTRY TABLE        133
         ST    R0,ETETOKEN            SAVE ENTRY TABLE TOKEN        134
         LTR   R15,R15                RC = 0 ;                      135
         BNZ   EXIT10                 NO; EXIT                      136
         WTO   'PCSET: ENTRY TABLE CREATED'                        137
*        *---------------------------------------*              138
*        *     GENERATE PC NUMBER FROM LX AND ET.*              139
*        *     SAVE PC # IN USER CONTROL BLOCK.  *              140
*        *---------------------------------------*              141
         LA    R7,ETESNUM             NUMBER OF DEFINED PC ROUTINES 142
         LA    R8,PCTAB               ADDRESS OF PC NUMBERS TABLE   143
         L     R2,LXVALUE             LINKAGE INDEX => R2           144
PCTBLP   DS    0H                                                   145
         ST    R2,0(R8)               PUT IN PCTABLE               146
         LA    R2,1(R2)               INCREMENT LX + EX             147
         LA    R8,4(R8)               POINT AT NEXT PCTAB ENTRY     148
         BCT   R7,PCTBLP              LOOP FOR NEXT PC NUMBER       149
*        *---------------------------------------*              150
*        *     SINCE PC ROUTINE IS DEFINED        *              151
*        *     SASN=OLD, WE NEED SSAR AUTHORITY   *              152
*        *---------------------------------------*              153
         LA    R2,1                   "1" IS MASTER AX             154
         AXSET AX=(R2)                SET AX TO 1                  155
*        *---------------------------------------*              156
*        *     CONNECT ENTRY TABLE TO THE  LX     *              157
*        *---------------------------------------*              158
         LA    R2,1                   1 ENTRY TABLE TO BE CONNECTED 159
         ST    R2,ETECOUNT            PUT IN TOKEN PARMLIST        160
*                                     CONNECT THE ENTRY TABLE TO LX 161
         ETCON LXLIST=LXL,TKLIST=ETE,MF=(E,ETCONLST)               162
         MODESET MODE=PROB            GET A PROBLEM STATE PSW      163
         B     WAIT                   WAIT FOR CONSOLE COMMANDS    164
*-------------------------------------------------------------------*  165
*       "STOP" AND "MODIFY" CONSOLE COMMANDS ARE PROCESSED IN LOOP  *  166
*-------------------------------------------------------------------*  167
CKCOM    DS    0H                     TOP OF COMMAND PROCESSING LOOP 168
         L     R4,COMCIBPT            ADDRESS OF COMMAND INPUT BUF  169
         CLI   CIBVERB,CIBSTOP        IS IT STOP ?                 170
         BNE   NOTSTOP                NO; CHECK IF "MODIFY"        171
```

Figure 10.10 *(Continued)*

```
*           *------------------------------------------*           172
*           *    DESTROY THE ENTRY TABLE.        *                 173
*           *------------------------------------------*           174
            MODESET MODE=SUP              GET A SUPERVISOR STATE PSW   175
            ETDES TOKEN=ETETOKEN,           ..DISCONNECT THE ENTRY TABLE   X 176
                  PURGE=YES,MF=(E,ETDLIST)  ..FROM ALL LNK TBLS AND DESTROY 177
            MODESET MODE=PROB            GET A PROBLEM STATE PSW      178
            WTO   'PCSET: ENTRY TABLE DESTROYED'                     179
            QEDIT ORIGIN=COMCIBPT,BLOCK=(R4)   FREE THE CIB          180
            B     EXIT00                                             181
NOTSTOP     DS    OH                                                 182
            CLI   CIBVERB,CIBMODFY        IS IT MODIFY ?             183
            BE    MODIFY                  YES; PROCESS "MODIFY" COMMAND 184
            WTO   'PCSET: INVALID COMMAND ISSUED'                    185
            B     WAIT                    WAIT FOR NEXT COMMAND      186
MODIFY      DS    OH                                                 187
*******     ADD   "MODIFY" COMMAND PROCESSING HERE                   188
*           *------------------------------------------*            189
*           *    GO INTO WAIT STATE UNTIL POSTED  *                 190
*           *    BY A CONSOLE COMMAND.            *                 191
*           *------------------------------------------*            192
WAIT        DS    OH                                                 193
            QEDIT ORIGIN=COMCIBPT,BLOCK=(R4)   FREE THE LAST CIB     194
            L     R6,COMECBPT             .. WAIT ON ECB             195
            WAIT  ECB=(6)                 .. IN COMM AREA            196
            B     CKCOM                   BOTTOM OF COMMAND LOOP     197
*------------------------------------------------------------------* 198
*           EXIT ROUTINES                                          * 199
*------------------------------------------------------------------* 200
EXIT00      DS    OH                      SUCCESSFUL EXIT            201
            LA    15,X'00'                                           202
            B     EXIT                                               203
EXIT10      DS    OH                      PERCOLATE RETRUN & REASON CODES 204
            PERCRC RC=X'10'                                          205
            B     EXIT                                               206
*------------------------------------------------------------------* 207
*           COMMON EXIT                                            * 208
*------------------------------------------------------------------* 209
EXIT        DS    OH                                                 210
            LR    R2,R15                  PRESERVE REGISTER 15       211
            MODESET MODE=PROB             GET A PROBLEM STATE PSW    212
            LR    R15,R2                  RESTORE REGISTER 15        213
            ENDMOD                                                   214
*------------------------------------------------------------------* 215
*           CONSTANTS                                              * 216
*------------------------------------------------------------------* 217
EYE         DC    CL4'PC@1'               EYCATCHER IN PC NUMBERS TABLE 218
TBLN        DC    CL8'PCTBL01'            NAME IN CDE ANCHOR FOR PC # TBL 219
*------------------------------------------------------------------* 220
*           ENTRY TABLE DEFINITION                                 * 221
*------------------------------------------------------------------* 222
MENTBL      ETDEF TYPE=INITIAL           BEGINNING OF ENTRY TABLE   223
METD1       ETDEF TYPE=ENTRY,ROUTINE=0,AKM=(0:15)                   224
*******     IF ADDITIONAL ENTRIES ARE NEEDED IN ENTRY TABLE,ADD HERE **** 225
ETESNUM     EQU   (*-METD1)/ETDELEN       NUMBER OF PC ROUTINES DEFINED 226
            ETDEF TYPE=FINAL                                         227
LENTABL     EQU   *-MENTBL                                           228
```

Figure 10.10 *(Continued)*

```
*-------------------------------------------------------------------*  227
*           WORK AREA                                            *     228
*-------------------------------------------------------------------*  229
WPCSET DSECT                                   WORK AREA                230
TRANSECB DS    F                               ECB FOR SYSEVENT        231
ECB1     DS    F                               ECB FOR THIS ADDRESS SPACE  232
ETDESC   DS    CL(LENTABL)                     ENTRY TABLE ENTRIES     233
ETD1     EQU   ETDESC+(METD1-MENTBL)           ADDRESS OF ENTRY TABLE ENTRY  234
ANKLIST  DS    OF,CL(LANKPRM)                  PARMLIST FOR ANCHOR1 SERVICE  235
LXLIST   LXRES MF=L                            PARMLIST FOR LXRES      236
ETCONLST ETCON MF=L                            PARMLIST FOR ETCON      237
ETDLIST  ETDES MF=L                            PARMLIST FOR ETDES      238
EXTLIST  EXTRACT ,MF=L                         PARMLIST FOR EXTRACT    239
XTRANSW  DS    F                               RESPONSE FROM QEDIT     240
LPCSET   EQU   *-WPCSET                        LENGTH OF WORK AREA     241
*-------------------------------------------------------------------*  242
*           OTHER DSECTS                                         *     243
*-------------------------------------------------------------------*  244
         ANKPRM                                MAP ANCHOR PARMLIST     245
         PCSERV                                MAP PC SERVICES ANCHOR BLOCK  246
         IEZCOM                                MAP COMMUNICATIONS AREA 247
CIB      DSECT                                 MAP COMMAND INPUT BUFFER  248
         IEZCIB                                                        249
         IHAETD LIST=YES,FORMAT=1              MAP ENTRY TABLE ENTRY   250
         END                                                          251
```

Figure 10.10 *(Continued)*

```
         MACRO                        MAP PC NUMBERS CONTROL BLOCK     1
         PCSERV                                                       2
.*+-------------------------------------------------------------+     3
.*|       THIS DSECT MAPS THE CONTROL BLOCK IN COMMON STORAGE THAT  | 4
.*|       CONTAINS PC NUMBERS FOR ROUTINES IN THE PCSET ADDRESS SPACE. | 5
.*+-------------------------------------------------------------+     6
PCSERV   DSECT                                                        7
PCSID    DS    CL4                             BLOCK IDENTIFIER        8
LXL      DS    OF                              LX LIST                 9
LXCOUNT  DS    F                               NUMBER OF LXES REQUIRED 10
LXVALUE  DS    F                               LX RETURNED BY LXRES    11
ETE      DS    OF                              TOKEN LIST              12
ETECOUNT DS    F                               NUMBER OF ETS CREATED   13
ETETOKEN DS    F                               TOKEN RETURNED BY ETCRE 14
PCTAB    DS    0A                              TABLE OF PC NUMBERS      15
PCSRTN1  DS    F                               PC NUMBER OF PC ROUTINE 1  16
PCSRTN2  DS    F                               PC NUMBER OF PC ROUTINE 2  17
PCSRTN3  DS    F                               PC NUMBER OF PC ROUTINE 3  18
PCSRTN4  DS    F                               PC NUMBER OF PC ROUTINE 4  19
.*       ADD   ADDITIONAL PC NUMBERS HERE  **************************   20
LPCSERV  EQU   *-PCSERV                        LENGTH OF PARMLIST      21
         MEND                                                         22
```

Figure 10.11 PCSERV DSECT.

issues the LXRES macro. LXRES returns the Linkage Index it obtains in the field LXVALUE on line 11 of the PCSERV DSECT. Note that the execute form of the macro is used against the LXRES MF = L on line 236 to preserve reentrancy.

Lines 96 through 100 load the PC routine module, CKXTALK, into the private area of the PCSET address space, and lines 102 through 106 load PCPERM, the table that CKXTALK examines before it calls XTALK. The address of the PCPERM table will be passed to CKXTALK as a latent parameter through the ETE.

10.11.3 ETDEF

Since the virtual addresses of CKXTALK and PCPERM are not available until the modules are LOADed, and since the parameter list that ETDEF uses to build the ETE will have to be modified to contain these addresses, line 111 copies the ETDEF macros in lines 220 through 228 to the work area to preserve reentrancy. Note that ETDEF does not have an MF = E or MF = L format. Rather, it has the TYPE = INITIAL, TYPE = ENTRY, and TYPE = FINAL formats on lines 220 through 228, which expand into parameter lists. These are equivalent to the MF = L format. The ETDEF TYPE = SET statements on lines 113 and 118 expand into instructions that modify the parameter lists built by TYPE = INITIAL, ENTRY, and FINAL. ETDEF TYPE = SET is equivalent to the MF = E format.

Since PCSET initializes only one PC routine, there is one ETDEF TYPE = ENTRY macro coded on line 224. If PCSET is modified to define additional PC routines, an ETDEF TYPE = ENTRY macro can be added where indicated by line 225 to build an ETE for each new routine. An ETDEF TYPE = SET macro can similarly be included where indicated on line 129 for each additional ETDEF TYPE = ENTRY.

Note that the EQU on line 226 sets the symbol ETESNUM equal to the number of ETEs in the Entry Table by subtracting the address of the first ETE from the address after the last ETE and dividing the difference by the length of an ETE. The symbol ETDELEN, which is the length of an ETE, is defined in the IBM-supplied macro IHAETD on line 250 that maps the ETE.

The ETDEF TYPE = SET macro on lines 113 through 114 modifies the ETDEF TYPE = INITIAL macro (moved to the work area from line 223) so that it contains the number of PC routines in the Entry Table. Line 112 uses the symbol ETESNUM defined on line 226.

The ETDEF TYPE = SET macro on lines 118 through 128 modifies the ETDEF TYPE = ENTRY macro (moved to the work area from line 224) so that it contains the values needed to build the ETE. Register 2, which contains the address where CKXTALK has been loaded, is the operand of the ROUTINE = operand on line 119. Register 7 contains the address of the PCPERM table that CKXTALK will examine when it executes. The PARM1 = operand on line 120 defines this table address as the first latent parameter specified by the ETE Latent Parmlist field (see Fig. 10.4).

Note that the ETDEF TYPE = SET completely replaces all the values coded in the ETDEF TYPE = ENTRY macro it modifies. All nondefault operand values, therefore, must be coded on the ETDEF TYPE = SET macro even if they have been coded on the TYPE = ENTRY macro.

10.11.4 ETCRE

The ETCRE macro on line 133 builds the actual Entry Table in LSQA based on what has been coded on the ETDEF macros. The ETDEF TYPE = INITIAL macro indicates how many ETEs will be in the table and how much LSQA storage ETCRE needs to obtain. ETCRE returns a token identifying this Entry Table in register 0 which line 134 saves in the PCSERV control block. This token is part of the parameter list for ETCON on line 162 and is used by ETDES on line 176.

10.11.5 Generating PC Numbers

The loop in lines 138 through 149 generates PC numbers for each of the PC routines defined by ETDEF (in this case there is only one routine) and stores the PC numbers in the PCSERV control block. Line 142 loads the loop counter with the number of PC routines defined; line 144 loads the LX returned by LXRES into register 2. Each repetition of the loop stores the LX into the PCSERV control block and increments register 2, in effect, creating a new LX/EX that indexes to the next ETE in the Entry Table.

10.11.6 SASN = OLD

The ETDEF macro on line 118 has defined CKXTALK as a space-switching PC routine with the SSWITCH = YES operand on line 122. This means that a program calling CKXTALK will, in effect, branch to the PCSET address space when it issues a PC instruction with the LX/EX for CKXTALK. After the branch, all virtual addresses will be translated by DAT using the Segment and Page Tables for PCSET rather than those of the calling program. Since any parameters that the calling program wishes to pass to CKXTALK still reside in the caller's address space, simply passing the virtual address of those parameters does not make them addressable. CKXTALK must use the caller's Segment and Page Tables to translate the virtual address of the caller's parameter list.

One way that CKXTALK could establish addressability to the caller's address space would be by issuing the SSAR instruction. Once the SSAR established the caller's address space as the secondary address space, CKXTALK could use access register addressing mode with an ALET of X'00000001' or secondary space mode to access data in the caller's virtual storage.

The same effect as the SSAR instruction can be achieved by including the SASN = OLD operand (line 124) on the ETDEF macro. When the PC instruction examines the ETE and sees SASN = OLD, it transfers control to the PC routine with the the secondary address space set to the caller's primary address space.

10.11.7 Authorization Index

Whenever a new secondary address space is set, either with a SSAR instruction or with ETDEF SASN = OLD, the Authorization Index (AX) in control register 4 is used to locate an entry in the target address space's Authority Table. If the SSAR bit in the Authority Table entry is 1, the operation proceeds. If the bit is 0, a program check 0025 occurs.

The instructions on 154 and 155 set an AX value of 1 for the PCSET address space, which gives it SSAR authority to every address space (1 is the master AX). Notice, in Fig. 10.3, how AXSET changes the AX both in control register 4 and in the primary space ASTE. When another address space issues a PC instruction to invoke CKXTALK and the PCSET address space is established as the new PASN, the AX value of 1 is loaded from the ASTE into control register 4, giving CKXTALK master SSAR authority.

10.11.8 ETCON

In response to the ETCON macro on line 162, PCAUTH puts the real address of the Entry Table created by ETCRE into the PC Linkage Table slot corresponding to the LX reserved by LXRES. Since LXRES reserved a system LX, the address of the Entry Table is placed in the PC Linkage Table of every address space in the system. At this point any address space can issue the PC instruction to invoke CKXTALK. Note that the execute and list forms of ETCON are used to preserve reentrancy.

Once the PCSET address space has established CKXTALK as a PC routine, it branches to line 193 where line 196 issues WAIT against the ECB in the COMM area. (The IEZCOM DSECT on line 247 maps the COMM area.) The PCSET task remains in WAIT state until the ECB is posted by an MVS console command. Note that since PC routines execute under the caller's TCB, a PC call to CKXTALK does not take the PCSET TCB out of WAIT state.

10.11.9 ETDES

When a STOP or MODIFY console command is issued against PCSET, the task becomes active, and control is given to line 168 where the command in the CIB is analyzed. If the command is STOP, lines 176 and 177 issue ETDES to disconnect the Entry Table from the PC Linkage Tables of all address spaces and to free the LSQA storage occupied by the Entry Table. PCSET does not presently process MODIFY commands. MODIFY command processing can be added at line 188 (a MODIFY to reload the PCPERM table if it is reassembled might be useful.)

10.12 ESAMOVE(PC)—INVOKE A PC ROUTINE

The ESAMOVE(PC) program is identical to the ESAMOVE program in Chap. 7 except for the few lines that call XTALK to build an access list entry. Figure 10.9 illustrates that, while ESAMOVE must issue MODESET to go into supervisor state before calling XTALK, ESAMOVE(PC) issues the CALLPC macro while still in problem state. CALLPC, whose expansion is illustrated in Fig. 10.12:

■ Saves the registers and addressing mode on the linkage stack (lines 68 and 69).

■ Retrieves the PC number for the CKXTALK program from the PCSERV control block (lines 70 through 80). Lines 71 through 75 call IEAQCDSR to locate the PCSERV control block on the LPAQ. Lines 79 and 80 load the PC number from PCSERV into register 14.

■ Loads the address of the parameter list for CKXTALK into register 1 (line 81).

■ Issues the PC instruction to invoke CKXTALK (line 84).

■ Restores the original registers and addressing mode (line 85).

The source code for the CALLPC macro is in Fig. 10.13.

10.13 CKXTALK—A PC ROUTINE

In the right section of Fig. 10.8, ESAMOVE(PC) issues the CALLPC macro, which retrieves the PC number from the PCSERV control block and issues the PC instruction. The PC instruction uses the LX portion of

```
          CALLPC PLIST=PARMLIST                                                        67
+         LAE    14,CP500025          ADDRESS AFTER STACK IS POPPED     68
+         BAKR   14,0                 SAVE REGISTERS AND ASC MODE       69
+         SAC    0                    GO INTO PRIMARY ASC MODE          70
+         L      3,CVTPTR             ADDRESS OF CVT                    71
+         LA     9,CP200025           ADDRESS OF ANCHOR CDE NAME        72
+         L      8,CVTQLPAQ-CVT(3)    HEAD OF LPAQ                      73
+         L      15,CVTQCDSR-CVT(3)   ADDRESS OF THE LPAQ SCAN RTN      74
+         BALR   14,15                INVOKE LPAQ SCAN ROUTINE          75
+         B      CP100025             CDE FOUND                         76
+         LA     15,8                 CDE NOT FOUND; SET RC=8           77
+         B      CP400025             BRANCH TO POP THE STACK           78
+CP100025 L      11,CDENTPT-CDENTRY(11) POINTER TO PC # TABLE IN CDE    79
+         L      14,PCSRTN1-PCSERV(11) LOAD PC NUMBER FOR THIS ROUTINE 80
+         LA     1,PARMLIST           PARMLIST ADDRESS TO REGISTER 1    81
+         B      CP300025                                               82
+CP200025 DC     CL8'PCTBL01'         NAME OF CDE THAT ANCHORS PCTBL    83
+CP300025 PC     0(14)                INVOKE THE PC ROUTINE             84
+CP400025 PR                          POP THE STACK                     85
+CP500025 DS     0H                                                     86
```

Figure 10.12 Expansion of CALLPC macro.

the PC number to index into the current address space's PC Linkage Table. Since PCSET obtained a system LX, every PC Linkage Table contains the address of the PCSET's Entry Table. The PC instruction uses the EX portion of the PC number to index into the Entry Table and locates the ETE for the CKXTALK routine.

Because the PC instruction was issued by a program with a problem-state PSW, the PC instruction ANDs the current PKM, which has a value of X'0080', with the AKM in the ETE, which has a value of X'FFFF'. Since the result of the AND is not 0, the PC instruction establishes an operating environment based on the contents of the ETE. In this case (see the ETDEF operands in PCSET), the PC instruction creates an entry on the linkage stack, loads the address space number (ASN) of the PCSET address space as the PASN, loads the ASN for the ESA-MOVE(PC) address space as the SASN, and ORs the PKM in control register 3 with the EKM in the ETE, which has a value of X'FFFF'.

The PC instruction then builds a key 8, problem-state, primary space mode PSW that contains the virtual address of the entry point of the

```
              MACRO                                                        1
&LABEL        CALLPC &PLIST=                                               2
              LCLB   &E1                                                   3
              LCLC   &LBL1,&LBL2,&LBL3,&LBL4                               4
.*+----------------------------------------------------------------+      5
.*|           &PLIST IS THE ADDRESS OF A REMOTE PARAMETER LIST      |      6
.*|           MAPPED BY THE XMSESA MACRO                            |      7
.*+----------------------------------------------------------------+      8
&LBL1         SETC   'CP1'.'&SYSNDX'                                       9
&LBL2         SETC   'CP2'.'&SYSNDX'                                      10
&LBL3         SETC   'CP3'.'&SYSNDX'                                      11
&LBL4         SETC   'CP4'.'&SYSNDX'                                      12
&LBL5         SETC   'CP5'.'&SYSNDX'                                      13
              AIF    (T'&PLIST NE 'O').OK1                                14
              MNOTE  8,'OPERAND "PLIST=" IS REQUIRED'                     15
&E1           SETB   1                                                    16
.OK1          ANOP                                                        17
              AIF    (&E1).MEND                                           18
.*+----------------------------------------------------------------+     19
.*|                                                                 |     20
.*+----------------------------------------------------------------+     21
&LABEL        LAE    14,&LBL5              ADDRESS AFTER STACK IS POPPED  22
              BAKR   14,0                 SAVE REGISTERS AND ASC MODE     23
              SAC    0                    GO INTO PRIMARY ASC MODE        24
              L      3,CVTPTR             ADDRESS OF CVT                  25
              LA     9,&LBL2              ADDRESS OF ANCHOR CDE NAME      26
              L      8,CVTQLPAQ-CVT(3)    HEAD OF LPAQ                    27
              L      15,CVTQCDSR-CVT(3)   ADDRESS OF THE LPAQ SCAN RTN    28
              BALR   14,15                INVOKE LPAQ SCAN ROUTINE        29
              B      &LBL1                CDE FOUND                       30
              LA     15,8                 CDE NOT FOUND; SET RC=8         31
              B      &LBL4                BRANCH TO POP THE STACK         32
&LBL1         L      11,CDENTPT-CDENTRY(11) POINTER TO PC # TABLE IN CDE  33
              L      14,PCSRTN1-PCSERV(11)  PC NUMBER FOR "ADD"           34
              INNERMM &PLIST,1            PARSE OPERAND                   35
              B      &LBL3                ISSUE PC INSTRUCTION            36
&LBL2         DC     CL8'PCTBL01'         NAME OF CDE THAT ANCHORS PCTBL  37
&LBL3         PC     0(14)                INVOKE THE PC ROUTINE           38
&LBL4         PR                          POP THE STACK                   39
&LBL5         DS     0H                                                   40
.MEND         MEND                                                        41
```

Figure 10.13 CALLPC macro source code.

CKXTALK routine and an AMODE of 31. PC loads this PSW on the processor where it is executing, and CKXTALK receives control.

10.13.1 The MODULE Macro: ENTRY = PCSTACK

CKXTALK (Fig. 10.14) begins with the MODULE macro on line 39. Since this module receives control when a PSW is loaded on the processor, rather than as the result of a branch, the ENTRY = PCSTACK operand is coded on the MODULE macro. This causes MODULE to generate the following instructions to load the base register and establish addressability:

```
*+------------------------------------------------------------------+    1
*|   FUNCTION:                                                       |    2
*|      CKXTALK IS A SPACE-SWITCHING PC ROUTINE THAT INVOKES XTALK   |    3
*|      TO BUILD AN ACCESS LIST ENTRY ON THE DU-AL ASSOCIATED WITH   |    4
*|      THE CALLING PROGRAM'S TCB.  BEFORE BUILDING THE ACCESS LIST  |    5
*|      ENTRY, CKXTALK CHECKS A TABLE TO DETERMINE IF THE CALLER IS  |    6
*|      AUTHORIZED TO ESTABLISH COMMUNICATION WITH THE TARGET SPACE. |    7
*|   LOGIC:                                                          |    8
*|      1) GET THE CALLER'S PARAMETER LIST BY LOADING 1 INTO ACCESS  |    9
*|         REGISTER 1, GOING INTO AR MODE, AND MOVING THE PARMLIST   |   10
*|         FROM THE CALLER'S ADDRESS SPACE TO THIS ADDRESS SPACE.    |   11
*|         THE ETDEF THAT DEFINED CKXTALK MUST CONTAIN SASN=OLD.     |   12
*|      2) GET THE NAME OF THE CALLER'S ADDRESS SPACE BY USING       |   13
*|         THE SASN AS AN INDEX INTO THE ASVT.                       |   14
*|      3) SEARCH THE PERMISSIONS TABLE WHOSE ADDRESS WAS PASSED     |   15
*|         AS A LATENT PARAMETER BY THE CALLER.  IF THE CALLING      |   16
*|         ADDRESS SPACE NAME AND THE TARGET ADDRESS SPACE NAME      |   17
*|         ARE BOTH FOUND IN AN ENTRY IN THE PERMISSIONS TABLE,      |   18
*|         CONTINUE.  ELSE EXIT.                                     |   19
*|      4) CALL THE XTALK ROUTINE TO BUILD THE ACCESS LIST ENTRY.    |   20
*|   INPUTS:                                                         |   21
*|      GR1 - ADDRESS OF CALLER'S PARMLIST                           |   22
*|            THIS PARMLIST HAS THE SAME FORMAT AS THE XTALK PARMLIST.|   23
*|      GR4 - ADDRESS OF LATENT PARAMETER LIST                       |   24
*|            1ST WORD - ADDRESS OF PERMISSIONS TABLE                |   25
*|      SASN  IS CALLER'S PASN.                                      |   26
*|   OUTPUTS:                                                        |   27
*|      GR15 - RETURN CODE                                           |   28
*|         0  - ACCESS LIST ENTRY IS BUILT                           |   29
*|         8  - CALLER IS NOT AUTHORIZED TO BUILD ACCESS LIST ENTRY  |   30
*|              TO TARGET.                                           |   31
*|        12  - XTALK ROUTINE IS NOT LINK-EDITED.                    |   32
*|        16  - XTALK ROUTINE FAILED.                                |   33
*|              R0 - CONTAINS RETURN CODE FROM XTALK.                |   34
*|              R1 - CONTAINS REASON CODE FROM XTALK.                |   35
*|   ATTRIBUTES:                                                     |   36
*|      AMODE 31, RMODE ANY, REENTRANT                               |   37
*+------------------------------------------------------------------+   38
         MODULE CKXTALK,BASE-12,AMODE=31,RMODE=ANY,ENTRY=PCSTACK,     X   39
               TEXT='PC RTN TO BUILD ACCESS LIST ENTRY'                  40
*        *------------------------------------------*                    41
*        *    GET THE NAME OF TARGET ADDRESS       *                     42
*        *    SPACE FROM CALLER'S PARMLIST.        *                     43
*        *------------------------------------------*                    44
         LAM   A1,A1,=A(X'00000001')    SECONDARY ADDRESS SPACE          45
         SAC   512                      GO INTO ACCESS REGISTER MODE.    46
         MVC   XTPARMS(XMSESAL),0(R1)   MOVE PARMLIST FROM CALLER'S SPC  47
         LAE   R3,XTPARMS               ADDRESS OF PARMLIST FOR XTALK    48
         USING XMSESA,R3                MAP PARMLIST                     49
         SAC   0                        SET PRIMARY SPACE MODE           50
*        *------------------------------------------*                    51
*        *    GET THE NAME OF CALLER'S              *                     52
*        *    ADDRESS SPACE.                        *                     53
*        *------------------------------------------*                    54
         L     R5,CVTPTR                ADDRESS OF CVT                   55
         L     R5,CVTASVT-CVT(R5)       ADDRESS OF ASVT                  56
         ESAR  R6                       EXTRACT SECONDARY ASID           57
```

Figure 10.14 CKXTALK.

```
         SLL   R6,2                          MULTIPLY BY 4                        58
         L     R5,ASVTFRST-ASVT(R5,R6)  LOAD ADDRESS OF CALLER'S ASCB            59
         USING ASCB,R5                       MAP THE ASCB                        60
         L     R7,ASCBJBNS                   POINTER TO JOBNAME FIELD            61
         CLC   0(L'INIT,R7),INIT             IS IT AN INITIATOR ?                62
         BNE   NOTINIT                       NO; USE ASCBJBNS                    63
         L     R7,ASCBJBNI                   ADDRESS OF JOBNAME FOR INIT         64
         MVC   CALLER(L'CALLER),0(R7)  MOVE CALLER'S NAME TO WORKAREA            65
NOTINIT  DS    0H                                                                66
*        *----------------------------------------*                             67
*        *    SEARCH PERMIT TABLE                  *                             68
*        *----------------------------------------*                             69
*                                       .. ADDRESS OF PERMISSIONS TABLE          70
         L     R7,0(R4)                      .. IS FIRST LATENT PARM             71
TLOOP    DS    0H                                                                72
         CLC   0(L'CALLER,R7),ENDTAB    END OF PERMISSIONS TABLE ?               73
         BE    EXIT08                        YES; MATCH NOT FOUND                74
         CLC   0(L'CALLER,R7),CALLER    IS THIS THE RIGHT CALLER ?               75
         BNE   NEXTENT                       NO; CHECK NEXT ENTRY                76
         CLC   8(L'XMNAME,R7),XMNAME    IS THIS THE RIGHT TARGET ?               77
         BE    FOUND                         YES; CALL XTALK                     78
NEXTENT  LA    R7,16(R7)                     POINT AT NEXT ENTRY                 79
         B     TLOOP                         CHECK NEXT PERMIT TABLE ENTRY       80
*        *----------------------------------------*                             81
*        *    CALL XTALK                           *                            82
*        *----------------------------------------*                             83
FOUND    DS    0H                                                                84
         LA    R7,8                          LENGTH OF ADDRESS SP NAME           85
         ST    R7,XMNAMEL                    PUT IN XTALK PARMLIST               86
         LAE   R1,0(0,R3)                    PARMLIST ADDRESS                    87
         ICM   R15,15,=V(XTALK)              ADDRESS OF XTALK ROUTINE            88
         BZ    EXIT0C                        NOT FOUND; EXIT                     89
         O     R15,=A(X'80000000')           SET 31 BIT ENTRY                    90
         BASSM R14,R15                        INVOKE THE ROUTINE                 91
         LTR   R15,R15                       RC = 0 ?                            92
         BNZ   EXIT10                        NO; EXIT RC = 16                    93
         EREG  R1,R1                         EXTRACT FROM STACK PARMLIST         94
         LAM   A1,A1,=A(X'00000001')   LOAD R1 WITH SECONDARY ADD/SP            95
         SAC   512                           GO INTO ACCESS REGISTER MODE        96
         MVC   0(XMSESAL,R1),XTPARMS   MOVE PARMLIST TO CALLERS ADD.SP          97
         SAC   0                             GO INTO PRIMARY SPACE MODE          98
         B     EXIT00                                                            99
*---------------------------------------------------------------------*         100
*        EXIT ROUTINES                                                *          101
*---------------------------------------------------------------------*         102
EXIT00   DS    0H                            SUCCESSFUL COMPLETION              103
         LA    R15,X'00'                                                         104
         B     EXIT                                                             105
EXIT08   DS    0H                            PERMISSION NOT ALLOWED             106
         LA    R15,X'08'                                                         107
         B     EXIT                                                             108
EXIT0C   DS    0H                            XTALK ROUTINE NOT LINKED           109
         LA    15,X'0C'                                                          110
         B     EXIT                                                             111
EXIT10   DS    0H                            XTALK SERVICE FAILED               112
         PERCRC RC=X'10'                                                         113
         B     EXIT                                                             114
```

Figure 10.14   *(Continued)*

```
*----------------------------------------------------------------*  115
*          COMMON EXIT                                           *  116
*----------------------------------------------------------------*  117
EXIT      DS    0H                                                  118
          ENDMOD                                                    119
*----------------------------------------------------------------*  120
*          CONSTANTS                                             *  121
*----------------------------------------------------------------*  122
INIT      DC    CL8'INIT'           TO TEST INITIATOR ASCB NAMES   123
ENDTAB    DC    8X'FF'              END OF PERMISSIONS TABLE LITERAL 124
*----------------------------------------------------------------*  125
*          WORK AREA                                             *  126
*----------------------------------------------------------------*  127
WCKXTALK  DSECT                                                     128
XTPARMS   DS    0F,CL(XMSESAL)      XTALK PARMLIST                 129
CALLER    DS    CL8                 XMNAME ADDRESS SPACE           130
LCKXTALK  EQU   *-WCKXTALK                                         131
*----------------------------------------------------------------*  132
*          OTHER DSECTS                                          *  133
*----------------------------------------------------------------*  134
          XMSESA                    MAP XTALK PARMLIST             135
          PCSERV                    MAP PC SERVICES ANCHOR BLOCK   136
          CVT       DSECT=YES       MAP CVT                       137
          IHAASVT DSECT=YES         MAP ASVT                      138
          IHAASCB DSECT=YES         MAP ASCB                      139
          END                                                     140
```

Figure 10.14 *(Continued)*

```
BALR   12,0
BCTR   12,0
BCTR   12,0
USING CKXTALK,12
LAE    12,0(12,0)
```

The calling program [ESAMOVE(PC) in this case] has supplied the address of a parameter list in general register 1. This is the same parameter list that will be used to call XTALK. Since the parameter list resides in the virtual storage of the calling program, CKXTALK establishes addressability to the caller's address space and copies the parameter list to its own address space. When CKXTALK calls XTALK using the copy of the parameter list in its own address space, XTALK stores the ALET for the access list entry it builds into that parameter list. CKXTALK, therefore, will copy the modified parameter list back to the caller's address space before it returns control.

10.13.2 AR Mode in a PC Routine

Since SASN = OLD was an operand for the ETDEF that defined CKXTALK as a PC routine, the caller's address space is now the secondary address space. Loading an ALET of X'00000001' into access register 1 on line 45 to indicate the secondary address space, and going into access register mode with the SAC 512 on line 46, allows the MVC on line 47 to copy the parameter list from the secondary address space [ESA-MOVE(PC)] to the primary address space (CKXTALK). After lines 48 and 49 map the copied parameter list with the DSECT in the XMSESA macro on line 135, SAC 0 on line 50 resets the PSW to primary space mode.

10.13.3 Finding the Name of the Caller's Address Space

The name of the caller's address space is one of the arguments used in the search of the PCPERM table (lines 67 through 80) to see if CKXTALK is permitted to build an access list entry. Lines 51 through 66 retrieve the name from a field whose address is in the caller's Address Space Control Block (ASCB). Lines 54 and 55 locate the Address Space Vector Table (ASVT) by its address in the Communications Vector Table (CVT). The ASVT contains the address of the ASCB for every active address space in order by ASN. Line 57 issues ESAR to extract the SASN (i.e., the caller's PASN) from control register 3 into general register 6. Line 58 multiplies the SASN by 4 (the size of an ASVT entry). Line 59 adds the resulting displacement to the address of the first ASVT entry to locate the address of the ASCB corresponding to the SASN. Lines 61 through 66 test the two pointers to the ASCB address space name field and move the address space name to working storage.

10.13.4 Searching the PCPERM Table

Lines 67 through 81 search the PCPERM table in Fig. 10.15. The address of the PCPERM table was specified as the first latent parameter by the PARM1 = operand on the ETDEF macro in PCSET. Before transferring control to CKXTALK, the PC instruction loads the address of the two fullwords that contain the latent parameters into general register 4. Lines 70 and 71 load the first latent parameter (the address of the PCPERM table) into register 7. There are two arguments for the search:

■ The name of the caller's address space—saved in the work area by lines 55 through 66

■ The name of the address space for which an access list entry is to be built—from the input parameter list

If an entry in PCPERM is found matching the arguments, permission is granted to create an access list entry. Otherwise CKXTALK branches to line 106 and returns control to ESAMOVE(PC) with a return code of 8. Lines 81 through 93 call XTALK to build an access list entry on the DU-AL for the current TCB. Notice, in Fig. 10.8 how the PC routine CKXTALK executes under the same TCB as its caller ESAMOVE(PC).

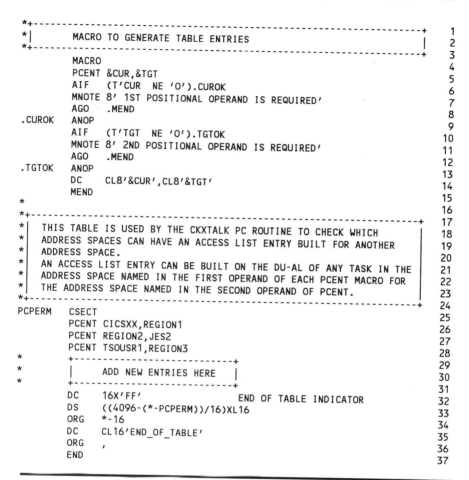

```
*+-------------------------------------------------------------------+     1
*|          MACRO TO GENERATE TABLE ENTRIES                          |     2
*+-------------------------------------------------------------------+     3
          MACRO                                                            4
          PCENT &CUR,&TGT                                                  5
          AIF    (T'CUR   NE  '0').CUROK                                   6
          MNOTE 8' 1ST POSITIONAL OPERAND IS REQUIRED'                    7
          AGO   .MEND                                                      8
.CUROK    ANOP                                                            9
          AIF    (T'TGT   NE  '0').TGTOK                                  10
          MNOTE 8' 2ND POSITIONAL OPERAND IS REQUIRED'                   11
          AGO   .MEND                                                     12
.TGTOK    ANOP                                                           13
          DC    CL8'&CUR',CL8'&TGT'                                      14
          MEND                                                           15
*                                                                        16
*+-------------------------------------------------------------------+    17
*|  THIS TABLE IS USED BY THE CKXTALK PC ROUTINE TO CHECK WHICH      |    18
*|  ADDRESS SPACES CAN HAVE AN ACCESS LIST ENTRY BUILT FOR ANOTHER   |    19
*|  ADDRESS SPACE.                                                   |    20
*|  AN ACCESS LIST ENTRY CAN BE BUILT ON THE DU-AL OF ANY TASK IN THE|    21
*|  ADDRESS SPACE NAMED IN THE FIRST OPERAND OF EACH PCENT MACRO FOR |    22
*|  THE ADDRESS SPACE NAMED IN THE SECOND OPERAND OF PCENT.          |    23
*+-------------------------------------------------------------------+    24
PCPERM    CSECT                                                           25
          PCENT CICSXX,REGION1                                            26
          PCENT REGION2,JES2                                              27
          PCENT TSOUSR1,REGION3                                           28
*         +---------------------------+                                   29
*         |     ADD NEW ENTRIES HERE  |                                   30
*         +---------------------------+                                   31
          DC    16X'FF'              END OF TABLE INDICATOR               32
          DS    ((4096-(*-PCPERM))/16)XL16                               33
          ORG   *-16                                                      34
          DC    CL16'END_OF_TABLE'                                       35
          ORG   ,                                                         36
          END                                                            37
```

Figure 10.15 The PCPERM Table.

XTALK stores the ALET for the new access list entry into the parameter list, so lines 95 through 98 copy the parameter list back to the caller's address space (see lines 45 through 50).

The expansion of the ENDMOD macro on line 119 issues the PR instruction, which pops the linkage stack. This restores ESAMOVE(PC)'s operating environment at the time it issued the PC instruction.

10.14 PC ROUTINES IN AN XA ENVIRONMENT

Since there is no linkage stack in 370/XA, only *basic* PC routines are available. Basic PC routines differ from stacking PC routines in four respects:

1. The parameters for ETDEF that create the fields labeled "ESA only" in the ETE in Fig. 10.4 are not available.

2. The PC instruction stores the address portion of the PSW into general register 14 and the caller's PKM and PASN from control register 3 into general register 3 before transferring control to a basic PC routine.

3. The calling program and the PC routine itself must preserve the calling environment in software rather than on the linkage stack.

   The *calling program* preserves the SASN and the contents of the general registers (there are no access registers in XA) in a save area it provides before issuing the PC instruction. The calling program restores these values after the PC routine returns control.

   When it receives control, the *PC routine* issues the PCLINK STACK macro to save register values on a software stack anchored in the ASCB. PCLINK STACK saves general registers 13 through 4:

   - Register 13 contains the virtual address of the caller's save area.
   - Register 14 contains the return address in the calling program.
   - Registers 15, 0, 1, and 2 contain values supplied by the calling program including parameters for the PC routine.
   - Register 3 contains the caller's PKM and PASN.
   - Register 4 contains the latent parameter list address.

   The PC routine issues PCLINK UNSTACK to restore these registers before returning control to its caller.

4. The PC routine uses the PT (Program Transfer) instruction rather than the PR instruction to return control to its caller.

   Unlike PR, which does no authority checking, PT uses the AX in control register 4 to index into the Authority Table of the caller's address space. If the PT bit in the Authority Table Entry is 1, PT loads the ASN and PKM from its second operand into control register 3 and the virtual address from its first operand into the address portion of the PSW. If the PT bit in the Authority Table entry is 0, PT fails with a program check 0024.

The underlined instructions in Fig. 10.16 illustrate how the caller of a basic PC routine and the PC routine itself save and restore the caller's environment. Note that if the PC routine in Fig. 10.16 wishes to call another PC routine, it needs to acquire an area of virtual storage it can use as a register save area and must issue instructions similar to those in the calling program to save and restore the SASN and general registers.

```
                         CALLER OF PC ROUTINE

          STM   14,12,12(13)          SAVE REGISTERS                68
          ESAR  2                     ..STORE THE SASN              69
          ST    2,16(13)              ..IN THE R15 SLOT IN SAVEAREA 70
          L     3,CVTPTR              ADDRESS OF CVT                71
          L     8,CVTQLPAQ-CVT(3)     HEAD OF LPAQ                  72
          L     15,CVTQCDSR-CVT(3)    ADDRESS OF THE LPAQ SCAN RTN  73
          BALR  14,15                 INVOKE LPAQ SCAN ROUTINE      74
          B     CP100025              CDE FOUND                     75
          LA    15,8                  CDE NOT FOUND; SET RC=8       76
          B     CP400025              BRANCH TO POP THE STACK       77
CP100025  L     11,CDENTPT-CDENTRY(11) POINTER TO PC # TABLE IN CDE 78
          L     14,PCSRTN1-PCSERV(11) LOAD PC NUMBER FOR THIS ROUTINE 79
          LA    1,PARMLIST            PARMLIST ADDRESS TO REGISTER 1 80
          B     CP300025                                            81
CP200025  DC    CL8'PCTBL01'          NAME OF CDE THAT ANCHORS PCTBL 82
CP300025  PC    0(14)                 INVOKE THE PC ROUTINE         83
CP400025  L     2,16(13)              ..RESET THE SASN TO THE       84
          SSAR  2                     ..VALUE BEFORE PC WAS ISSUED  85
          LM    2,12,28(13)           ..RESTORE ALL GENERAL REGS    86
          L     14,12(13)             ..EXCEPT 0,1 AND 15           87


                            PC ROUTINE

PCRTN     CSECT                                                     1
          BALR  6,0                   LOAD BASE REGISER             2
          USING PCRTN,6               SET UP ADDRESSING             3
          PCLINK STACK,SAVE=NO        SAVE REGS 13 THRU 4           4
          ..     ..                   ..
          PCLINK UNSTACK,SAVE=NO      RESTORE REGS 13 THRU 4        100
          PT    3,14                  RETURN TO CALLER              101
```

Figure 10.16 Calling a basic PC routine.

To acquire the virtual storage for a register save area, the PC routine must use the BRANCH = YES operand on GETMAIN since it cannot use the SVC expansion in a PC routine.

11

Dataspaces
and Hiperspaces

11.1 DATASPACES, HIPERSPACES, AND ADDRESS SPACES

In versions of MVS before ESA, all virtual storage was defined within the context of an address space. MVS/ESA introduced two new types of virtual storage spaces, data-only spaces (dataspaces) and high-performance spaces (hiperspaces). Dataspaces and hiperspaces have two principal uses:

- Extending *common* virtual storage: Dataspaces and hiperspaces can provide commonly addressable storage without using the common areas in address spaces. The common areas of virtual storage, while greatly increased in size in MVS/XA, are finite resources. As applications, particularly databases, increase their use of common storage, they produce corresponding reductions in the amount of private storage available to individual applications.

  Since dataspaces and hiperspaces can be made selectively addressable to some applications and not to others and are not automatically addressable by all applications as with common storage, they provide a method for isolating and protecting data.

- There is a good deal of MVS overhead in creating and maintaining an address space. Dataspaces and hiperspaces provide addressable virtual storage that, because it is not dispatched and cannot contain dispatch-able units of work, requires very little support from MVS.

Dataspaces are true virtual storage spaces. They are backed by real and auxiliary storage (expanded storage or DASD) and are byte-addressable. When a dataspace page is not in real storage, RSM and ASM will page it in.

Hiperspaces are not complete virtual storage spaces. They are backed *only* by auxiliary storage. Hiperspaces can be addressed only by 4K block. Hiperspace pages must be brought into real storage by issuing the HSPSERV macro before the data they contain can be accessed.

Figure 11.1 summarizes the differences between the three types of virtual storage spaces: address spaces, dataspaces, and hiperspaces.

11.1.1 STOKENs

In versions of 370 architecture before ESA, address spaces were identi-fied by address space numbers. Loading an ASN into control register 3 to make it the SASN or into control register 4 to make it the PASN were the only ways to get addressability to an address space. Changing the ASN in one of these control registers caused ASN Translation to locate the ASN Second Table Entry (ASTE) that contained the STD for the address space.

In MVS/ESA, every address space, dataspace and hiperspace is de-scribed by an ASTE. But the ASTEs for dataspaces and hiperspaces do not reside in ASN Second Tables. ASTEs, and the virtual storage spaces they define, are now identified by unique 8 byte STOKENs. While address spaces are identified by ASNs as well as STOKENs, dataspaces and hiperspaces are identified only by STOKENs.

Unlike ASN, which is a structure for 370 architecture, an STOKEN exists only in MVS software. The STOKEN value is specified when in-voking various MVS/ESA services, such as ALESERV, DSPSERV, HSPSERV, and TCBTOKEN to direct these services to a particular virtual storage space. The services themselves, rather than 370 architecture ASN Translation, locate the ASTE that describes the vir-tual storage. When an address space, dataspace, or hiperspace termin-ates, its STOKEN is not reused until MVS is initialized again. ASNs, B, contrast are reused within an IPL.

11.1.2 Task Ownership of Dataspaces and Hiperspaces

Every dataspace or hiperspace is associated with a particular task. When the address space in which the TCB for that task resides is swapped in,

Address Space	Dataspace	Hiperspace
Has an STOKEN; has an ASTE.	Has an STOKEN; has an ASTE.	Has an STOKEN; has an ASTE.
Has an Address Space Number (ASN).	Does not have an ASN.	Does not have an ASN.
ASTE is in an ASN Second Table.	ASTE is not in an ASN Second Table.	ASTE is not in an ASN Second Table.
Can be Primary, Secondary or Home Space.	Cannnot be Primary, Secondary or Home Space.	Cannnot be Primary, Secondary or Home Space.
Is addressable in Primary, Secondary, or Access Register Modes.	Is only addressable in Access Register Mode.	Is not byte addres-sable. Accessed with the HPSERV macro.
Is backed by real and auxiliary storage; experiences paging.	Is backed by real and auxiliary storage; experiences paging.	Is only backed by auxiliary storage.
PSW fetches and executes instructions from an address space.	PSW does not fetch or execute instructions from a dataspace.	PSW does not fetch or execute instructions from a hiperspace.
MVS maintains ASCB and related structures.	Does not have an ASCB.	Does not have an ASCB.
Contains MVS Control blocks in LSQA (TCBs, CDEs, etc.)	Does not contain MVS Control Blocks.	Does not contain MVS Control Blocks.
Contains Common and Private areas.	Contains only Private area.	Does not have virtual storage.
Created by ASCRE macro or equivalent.	Created by DSPSERV macro.	Created by DSPSERV macro.

Figure 11.1 Dataspaces, hiperspaces and address spaces.

the dataspace or hiperspace is addressable. When the task that owns a dataspace or hiperspace terminates, the dataspace or hiperspace is destroyed. A dataspace or hiperspace is owned by either:

- The TCB under which the program that issued DSPSERV was executing. This is the default if the TTOKEN= operand is not used.

- By a TCB to which the dataspace was assigned when it was created.

The TTOKEN= operand on the DSPSERV macro assigns ownership of a dataspace or hiperspace to a TCB. TTOKENs identify TCBs in much the same way STOKENs identify virtual storage spaces. In MVS/ESA, each TCB is assigned a unique TTOKEN when it is built. TTOKENs are not reused within an IPL. The TCBTOKEN macro can extract a TCB's TTOKEN for use by the DSPSERV TTOKEN= operand.

SRBs can create dataspaces but cannot own them. If an SRB creates a dataspace, it assigns ownership to a TCB in the address space where it is executing with the TTOKEN= operand.

11.1.3 Accessing Data in a Dataspace

Dataspaces can be accessed only in AR addressing mode. Addressability to a dataspace is established by issuing ALESERV, using the STOKEN returned by DSPSERV CREATE. After the ALET returned by ALESERV is loaded into an access register and SAC 512 sets the addressing mode bits in the PSW, the bytes in a dataspace can be addressed by their virtual addresses. The virtual addresses in a dataspace begin at the address returned by the ORIGIN= parameter on DSPSERV and end at the ORIGIN address plus the size of the dataspace specified in the DSPSERV BLOCKS= parameter.

11.2 Global Resource Serialization (GRS)

GRS is the MVS component that serializes resources not controlled by MVS locks (see Chap. 8). GRS, like the MVS Lock Manager, does not deal with the resources themselves, but with tokens that represent the resources. All programs using a resource must refer to that resource by its token name if it wants GRS to serialize its use. If any program violates the honor system and uses a resource without serializing it by its token, GRS is unable to regulate the resource.

Programs request GRS serialization with the ENQ macro. The first two positional operands of ENQ (the QNAME and RNAME) constitute the token that GRS recognizes. If a second program issues an ENQ with the same token, GRS will put that program's TCB into WAIT state until the first program releases the ENQ by issuing the DEQ macro.

Many MVS components define QNAMEs and RNAMEs that are respected by other MVS components. SYSDSN, for example, is the QNAME for data sets (the RNAME is the data set name). Whenever a program allocates a data set with DISP = OLD, Allocation issues ENQ with the QNAME "SYSDSN" to request exclusive use of that data set. *MVS Debugging Handbook Volume 1* lists all the system-defined QNAMES and RNAMES.

Whenever an application program wants to serialize on a resource for which MVS has predefined a QNAME and/or an RNAME, the program should use the same tokens. If an application wants to serialize the use of a resource for which there is no MVS-defined token, it can create its own QNAME and RNAME. GRS will serialize the use of the resource represented by the QNAME/RNAME as long as all the programs in the application use the same QNAME/RNAME combination to refer to the resource.

11.2.1 GRS Control Structures

Figure 11.2 illustrates the control structures that GRS uses to serialize resources. When an ENQ is first issued for a resource, GRS builds a Queue Control Block (QCB) that contains the QNAME/RNAME combination and adds it to the QCB queue anchored in the GRS Vector Table (GVT). GRS also builds a Queue Element (QEL) on a queue anchored in that QCB that points to the requestor TCB. GRS adds a QEL for each subsequent outstanding request. Notice that the task in address space 1 has issued an exclusive ENQ, represented by a QEL, for a resource named in a QCB. GRS has placed the task in address space 2 in WAIT state because it has issued ENQ for the same resource and its QEL is behind the first task's QEL.

The task in address space 1 releases its ENQ by naming the same QNAME/RNAME on the DEQ macro. If the task terminates while holding the ENQ, RTM2, as part of task cleanup, issues DEQ to release the resource. DEQ causes GRS to dequeue the task's QEL and to take the task represented by the next QEL on the QCB queue out of WAIT state.

11.2.2 The SCOPE of an ENQ

The last positional parameter of the ENQ macro describes the scope of the ENQ:

- STEP serializes resources among tasks within an address space. A scope of STEP does not prevent a task in another address space from obtaining an ENQ with the same QNAME and RNAME.
- SYSTEM serializes the resource among all tasks in all address spaces in the system but does not serialize a resource if it is shared among MVS systems.

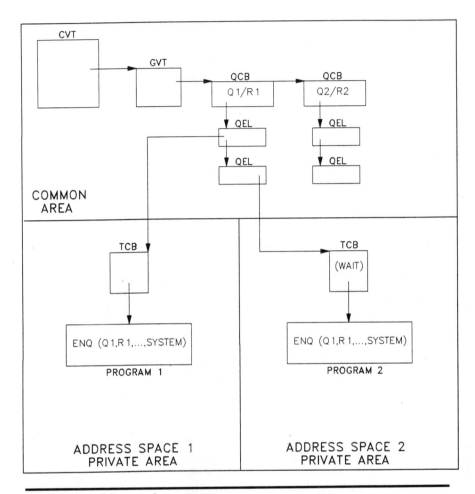

Figure 11.2 GRS control structures.

- SYSTEMS serializes the resource among all tasks in all MVS systems that can access the resource. For GRS to regulate ENQs with the scope of SYSTEMS, a global resource serialization facility, such as GRS using CTCs or a vendor product such as MSX, must be active.

ENQs with a scope of SYSTEMS are most frequently used by programs that access data sets on DASD shared among MVS systems. If a global serialization facility is not active, a program that accesses data on a shared DASD volume can issue the RESERVE macro to gain exclusive control of the entire DASD volume. RESERVE causes the DASD controller hardware to lock out I/Os from other systems to any data set on the volume and can result in long access delays for the locked-out systems.

The GRSRNLxx member of SYS1.PARMLIB contains three lists. When a QNAME or QNAME/RNAME combination is included in one of the lists, GRS may change the scope of an ENQ using that QNAME or QNAME/RNAME. By including a resource name in one of the lists, programs do not have to be modified when the system configuration changes.

- *SYSTEM Inclusion List:* When a resource name is included in this list, GRS will change a SYSTEM ENQ for that resource to a SYSTEMS ENQ. Programs written to serialize resources on single MVS systems can be made to serialize the resource across multiple systems by including the resource name in the SYSTEM Inclusion List on each system.

- *SYSTEMS Exclusion List:* When a resource name is included in this list, GRS will change a SYSTEMS ENQ for the resource to a SYSTEM ENQ. You might add a resource name to this list if two MVS systems use the same QNAME/RNAME combination to represent different resources.

- *RESERVE Conversion List:* GRS will change any RESERVE issued for a resource to an ENQ if its name is included in this list. Resource names are most typically added to this list when a multisystem serialization facility is installed and there is no longer a need to incur the delays caused by RESERVE.

11.3 PROGRAMS IN THIS CHAPTER

The programs in this chapter illustrate how a task in one address space can create dataspaces and how tasks in other address spaces can move data into and out of those dataspaces.

DSPACE, which executes as a started task, creates SCOPE = ALL dataspaces in response to console commands and builds control blocks in common storage to manage the dataspaces.

DSPFIND locates the control block for one of the dataspaces built by DSPACE and issues ALESERV to establish AR mode communication with the dataspace.

DSPUT writes data to dataspaces created by DSPACE. DSPUT calls DSPFIND to establish addressability to the dataspaces.

11.4 DSPACE WALKTHROUGH

DSPACE, illustrated in Fig. 11.3, begins execution when the operator issues a START DSPACE command at the MVS console. In response to operator MODIFY commands, DSPACE creates or deletes dataspaces. Whenever DSPACE creates a dataspace, it builds in common storage its

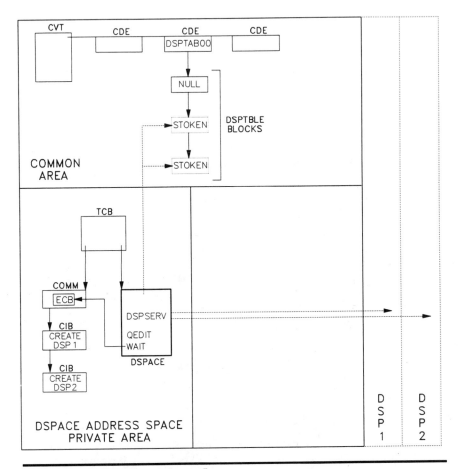

Figure 11.3   DSPACE—program flow.

own control block, DSPTBLE, which contains the STOKEN for that dataspace. Programs in other address spaces can locate the DSPTBLE control block for a dataspace and use the STOKEN to establish access register mode communication with that dataspace.

Immediately after DSPACE (Fig. 11.4) has saved the caller's registers and set up a reentrant environment with the MODULE macro, line 46 issues ENQ to obtain exclusive control of the DSPTBLE chain. This chain is represented by the combination of the major and minor names defined on lines 379 and 380. This major name/minor name combination will be used by any program that attempts to modify the DSPTBLE chain. DSPACE obtains exclusive control of the chain since it is quite possible for another dataspace-owning region to put its DSPTBLE blocks on the same chain as DSPACE.

```
*+---------------------------------------------------------------------+   1
*| FUNCTION:                                                           |   2
*|   DSPACE EXECUTES AS A STARTED TASK.  IN RESPONSE TO CONSOLE         |   3
*|   COMMANDS, DSPACE WILL CREATE OR DELETE SCOPE=ALL DATASPACES.       |   4
*|   DSPACE INITIALIZES AND MAINTAINS A QUEUE OF CONTROL BLOCKS THAT    |   5
*|   DESCRIBE EACH DATASPACE IT HAS CREATED.  ANY PROGRAM THAT WISHES   |   6
*|   TO ACCESS ANY OF THE DATASPACES (SUCH AS DSPUT) CAN LOCATE ITS     |   7
*|   CONTROL BLOCK AND USE ITS CONTENTS TO ESTABLISH ACCESS REGISTER    |   8
*|   MODE COMMUNICATION WITH THE DATASPACE.                             |   9
*| INPUTS:                                                             |  10
*|   COMMANDS FROM THE MVS CONSOLE:                                     |  11
*|     F DSPACE,CREATE(NNNNNNNN) - CREATES DATASPACE NNNNNNNN           |  12
*|     F DSPACE,DELETE(NNNNNNNN) - DELETES DATASPACE NNNNNNNN           |  13
*|     P DSPACE                  - STOPS DSPACE                         |  14
*| OUTPUTS:                                                            |  15
*|   R15 - RETURN CODE                                                 |  16
*|         0 - DSPACE SUCCESSFULLY INITIALIZED                         |  17
*|         8 - INITIALIZATION FAILED                                   |  18
*|   CONSOLE MESSAGES DURING INITIALIZAION, SHUTDOWN, AND IN           |  19
*|   RESPONSE TO MODIFY COMMANDS.                                      |  20
*| MAINLINE LOGIC:                                                     |  21
*|   1) PREPARE TO ACCEPT COMMANDS FROM THE MVS CONSOLE.               |  22
*|   2) CALL INITRTN SUBROUTINE TO ANCHOR DATASPACE CONTROL BLOCK      |  23
*|      CHAIN ON AN LPAQ CDE.                                          |  24
*|   3) DEQUEUE THE "START" CIB AND WAIT FOR CONSOLE COMMANDS.         |  25
*|   4) WHEN A CONSOLE COMMAND POSTS THE COMMAREA ECB, GO TO THE       |  26
*|      TOP OF THE COMMAND PROCESSING LOOP AND DETERMINE WHETHER       |  27
*|      THE COMMAND IS "STOP" OR "MODIFY".                            |  28
*|      A) IF THE COMMAND IS "STOP", EXIT.                            |  29
*|      B) IF THE COMMAND IS "MODIFY" CALL THE PARSRTN SUBROUTINE      |  30
*|         PARSE THE COMMAND TEXT.                                    |  31
*|         1) IF THE COMMAND IS "CREATE",CALL THE CREATRN SUBROUTINE   |  32
*|            TO CREATE A DATASPACE AND ITS CONTROL BLOCK.            |  33
*|         2) IF THE COMMAND IS "DELETE",CALL THE DELERTN SUBROUTINE  |  34
*|            TO DELETE THE DATASPACE AND ITS CONTROL BLOCK.          |  35
*|   5) WAIT FOR THE NEXT CONSOLE COMMAND.                            |  36
*| ATTRIBUTES:                                                         |  37
*|   AMODE 31, RMODE ANY, REENTRANT, REQUIRES APF AUTHORIZATION        |  38
*+---------------------------------------------------------------------+  39
          MODULE DSPACE,BASE=12,LOC=BELOW,AMODE=31,RMODE=ANY,       X  40
                TEXT='SETUP DATA SPACES ADDRESS SPACE'                 41
*         *-------------------------------------*                     42
*         *    PREPARE MVS CONSOLE INTERFACE    *                     43
*         *-------------------------------------*                     44
*                             ENQUEUE ON CONTROL BLOCK CHAIN           45
          ENQ   (QNAME,DSPTNAME,E,L'DSPTNAME,SYSTEM)                   46
          LA    R1,EXTLIST         PARMLIST FOR EXTRACT                47
          LA    R3,QEDANSW         ANSWER AREA FOR EXTRACT             48
*                                  GET ADDRESS COMMUNICATION AREA      49
          EXTRACT (R3),'S',FIELDS=(COMM),MF=(E,(1))                    50
          L     R3,QEDANSW         A(COMMUNICATIONS AREA) => R3        51
          USING COMLIST,R3         MAP COMMUNICATIONS AREA             52
          L     R4,COMCIBPT        A(COMMAND INPUT BUFFER)             53
          USING CIB,R4             MAP CIB                             54
          QEDIT ORIGIN=COMCIBPT,CIBCTR=4 SET LIMIT ON QUEUED COMMANDS  55
          USING DSPTBLE,R5         MAP DSPTBLE BLOCK                   56
```

Figure 11.4 DSPACE.

```
*          *------------------------------------------*          57
*          *      CALL INITIALIZATION ROUTINE      *          58
*          *------------------------------------------*          59
           LA      R15,INITRTN          ..INVOKE                 60
           BAKR    0,R15                ..INITIALIZATION ROUTINE 61
           LTR     R15,R15              RC = 0 ?                 62
           BZ      CONT1                YES; CONTINUE            63
           WTO     'DSPACE: INITIALIZATION FAILED'              64
           B       EXIT08               NO; EXIT                 65
CONT1      DS      0H                                            66
           LA      R1,TRANSECB          ..MAKE THIS              67
           SYSEVENT TRANSWAP            ..ADDRESS SPACE NON-SWAPABLE 68
           B       WAIT                 WAIT FOR CONSOLE COMMANDS 69
*          *------------------------------------------*          70
*          *      TOP OF COMMAND PROCESSING LOOP   *          71
*          *------------------------------------------*          72
CKCOM      DS      0H                   TOP OF COMMAND PROCESSING LOOP 73
           L       R4,COMCIBPT          ADDRESS OF COMMAND INPUT BUFR 74
           CLI     CIBVERB,CIBSTOP      IS THE COMMAND "STOP" ?  75
           BNE     NOTSTOP              NO; CHECK IF "MODIFY"    76
*          *------------------------------------------*          77
*          *      PROCESS "STOP" COMMAND           *          78
*          *------------------------------------------*          79
           QEDIT   ORIGIN=COMCIBPT,BLOCK=(R4)   FREE THE CIB    80
           B       EXIT00               EXIT WITH RC=0          81
NOTSTOP    DS      0H                                            82
           CLI     CIBVERB,CIBMODFY     IS THE COMMAND "MODIFY" ? 83
           BE      MODIFY               YES; PROCESS "MODIFY" COMMAND 84
           WTO     'DSPACE: INVALID COMMAND ISSUED'             85
           B       WAIT                 WAIT FOR NEXT COMMAND   86
MODIFY     DS      0H                                            87
*          *------------------------------------------*          88
*          *      PROCESS "MODIFY" COMMAND         *          89
*          *------------------------------------------*          90
           LA      R15,PARSRTN          ..INVOKE                 91
           BAKR    0,R15                ..COMMAND PARSE ROUTINE  92
*                                       ENQUEUE ON CONTROL BLOCK CHAIN 93
           ENQ     (QNAME,DSPTNAME,E,L'DSPTNAME,SYSTEM)         94
           CLC     PARSAREA(L'COMM1),COMM1 IS THE COMMAND "CREATE" ? 95
           BNE     NCOMM1               NO; CHECK NEXT COMMAND  96
           LA      R15,CREATRN          ..INVOKE                 97
           BAKR    0,R15                ..DATASPACE CREATE ROUTINE 98
           B       WAIT                 WAIT FOR NEXT COMMAND   99
NCOMM1     DS      0H                                            100
           CLC     PARSAREA(L'COMM2),COMM2 IS THE COMMAND "DELETE" ? 101
           BNE     NCOMM2               NO; CHECK NEXT COMMAND  102
           LA      R15,DELERTN          ..INVOKE                 103
           BAKR    0,R15                ..DATASPACE DELETE ROUTINE 104
           B       WAIT                 WAIT FOR NEXT COMMAND   105
NCOMM2     DS      0H                                            106
*          *------------------------------------------*          107
*          *      UNKNOWN COMMAND                  *          108
*          *------------------------------------------*          109
           WTO     'DSPACE: UNKNOWN OPERAND'                    110
           B       WAIT                 WAIT FOR NEXT COMMAND   111
WAIT       DS      0H                                            112
*                                       DEQUEUE CONTROL BLOCK CHAIN 113
```

Figure 11.4 *(Continued)*

```
          DEQ   (QNAME,DSPTNAME,L'DSPTNAME,SYSTEM),RET=HAVE            114
          QEDIT ORIGIN=COMCIBPT,BLOCK=(R4)    FREE THE PROCESSED CIB   115
          L     R6,COMECBPT           .. WAIT ON ECB                   116
          WAIT  ECB=(6)               .. IN COMM AREA                  117
          B     CKCOM                 BOTTOM OF COMMAND LOOP           118
*-----------------------------------------------------------------*   119
*         INITIALIZATION ROUTINE                                  *   120
*         1)  CALL PGMNAME TO GET CURRENT ADDRESS SPACE NAME      *   121
*         2)  ISSUE ALESERV EXTRACTH TO GET STOKEN FOR CURRENT SPACE * 122
*         3)  CALL ANCHOR TO GET LPAQ CDE TO ANCHOR CONTROL BLOCKS *  123
*         4)  INITIALIZE THE FIRST CONTROL BLOCK ON THE CHAIN     *   124
*-----------------------------------------------------------------*   125
INITRTN   DS    0H                                                     126
          LA    R1,PPGPARM            PARMLIST FOR PGMNAME SERVICE     127
          ICM   R15,B'1111',=V(PGMNAME) A(PGNMNAM SERVICE)             128
          BNZ   CONTI0                ^=0; MODULE IS LINK-EDITED       129
          LA    R15,8                 SET BAD RETURN CODE              130
          B     INITRTNE              EXIT THIS SUBROUTINE             131
CONTI0    DS    0H                                                     132
          O     R15,=A(X'80000000')   TURN ON HIGH ORDER BIT          133
          BASSM R14,R15               INVOKE SERVICE                   134
*                                     SAVE HOME ADDRESS SPACE NAME     135
          MVC   HOMENAME(L'HOMENAME),PPGNAME-PPGNM(R1)                 136
          ALESERV EXTRACTH,           GET STOKEN FOR THIS ADDRESS SPC X 137
                STOKEN=HOMETOKN,      RETURN STOKEN TO HOMETOKN      X 138
                MF=(E,ALELIST)                                         139
          LTR   R15,R15               RC = 0?                          140
          BZ    CONTI1                YES; CONTINUE                    141
          WTO   'DSPACE: ALESERV EXTRACT FAILED'                       142
          B     INITRTNE              EXIT THIS SUBROUTINE             143
CONTI1    DS    0H                                                     144
          LA    R1,ANKPARMS           PARMLIST FOR ANCHOR SERVICE      145
          USING ANKPRM,R1             MAP PARMLIST                     146
          LA    R15,LDSPTABE          ..LENGTH OF DSPTBLE              147
          ST    R15,ANKLEN            ..TO PARMLIST                    148
          MVI   ANKSP,ANKPOOL         SET SUBPOOL IN PARMLIST          149
          MVC   ANKNAME(8),DSPTNAME   MODULE NAME TO PARMLIST          150
          MVC   ANKEYE(L'ANKEYE),EYEID EYECATCHER TO PARMLIST          151
          XC    ANKEP(L'ANKEP),ANKEP  INITIALIZE ENTRYPOINT TO X'00'   152
          ICM   R15,B'1111',=V(ANCHOR) A(ANCHOR SERVICE)               153
          BNZ   CONTI2                                                 154
          WTO   'DSPACE: ANCHOR NOT LINKED'                            155
          LA    R15,8                 SET BAD RETURN CODE              156
          B     INITRTNE              EXIT THIS SUBROUTINE             157
CONTI2    DS    0H                                                     158
          O     R15,=A(X'80000000')   TURN ON HIGH ORDER BIT          159
          BASSM R14,R15               INVOKE SERVICE                   160
          C     R15,=F'4'             RC LE 4?                         161
          BNH   CONTI3                YES; CONTINUE                    162
          WTO   'DSPACE: ANCHOR FAILED'                                163
          B     INITRTNE              EXIT THIS SUBROUTINE             164
CONTI3    DS    0H                                                     165
          LA    R5,ANKPARMS           PARMLIST FOR ANCHOR SERVICE      166
          L     R5,ANKEP-ANKPRM(R5)   LOAD ADDRESS OF FIRST TBLENTRY   167
          ST    R5,ENTRY1             SAVE A(FIRST ENTRY)              168
*                                     TABLE INITIALIZED ?              169
          CLC   DSP_XNAME(L'DSP_XNAME),=C'@@NULL@@'                    170
```

Figure 11.4 *(Continued)*

```
            BE      ALLSET                    YES; BYPASS INITIALIZATION       171
*                                             SET NEXT ENTRY FIELD TO X'00'    172
            XC      DSP_NEXT_ENTRY(L'DSP_NEXT_ENTRY),DSP_NEXT_ENTRY            173
*                                             SET NAME FIELD TO DUMMY          174
            MVC     DSP_XNAME(L'DSP_XNAME),=C'@@NULL@@'                        175
*                                             SET NAME FIELD TO DUMMY          176
            MVC     DSP_XOUTNAME(L'DSP_XOUTNAME),=C'@@NULL@@'                  177
ALLSET      DS      0H                                                        178
            WTO     'DSPACE: INITIALIZED '  ISSUE INITIALIZED MESSAGE         179
INITRTNE    DS      0H                                                        180
            PR                                POP STACK AND RETURN            181
*----------------------------------------------------------------------*     182
*           COMMAND PARSE ROUTINE                                     *       183
*----------------------------------------------------------------------*     184
PARSRTN     DS      0H                                                        185
            MVI     OPERAND,X'40'                     ..SET OPERAND           186
            MVC     OPERAND+1(L'OPERAND-1),OPERAND    ..AREA TO SPACES        187
            MVI     PARSAREA,X'40'                    ..SET COMMAND PARSE      188
            MVC     PARSAREA+1(L'PARSAREA-1),PARSAREA ..AREA TO SPACES        189
            LH      R6,CIBDATLN        LENGTH OF CIBDATA                      190
            BCTR    R6,0               LESS 1 FOR EXECUTE                     191
            EX      R6,MVCIBDAT        MOVE COMMAND TO PARSE AREA             192
            B       AFT1                                                      193
MVCIBDAT    MVC     PARSAREA(0),CIBDATA *** EXECUTE ONLY ***                  194
AFT1        DS      0H                                                        195
            LA      R7,PARSAREA+7      POINT AT OPERAND                       196
            S       R6,=F'7'           DECREMENT LENGTH                       197
            BNH     PARSRTNE           LE 0; EXIT                             198
            EX      R6,TRTIBDAT        TEST FOR DELIMETER                     199
            B       AFT2                                                      200
TRTIBDAT    TRT     0(0,R7),CMDDLM     *** EXECUTE ONLY ***                   201
AFT2        DS      0H                                                        202
            LR      R9,R1              A(DELIMETER)                           203
            SR      R9,R7              LENGTH OF OPERAND                      204
            BCTR    R9,0               DECREMENT FOR EXECUTE                  205
            EX      R9,MVCOBDAT        MOVE OPERAND                           206
            B       AFT3                                                      207
MVCOBDAT    MVC     OPERAND(0),0(R7)   *** EXECUTE ONLY ***                   208
AFT3        DS      0H                                                        209
PARSRTNE    DS      0H                                                        210
            PR                                POP STACK AND RETURN           211
*           *----------------------------------------*                       212
*           *     TABLE OF DELIMETERS USED           *                       213
*           *     TO PARSE COMMANDS                  *                       214
*           *----------------------------------------*                       215
CMDDLM      DC      XL256'00'                                                 216
            ORG     CMDDLM+X'40'                                              217
            DC      X'40'                                                     218
            ORG     CMDDLM+C','                                               219
            DC      C','                                                      220
            ORG     CMDDLM+C'('                                               221
            DC      C'('                                                      222
            ORG     CMDDLM+C')'                                               223
            DC      C')'                                                      224
            ORG                                                               225
```

Figure 11.4 *(Continued)*

```
*----------------------------------------------------------------------*   226
*          DATASPACE CREATE ROUTINE                                    *   227
*          1)   ISSUE DSPSERV CREATE TO BUILD DATASPACE                *   228
*          2)   FIND END OF DSPTBLE CHAIN, BUILD DSPTBLE BLOCK FOR     *   229
*               NEW DATASPACE AND ADD THE BLOCK TO THE DSPTBLE CHAIN   *   230
*----------------------------------------------------------------------*   231
CREATRN   DS    0H                                                        232
          MODESET MODE=SUP,           ..GET A SUPERVISOR STATE         X 233
                  KEY=ZERO            ..ZERO KEY PSW                      234
*                                                                         235
          DSPSERV CREATE,             CREATE A DATASPACE               X 236
                  SCOPE=ALL,          ACCESS PERMITTED TO ALL          X 237
                  NAME=OPERAND,       NAME OF DATASPACE FROM COMMAND   X 238
                  BLOCKS=DSPBLOCK,    SIZE OF THE DATASPACE            X 239
                  KEY=KEY,            DATASPACE STORAGE KEY            X 240
                  STOKEN=DSPTOKEN,    STOKEN OF NEW DATASPACE          X 241
                  ORIGIN=DSPORG,      FIRST VIRTUAL ADDR IN DATASPACE X 242
                  MF=(E,DSPLIST,COMPLETE)                                 243
          LTR   R15,R15               RETURN CODE = 0 ?                  244
          BZ    CONTC1                YES; CONTINUE                      245
          WTO   'DSPACE: DPSERV CREATE FAILED'                          246
          B     CREATRNE              EXIT THIS ROUTINE                  247
CONTC1    DS    0H                                                        248
*         *----------------------------------------*                      249
*         *    BUILD DSPTBLE CONTROL BLOCK         *                      250
*         *    FOR DATASPACE AND CHAIN IT ON       *                      251
*         *----------------------------------------*                      252
          L     R5,ENTRY1             A(FIRST DSPTBLE CONTROL BLOCK)     253
CKNXTE    DS    0H                                                        254
*                                     WAS THIS CREATED BY ADDRESS        255
*                                     SPACE WITH THIS NAME               256
          CLC   DSP_OWNER_NAME(L'DSP_OWNER_NAME),HOMENAME                257
          BNE   CKNXT                 NO; CHECK THE NEXT ENTRY           258
*                                     DOES THIS HAVE SAME DSPACE NAME?   259
          CLC   DSP_XNAME(L'DSP_XNAME),OPERAND                           260
          BE    STUPENT               YES; MUST NOT HAVE BEEN            261
*                                     CLEANED UP SO REUSE IT             262
CKNXT     DS    0H                                                        263
*                                     IS THIS THE LAST IN CHAIN ?        264
          ICM   R6,B'1111',DSP_NEXT_ENTRY                                265
          BZ    NEWENT                YES; GET A NEW DSPTBLE BLOCK       266
          LR    R5,R6                 POINT AT NEXT DSPTBLE BLOCK        267
          B     CKNXTE                CHECK NEXT BLOCK                   268
NEWENT    DS    0H                                                        269
          ICM   R15,B'0001',=AL1(ANKPOOL)                                270
          LA    R0,LDSPTBLE           LENGTH OF DSPTBLE BLOCK            271
          STORAGE OBTAIN,COND=YES,    GET STORAGE FOR NEW BLOCK        X 272
                  LENGTH=(0),         LENGTH OF DSPTBLE BLOCK          X 273
                  SP=(15),            SAME SUBPOOL AS CDE              X 274
                  ADDR=(1)            RETURN STORAGE ADDRESS TO R1       275
          LTR   R15,R15                                                  276
          BZ    CONTC2                YES; CONTINUE                      277
          WTO   'DSPACE: STORAGE OBTAIN FAILED FOR CREATE'              278
          B     CREATRNE              EXIT THIS ROUTINE                  279
CONTC2    DS    0H                                                        280
          ST    R1,DSP_NEXT_ENTRY     PUT ADDRESS IN PREVIOUS BLOCK     281
          LR    R5,R1                 POINT AT THIS BLOCK                282
```

Figure 11.4   *(Continued)*

```
STUPENT  DS    OH                                                   283
*                                  PUT EYECATCHER IN BLOCK          284
         MVC   DSP_BLOCK_ID(L'DSP_BLOCK_ID),EYEID                   285
*                                  COPY DSPSERV PARMLIST TO BLOCK   286
         MVC   DSP(DSPL),DSPLIST                                    287
*                                  COPY CREATOR'S STOKEN TO BLOCK   288
         MVC   DSP_OWNER_STOKEN(L'DSP_OWNER_STOKEN),HOMETOKN        289
*                                  COPY CREATOR'S NAME  TO BLOCK    290
         MVC   DSP_OWNER_NAME(L'DSP_OWNER_NAME),HOMENAME            291
         MVC   WTOAREA(WTO1L),WTO1    COPY WTO PARMLIST TO USER STORAG 292
         MVC   WTO1VAR(L'WTO1VAR),OPERAND   MOVE DSPACE NAME TO WTO 293
         LA    R1,WTOAREA            ..ISSUE                        294
         WTO   ,MF=(E,(R1))          ..WTO                          295
CREATRNE DS    OH                                                   296
         MODESET MODE=PROB,KEY=NZERO  GET A PROBLEM STATE AND KEY PSW 297
         PR                          POP STACK AND RETURN           298
*------------------------------------------------------------------*  299
*         DATASPACE DELETE ROUTINE                                 *   300
*------------------------------------------------------------------*  301
DELERTN  DS    OH                                                   302
*        *--------------------------------------------*            303
*        *    SEARCH CHAIN FOR DSPTBLE ENTRY      *                304
*        *    FOR THE DATASPACE TO DELETE         *                305
*        *--------------------------------------------*            306
         L     R5,ENTRY1             A(FIRST DSPTBLE BLOCK)         307
CKNXTE1  DS    OH                                                   308
*                                  A(NEXT DSPTBLE BLOCK)           309
         ICM   R6,B'1111',DSP_NEXT_ENTRY                           310
*                                  WAS THIS DATASPACE CREATED BY   311
*                                  ADDRESS SPACE WITH THIS NAME    312
         CLC   DSP_OWNER_NAME(L'DSP_OWNER_NAME),HOMENAME           313
         BNE   CKNXT1                NO; CHECK THE NEXT ENTRY       314
*                                  DOES THIS HAVE SAME DSPACE NAME? 315
         CLC   DSP_XNAME(L'DSP_XNAME),OPERAND                      316
         BE    DELETEIT              YES; DELETE IT                 317
CKNXT1   DS    OH                                                   318
         LTR   R6,R6                 DOES NEXT BLOCK EXIST ?        319
         BZ    NODELETE              NO; DO NOT DELETE              320
         LR    R7,R5                 SAVE ADDRESS PREVIOUS BLOCK    321
         LR    R5,R6                 POINT AT NEXT BLOCK            322
         B     CKNXTE1               CHECK NEXT BLOCK              323
DELETEIT DS    OH                                                   324
*        *--------------------------------------------*            325
*        *    DELETE DATA SPACE                    *                326
*        *--------------------------------------------*            327
         MODESET MODE=SUP,           ..GET A SUPERVISOR STATE   X  328
                 KEY=ZERO            ..ZERO KEY PSW                 329
*                                                                  330
         DSPSERV DELETE,             ..DELETE THE DATASPACE USING X 331
                 STOKEN=DSP_XSTOKEN, ..THE STOKEN FROM DSPTBLE BLOCK X 332
                 MF=(E,DSPLIST,COMPLETE)                           333
         LTR   R15,R15               RETURN CODE = 0?              334
         BZ    CDELETE               YES; CONTINUE                 335
NODELETE DS    OH                                                   336
         WTO   'DSPACE: DSPSERV DELETE FAILED'                     337
         B     DELERTNE              EXIT THIS SUBROUTINE          338
CDELETE  DS    OH                                                   339
```

Figure 11.4 *(Continued)*

```
*                                        ADDR NEW BLOCK INTO OLD BLOCK   340
        ST    R6,DSP_NEXT_ENTRY-DSPTBLE(R7)                              341
        MVC   WTOAREA(WTO2L),WTO2     MOVE WTO TO USER STORAGE           342
        MVC   WTO2VAR(L'WTO2VAR),OPERAND   MOVE DSPACE NAME TO WTO       343
        LA    R1,WTOAREA              ..ISSUE                            344
        WTO   ,MF=(E,(R1))            ..WTO                              345
*       *---------------------------------------*                       346
*       *   DELETE DSPTBLE BLOCK                 *                       347
*       *---------------------------------------*                       348
        ICM   R15,B'0001',=AL1(ANKPOOL)  SUBPOOL OF DSPTBLE BLOCK        349
        LA    R0,LDSPTBLE            LENGTH OF BLOCK                     350
        STORAGE RELEASE,COND=YES,    FREE THE STORAGE FOR DSPTBLE      X 351
              LENGTH=(0),            LENGTH OF BLOCK                   X 352
              ADDR=(5),              ADDRESS OF BLOCK                  X 353
              SP=(15)                SUBPOOL OF BLOCK                    354
        LTR   R15,R15                RC = 0?                            355
        BZ    DELERTNE               YES; EXIT THIS SUBROUTINE           356
        WTO   'DSPACE: STORAGE RELEASE FAILED'                          357
DELERTNE DS   OH                                                        358
        MODESET MODE=PROB,KEY=NZERO  GET A PROBLEM STATE AND KEY PSW     359
        PR                           POP STACK AND RETURN               360
*-----------------------------------------------------------------*     361
*       EXIT ROUTINES                                             *      362
*-----------------------------------------------------------------*     363
EXIT00  DS    OH                     SUCCESSFUL                         364
        LA    15,X'00'                                                  365
        B     EXIT                                                      366
EXIT08  DS    OH                     INITIALIZATION FAILED              367
        PERCRC RC=X'08'                                                 368
        B     EXIT                                                      369
*-----------------------------------------------------------------*     370
*       COMMON EXIT                                              *       371
*-----------------------------------------------------------------*     372
EXIT    DS    OH                                                        373
        ENDMOD                                                          374
*-----------------------------------------------------------------*     375
*       CONSTANTS                                                *       376
*-----------------------------------------------------------------*     377
EYEID    DC   CL4'DS@P'              EYECATCHER IN DUMMY DSPSERV         378
QNAME    DC   CL8'DSPCDE'            QNAME FOR ENQ/DEQ                   379
DSPTNAME DC   CL8'DSPTAB00'          RNAME FOR ENQ/DEQ                   380
COMM1    DC   C'CREATE('             F DSPACE,CREATE - COMMAND TEXT      381
COMM2    DC   C'DELETE('             F DSPACE,DELETE - COMMAND TEXT      382
DSPBLOCK DC   A((DSPBYTES+4095)/4096) DATASPACE SIZE IN BLOCKS          383
DSPBYTES EQU  100000                 DATASPACE SIZE IN BYTES            384
WTO1     WTO  'DATASPACE CREATED.  NAME OF DATASPACE IS XXXXXXXX',MF=L   385
WTO1L    EQU  *-WTO1                 PARMLIST AND LENGTH FOR WTO         386
WTO1VAR  EQU  WTOAREA+4+41,8         WTO MODIFIED FIELD DISPLACEMENT     387
WTO2     WTO  'DATASPACE DELETED.  NAME OF DATASPACE IS XXXXXXXX',MF=L   388
WTO2L    EQU  *-WTO2                 PARMLIST AND LENGTH FOR WTO         389
WTO2VAR  EQU  WTOAREA+4+41,8         WTO MODIFIED FIELD DISPLACEMENT     390
KEY      DC   X'80'                  STORAGE KEY FOR DATASPACE           391
ANKPOOL  EQU  228                    SUBPOOL FOR ANCHOR                  392
*-----------------------------------------------------------------*     393
*       WORK AREA                                               *        394
*-----------------------------------------------------------------*     395
```

Figure 11.4 *(Continued)*

```
WDSPACE DSECT                                                              396
TRANSECB DS    F                     ECB FOR SYSEVENT                      397
         DSPSERV MF=(L,DSPLIST)      PARMLIST FOR DSPSERV                  398
ALELIST  ALESERV MF=L                PARMLIST FOR ALESERV                  399
EXTLIST  EXTRACT ,MF=L               PARMLIST FOR EXTRACT                  400
PPGPARM  DS    CL(PPGNML)            PARMLIST FOR PGMNAME SERVICE          401
DSPALET  DS    F                     DATASPACE ALET                        402
DSPORG   DS    F                     DATASPACE ORIGIN                      403
DSPTOKEN DS    CL8                   DATASPACE STOKEN                      404
HOMETOKN DS    CL8                   HOME ASN TOKEN                        405
QEDANSW  DS    F                     RESPONSE FROM EXTRACT                 406
ANKPARMS DS    OF,CL(LANKPRM)        PARMLIST FOR ANCHOR1 SERVICE          407
PARSAREA DS    CL100                 COMMAND PARSE AREA                    408
WTOAREA  DS    OF,CL100              WTO                                   409
OPERAND  DS    CL8                   OPERAND FROM COMMAND PARSE            410
HOMENAME DS    CL8                   HOME ADDRESS SPACE NAME               411
ENTRY1   DS    F                     ADDR FIRST ENTRY) IN DSPTABLE         412
LDSPACE  EQU   *-WDSPACE             LENGTH OF THE WORK AREA               413
*-----------------------------------------------------------------*       414
*        OTHER DSECTS                                             *        415
*-----------------------------------------------------------------*       416
         IEZCOM                      MAPPING FOR COMMUNICATIONS AREA       417
CIB      DSECT                       DSECT CARD FOR CIB                    418
         IEZCIB                      MAPPING FOR COMMAND INPUT BUFFER      419
         ANKPRM                      MAP PARMLIST FOR ANCHOR SERVICE       420
         DSPTBLE                     MAP DSPTBLE ENTRY                     421
         PPGNM                       MAP PARMLIST FOR PGMNAME SERVICE      422
         END                                                              423
```

Figure 11.4 *(Continued).*

Note that it does not matter whether the DSPTBLE chain exists at this point or not. ENQ serializes on the major name/minor name tokens and not on the underlying resource. Just as with MVS locks, other programs are prevented from using the underlying resource only if they issue ENQ for the same tokens. Note that the scope of the ENQ is SYSTEM since there is one LPAQ per MVS system.

11.4.1 Command Input Buffer (CIB)

Before DSPACE can processes console commands, it must establish addressability to the Command Input Buffer (CIB) queue anchored off the TCB. When an operator issues a command for the DSPACE task, CONSOLE queues a CIB that contains the command text to DSPACE's TCB. In Fig. 11.3, two MODIFY DSPACE,CREATE commands have resulted in two CIBs queued to DSPACE's TCB through the Command Scheduler Communications Parameter List (COMM Area).

Lines 47 through 52 in DSPACE obtain the address of the COMM area by issuing the EXTRACT macro. EXTRACT invokes a Task Management service that locates the addresses of control structures related to the current TCB or one of its subtasks. Line 48 loads the address of field QEDANSW on line 406, whose length in fullwords corresponds to the number of addresses EXTRACT will return. Since EXTRACT specifies one field in the FIELDS= parameter, the QEDANSW is only one full-word. Notice that line 50 issues the execute form of EXTRACT against the parameter list on line 400.

After line 51 loads the address of the COMM area returned by EX-TRACT into register 3, line 52 issues USING so that fields in the COMM area can be referenced by names in the COMLIST DSECT. (This DSECT is produced by the expansion of the IEZCOM macro on line 417.) Similarly, lines 53 and 54 get the address of the first CIB in the queue from the COMM area and map the CIB by the fields in the IEZCIB data area (line 419). Since IEZCIB does not expand with a DSECT statement, line 418 provides the DSECT statement.

11.4.2 QEDIT

QEDIT is the interface to the Task Management service that manipulates the CIB queue. The QEDIT CIBCTR= on line 55 sets a limit on the number of CIBs that can be on the CIB queue at any one time. When a command is issued for a task and the CONSOLE address space detects that the limit on queued CIBs has been reached for that task, CONSOLE issues the message "IEE342I Task busy" and discards the command. QEDIT is also used to remove CIBs from the queue after a program has processed them. DSPACE dequeues the most recently processed CIB with QEDIT BLOCK= on line 115. Line 56 issues USING so that labels in the DSPTBLE DSECT, produced by the expansion of the macro on line 421, can be used to reference fields in the DSPTBLE block.

11.4.3 Building the DSPTBLE Queue

Lines 57 through 66 invoke the subroutine INITRTN on lines 119 through 181. INITRTN calls the ANCHOR program from Chap. 8 to obtain a CDE on the LPAQ. DSPACE will chain the DSPTBLE control blocks it builds when it creates dataspaces from this CDE so that other address spaces can obtain their STOKENs. Note in Fig. 11.3, that the first DSPTBLE block (labeled NULL) on the chain does not represent a dataspace but only serves as the head of the chain. This "dummy" control block allows DSPACE to manipulate the DSPTBLE chain without having to change the anchoring CDE. This means that DSPACE acts only once on the LPAQ CDEs, when it calls ANCHOR, and thus it allows the program's control blocks to be isolated from MVS control blocks.

Line 61 invokes INITRTN with the BAKR 0,R15. Remember that when the first operand of BAKR is 0, the current PSW (which points to the instruction following BAKR) is stored in the stack state entry that BAKR creates. Whenever BAKR is used to transfer control to a subroutine in this way, the subroutine must return control with a PR instruction (line 181) in order to load the PSW from the stack state entry.

When INITRTN receives control, lines 126 through 134 invoke the PGMNAME routine (Appendix B) and lines 137 through 144 issue ALESERV EXTACTH to obtain the name and STOKEN, respectively, of the current address space. The name and STOKEN will be placed in the DSPTBLE block for any dataspace that DSPACE creates.

Lines 145 through 165 call the ANCHOR routine to build the LPAQ CDE that anchors the DSPTBLE queue. ANCHOR also builds the dummy DSPTBLE block that is first in the chain. Lines 166 and 167 load the address of the dummy DSPTBLE block returned by ANCHOR into register 5.

Figure 11.5 contains the DSPTBLE macro. Lines 3 through 12 of this macro expand into the DSECT that maps the DSPTBLE block. ANCHOR uses the length of this DSECT (line 12 of the macro) on lines 147 and 148 when it GETMAINs storage for the dummy DSPTBLE.

11.4.4 DSPSERV

Line 11 of the macro contains the MF = L form of DSPSERV. After DSPACE issues DSPSERV MF = E to create a new dataspace, the program copies the DSPSERV MF = L parameter list into the new dataspace's DSPTBLE block. Note how DSPSERV is coded:

```
DSPSERV  MF = (L,DSP)
```

DSP, the second suboperand of MF = causes the macro to expand into a

```
            MACRO                     MAP DSPTBLE BLOCK/PARMS - DSPFIND    1
            DSPTBLE                                                        2
DSPTBLE   DSECT                                                            3
.*                  *---------------------------------------*             4
.*                  * THIS SECTION MAPS DSPTBLE BLOCK       *             5
.*                  *---------------------------------------*             6
DSP_BLOCK_ID    DS    CL4              EYECATCHER                          7
DSP_NEXT_ENTRY  DS    F                ADDRESS NEXT DSPTBLE BLOCK          8
DSP_OWNER_NAME  DS    CL8              NAME OF OWNING ADDRESS SPACE        9
DSP_OWNER_STOKEN DS   CL8              STOKEN OF OWNING ADDRESS SPACE     10
            DSPSERV MF=(L,DSP)         LIST FORM DSPSERV MACRO            11
LDSPTABE EQU        *-DSPTBLE          LENGTH OF DSPTBLE BLOCK            12
.*                  *----------------------------------------*           13
.*                  * THIS SECTION CONTAINS PARMS FOR THE    *           14
.*                  * DSPFIND SERVICE                        *           15
.*                  *----------------------------------------*           16
DSP_FUNCTION    DS    X                FUNCTION CODE FOR DSPFIND          17
@GETDUAL        EQU   B'10000000'      CREATE DU-AL ACCESS LIST ENTRY     18
@GETPSAN        EQU   B'01000000'      CREATE PS-AL ACCESS LIST ENTRY     19
@FREEAL         EQU   B'00100000'      DELETE ACCESS LIST ENTRY           20
                DS    XL3              NOT USED                           21
DSP_ALET        DS    A                ALET FROM CREATE OR FOR DELETE     22
*                                      (CALLER MUST SUPPLY FOR DELETE)    23
DSP_TBLENTRY    DS    A                ADDRESS OF DSPTBLE BLOCK           24
LDSPTBLE EQU        *-DSPTBLE          LENGTH OF DSPTBLE DSECT            25
            MEND                                                          26
```

Figure 11.5 DSPTBLE DSECT.

DSECT named DSP with field labels that begin DSP___. When DSPACE references a field in the control block, as in line 260, it names a label beginning DSP___. Because the macro expands in this way (the second suboperand for MF = is required), the other fields in the DSECT (lines 7 through 10) are assigned labels beginning DSP___ for consistency.

After lines 169 through 179 initialize the dummy DSPTBLE block, INITRTN returns control with the PR on line 181 to line 62. Lines 62 through 65 test the return code from INITRTN and exit if initialization was not successful. Since a dataspace is swapped when the address space that contains the TCB that owns the dataspace is swapped, lines 67 and 68 issue SYSEVENT TRANSWAP to make DSPACE's address space nonswappable. This is necessary since programs in other address spaces will establish access register mode communication with DSPACE's dataspaces. Making DSPACE nonswappable insures that the dataspaces' Segment and Page Tables will be in storage when programs in other address spaces access dataspace storage.

Line 69 branches to line 112 where DEQ on line 114 releases the ENQ for the DSPTBLE chain, and line 115 dequeues the CIB that contained the START command.

Lines 116 and 117 issue WAIT against the ECB in the COMM area. WAIT invokes the Task Manager service that marks the DSPACE TCB as nondispatchable, and DSPACE remains in a WAIT state until a command directed at DSPACE is issued at the MVS console. The command causes CONSOLE to build a CIB and queue it on DSPACE's CIB chain. CONSOLE then issues POST against the COMM area ECB, causing Task Manager to make DSPACE dispatchable.

11.4.5 Processing Console Commands

DSPACE receives control at line 118, the instruction immediately following WAIT, which branches to line 73. Line 74 then loads the address of the CIB into register 4. This corresponds to the USING for the CIB DSECT on line 54. Lines 75 through 86 examine the command verb flag in the CIB, and exit the command loop on lines 77 through 81 if the verb is STOP. Note that when the DSPACE task terminates, any dataspaces it owns will be deleted.

If the verb flag in the CIB indicates that a MODIFY command has been issued, lines 91 and 92 invoke the PARSRTN subroutine on lines 182 through 225 to parse the command text in the CIB. This text contains whatever was entered at the MVS console after the MODIFY DSPACE command. For example, if the operator entered

```
F   DSPACE,CREATE(DSP1)
```

(F is an abbreviation for MODIFY) the CIBDATA field in the CIB would contain

CREATE(DSP1)

PARSRTN uses the TRT on line 201 to isolate the name of the dataspace that is to be created or deleted. After the execution of PARSRTN against the command text

CREATE(DSP1)

the field OPERAND on line 410 would contain

DSP1

Note that the table in lines 212 through 225 that is used by TRT recognizes several command delimiters. This allows the console command to be entered in any of the following ways:

```
F   DSPACE,CREATE(DSP1)
F   DSPACE,CREATE(DSP1
F   DSPACE,CREATE(DSP1,
F   DSPACE,CREATE(DSP1)
```

PARSRTN returns control to line 94, which issues ENQ against the DSPTBLE chain. Lines 95 through 104 invoke the CREATRN or DELERTN subroutine to create or delete a dataspace depending on the contents of the command text from the CIB.

11.4.6 Creating a Dataspace

When CREATRN on lines 226 through 298 receives control, it issues MODESET on lines 233 through 234. This is necessary because the DSPSERV CREATE macro contains the SCOPE = ALL operand on line 237. The SCOPE = parameter determines whether tasks in other address spaces can issue ALESERV to build an access list entry for the dataspace. Tasks in other address spaces:

■ Cannot issue ALESERV for SCOPE = SINGLE dataspaces.

■ Can issue ALESERV for SCOPE = ALL or SCOPE = COMMON dataspaces providing they are executing with a supervisor-state or key-zero PSW. Additionally, whenever any program issues ALESERV AL = PASN for a SCOPE = COMMON dataspace, ALESERV builds an access list entry for the dataspace on the PS-AL of every address space in the system.

NAME = on line 238 causes DSPSERV to create a dataspace with the name specified in the MODIFY command. This name must not be the same as that of another dataspace already owned by DSPACE. BLOCKS= on line 239 defines the amount of virtual storage in the new dataspace in units of 4K. Note how DSPBLOCK on line 383 uses the assembler to calculate the number of 4K blocks required to contain the number of bytes in DSPBYTES on line 384.

The KEY= operand on line 240 insures that the new dataspace will have a storage-protect key of 8. This allows TCB key programs in other address spaces to access storage in the dataspace. If KEY= were not coded, the dataspace storage would have the same key as the current PSW, which is 0. This is the same consideration that applies when a key-zero program, such as ANCHOR, issues GETMAIN for CSA storage that will be referenced by key-8 programs.

DSPSERV CREATE returns the STOKEN for the new dataspace into field DSPTOKEN on line 404 as specified by the STOKEN= operand on line 241. Any program that now wishes to establish access register mode communication with the dataspace, such as DSPFIND, uses this STOKEN when it issues ALESERV to build an access list entry.

In addition to the STOKEN that identifies the new dataspace, DSPSERV CREATE returns the virtual address of the first byte of the dataspace. This is a virtual address *in the dataspace's, not the creator's, virtual storage.* The ORIGIN= operand on line 242 of DSPACE causes DSPSERV to save the address of the first byte of the dataspace in field DSPORG on line 403.

Lines 253 through 268 constitute a loop in which each DSPTBLE block on the chain is examined to see whether it has the same address space name in the DSP_OWNER_NAME field as the current address space and the same dataspace name in the DSP_XNAME field as the one that DSPSERV just created. Since an address space cannot own two dataspaces with the same name, any DSPTBLE block that has that address space name/dataspace name combination must not have been cleaned up when the dataspace it represented ceased to exist. In that case, line 261 branches around the STORAGE OBTAIN macro for new DSPTBLE block and reuses the block for the nonexistent dataspace. If a new block is required, lines 270 through 280 obtain storage in the same key as the dummy DSPTBLE block (line 270). Lines 281 and 282 add the new DSPTBLE block onto the queue by storing its address in the last block's chain field.

Lines 283 through 295 initialize the DSPTBLE block. Note that line 287 copies the parameter list used by DSPSERV on line 243 into the block. This parameter list contains information returned by the DSPSERV service about the dataspace. The MODESET on line 297 is not really necessary. The PR instruction on line 298 loads the PSW from the stack state entry that contains the state and key in effect when BAKR on line 98 created the stack state entry.

11.4.7 Deleting a Dataspace

The DELRTN on lines 299 through 360 is similar in structure to the CREATRN. Lines 303 through 324 examine the DSPTBLE blocks for one that contains an address space name/dataspace name combination that matches the current address space and dataspace to be deleted. If a DSPTBLE block is found, line 317 branches to lines 325 through 335, which issue DSPSERV DELETE. The STOKEN= operand on line 332 uses the STOKEN from the DSPSERV parameter list that was copied into the DSPTBLE block.

Line 341 removes the DSPTBLE block for the deleted dataspace from the chain of DSPTBLE blocks by storing the address of the following block in the NEXT_ENTRY field of the previous block. (Line 321 has loaded the address of the previous block into register 7 for this purpose.) Once the DSPTBLE block has been unchained, lines 346 through 357 issue STORAGE RELEASE to free the block's virtual storage.

11.5 DSPFIND WALKTHROUGH

Any program that wishes to access one of the dataspaces built by DSPACE can call program DSPFIND (Fig. 11.6). When entered, DSPFIND saves the address of the parameter list supplied by the caller in register 3 (line 27) and issues ENQ on line 31 so that no other program will change the chain of DSPTBLE blocks until DSPFIND is through examining them. The parameter list is mapped by the same macro that maps the DSPTBLE block (Fig. 11.5).

Lines 33 through 42 invoke the same LPAQ search routine used by the ANCHOR program in Chap. 8 to locate the LPAQ CDE that anchors the chain of DSPTBLE blocks. This routine (IEAQCDSR) returns control to the instruction immediately following the BALR on line 39 if it locates the CDE, or to the instruction 4 bytes after BALR if it does not.

If IEAQCDSR finds the CDE, lines 43 through 62 search the chain of DSPTBLE blocks until it finds a block that contains the same address space name/dataspace name combination that the caller specified in the input parameter list. Line 46 loads register 5 with the address of the first DSPTBLE block from the CDE whose address is returned in register 11 by IEAQCDSR. Note that because of the USING statement on line 47, the assembler treats the first operands of the CLC instructions on lines 51 and 55 as displacements off register 5 (which contains the address of a DSPTBLE block). Explicit notation in these instructions' second operands specifies a displacement off register 3 (which contains the address of the input parameter list).

If DSPFIND is able to locate a DSPTBLE block for the target dataspace, line 63 copies the contents of that block to the input parameter list. The USING on line 65 allows the following instructions to access fields in

```
*+---------------------------------------------------------------------+    1
*|  FUNCTION:                                                          |    2
*|    FINDS THE DSPTBLE CONTOL BLOCK FOR A DATASPACE CREATED BY        |    3
*|    THE DSPACE ROUTINE.  DSPFIND WILL OPTIONALLY BUILD OR DELETE     |    4
*|    AN ACCESS LIST ENTRY ON THE CALLER'S DU-AL OR PS-AL ACCORDING    |    5
*|    TO A FUNCTION CODE SUPPLIED IN THE INPUT PARAMETER LIST.         |    6
*|  INPUTS:                                                            |    7
*|    R1  - ADDRESS OF A PARMLIST MAPPED BY DSPTBLE MACRO              |    8
*|          (FOR DELETE REQUEST CALLER MUST SUPPLY ALET IN PARMLIST)   |    9
*|  OUTPUTS:                                                           |   10
*|    R15 - RETURN CODE                                                |   11
*|           0 - DATASPACE FOUND / ACCESS LIST ENTRY BUILT             |   12
*|           8 - LPAQ CDE NOT FOUND FOR DSPTBLE BLOCK CHAIN            |   13
*|          12 - DSPTBLE BLOCK FOR THE TARGET DATASPACE NOT ON CHAIN   |   14
*|          16 - ACCESS LIST ENTRY CREATION FAILED                     |   15
*|          20 - ACCESS LIST ENTRY DELETION FAILED                     |   16
*|  LOGIC:                                                             |   17
*|    1) ENQUEUE ON THE CHAIN OF DSPTBLE BLOCKS                        |   18
*|    2) CALL LPAQ SEARCH ROUTINE TO FIND ANCHOR FOR DSPTBLE CHAIN     |   19
*|    3) SEARCH FOR DSPTBLE BLOCK FOR TARGET DATASPACE                 |   20
*|    4) ACCORDING TO FUNCTION CODE ISSUE ALSERV ADD OR DELETE         |   21
*|  ATTRIBUTES:                                                        |   22
*|    AMODE 31, RMODE ANY, REENTRANT, REQUIRES APF OR PKM 0 AUTHORITY  |   23
*+---------------------------------------------------------------------+   24
            MODULE DSPFIND,BASE=12,LOC=BELOW,AMODE=31,RMODE=ANY,       X   25
                   TEXT='FIND STOKEN FOR DATASPACE'                        26
            LR    R3,R1                     ADDRESS OF PARMLIST             27
*           *-----------------------------------------*                    28
*           *    ENQUEUE ON TABLE CHAIN               *                    29
*           *-----------------------------------------*                    30
            ENQ   (QNAME,DSPTNAME,E,L'DSPTNAME,SYSTEM)                      31
*           *-----------------------------------------*                    32
*           *    FIND LPAQ CDE FOR DSPTBLE CHAIN      *                    33
*           *-----------------------------------------*                    34
            L     R2,CVTPTR                 ADDRESS OF CVT                  35
            LA    R9,DSPTNAME               ADDRESS OF ANCHOR CDE NAME      36
            L     R8,CVTQLPAQ-CVT(R2)       HEAD OF LPAQ                    37
            L     R15,CVTQCDSR-CVT(R2)      ADDRESS OF THE LPAQ SCAN RTN    38
            BALR  R14,R15                   INVOKE LPAQ SCAN ROUTINE        39
            B     FNDCDE                    CDE FOUND                       40
            B     EXIT08                    CDE NOT FOUND                   41
FNDCDE      DS    0H                                                       42
*           *-----------------------------------------*                    43
*           *    SEARCH DSPTBLE BLOCKS FOR TARGET     *                    44
*           *-----------------------------------------*                    45
            L     R5,CDENTPT-CDENTRY(R11)   A(FIRST BLOCK FROM CDE E.P)     46
            USING DSPTBLE,R5                MAP DSPTBLE BLOCK               47
CKNXTE      DS    0H                                                       48
*                                          ..OWNER NAME IN DSPTBLE SAME AS 49
*                                          ..OWNER NAME IN PARMLIST?       50
            CLC   DSP_OWNER_NAME,DSP_OWNER_NAME-DSPTBLE(R3)                 51
            BNE   CKNXT                     NO; CHECK THE NEXT ENTRY        52
*                                          ..DSPACE NAME IN DSPTBLE SAME AS 53
*                                          ..DSPACE NAME IN PARMLIST?      54
            CLC   DSP_XNAME,DSP_XNAME-DSPTBLE(R3)                          55
            BE    FOUNDIT                   YES; CHECK FUNCTION CODE        56
CKNXT       DS    0H                                                       57
```

Figure 11.6 DSPFIND.

```
×                                    LAST DSPTBLE BLOCK?              58
        ICM    R5,B'1111',DSP_NEXT_ENTRY                              59
        BZ     EXITOC              YES; EXIT                          60
        B      CKNXTE              CHECK NEXT DSPTBLE BLOCK           61
FOUNDIT DS     OH                                                     62
        MVC    O(LDSPTABE,R3),DSPTBLE  COPY BLOCK TO INPUT PARMLIST   63
        DROP   R5                  DROP ADDRESSING ON DSPTBLE         64
        USING DSPTBLE,R3           MAP INPUT PARMLIST                 65
        ST     R5,DSP_TBLENTRY     SAVE DSPTBLE ADDRESS IN PARMLIST   66
        TM     DSP_FUNCTION,X'FF'  ANY FUNCTION CODE?                 67
        BZ     ENDFUNCT            NO; EXIT                           68
        SPKA   0                   GET A KEY ZERO PSW                 69
*       *-------------------------------------*                      70
*       *   CREATE ENTRY IN DU-AL ACCESS LIST *                      71
*       *-------------------------------------*                      72
        TM     DSP_FUNCTION,@GETDUAL  CREATE DU-AL ACCESS LIST ENTRY? 73
        BNE    NOTDUAL             NO; TEST NEXT CODE                 74
        ALESERV ADD,               CREATE ACCESS LIST ENTRY        X  75
               STOKEN=DSP_XSTOKEN, STOKEN FROM COPIED DSPTBLE BLOCKX  76
               ALET=DSP_ALET,      SAVE ALET IN INPUT PARMLIST     X  77
               CHKEAX=NO,          DO NOT CHECK EAX                X  78
               AL=WORKUNIT,        BUILD DU-AL ACCESS LIST ENTRY   X  79
               ACCESS=PUBLIC,      PUBLIC ACCESS LIST ENTRY        X  80
               MF=(E,ALELIST)                                         81
        LTR    R15,R15             RETURN CODE = 0?                   82
        BNZ    EXIT10              NO; EXIT PEROLATING ALESERV RC     83
        B      ENDFUNCT            EXIT RC=0                          84
NOTDUAL DS     OH                                                     85
*       *-------------------------------------*                      86
*       *   CREATE ENTRY IN PS-AL ACCESS LIST *                      87
*       *-------------------------------------*                      88
        TM     DSP_FUNCTION,@GETPSAN  CREATE PS-AL ACCESS LIST ENTRY? 89
        BNE    NOTPSAN             NO; TEST NEXT FLAG                 90
        ALESERV ADD,                                               X  91
               STOKEN=DSP_XSTOKEN, STOKEN FROM COPIED DSPTBLE BLOCKX  92
               ALET=DSP_ALET,      SAVE ALET IN INPUT PARMLIST     X  93
               CHKEAX=NO,          DO NOT CHECK EAX                X  94
               AL=PASN,            BUILD PS-AL ACCESS LIST ENTRY   X  95
               ACCESS=PUBLIC,      PUBLIC ACCESS LIST ENTRY        X  96
               MF=(E,ALELIST)                                         97
        LTR    R15,R15             RETURN CODE = 0?                   98
        BNZ    EXIT10              NO; EXIT PEROLATING ALESERV RC     99
        B      ENDFUNCT            EXIT RC=0                         100
NOTPSAN DS     OH                                                    101
*       *-------------------------------------*                     102
*       *   DELETE ACCESS LIST ENTRY          *                     103
*       *-------------------------------------*                     104
        TM     DSP_FUNCTION,@FREEAL  DELETE ACCESS LIST ENTRY ?      105
        BNE    NOTFREE             NO; TEST NEXT FLAG                106
        ALESERV DELETE,            DELETE ACCESS LIST ENTRY        X 107
               ALET=DSP_ALET,      CALLER MUST SUPPLY ALET         X 108
               MF=(E,ALELIST)                                        109
        LTR    R15,R15             RETURN CODE = 0?                  110
        BNZ    EXIT14              NO; EXIT PEROLATING ALESERV RC    111
        B      ENDFUNCT            EXIT RC=0                         112
NOTFREE DS     OH                                                    113
ENDFUNCT DS    OH                                                    114
```

Figure 11.6 *(Continued)*

```
        B     EXIT00                                              115
*-----------------------------------------------------------*    116
*       EXIT ROUTINES                                        *    117
*-----------------------------------------------------------*    118
EXIT00  DS    0H                    SUCCESSFUL                    119
        LA    15,X'00'                                            120
        B     EXIT                                                121
EXIT08  DS    0H                    ANCHOR FOR DSPTBLE NOT FOUND  122
        PERCRC RC=X'08'                                           123
        WTO   'DSPFIND: CDE NOT FOUND'                            124
        B     EXIT                                                125
EXIT0C  DS    0H                    NO DSPTBLE BLOCK FOR DATASPACE 126
        LA    15,X'0C'                                            127
        WTO   'DSPFIND: DSPACE ENTRY NOT FOUND'                   128
        B     EXIT                                                129
EXIT10  DS    0H        CREATION OF ACCESS LIST ENTRY FAILED      130
        PERCRC RC=X'10'                                           131
        WTO   'DSPFIND: ALESERV CREATE FAILED'                    132
        B     EXIT                                                133
EXIT14  DS    0H        DELETION OF ACCESS LIST ENTRY FAILED      134
        PERCRC RC=X'14'                                           135
        WTO   'DSPFIND: ALESERV DELETE FAILED'                    136
        B     EXIT                                                137
*-----------------------------------------------------------*    138
*       COMMON EXIT                                          *    139
*-----------------------------------------------------------*    140
EXIT    DS    0H                                                  141
        LR    R2,R15              SAVE RETURN CODE                142
*       *-----------------------------------*                     143
*       *   DEQUEUE ON TABLE CHAIN          *                     144
*       *-----------------------------------*                     145
        DEQ   (QNAME,DSPTNAME,L'DSPTNAME,SYSTEM),RET=HAVE         146
        LR    R15,R2              RESTORE RETURN CODE             147
        ENDMOD                                                    148
*-----------------------------------------------------------*    149
*       CONSTANTS                                           *    150
*-----------------------------------------------------------*    151
QNAME    DC   CL8'DSPCDE'        ENQ/DEQ MAJOR NAME               152
DSPTNAME DC   CL8'DSPTAB00'      NAME OF CDE THAT ANCHORS DSPTBL  153
*-----------------------------------------------------------*    154
*       WORK AREA                                           *    155
*-----------------------------------------------------------*    156
WDSPFIND DSECT                                                   157
ALELIST  ALESERV MF=L            ALESERV PARMLIST                158
LDSPFIND EQU   *-WDSPFIND                                        159
*-----------------------------------------------------------*    160
*       OTHER DSECTS                                        *    161
*-----------------------------------------------------------*    162
         DSPTBLE               DSPTBLE ENTRY                     163
         IHACDE                MAP CDE                           164
LCDE     EQU   *-CDENTRY       LENGTH OF CDE                     165
         CVT   DSECT=YES,LIST=NO  MAP CVT                        166
         END                                                    167
```

Figure 11.6 *(Continued)*

the parameter list, including the copied DSPTBLE block, by the labels in the DSPTBLE macro (Fig. 11.5).

Lines 67, 73, 89, and 105 test bits in the DSP_FUNCTION byte of the parameter list. Depending on the value, DSPFIND builds an access list entry for the target dataspace on the caller's Dispatchable Unit Access List (lines 70 through 84) or Primary Space Access List (lines 86 through 100) or deletes the access list entry corresponding to an ALET supplied by the caller (lines 102 through 112).

Both of the ALESERV ADD macros specify CHKEAX = NO (lines 78 and 94), which requires a PSW key of 0 or supervisor state. Line 69 has issued the SPKA instruction to set a zero PSW key rather than the SVC 107 expansion of MODESET. Because DSPFIND contains no SVC instructions, it could be defined as a PC routine in the same way as CKXTALK in Chap. 10. Just as nonauthorized programs can invoke the PC routine CKXTALK to build access list entries for address spaces, they could invoke DSPFIND to build access list entries for dataspaces.

11.6 DSPUT WALKTHROUGH

DSPUT, illustrated in Fig. 11.7, moves data between its own address space and two dataspaces named DSP1 and DSP2 owned by DSPACE. These dataspaces are created by issuing the following MODIFY commands for DSPACE at the MVS console:

    F   DSPACE,CREATE(DSP1)

and

    F   DSPACE,CREATE(DSP2)

As a result of the commands, DSPACE creates the two dataspaces illustrated in Fig. 11.3.

DSPUT (Fig. 11.8) makes two calls to DSPFIND in lines 25 through 44 and lines 45 through 60 to build access list entries for the dataspaces.

In the first call, lines 29 through 34 establish addressability to the parameter list that will be passed to DSPFIND and initialize the function code, address space name and dataspace name fields in the parameter list. (Figure 11.5 contains the parameter list mapping.) After issuing MODESET on line 35 (because of the SPKA instruction in DSPFIND), lines 36 through 42 load the parameter list address into register 1 and branch to DSPFIND.

DSPFIND locates the DSPTBLE block for the dataspace and, based on the function code in the parameter list, builds an access list entry for the dataspace on DSPUT's Dispatchable Unit Access List. DSPFIND

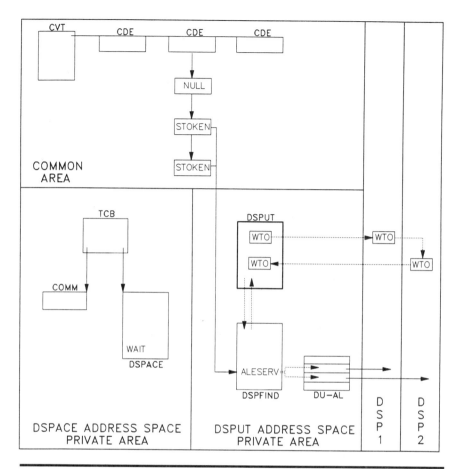

Figure 11.7 DSPUT—program flow.

returns the ALET corresponding to this access list entry as well as the dataspace origin in the parameter list it received from DSPUT. Since DSPUT uses the same parameter list (line 135) for the second call to DSPFIND, lines 43 and 44 save the ALET and the dataspace origin from the first call in the fields in lines 136 and 137.

Since another program might access the same storage in the DSP1 and DSP2 dataspaces while DSPUT is changing that storage, lines 65 and 66 issue ENQs. If other programs that access the same addresses in the two dataspaces as DSPUT issue ENQ for the same major name/minor name combination (lines 128 through 130), GRS will cause them to wait until DSPUT issues DEQ. Note that other programs that issue the same ENQs should do so in the same order as DSPUT. Otherwise an interlock could occur, with each program holding the ENQ needed by the other

```
*+-----------------------------------------------------------------+   1
*|  FUNCTION:                                                       |   2
*|    DSPUT IS A TEST PROGRAM FOR THE DATASPACES CREATED BY DSPACE. |   3
*|    AFTER DSPACE IS STARTED AT THE CONSOLE, THE OPERATOR ISSUES:  |   4
*|      F DSPACE,CREATE(DSP1) - TO CREATE A DATASPACE NAMED "DSP1"  |   5
*|      F DSPACE,CREATE(DSP2) - TO CREATE A DATASPACE NAMED "DSP2"  |   6
*|    WHEN DSPUT IS NOW EXECUTED, IT WILL MOVE A WTO PARAMETER LIST |   7
*|    FROM THIS ADDRESS SPACE TO DATASPACE DSP1, FROM DSP1 TO DSP2, |   8
*|    AND FROM DSP2 TO A LOCATION IN THIS ADDRESS SPACE.  DSPUT THEN|   9
*|    WRITES A CONSOLE MESSAGE BY ISSUING WTO MF=E USING THE PARMLIST.| 10
*|  INPUTS:                                                         |  11
*|    NONE                                                          |  12
*|  OUTPUTS:                                                        |  13
*|    R15 - RETURN CODE                                             |  14
*|        0 - SUCCESSFUL COMPLETION                                 |  15
*|        8 - DSPFIND ROUTINE NOT LINK EDITED                       |  16
*|       16 - DSPFIND DID NOT LOCATE DSP1 OR DSP2                   |  17
*|  LOGIC:                                                          |  18
*|    1) PREPARE TO ACCEPT COMMANDS FROM THE MVS CONSOLE.           |  19
*|  ATTRIBUTES:                                                     |  20
*|    AMODE 31, RMODE ANY, REENTRANT, REQUIRES APF AUTHORIZATION    |  21
*+-----------------------------------------------------------------+  22
         MODULE DSPUT,BASE=12,LOC=BELOW,AMODE=31,RMODE=ANY,       X  23
               TEXT='MOVE DATA INTO DATASPACES'                      24
*        *------------------------------------------*                25
*        *    CALL DSPFIND TO BUILD ACCESS          *                26
*        *    LIST ENTRY FOR DSP1 DATASPACE         *                27
*        *------------------------------------------*                28
         LA    R3,DSPPARMS            PARMLIST FOR FIND SERVICE       29
         USING DSPTBLE,R3             MAP PARMLIST                    30
         OI    DSP_FUNCTION,@GETDUAL  SET FLAG TO BUILD DU-AL ENTRY   31
*                                     DSP1 OWNER NAME TO PARMLIST     32
         MVC   DSP_OWNER_NAME(L'DSP_OWNER_NAME),=CL8'DSPACE'          33
         MVC   DSP_XNAME(L'DSP_XNAME),DSNAME1                         34
         MODESET MODE=SUP             GET A SUPERVISOR STATE PSW      35
         LR    R1,R3                  PARMLIST ADDRESS TO R1          36
         ICM   R15,B'1111',=V(DSPFIND) A(DSPFIND SERVICE)            37
         BZ    EXIT08                 =0; SERVICE NOT LINK-EDITED     38
         O     R15,=A(X'80000000')    SET FOR 31 BIT ENTRY           39
         BASSM R14,R15                INVOKE SERVICE                  40
         LTR   R15,R15                RC=0?                           41
         BNZ   EXIT10                 NO; EXIT                        42
         MVC   ALET1,DSP_ALET         ALET FOR DSP1                   43
         MVC   ORIGIN1,DSP_XORIGIN    ORIGIN FOR DSP1                 44
*        *------------------------------------------*                45
*        *    CALL DSPFIND TO BUILD ACCESS          *                46
*        *    LIST ENTRY FOR DSP2 DATASPACE         *                47
*        *------------------------------------------*                48
*                                     DSP2 OWNER NAME TO PARMLIST     49
         MVC   DSP_OWNER_NAME(L'DSP_OWNER_NAME),=CL8'DSPACE'          50
         MVC   DSP_XNAME(L'DSP_XNAME),DSNAME2                         51
         LR    R1,R3                  PARMLIST ADDRESS TO R1          52
         ICM   R15,B'1111',=V(DSPFIND) A(DSPFIND SERVICE)            53
         O     R15,=A(X'80000000')    SET FOR 31 BIT ENTRY           54
         BASSM R14,R15                INVOKE SERVICE                  55
         LTR   R15,R15                RC=0?                           56
         BNZ   EXIT10                 NO; EXIT                        57
```

Figure 11.8 DSPUT.

```
        MODESET MODE=PROB            GET A PROBLEM STATE PSW         58
        MVC   ALET2,DSP_ALET         ALET FOR DSP2                  59
        MVC   ORIGIN2,DSP_XORIGIN    ORIGIN FOR DSP2                60
*       *----------------------------------------*                  61
*       *    ISSUE ENQ TO SERIALIZE ACCESS TO  *                    62
*       *    DATASPACE STORAGE                  *                    63
*       *----------------------------------------*                  64
        ENQ   (DSNAME1,DSRANGE,E,L'DSRANGE,SYSTEM)                   65
        ENQ   (DSNAME2,DSRANGE,E,L'DSRANGE,SYSTEM)                   66
*       *----------------------------------------*                  67
*       *    GO INTO ACCESS REGISTER MODE       *                    68
*       *----------------------------------------*                  69
        SAC   512                    GO INTO ACCESS REGISTER MODE   70
        LAE   R12,0(R12,0)           LOAD BASE AR WITH X'00'        71
        CPYA  A13,A12                LOAD WORK AREA AR WITH X'00'   72
        SYSSTATE ASCENV=AR           SET FOR AR MACRO EXPANSIONS    73
*       *----------------------------------------*                  74
*       *    MOVE A WTO PARMLIST FROM THIS      *                    75
*       *    ADDRESS SPACE TO 1ST DATASPACE     *                    76
*       *    THEN FROM 1ST DATASPACE TO 2ND     *                    77
*       *    DATASPACE, THEN FROM 2ND DATASPC   *                    78
*       *    BACK TO THIS ADDRESS SPACE.        *                    79
*       *----------------------------------------*                  80
        LAM   A6,A6,ALET1            LOAD ACCESS REG W/DSP1 ALET    81
        L     R6,ORIGIN1             LOAD GEN REG W/DSP1 ORIGIN     82
        LAM   A7,A7,ALET1            LOAD ACCESS REG W/DSP2 ALET    83
        L     R7,ORIGIN2             LOAD GEN REG W/DSP2 ORIGIN     84
        MVC   0(LWTOLIST,R6),WTOLIST MOVE WTO PARMLIST TO DSP1      85
        MVC   0(LWTOLIST,R7),0(R6)   MOVE FROM DSP1 TO DSP2         86
        MVC   WTOPARM(LWTOLIST),0(7) MOVE FROM DSP2 TO THIS SPACE   87
*       *----------------------------------------*                  88
*       *    GO INTO PRIMARY SPACE MODE         *                    89
*       *----------------------------------------*                  90
        SAC   0                      GO INTO PRIMARY SPACE MODE     91
        SYSSTATE ASCENV=P            SET FOR PRIMARY SPC EXAPNSIONS 92
*       *----------------------------------------*                  93
*       *    ISSUE WTO AGAINST PARMLIST THAT    *                    94
*       *    WAS MOVED AROUND                   *                    95
*       *----------------------------------------*                  96
        WTO   ,MF=(E,WTOPARM)        ISSUE WTO                      97
        B     EXIT00                                                98
*---------------------------------------------------------------*   99
*       EXIT ROUTINES                                           *  100
*---------------------------------------------------------------*  101
EXIT00  DS    0H                     SUCCESSFUL                    102
        LA    15,X'00'                                             103
        B     EXIT                                                 104
EXIT08  DS    0H                     DSPFIND NOT LINK-EDITED       105
        LA    15,X'08'                                             106
        B     EXIT                                                 107
EXIT10  DS    0H                     DSPFIND DID NOT FIND DATASPACE 108
        PERCRC RC=X'10'                                            109
        B     EXIT                                                 110
*---------------------------------------------------------------*  111
*       COMMON EXIT                                             *  112
*---------------------------------------------------------------*  113
```

Figure 11.8 *(Continued)*

```
EXIT      DS    OH                                                       114
          LR    R2,R15                    PRESERVE RETURN CODE IN R2     115
*         *-----------------------------------------*                   116
*         *   DEQ DATASPACE STORAGE           *                         117
*         *-----------------------------------------*                   118
          DEQ   (DSNAME1,DSRANGE,L'DSRANGE,SYSTEM),RET=HAVE              119
          DEQ   (DSNAME2,DSRANGE,L'DSRANGE,SYSTEM),RET=HAVE              120
          LR    R15,R2                    RESTORE RETURN CODE TO R15     121
          ENDMOD                                                        122
*--------------------------------------------------------------*        123
*         CONSTANTS                                             *        124
*--------------------------------------------------------------*        125
WTOLIST   WTO   'WTO PARMLIST MOVED: HOME => DSP1 => DSP2 => HOME',MF=L  126
LWTOLIST  EQU   *-WTOLIST                                               127
DSNAME1   DC    CL(L'DSP_XNAME)'DSP1'                                   128
DSNAME2   DC    CL(L'DSP_XNAME)'DSP2'                                   129
DSRANGE   DC    C'LOW100'                                               130
*--------------------------------------------------------------*        131
*         WORK AREA                                             *        132
*--------------------------------------------------------------*        133
WDSPUT    DSECT                                                         134
DSPPARMS  DS    OF,CL(LDSPTBLE)           PARMLIST FOR DSPFIND SERVICE   135
ALET1     DS    F                         ALET FOR DSP1                  136
ORIGIN1   DS    F                         ORIGIN FOR DSP1                137
ALET2     DS    F                         ALET FOR DSP2                  138
ORIGIN2   DS    F                         ORIGIN FOR DSP2                139
WTOPARM   DS    OF,CL(LWTOLIST)           WTO PARMLIST                   140
LDSPUT    EQU   *-WDSPUT                                                141
*--------------------------------------------------------------*        142
*         OTHER DSECTS                                          *        143
*--------------------------------------------------------------*        144
          DSPTBLE                         MAP DSPTBLE BLOCK              145
          END                                                          146
```

Figure 11.8 (*Continued*)

program. ENQs are similar in this way to MVS locks which must be obtained according to a defined hierarchy.

ENQ major and minor names are arbitrary tokens that are application dependent. In this case, each major name/minor name combination represents the first 100 bytes of storage in a dataspace. Other major name/minor name combinations could have been defined to represent other shareable resources. Devising an appropriate major name/minor name structure to which all applications in a system adhere to is an essential part of the design of a system that has shareable resources.

After the second call to DSPFIND, the SAC 512 instruction on line 70 changes bits 16 and 17 in the PSW to 10 initiating access register addressing mode. Lines 71 and 72 load X'00000000' into the access registers corresponding to the program's base register (register 12) and reentrant work area (register 13) so that addresses based on these registers will reference storage in the primary address space.

Line 73 sets the global variable &SYSASCE so that macros will expand with ALET-qualified parameter lists (see Chap. 2). Even though no macros are invoked while DSPUT is in access register mode, it is good practice to issue SYSSTATE whenever changing to AR mode, since enhancements to the program might introduce macros.

Lines 81 through 84 load the ALETs for the two dataspaces into access registers 6 and 7 and the virtual addresses of the first bytes in each of the dataspaces (the dataspace origins) into general registers 6 and 7. Since DSPUT is in access register addressing mode, the MVCs on lines 85 through 87 cause access register translation (ART) of the ALETs in the access registers as well as Dynamic Address Translation (DAT) of the virtual addresses in the general registers. The MVCs thus move a WTO parameter list from DSPUT's address space to the DSP1 dataspace, from the DSP1 dataspace to the DSP2 dataspace, and from the DSP2 dataspace to a different location in the DSPUT address space.

After returning to primary space addressing mode with SAC 0 on line 91 and setting &SYSASCE for primary space macro expansions (line 92), line 97 issues WTO against the parameter list that was moved through the dataspaces.

Macros for Reentrant Code

```
        MACRO                                                               1
        MODULE &CNAME,&AMODE=31,&RMODE=ANY,&SP=1,&LOC=,&BASE=12,        X    2
              &ENTRY=BRANCH,&FLOATSV=NO,&RENT=YES,&WORK=YES,            X    3
              &TEXT=' '                                                      4
.**********************************************************************      5
.*   BEGIN MODULE WITH THIS MACRO                                     *      6
.*      &CNAME    - NAME OF MODULE (7 CHARACTERS OR LESS)             *      7
.*      &AMODE    - "24" OR "31"                                      *      8
.*      &RMODE    - "24" OR "ANY"                                     ^      9
.*      &SP       - SUBPOOL FOR RENTRANT STORAGE THIS MODULE          *     10
.*      &LOC      - "BELOW" IF GETMAINED STORAGE BELOW 16M            *     11
.*      &BASE     - BASE REGISTER (NOT R1, R2 OR R13)                 *     12
.*      &ENTRY    - "BRANCH" "PCSTACK" "PCBASIC" "SRB" OR "SVC"       *     13
.*      &FLOATSV  - SAVE FLOATING POINT REGISTERS                     *     14
.*      &RENT     - WORK AREA DYNAMICALLY OBTAINED (DEFAULT = YES)    *     15
.*      &WORK     - WORK AREA TO BE GOTTEN (DEFAULT = YES)            *     16
.*      &TEXT     - COMMENT THAT IS ASSEMBLED INTO OBJECT CODE        *     17
.**********************************************************************     18
        GBLA  &POOL                                                        19
        GBLB  &EQU                                                         20
        GBLB  &CALSA,&WORKA,&FLOAT,&RENTA                                  21
        GBLC  &SYSSPLV,&SYSASCE                                            22
        GBLC  &DSCTLEN,&NRENTWK,&DNAME                                     23
        GBLC  &SAVEGEN,&SAVELEN,&SAVEFLT,&SPLEVI                           24
        LCLB  &E1                                                          25
        LCLC  &BEGIN,&TXT,&ONSTACK                                         26
        SPLEVEL  TEST                                                      27
```

Figure A.1 MODULE.

```
.****************************************************       28
.*        CHECK ERROR CONDITIONS                    *       29
.****************************************************       30
&E1       SETB  0                                           31
          AIF   (T'&CNAME NE 'O').OK1                       32
          MNOTE 8,'MODULE NAME IS REQUIRED'                 33
&E1       SETB  1                                           34
.OK1      ANOP                                              35
          AIF   (K'&CNAME LE 7).OK2                         36
          MNOTE 8,'MODULE NAME MUST BE LESS THAN 7 CHARACTERS'  37
&E1       SETB  1                                           38
.OK2      ANOP                                              39
          AIF   (&BASE GT 2 AND &BASE LT 13).OK3            40
          MNOTE 8,'ONLY REGISTERS 3 THROUGH 12 CAN BE BASE REGISTERS'  41
&E1       SETB  1                                           42
.OK3      ANOP                                              43
          AIF   ('&ENTRY' EQ 'BRANCH' OR '&ENTRY' EQ 'PCSTACK').OK4   44
          AIF   ('&ENTRY' EQ 'PCBASIC' OR '&ENTRY' EQ 'SRB').OK4      45
          AIF   ('&ENTRY' EQ 'SVC').OK4                     46
          MNOTE 8,'"ENTRY="  "BRANCH","PCSTACK","PCBASIC","SRB","SVC"'  47
&E1       SETB  1                                           48
.OK4      ANOP                                              49
          AIF   ('&ENTRY' NE 'PCSTACK' OR '&SYSSPLV' GT '2').OK5   50
          MNOTE 8,'"ENTRY=PCSTACK" MUST BE ASSEMBLED "SPLEVEL > 2" '  51
&E1       SETB  1                                           52
.OK5      ANOP                                              53
          AIF   ('&ENTRY' NE 'SVC').OK6                     54
          AIF   ('&BASE' EQ '6').OK6                        55
          MNOTE 8,'BASE REGISTER MUST BE 6 WITH "ENTRY=SVC" '  56
&E1       SETB  1                                           57
.OK6      ANOP                                              58
          AIF   (&E1).MEND                                  59
.****************************************************       60
.*        SET GLOBAL SYMBOLS                        *       61
.****************************************************       62
&POOL     SETA  &SP                                         63
&SPLEVI   SETC  '&SYSSPLV'                                  64
&DSCTLEN  SETC  'L'.'&CNAME'                                65
&NRENTWK  SETC  'N'.'&CNAME'                                66
&DNAME    SETC  'W'.'&CNAME'                                67
&BEGIN    SETC  'BEG'.'&SYSNDX'                             68
&SAVEGEN  SETC  'GEN'.'&SYSNDX'                             69
&SAVEFLT  SETC  'FLT'.'&SYSNDX'                             70
&SAVELEN  SETC  'LEN'.'&SYSNDX'                             71
&ONSTACK  SETC  'STK'.'&SYSNDX'                             72
&TXT      SETC  '&TEXT'                                     73
          AIF   ('&TXT'(1,1) EQ '''').STRIP                 74
          AIF   ('&TXT'(1,1) EQ '(').STRIP                  75
          AGO   .NOSTRIP                                    76
.STRIP    ANOP                                              77
&TXT      SETC  '&TXT'(2,K'&TXT-2)                          78
.NOSTRIP  ANOP                                              79
```

Figure A.1 *(Continued)*

```
.*****************************************************    80
.*          SET GLOBAL SWITCHES                      *    81
.*****************************************************    82
&WORKA   SETB  0     OBTAIN REENTRANT WORKAREA ?          83
         AIF   ('&WORK'(1,1) EQ 'N').NWORK               84
         AIF   ('&ENTRY' EQ 'PCBASIC' AND '&SPLEVI' LT '3').NWORK    85
         AIF   ('&ENTRY' EQ 'SVC' AND '&SPLEVI' LT '3').NWORK        86
&WORKA   SETB  1                                         87
.NWORK   ANOP                                            88
&RENTA   SETB  0     OBTAIN WORK AREA AND NON-REENTRANT   89
         AIF   ('&RENT'(1,1) EQ 'N').NRENT               90
         AIF   ('&ENTRY' EQ 'SRB' AND '&SPLEVI' LT '3').NRENT        91
&RENTA   SETB  1                                         92
.NRENT   ANOP                                            93
&CALSA   SETB  0     IS SAVE AREA PROVIDED BY CALLER ?    94
         AIF   ('&ENTRY'(1,2) EQ 'PC').NSAVE             95
         AIF   ('&ENTRY' EQ 'SRB').NSAVE                 96
         AIF   ('&ENTRY' EQ 'SVC').NSAVE                 97
&CALSA   SETB  1                                         98
.NSAVE   ANOP                                            99
&FLOAT   SETB  0     ARE FLOATING POINT REGISTERS SAVED ? 100
         AIF   ('&FLOATSV'(1,1) EQ 'N').NFLOT            101
         AIF   (&WORKA EQ 0).NFLOT                       102
&FLOAT   SETB  1                                         103
.NFLOT   ANOP                                            104
&CNAME   CSECT                                           105
         AIF   ('&SPLEVI' LT '2').NOAMODE                106
*        *-------------------------------------*         107
*        *    SPECIFY AMODE AND RMODE          *         108
*        *-------------------------------------*         109
&CNAME   AMODE &AMODE                                    110
&CNAME   RMODE &RMODE                                    111
.NOAMODE ANOP                                            112
         AIF   (&WORKA NE 1).NOWORKO                     113
*        +-------------------------------------+         114
*        |    SAVE AREAS                       |         115
*        +-------------------------------------+         116
&DNAME   DSECT                   USER ACQUIRED STORAGE FOR REENTRABLE  117
&SAVEGEN DS    18F               GENERAL REGISTER SAVE AREA  118
         AIF   (&FLOAT NE 1).NOF1                        119
&SAVEFLT DS    4D                FLOATING POINT REGISTER SAVE AREA  120
.NOF1    ANOP                                            121
&SAVELEN DS    F                 LENGTH OF ACQUIRED STORAGE  122
&CNAME   CSECT                                           123
.NOWORKO ANOP                                            124
         AIF   (&EQU).NOEQU                              125
&EQU     SETB  1                                         126
*        *-------------------------------------*         127
*        *    REGISTER EQUATES                 *         128
*        *-------------------------------------*         129
         PRINT NOGEN                                     130
         COPY  EQUATES                                   131
         PRINT GEN                                       132
.NOEQU   ANOP                                            133
*        *-------------------------------------*         134
*        *    ENTRY POINT                      *         135
*        *-------------------------------------*         136
         AIF   ('&ENTRY'(1,2) EQ 'PC').PCENT             137
         AIF   ('&ENTRY' EQ 'SVC').SVCENT                138
```

Figure A.1 *(Continued)*

```
.*************************************************            139
.*          ENTRY = BRANCH AND SRB                *           140
.*************************************************            141
          USING &CNAME,15              SET ADDRESSING ON ENTRY POINT     142
          B     &BEGIN                 BRANCH AROUND EYECATCHER          143
          DC    C' &CNAME '            NAME OF CSECT                     144
          DC    C' &SYSDATE '          DATE OF ASSEMBLY                  145
          DC    C' &SYSTIME '          TIME OF ASSEMBLY                  146
          DC    C' &TXT '                                                147
          AIF   ('&SPLEVI' LT '3').XA1                                   148
          AIF   (&WORKA EQ 0).NL1                                        149
&ONSTACK  DC    C'F1SA'                CALLER'S SAVE AREA ON STACK       150
.NL1      ANOP                                                           151
&BEGIN    BAKR  14,0                   PUSH REGS AND PSW ONTO STACK      152
          LAE   &BASE,0(15,0)          LOAD BASE REGISTER WITH ENTRYPNT  153
          MSTA  0                      PUSH REGS AND PSW ONTO STACK      154
          AGO   .DROP15                DROP ADDRESSING ON ENTRY POINT    155
.XA1      ANOP                                                           156
          AIF   (&CALSA NE 1).NOSA1                                      157
&BEGIN    SAVE  (14,12)                CALLER'S REGS => CALLER'S SAVEAREA 158
          LR    &BASE,15               LOAD BASE REGISTER WITH ENTRY POINT 159
          AGO   .DROP15                DROP ADDRESSING ON ENTRY POINT    160
.NOSA1    ANOP                                                           161
&BEGIN    LR    &BASE,15               LOAD BASE REGISTER WITH ENTRY POINT 162
.DROP15   ANOP                                                           163
          DROP  15                     DROP ADDRESSING ON ENTRY POINT    164
          USING &CNAME,&BASE           SET ADDRESSING ON BASE REGISTER   165
          AGO   .CKSTG                                                   166
.*************************************************            167
.*          ENTRY = PCSTACK AND PCBASIC           *           168
.*************************************************            169
.PCENT    ANOP                                                           170
          BALR  &BASE,0                LOAD BASE REGISTER                171
          BCTR  &BASE,0                .. SUBTRACT 2 FROM                172
          BCTR  &BASE,0                .. BASE REGISTER                  173
          USING &CNAME,&BASE           SET ADDRESSING ON ENTRY POINT     174
          AIF   ('&SPLEVI' LT '3').PC2                                   175
          LAE   &BASE,0(&BASE,0)       CLEAR BASE ACCESS REGISTER        176
          MSTA  0                      SAVE REGS 1 AND 2 IN USER STACK   177
.PC2      ANOP                                                           178
          B     &BEGIN                 BRANCH AROUND EYECATCHER          179
          DC    C' &CNAME '            NAME OF CSECT                     180
          DC    C' &SYSDATE '          DATE OF ASSEMBLY                  181
          DC    C' &SYSTIME '          TIME OF ASSEMBLY                  182
          DC    C' &TXT '                                                183
          AIF   (&WORKA EQ 0).NL2                                        184
&ONSTACK  DC    C'F1SA'                CALLER'S SAVE AREA ON STACK       185
.NL2      ANOP                                                           186
&BEGIN    DS    0H                                                       187
          AGO   .CKSTG                                                   188
.SVCENT   ANOP                                                           189
```

Figure A.1 *(Continued)*

```
.********************************************************        190
.*        ENTRY = SVC                              *        191
.********************************************************        192
         USING &CNAME,6           SET ADDRESSING ON ENTRY POINT   193
         B     &BEGIN             BRANCH AROUND EYECATCHER        194
         DC    C' &CNAME '        NAME OF CSECT                   195
         DC    C' &SYSDATE '      DATE OF ASSEMBLY                196
         DC    C' &SYSTIME '      TIME OF ASSEMBLY                197
         DC    C' &TXT '                                          198
         AIF   ('&SPLEVI' LT '3').XA3                             199
         AIF   (&WORKA EQ 0).NL3                                  200
&ONSTACK DC    C'F1SA'            CALLER'S SAVE AREA ON STACK     201
.NL3     ANOP                                                     202
&BEGIN   BAKR  14,0               PUSH REGS AND PSW ONTO STACK    203
         MSTA  0                  PUSH REGS AND PSW ONTO STACK    204
         AGO   .ESVCE             DROP ADDRESSING ON ENTRY POINT  205
.XA3     ANOP                                                     206
&BEGIN   DS    0H                                                 207
.ESVCE   ANOP                                                     208
.CKSTG   ANOP                                                     209
.********************************************************        210
.*        GET A WORK AREA FOR REENTRANCY            *        211
.********************************************************        212
         AIF   (&WORKA EQ 0).NOWORK                               213
         AIF   (&RENTA EQ 1).YESRENT                              214
         LA    13,&NRENTWK        ADDRESS OF WORK AREA            215
         AGO   .MAPDSECT                                          216
.YESRENT ANOP                                                     217
*        *---------------------------------------*               218
*        *     GET STORAGE FOR WORK AREA         *               219
*        *---------------------------------------*               220
         LA    0,&DSCTLEN         LENGTH OF STORAGE               221
         AIF   (T'&LOC EQ '0' OR '&SPLEVI' LT '2').NOLOC          222
         AIF   ('&SPLEVI' LT '3').NOSTOR                          223
         STORAGE OBTAIN,COND=NO,                                X 224
               LENGTH=(0),                                      X 225
               LOC=&LOC,                                        X 226
               SP=&POOL,                                        X 227
               ADDR=(1)                                           228
         AGO   .GOT                                               229
.NOSTOR  ANOP                                                     230
         GETMAIN RU,                                            X 231
               LV=(0),                                          X 232
               LOC=&LOC,                                        X 233
               SP=&POOL                                           234
         AGO   .GOT                                               235
.NOLOC   ANOP                                                     236
         AIF   ('&SPLEVI' LT '3').NOSTOR1                         237
         STORAGE OBTAIN,COND=NO,                                X 238
               LENGTH=(0),                                      X 239
               SP=&POOL,                                        X 240
               ADDR=(1)                                           241
         AGO   .GOT                                               242
.NOSTOR1 ANOP                                                     243
         GETMAIN RU,                                            X 244
               LV=(0),                                          X 245
               SP=&POOL                                           246
```

Figure A.1 *(Continued)*

```
.GOT        ANOP                                                           247
            AIF    ('&SPLEVI' GT '2').ESA2                                 248
            AIF    (&CALSA EQ 0).NOCSA0                                    249
            LR     2,13              PRESERVE ADDRESS CALLER'S SAVEAREA    250
            ST     13,4(1)           SAVE A(CALLER'S SAVE AREA)            251
            ST     1,8(13)           A(SAVE AREA) => CALLER'S SAVE AREA    252
.NOCSA0     ANOP                                                          253
            LR     13,1              A(SAVE AREA THIS CSECT) => R13        254
            AGO    .MAPDSECT                                              255
.ESA2       ANOP                                                         256
            AIF    (&CALSA EQ 0).NOCSA                                   257
            ST     1,8(0,13)         A(SAVE AREA) => CALLER'S SAVE AREA   258
.NOCSA      ANOP                                                         259
            LAE    13,0(1,0)         LOAD SAVE AREA GEN AND ACC REGS      260
*                                    INDICATE CALLER'S SAVEAREA ON STACK  261
            MVC    4(L'&ONSTACK,13),&ONSTACK                             262
.MAPDSECT   ANOP                                                         263
            USING  &DNAME,13         ADDRESSING FOR SAVE AREA             264
            ST     0,&SAVELEN        SAVE SUBPOOL AND LENGTH              265
.****************************************************                     266
.*          RESTORE REGISTERS FROM STACK OR          *                   267
.*          CALLER'S SAVE AREA                       *                   268
.****************************************************                     269
.NOWORK     ANOP                                                         270
            AIF    ('&SPLEVI' LT '3').XA2                                271
            EREG   14,1              RESTORE REGS FROM STACK              272
            AGO    .NOCSA2                                               273
.XA2        ANOP                                                         274
            AIF    (&CALSA EQ 0 OR &WORKA EQ 0).NOCSA2                   275
            LM     14,2,12(2)        RESTORE REGS FROM CALLER'S SAVEAREA  276
.NOCSA2     ANOP                                                         277
.******     SAVE FLOATING POINT REGISTERS **********                    278
            AIF    (&FLOAT EQ 0).MEND                                    279
            STD    0,&SAVEFLT        ..SAVE                              280
            STD    2,&SAVEFLT+8      ..FLOATING                          281
            STD    4,&SAVEFLT+16     ..POINT                             282
            STD    6,&SAVEFLT+24     ..REGISTERS                         283
.MEND       MEND                                                         284
```

Figure A.1 *(Continued)*

```
        MACRO                                                               1
        ENDMOD                                                              2
.*******************************************************************         3
.*          END MODULE WITH THIS MACRO                          *            4
.*******************************************************************         5
        GBLA  &POOL                                                         6
        GBLB  &CALSA,&WORKA,&FLOAT,&RENTA                                   7
        GBLC  &SYSSPLV,&SYSASCE                                             8
        GBLC  &DSCTLEN,&NRENTWK,&DNAME                                      9
        GBLC  &SAVEGEN,&SAVELEN,&SAVEFLT,&SPLEVI                           10
        LCLC  &AROUND                                                      11
&AROUND SETC  'AWK'.'&SYSNDX'                                              12
*----------------------------------------------------------------*          13
*          COMMON EXIT                                           *           14
*----------------------------------------------------------------*          15
        AIF   (&FLOAT EQ 0).NOFLT                                          16
        LD    0,&SAVEFLT            .. RESTORE                             17
        LD    2,&SAVEFLT+8          ..FLOATING                            18
        LD    4,&SAVEFLT+16         ..POINT                               19
        LD    6,&SAVEFLT+24         ..REGISTERS                           20
.NOFLT  ANOP                                                              21
        AIF   (&WORKA EQ 0).NOWORK                                        22
        AIF   (&RENTA EQ 1).YRENT                                         23
        B     &AROUND              BRANCH AROUND WORK AREA                24
        CNOP  0,8                  FORCE DOUBLEWORD ALIGNMENT             25
&NRENTWK DS   CL(&DSCTLEN)         WORK AREA                              26
&AROUND DS    0H                                                          27
        AGO   .NOWORK                                                     28
.YRENT  ANOP                                                              29
        L     0,&SAVELEN           LENGTH OF STORAGE                      30
        AIF   ('&SPLEVI' GT '2').ESA1                                     31
        LR    1,13                 A(SAVE AREA) => R2                     32
        AIF   (&CALSA EQ 0).NOCSA                                         33
        L     13,&SAVEGEN+4        A(CALLER'S SAVE AREA)                  34
*                                  FREE WORK AREA STORAGE                 35
.NOCSA  ANOP                                                              36
        LR    2,15                                                        37
        FREEMAIN RU,                                              X        38
              LV=(0),                                             X        39
              SP=&POOL,                                           X        40
              A=(1)                                                        41
        LR    15,2                                                        42
        AGO   .NOWORK                                                     43
.ESA1   ANOP                                                              44
        LR    2,15                 RETURN CODE => R2                      45
*                                  FREE WORK AREA STORAGE                 46
        STORAGE RELEASE,COND=NO,                                 X        47
              LENGTH=(0),                                         X        48
              ADDR=(13),                                          X        49
              SP=&POOL                                                     50
        LR    15,2                 RETURN CODE => R15                     51
.NOWORK ANOP                                                              52
        AIF   ('&SPLEVI' LT '3').NOESA1                                   53
        LA    0,3                  ..RESTORE REGS 0 AND 1                 54
        ESTA  0,0                  ..FROM STACK MODIFIABLE AREA           55
        PR                         RESTORE REGS AND RETURN                56
        AGO   .MEND                                                       57
```

Figure A.2 ENDMOD.

```
.NOESA1   ANOP                                                            58
          AIF    (&CALSA EQ 0).NOCSA1                                     59
          ST     15,16(,13)                                               60
          LM     14,12,12(13)         RESTORE CALLER'S REGISTERS          61
.NOCSA1   ANOP                                                            62
          AIF    ('&SYSSPLV' EQ '1').NOXA1                                63
          BSM    0,14                RESTORE AMODE AND RETURN             64
          AGO    .MEND                                                    65
.NOXA1    ANOP                                                            66
          BR     14                  RETURN TO CALLER                     67
          AGO    .MEND                                                    68
*         *-----------------------------------*                          69
*         *    LITERALS                       *                          70
*         *-----------------------------------*                          71
.MEND     ANOP                                                           72
          LTORG                                                           73
          MEND                                                           74
```

Figure A.2 *(Continued)*

```
          MACRO                                                            1
          PERCRC  &RC=X'10'                                                2
*****************************************************************          3
.*        PERCOLATE RETURN AND REASON CODE FROM INVOKED SERVICE  *         4
*****************************************************************          5
          GBLB   &CALSA,&WORKA,&FLOAT                                      6
          GBLC   &SAVEGEN,&SAVEFLT,&SAVELEN,&DNAME,&SPLEVI                 7
          GBLC   &SYSSPLV,&SYSASCE                                         8
*         *-----------------------------------*                           9
*         *    PERCOLATE RETURN AND REASON CODES *                       10
*         *-----------------------------------*                          11
          LR     1,0                 REASON CODE FROM SERVICE             12
          LR     0,15                RETURN CODE FROM SERVICE             13
          AIF    ('&SPLEVI' LT '3').NOTSTK                                14
          MSTA   0                   REGS 0 AND 1 TO STACK MODIFIYABLE    15
          AGO    .RCODE                                                   16
.NOTSTK   ANOP                                                           17
          AIF    (&WORKA EQ 0 OR &CALSA EQ 0).R1                         18
          L      14,&SAVEGEN+4       A(CALLER'S SAVE AREA)               19
          STM    0,1,20(14)          REGS 0,1 TO CALLER'S SAVEAREA       20
          AGO    .RCODE                                                   21
.R1       ANOP                                                           22
          AIF    (&CALSA EQ 0).RCODE                                     23
          STM    0,1,20(13)          REGS 0,1 TO CALLER'S SAVEAREA       24
.RCODE    ANOP                                                           25
          INNERMM &RC,15                                                 26
.MEND     MEND                                                           27
```

Figure A.3 PERCRC.

```
        MACRO                                                              1
        INNERMM &OP,&REG                                                   2
.*********************************************************************     3
.*      INNER MACRO FOR PARSING REGISTER OPERANDS OF MACROS        *       4
.*********************************************************************     5
        LCLC  &R,&OP1                                                      6
        AIF   (T'&OP  EQ 'O').MEND                                         7
&OP1    SETC  '&OP'                                                        8
&R      SETC  'A'                                                          9
        AIF   ('&OP1'(1,1) NE '(').NOTREG                                 10
&R      SETC  'R'                                                         11
&OP1    SETC  '&OP'(2,K'&OP-2)                                            12
.NOTREG ANOP                                                              13
        L&R   &REG,&OP1                                                   14
.MEND   MEND                                                              15
```

Figure A.4 INNERMM.

```
A0      EQU   0        ACCESS REGISTER  0                  1
..      ..    ..       ..
A15     EQU   15       ACCESS REGISTER  15                16
C0      EQU   0        CONTROL REGISTER 0                 17
..      ..    ..       ..
C15     EQU   15       CONTROL REGISTER 15                32
R0      EQU   0        GENERAL REGISTER 0                 33
..      ..    ..       ..
R15     EQU   15       GENERAL REGISTER 15                48
V0      EQU   0        VECTOR REGISTER 0                  49
..      ..    ..       ..
V15     EQU   15       VECTOR REGISTER 15                 64
F0      EQU   0        FLOATING POINT REGISTERS 0/1       65
..      ..    ..       ..
F6      EQU   6        FLOATING POINT REGISTERS 6/7       68
```

Figure A.5 EQUATES.

Programs and Macros Invoked by Programs in Chapters 4–11

```
          MACRO                                                          1
&LABEL    XTOC  &PLIST=,&ADOUT=,&LOUT=,&ADIN=,&LIN=                      2
.*********************************************************************   3
.*        GENERATES CALLING SEQUENCE FOR HEXPRT SERVICE            *     4
.*                  (CONVERT HEX TO PRINTABLE CHARACTERS)          *     5
.*        &PLIST  -  ADDRESS OF PARAMETER LIST                     *     6
.*        &ADOUT  -  ADDRESS OF OUTPUT STRING                      *     7
.*        &LOUT   -  LENGTH OF OUTPUT STRING                       *     8
.*        &ADIN   -  ADDRESS OF INPUT STRING                       *     9
.*        &LIN    -  LENGTH OF INPUT STRING                        *    10
.*********************************************************************  11
          LCLB  &E1                                                     12
          LCLC  &OP,&R,&LBL1,&LBL2                                      13
&LBL1     SETC  'PHX'.'&SYSNDX'                                         14
&LBL2     SETC  'PXX'.'&SYSNDX'                                         15
          AIF   (T'&PLIST NE '0').OK1                                   16
          MNOTE 8,'OPERAND "PLIST" IS REQUIRED'                         17
&E1       SETB  1                                                       18
.OK1      ANOP                                                          19
          AIF   (T'&ADOUT NE '0').OK2                                   20
          MNOTE 8,'OPERAND "ADOUT" IS REQUIRED'                         21
&E1       SETB  1                                                       22
.OK2      ANOP                                                          23
          AIF   (T'&LOUT NE '0').OK3                                    24
          MNOTE 8,'OPERAND "LOUT" IS REQUIRED'                          25
&E1       SETB  1                                                       26
.OK3      ANOP                                                          27
          AIF   (T'&ADIN NE '0').OK4                                    28
          MNOTE 8,'OPERAND "ADIN" IS REQUIRED'                          29
&E1       SETB  1                                                       30
.OK4      ANOP                                                          31
          AIF   (T'&LIN NE '0').OK5                                     32
          MNOTE 8,'OPERAND "LIN" IS REQUIRED'                           33
```

Figure B.1 XTOC.

```
&E1      SETB  1                                                              34
.OK5     ANOP                                                                 35
         AIF   (&E1).MEND                                                     36
.********************************************************************         37
.*       BUILD PARM LIST AND INVOKE SERVICE                         *         38
.********************************************************************         39
         INNERMM &PLIST,1                                                     40
         INNERMM &ADOUT,15                                                    41
         ST    15,0(1)            .. TO PLIST                                 42
         INNERMM &LOUT,15                                                     43
         ST    15,4(1)            .. TO PLIST                                 44
         INNERMM &ADIN,15                                                     45
         ST    15,8(1)            .. TO PLIST                                 46
         INNERMM &LIN,15                                                      47
         ST    15,12(1)           .. TO PLIST                                 48
         ICM   15,B'1111',=V(HEXPRT) .. ADDRESS OF OUTPUT STRING              49
         BNZ   &LBL1              =0; ROUTINE IS NOT LINKED                   50
         LA    15,13              LOAD RETURN CODE = 13                       51
         B     &LBL2              DO NOT INVOKE ROUTINE                       52
&LBL1    DS    0H                 INVOKE THE ROUTINE                          53
         O     15,=A(X'80000000') SET 31BIT ENTRY                            54
         BASSM 14,15              INVOKE THE ROUTINE                          55
&LBL2    DS    0H                                                             56
.MEND    MEND                                                                 57
```

Figure B.1   *(Continued)*.

```
*+----------------------------------------------------------------+   1
*|  FUNCTION:                                                      |   2
*|     CONVERT HEX STRING TO HEX IN CHARACTER FORMAT.              |   3
*|  INPUT:                                                         |   4
*|     R1 - ADDRESS OF 4 WORD PARMLIST                             |   5
*|             1ST WORD - ADDRESS OF OUTPUT STRING                 |   6
*|             2ND WORD - LENGTH OF OUTPUT STRING                  |   7
*|             3RD WORD - ADDRESS OF INPUT STRING                  |   8
*|             4TH WORD - LENGTH OF INPUT STRING                   |   9
*|  OUTPUT:                                                        |  10
*|     R15 -RETURN CODE                                            |  11
*|         0 - INPUT STRING TRANSLATED TO OUTPUT STRING            |  12
*|         4 - OUTPUT AREA LONGER  THAN 2*INPUT (PADDING)          |  13
*|         8 - OUTPUT AREA SHORTER THAN 2*INPUT (TRUNCATION)       |  14
*|        12 - OUTPUT AREA NOT ALLOCATED BY CALLER.                |  15
*|  LOGIC:                                                         |  16
*|     THE HIGH AND LOW ORDER 4 BITS OF EACH INPUT BYTE ARE        |  17
*|         PUT IN THE LOW ORDER 4 BITS OF 2 OUTPUT BYTES:          |  18
*|         INPUT:  |A5|37| ==> OUTPUT: |0A|05|03|07|               |  19
*|                                                                |  20
*|     THE TR INSTRUCTION IS USED TO TRANSLATE TO PRINTABLE HEX    |  21
*|         OUTPUT: |0A|05|03|07| ==>    |C1|F5|F3|F7|              |  22
*|  ATTRIBUTES:                                                    |  23
*|     REENTRANT AMODE 31 RMODE ANY                                |  24
*+----------------------------------------------------------------+  25
            MODULE HEXPRT,BASE=12,LOC=BELOW,AMODE=31,RMODE=ANY,     X  26
                 TEXT='CONVERT HEX STRING TO PRINTABLE'                27
            LR   R3,R1                   PARMLIST ADDRESS TO R3        28
            LM   R4,R7,0(R3)             LOAD PARMS                    29
*           *----------------------------------------*                30
*           *   R4 = ADDRESS OF OUTPUT STRING    *                    31
*           *   R5 = LENGTH   OF OUTPUT STRING   *                    32
*           *   R6 = ADDRESS OF INPUT STRING     *                    33
*           *   R7 = LENGTH   OF INPUT STRING    *                    34
*           *----------------------------------------*                35
*           *----------------------------------------*                36
*           *    TEST IF OUTPUT IS ALLOCATED     *                    37
*           *----------------------------------------*                38
            VSMLOC PVT,AREA=((R4),(R5)) .. OUTPUT ALLOCATED           39
            LTR  R15,R15                 .. IN USER PRIVATE AREA ?     40
            BNZ  EXIT0C                  NO; EXIT                      41
*           *----------------------------------------*                42
*           *    CLEAR OUTPUT STRING             *                    43
*           *----------------------------------------*                44
            XR   R7,R7                   .. SET                       45
            ICM  R7,B'1000',=X'40'       .. OUTPUT                    46
            MVCL R4,R6                    .. TO X'40'                  47
*           *----------------------------------------*                48
*           *    INPUT TO OUTPUT AND TRANSLATE   *                    49
*           *----------------------------------------*                50
            LM   R4,R7,0(R3)             LOAD PARMS                    51
HLOOP       DS   0H                                                   52
            CH   R5,=H'2'                AT LEAST 2 BYTES IN OUPUT ?   53
            BNL  MOREOP                  YES; CONTINUE                 54
            CH   R7,=H'1'                AT LEAST 1 BYTES IN INPUT ?   55
            BNL  EXIT08                  YES; EXIT INDICATING TRUNCATION 56
            B    EXIT00                  NO INPUT STRING/NO OUTPUT STRING 57
```

Figure B.2 HEXPRT.

```
MOREOP   DS    0H                                                              58
         CH    R7,=H'1'               AT LEAST 1 BYTES IN INPUT ?              59
         BL    EXIT04                 NO; EXIT INDICATING PADDING              60
         ICM   R8,B'0010',0(R6)       INPUT BYTE TO REGISTER                   61
         SRL   R8,4                   SHIFT HIGH NYBBLE TO LOW NYBBLE          62
         ICM   R8,B'0001',0(R6)       INPUT BYTE TO REGISTER                   63
         N     R8,=A(X'00000F0F')     MASK OFF IRRELVANT BITS                  64
         STCM  R8,B'0011',0(R4)       STORE 2 BYTES TO OUTPUT                  65
*                                     TRANSLATE OUTPUT                         66
         TR    0(2,R4),=C'0123456789ABCDEF'                                    67
         SH    R5,=H'2'               DECREMENT OUTPUT LENGTH                  68
         LA    R4,2(R4)               BUMP IN OUTPUT STRING                    69
         LA    R6,1(R6)               BUMP IN INPUT STRING                     70
         BCTR  R7,0                   DECREMENT INPUT LENGTH                   71
         B     HLOOP                  CHECK NEXT BYTES                         72
*-------------------------------------------------------------------*         73
*        EXIT ROUTINES                                              *         74
*-------------------------------------------------------------------*         75
EXIT00   DS    0H                     NO PADDING OR TRUNCATION                 76
         LA    R15,X'00'                                                       77
         B     EXIT                                                            78
EXIT04   DS    0H                     OUTPUT STRING PADDED                     79
         LA    R15,X'04'                                                       80
         B     EXIT                                                            81
EXIT08   DS    0H                     INPUT STRING TRUNCATED                   82
         LA    R15,X'08'                                                       83
         B     EXIT                                                            84
EXIT0C   DS    0H                     OUTPUT STRING AREA NOT ALLOCATED         85
         LA    R15,X'0C'                                                       86
         B     EXIT                                                            87
*-------------------------------------------------------------------*         88
*        COMMON EXIT                                                *         89
*-------------------------------------------------------------------*         90
EXIT     DS    0H                                                              91
         ENDMOD                                                                92
*-------------------------------------------------------------------*         93
*        WORK AREA                                                  *         94
*-------------------------------------------------------------------*         95
WHEXPRT  DSECT                                                                 96
LHEXPRT  EQU   *-WHEXPRT                                                       97
         END                                                 .                 98
```

Figure B.2 *(Continued)*

```
        MACRO                                                            1
&LABEL  GET24  &DCB,&AREA,&RPL=,&REG=                                    2
        LCLB   &E1                                                       3
        LCLC   &LBL1,&LBL2                                               4
.*****************************************************************        5
.*             PERFORM 24 BIT I/O IN 31 BIT PROGRAM              *        6
.*             REG = PARAMETER NAMES A WORK REGISTER             *        7
.*****************************************************************        8
        AIF    (T'&REG NE '0').OK1                                       9
        MNOTE 8,'OPERAND "REG" IS REQUIRED'                             10
&E1     SETB   1                                                        11
.OK1    ANOP                                                            12
        AIF    (&E1).MEND                                               13
&LBL1   SETC   'GTT'.'&SYSNDX'                                          14
&LBL2   SETC   'GTX'.'&SYSNDX'                                          15
        LA     &REG,&LBL1                                               16
        LA     15,&LBL2                                                 17
        BSM    &REG,15                                                  18
&LBL2   DS     0H                                                       19
        GET    &DCB,&AREA,&RPL=                                         20
        BSM    0,&REG                                                   21
&LBL1   DS     0H                                                       22
.MEND   MEND                                                            23
```

Figure B.3 GET24.

```
        MACRO                                                            1
&LABEL  PUT24  &DCB,&AREA,&RPL=,&REG=                                    2
        LCLB   &E1                                                       3
        LCLC   &LBL1,&LBL2                                               4
.*****************************************************************        5
.*             PERFORM 24 BIT I/O IN 31 BIT PROGRAM              *        6
.*             REG = PARAMETER NAMES A WORK REGISTER             *        7
.*****************************************************************        8
        AIF    (T'&REG NE '0').OK1                                       9
        MNOTE 8,'OPERAND "REG" IS REQUIRED'                             10
&E1     SETB   1                                                        11
.OK1    ANOP                                                            12
        AIF    (&E1).MEND                                               13
&LBL1   SETC   'PTT'.'&SYSNDX'                                          14
&LBL2   SETC   'PTX'.'&SYSNDX'                                          15
        LA     &REG,&LBL1                                               16
        LA     15,&LBL2                                                 17
        BSM    &REG,15                                                  18
&LBL2   DS     0H                                                       19
        PUT    &DCB,&AREA,&RPL=                                         20
        BSM    0,&REG                                                   21
&LBL1   DS     0H                                                       22
.MEND   MEND                                                            23
```

Figure B.4 PUT24.

```
*+-------------------------------------------------------------------+   1
*|  FUNCTION:                                                        |   2
*|     GIVEN THE NAME OF AN ADDRESS SPACE (JOBNAME FOR BATCH JOB,    |   3
*|     PROC NAME FOR STARTED TASK OR LOGON ID FOR TSO ADDRESSS       |   4
*|     SPACE), RETURNS THE ADDRESS OF THE ASCB FOR THAT ADDRESS SPACE|   5
*|  INPUTS:                                                          |   6
*|     R1 - ADDRESS OF PARMLIST                                      |   7
*|          1ST PARM - LENGTH OF ADDRESS SPACE NAME     F            |   8
*|          2ST PARM - ADDRESS SPACE NAME               CL8          |   9
*|          3RD PARM - SEE OUTPUTS                      A            |  10
*|  OUTPUTS:                                                         |  11
*|     R15 - RETURN CODE                                             |  12
*|           00 - FOUND                                              |  13
*|           08 - NOT FOUND                                          |  14
*|     IF ADDRESS SPACE NAME FOUND, 3RD PARM IN PARMLIST             |  15
*|        (SEE INPUTS) CONTAINS ADDRESS OF ASCB                      |  16
*|  PROGRAM LOGIC:                                                   |  17
*|     1) LOCATE THE ADDRESS SPACE VECTOR TABLE (ASVT).              |  18
*|     2) LOOP THROUGH THE ASVT, COMPARING THE ADDRESS SPACE NAME    |  19
*|        FROM THE PARMLIST WITH THE NAME POINTED TO BY EACH ASCB.   |  20
*|     3) IF ADDRESS SPACE FOUND, PUT THE ASCB ADDRESS INTO PARMLIST.|  21
*|  ATTRIBUTES:                                                      |  22
*|     REENTERABLE, AMODE=31, RMODE=ANY                              |  23
*+-------------------------------------------------------------------+  24
          MODULE GETASCB,BASE=12,AMODE=31,RMODE=ANY,             X   25
                 TEXT='SCAN ASVT FOR ADDRESS SPACE'                  26
*         *-----------------------------------------*                27
*         *     LOCATE THE ASVT                     *                28
*         *-----------------------------------------*                29
          LR    R8,R1                 ADDRESS OF PARMLIST TO R8       30
          L     R4,CVTPTR             ADDRESS OF CVT TO REGISTER 4    31
          USING CVT,R4                SET UP ADDRESSING FOR CVT       32
          L     R4,CVTASVT            ADDRESS OF ASVT                 33
          USING ASVT,R4               SET UP ADDRESSING FOR ASVT      34
*         *-----------------------------------------*                35
*         *     LOOP THROUGH THE ASVT COMPARING     *                36
*         *     ADDRESS SPACE NAME WITH PARMLIST    *                37
*         *-----------------------------------------*                38
          LA    R5,ASVTFRST           ADDRESS OF FIRST ENTRY IN ASVT  39
          L     R6,ASVTMAXU           ASVT MAXIMUM ADDRESS SPACES     40
A$SVTLP1  DS    0H                                                    41
          TM    0(R5),ASVTAVAI        ADDRESS SPACE NUMBER UNUSED?    42
          BNO   A$CNT                 NO; CHECK THE ASCB              43
          C     R5,=A(X'80000000')    IS THIS THE LAST ASVT ENTRY ?   44
          BE    A$NTFND               YES; ASID NOT FOUND             45
          B     A$BMP                 NO; CHECK NEXT ASCB             46
A$CNT     DS    0H                                                    47
          L     R4,0(R5)              ADDRESS OF ASCB FROM ASVT       48
          USING ASCB,R4               SET UP ADDRESSING FOR ASCB      49
          MVC   PGM(L'PGM),SPACES     INITIALIZE FORMAT AREA          50
          L     R9,0(R8)              LENGTH OF ADDRESS SPACE NAME    51
          BCTR  R9,0                  LESS 1 FOR EXECUTE              52
          EX    R9,A$MVIT             MOVE TO FORMAT AREA             53
          B     A$MVITA                                               54
A$MVIT    MVC   PGM(0),4(R8)          ** EXECUTE ONLY **              55
A$MVITA   DS    0H                                                    56
          L     R7,ASCBJBNS           ASCB POINTER TO JOBNAME FIELD   57
```

Figure B.5 GETASCB.

```
           CLC   0(L'INIT,R7),INIT          IS THIS AN INITIATOR ?               58
           BNE   A$NTINIT                   NO; USE ASCBJBNS FOR COMPARE         59
           ICM   R7,15,ASCBJBNI             ADDRESS OF JOBNAME FIELD IN INIT     60
           BZ    A$BMP                      =0; UNUSED INITIATOR                 61
A$NTINIT   DS    0H                                                              62
           CLC   0(L'PGM,R7),PGM            IS THIS THE ADDRESS SPACE ?          63
           BE    A$YFND                     YES; ASCB ADDRESS TO PARMLIST        64
A$BMP      DS    0H                                                              65
           LA    R5,L'ASVTENTY(R5)          BUMP TO NEXT ENTRY                   66
           BCT   R6,A$SVTLP1                CHECK NEXT ASVT ENTRY                67
A$NTFND    DS    0H                                                              68
           B     EXIT08                     ADDRESS SPACE NOT FOUND              69
A$YFND     DS    0H                                                              70
*          *---------------------------------------*                            71
*          *    PUT ASCB ADDRESS IN PARMLIST   *                                72
*          *---------------------------------------*                            73
           ST    R4,12(R8)                  PUT ASCB ADDRESS IN PARMLIST         74
           B     EXIT00                     ADDRESS SPACE FOUND                  75
*-----------------------------------------------------------------------*       76
*          EXIT ROUTINES                                                *        77
*-----------------------------------------------------------------------*       78
EXIT00     DS    0H                         ADDRESS SPACE FOUND                  79
           LA    R15,X'00'                                                       80
           B     EXIT                                                            81
EXIT08     DS    0H                         ADDRESS SPACE NOT FOUND              82
           LA    R15,X'08'                                                       83
           B     EXIT                                                            84
*-----------------------------------------------------------------------*       85
EXIT       DS    0H                                                              86
           ENDMOD                                                                87
*-----------------------------------------------------------------------*       88
*          CONSTANTS                                                    *        89
*-----------------------------------------------------------------------*       90
SPACES     DC    CL8' '                     8 BYTES OF X'40'                     91
INIT       DC    CL8'INIT'                  ADDRESS SPACE NAME FOR INITIATOR     92
*-----------------------------------------------------------------------*       93
*          WORK AREA                                                    *        94
*-----------------------------------------------------------------------*       95
WGETASCB   DSECT                                                                 96
PGM        DS    CL8                        FORMAT AREA-ADDRESS SPACE NAME       97
LGETASCB   EQU   *-WGETASCB                                                      98
*-----------------------------------------------------------------------*       99
*          OTHER DSECTS                                                 *        100
*-----------------------------------------------------------------------*       101
           PRINT NOGEN                                                           102
           CVT   DSECT=YES,LIST=NO          MAP CVT                              103
           IHAASVT DSECT=YES                MAP ASVT                             104
           IHAASCB DSECT=YES                MAP ASCB                             105
           END                                                                   106
```

Figure B.5 *(Continued)*

```
          MACRO                         PARMLIST FOR XTALK SERVICE      1
          GETPRM                                                        2
.*+----------------------------------------------------------------+   3
.*|      PARMLIST FOR GETASCB                                       |   4
.*+----------------------------------------------------------------+   5
GETPRM    DSECT                                                         6
GETNAMEL  DS    F               LENGTH OF ADDRESS SPACE NAME            7
GETNAME   DS    CL8             ADDRESS SPACE NAME                      8
GETADDR   DS    A               ADDRESS OF ASCB                         9
GETPRML   EQU   *-GETPRM                                               10
          MEND                                                         11
```

Figure B.6 GETPRM.

```
*+------------------------------------------------------------------+   1
*|  FUNCTION:                                                       |   2
*|    GET ADDRESS SPACE NAME AND LENGTH                             |   3
*|  INPUT:                                                          |   4
.*|    R1 = A(PARAMETER LIST) MAPPED BY PPGNM DSECT                 |   5
*|  OUTPUT:                                                         |   6
*|    R15 - RETURN CODE                                            |   7
*|  LOGIC:                                                          |   8
*|    1) GET CURRENT ASCB ADDRESS FROM PSA                         |   9
*|    2) SEE IF ASCBJBNI OR ASCBJBNS POINTS TO ADDRESS SPACE NAME  |  10
*|    3) MOVE ALL 8 BYTES OF NAME TO INPUT PARMLIST                |  11
*|    4) FIND ADDRESS OF FIRST X'40' IN ADDRESS SPACE NAME AND     |  12
*|       CALCULATE LENGTH OF ADDRESS SPACE NAME                    |  13
*|  ATTRIBUTES:                                                     |  14
*|    AMODE 31, RMODE ANY, REENTRANT                               |  15
*+------------------------------------------------------------------+  16
          MODULE PGMNAME,BASE=12,AMODE=31,RMODE=ANY,            X      17
                TEXT='GET ADDRESS SPACE NAME'                          18
*         *----------------------------------------*                   19
*         *    DETERMINE LENGTH OF NAME        *                       20
*         *----------------------------------------*                   21
          LR    R3,R1                   ADDRESS OF INPUT PARMLIST      22
          USING PPGNM,R3                MAP PARMLIST                   23
          L     R4,PSAAOLD-PSA          A(CURRENT ASCB) FROM PSA       24
*                                       INITIATED JOBNAME POINTER => R2 25
          ICM   R5,B'1111',ASCBJBNI-ASCB(R4)                          26
          BNZ   INITIAT                 ^= 0; POINTER IS FOR INIT JOB  27
          L     5,ASCBJBNS-ASCB(4)      POINTER IS FOR TSO LOGON OR STC 28
INITIAT   DS    0H                                                    29
          MVC   PPGNAME(L'PPGNAME),0(R5) MOVE NAME TO PARMLIST        30
*         *----------------------------------------*                   31
*         *    DETERMINE LENGTH OF NAME        *                       32
*         *----------------------------------------*                   33
          LA    R1,8                    DEFAULT IF NO HIT ON TRT       34
*                                       SCAN THE NAME FOR X'40'        35
          TRT   PPGNAME(L'PPGNAME),TRTTBL                             36
          BC    8,NOHIT                 NO SPACES IN NAME              37
          LA    R5,PPGNAME              .. ADDRESS OF X'40'            38
          SR    R1,R5                   .. SUBTRACTED FROM ADDRESS NAME 39
```

Figure B.7 PGMNAME.

```
NOHIT    DS   OH                                                              40
         ST   R1,PPGNLEN           STORE LENGTH IN PARMLIST                   41
         B    EXIT00                                                          42
*-------------------------------------------------------------------*         43
*        EXIT ROUTINES                                              *         44
*-------------------------------------------------------------------*         45
EXIT00   DS   OH                   SUCCESSFUL                                 46
         LA   R15,X'00'                                                       47
         B    EXIT                                                            48
*-------------------------------------------------------------------*         49
*        COMMON EXIT                                                *         50
*-------------------------------------------------------------------*         51
EXIT     DS   OH                                                              52
         ENDMOD                                                               53
*-------------------------------------------------------------------*         54
*        CONSTANTS                                                  *         55
*-------------------------------------------------------------------*         56
TRTTBL   DC   XL256'00'            TABLE FOR TRT                              57
         ORG  TRTTBL+X'40'                                                    58
         DC   X'08'                                                           59
         ORG                                                                  60
*-------------------------------------------------------------------*         61
*        WORK AREA                                                  *         62
*-------------------------------------------------------------------*         63
WPGMNAME DSECT                                                                64
LPGMNAME EQU  *-WPGMNAME                                                      65
*-------------------------------------------------------------------*         66
*        OTHER DSECTS                                               *         67
*-------------------------------------------------------------------*         68
         PPGNM                     MAP INPUT PARMLIST                         69
         PRINT NOGEN                                                          70
         IHAPSA                    MAP PSA                                    71
         IHAASCB                   MAP ASCB                                   72
         END                                                                 73
```

Figure B.7 *(Continued)*

```
         MACRO                                                                1
         PPGNM                                                                2
*-------------------------------------------------------------------*         3
*        MAPS PARMLIST PASSED TO PGMNAME                            *         4
*-------------------------------------------------------------------*         5
PPGNM    DSECT                                                                6
PPGNLEN  DS   F                    LENGTH OF PROGRAM NAME                     7
PPGNAME  DS   CL8                  PROGRAM NAME                               8
PPGNML   EQU  *-PPGNM              LENGTH OF PARMLIST                         9
         MEND                                                                10
```

Figure B.8 PPGNM.

Additional Programs and Macros

```
*+-------------------------------------------------------------------+    1
*|  FUNCTION:                                                        |    2
*|    INVOKE THE HOOKIN PROGRAM TO INSTALL AN SVC FRONT-END.         |    3
*|  INPUTS:                                                          |    4
*|    NONE                                                           |    5
*|  OUTPUTS:                                                         |    6
*|    SVC FRONT-END INSTALLED                                        |    7
*|  LOGIC:                                                           |    8
*|    1) COPY SVC UPDATE MF=L TO USER PARMLIST                       |    9
*|    2) PUT NAME OF FRONT-END PROGRAM IN PARMLIST                   |   10
*|    3) INVOKE THE HOOKIN PROGRAM TO INSTALL THE FRONT-END          |   11
*|  FUNCTION:                                                        |   12
*|    AMODE 31, RMODE ANY, REENTRANT, REQUIRES APF AUTHORIZATION     |   13
*+-------------------------------------------------------------------+   14
           MODULE HOOKDRV,BASE=12,AMODE=31,RMODE=ANY,             X   15
                  TEXT='CALL HOOKIN TO INSTALL SVC FRONT-END'         16
           LA    R3,PARMLIST            ADDRESS OF PARMLIST => R3      17
           USING HOOKPRM,R3             MAP PARMLIST                   18
*                                       ..COPY SVCUPDTE PARMLIST       19
           MVC   HOSVCUL(LHOSVCUL),SVCINSTL  ..MODEL TO USER PARMLIST  20
           LA    R1,L'HOOKNAME          LENGTH OF MODULE NAME          21
           STH   R1,HOLNAME             PUT IN PARMLIST                22
           MVC   HONAME(L'HOOKNAME),HOOKNAME MODULE NAME TO PARMLIST   23
           LOAD  EP=HOOKIN,ERRET=EXIT08 LOAD THE INSTALL ROUTINE       24
           LR    R15,R0                 HOOKIN ENTRYPOINT TO R15       25
           LA    R1,PARMLIST            PARMLIST ADDRESS TO R1         26
           BASSM R14,R15                INVOKE THE INSTALL ROUTINE     27
           LTR   R15,R15                RETURN CODE = 0 ?              28
           BNZ   EXITOC                 NO; EXIT                       29
           B     EXIT00                                                30
```

Figure C.1 HOOKDRV.

```
*-------------------------------------------------------------------*   31
*           EXIT ROUTINES                                       *   32
*-------------------------------------------------------------------*   33
EXIT00   DS    OH                      SUCCESSFUL INSTALL          34
         LA    15,X'00'                                            35
         B     EXIT                                                36
EXIT08   DS    OH                      LOAD FOR HOOKIN FAILED      37
         LA    15,X'08'                                            38
         B     EXIT                                                39
EXIT0C   DS    OH                      HOOKIN SERVICE FAILED       40
         PERCRC RC=X'0C'                                           41
         B     EXIT                                                42
*-------------------------------------------------------------------*   43
*           COMMON EXIT                                         *   44
*-------------------------------------------------------------------*   45
EXIT     DS    OH                                                  46
         ENDMOD                                                    47
*-------------------------------------------------------------------*   48
*           NAME OF THE SVC FRONT-END MODULE AND                *   49
*           SVCUPDTE PASSED TO HOOKIN PROGRAM IN PARMLIST       *   50
*-------------------------------------------------------------------*   51
HOOKNAME DC    CL8'HOOKSVC'            NAME OF THE SVC HOOK MODULE  52
SVCINSTL SVCUPDTE 200,REPLACE,TYPE=4,MF=L                          53
*-------------------------------------------------------------------*   54
*           WORK AREA                                           *   55
*-------------------------------------------------------------------*   56
WHOOKDRV DSECT                                                     57
PARMLIST DS    0F,CL(LHOOKPRM)         PARMLIST FOR HOOKIN SERVICE  58
LHOOKDRV EQU   *-WHOOKDRV              LENGTH OF WORK AREA          59
*-------------------------------------------------------------------*   60
*           OTHER DSECTS                                        *   61
*-------------------------------------------------------------------*   62
         HOOKPRM                       MAP PARMLIST                63
         END                                                       64
```

Figure C.1 *(Continued)*

```
         MACRO                         PARMLIST FOR HOOKIN          1
         HOOKPRM                                                    2
 .*+---------------------------------------------------------------+   3
 .*|     PARMLIST FOR THE SVC FRONT-END INSTALL PROGRAM, HOOKIN    |   4
 .*+---------------------------------------------------------------+   5
HOOKPRM  DSECT                                                     6
HOLNAME  DS    H,CL8                   LENGTH OF MODULE NAME        7
HONAME   EQU   HOLNAME+2,8             MODULE NAME                  8
         DS    0F                                                   9
 .*                                    SVCUPDTE PARMLIST           10
HOSVCUL  SVCUPDTE 200,REPLACE,TYPE=4,MF=L                          11
HOSVC    EQU   HOSVCUL+3,1             SVC NUMBER                  12
LHOSVCUL EQU   *-HOSVCUL               L'HOSVCUL                   13
LHOOKPRM EQU   *-HOOKPRM               LENGTH OF PARMLIST          14
         MEND                                                      15
```

Figure C.2 HOOKPRM.

```
*+-----------------------------------------------------------------+  1
*|  FUNCTION:                                                       |  2
*|    INSTALL AN SVC FRONT-END (HOOK). THE HOOK MODULE MUST BEGIN   |  3
*|    WITH THE PREFIX MAPPED BY THE HOOKPRE DSECT.                  |  4
*|  LOGIC:                                                          |  5
*|    1) CALL REPMOD TO INSTALL HOOK MODULE ON LPAQ.               |  6
*|    2) PUT LENGTH OF HOOK MODULE IN HOOK PREFIX.                  |  7
*|    3) ENQUE ON SVC TABLE.                                        |  8
*|    4) LOCATE SVC TABLE FOR SVC.                                  |  9
*|       PUT ORIGINAL SVC ENTRYPOINT INTO HOOK MODULE PREFIX.      | 10
*|    5) ISSUE SVCUPDTE AGAINST SVCUPDTE MF=L IN INPUT PARMLIST    | 11
*|    6) DEQUE ON SVC TABLE.                                        | 12
*|  INPUT:                                                          | 13
*|    R1 -  ADDRESS OF PARMLIST MAPPED BY HOOKPRM DSECT            | 14
*|  OUTPUT:                                                         | 15
*|    R15 - RETURN CODE                                             | 16
*|          0 = HOOK SUCCESSFULLY INSTALLED                         | 17
*|          4 = REPMOD NOT LINK-EDITED                              | 18
*|          8 = REPMOD SERVICE FAILED                               | 19
*|         12 = UPDATE OF SVC TABLE FAILED                          | 20
*|  ATTRIBUTES:                                                     | 21
*|    AMODE 31 RMODE ANY REENTRANT                                  | 22
*+-----------------------------------------------------------------+ 23
         MODULE HOOKIN,BASE=12,AMODE=31,RMODE=ANY,             X  24
                TEXT='INSTALL SVC HOOK ROUTINE'                   25
         LR    R3,R1                   ADDRESS OF INPUT PARMLIST  26
         USING HOOKPRM,R3              MAP INPUT PARMLIST         27
*        *------------------------------------*                  28
*        *   CALL REPMOD TO INSTALL HOOK       *                  29
*        *   MODULE ON LINK-PACK-AREA-QUEUE.   *                  30
*        *   REPMOD IS USUALLY CALLED:         *                  31
*        *     // EXEC PGM=REPMOD,PARM=HOOKMOD *                  32
*        *------------------------------------*                  33
         LA    R1,HOLNAME              ..STORE ADDRESS OF FIELD WITH 34
         ST    R1,ADHOLNAM             ..LNGTH AND NAME OF HOOK MODULE 35
         LA    R1,ADHOLNAM             LOAD ADDRESS OF ADDRESS INTO R1 36
         ICM   R15,15,=V(REPMOD)       ADDRESS OF REPMOD ROUTINE  37
         BZ    EXIT04                  =0; NOT LINKED, EXIT       38
         O     R15,=A(X'80000000')     SET FOR 31-BIT ENTRY       39
         BASSM R14,R15                 INVOKE REPMOD SERVICE      40
         LTR   R15,R15                 RETURN CODE= 0 ?           41
         BNZ   EXIT08                  NO; EXIT                   42
*        *------------------------------------*                  43
*        *   UPDATE HOOK MODULE PREFIX         *                  44
*        *------------------------------------*                  45
         LR    R5,R0                   ADDRESS OF HOOK MODULE     46
         USING HOOKPRE,R5              MAP PREFIX IN HOOK MODULE  47
         ST    R1,HOPLSTG              STORE HOOK MOD LENGTH IN PREFIX 48
         LA    R2,LHOOKPRE             ..LENGTH OF PREFIX         49
         ST    R2,HOPLPRE              ..INTO PREFIX              50
*        *------------------------------------*                  51
*        *   ENQUE ON SVCTABLE                 *                  52
*        *------------------------------------*                  53
         MODESET MODE=SUP,KEY=ZERO     SUPERVISOR STATE/KEY 0 PSW 54
         ENQ   (QNAME,RNAME,E,L'RNAME,SYSTEM) ENQUE ON SVC TABLE 55
```

Figure C.3 HOOKIN.

```
*       *------------------------------------------*           56
*       *       LOCATE SVCTABLE ENTRY FOR SVC.   *              57
*       *       PUT SVC ENTRYPOINT IN HOOK PREFIX.*             58
*       *------------------------------------------*           59
        L     R2,CVTPTR               ADDRESS OF THE CVT        60
        L     R2,CVTABEND-CVT(R2)     ADDRESS OF THE SCVT       61
        L     R2,SCVTSVCT-SCVTSECT(R2)  ADDRESS OF THE SVC TABLE 62
        XR    R6,R6                   CLEAR R6                  63
        ICM   R6,1,HOSVC              SVC NUMBER                64
        SLL   R6,3                    * 8                       65
        AR    R2,R6                   = ADDRESS OF ENTRY        66
        L     R6,0(R2)                LOAD SVC ROUTINE ENTRY POINT 67
        ST    R6,HOPORIG              STORE ENTRYPOINT IN HOOK PREFIX 68
*       *------------------------------------------*           69
*       *       POINT SVCTABLE ENTRY TO HOOK MOD  *             70
*       *------------------------------------------*           71
                                      ..ADDRESS OF HOOK MODULE + 72
        LA    R7,LHOOKPRE(R5)         ..LENGTH OF PREFIX = ENTRYPT 73
        LA    R2,HOSVCUL              ..ISSUE SVCUPDTE USING SVCUPDT 74
        SVCUPDTE EP=(R7),MF=(E,(2))   ..PARMLIST FROM CALLER    75
        LR    R6,R15                  PRESERVE RETURN CODE      76
*       *------------------------------------------*           77
*       *       DEQUE ON SVCTABLE                 *             78
*       *------------------------------------------*           79
        DEQ   (QNAME,RNAME,L'RNAME,SYSTEM)   DEQUE ON SVCTABLE  80
        MODESET MODE=PROB,KEY=NZERO   SET PROBLEM STATE/KEY 8 PSW 81
        LTR   R6,R6                   RETURN CODE FROM SVCUPDTE = 0 ? 82
        BNZ   EXITOC                  NO; EXIT                  83
        B     EXIT00                                            84
*--------------------------------------------------------------* 85
*       EXIT ROUTINES                                         * 86
*--------------------------------------------------------------* 87
EXIT00  DS    OH                      SUCCESSFUL INSTALL        88
        LA    15,X'00'                                          89
        B     EXIT                                              90
EXIT04  DS    OH                      REPMOD NOT LINK-EDITED    91
        LA    15,X'04'                                          92
        B     EXIT                                              93
EXIT08  DS    OH                      REPMOD SERVICE FAILED     94
        LA    15,X'08'                                          95
        B     EXIT                                              96
EXITOC  DS    OH                      SVCUPDTE FAILED           97
        PERCRC RC=X'0C'                                         98
        B     EXIT                                              99
*--------------------------------------------------------------* 100
*       COMMON EXIT                                          * 101
*--------------------------------------------------------------* 102
EXIT    DS    OH                                               103
        ENDMOD                                                 104
*--------------------------------------------------------------* 105
*       CONSTANTS                                            * 106
*--------------------------------------------------------------* 107
QNAME   DC    CL8'SYSZSVC'            ENQ/DEQ MAJOR NAME        108
RNAME   DC    C'TABLE'                ENQ/DEQ MINOR NAME        109
*--------------------------------------------------------------* 110
*       WORK AREA                                            * 111
*--------------------------------------------------------------* 112
```

Figure C.3 *(Continued)*

```
WHOOKIN  DSECT                            AQUIRED STORAGE FOR REENTRABLE   113
ADHOLNAM DS    F                          ADDRESS ADHOLNAM                 114
LHOOKIN  EQU   *-WHOOKIN                   LENGTH OF WORK AREA              115
*-----------------------------------------------------------------*       116
*         OTHER DSECTS                                             *       117
*-----------------------------------------------------------------*       118
         HOOKPRM                          MAP INPUT PARMLIST               119
         HOOKPRE                          MAP HOOK PREFIX                  120
         CVT DSECT=YES,LIST=NO            MAP THE CVT                      121
         IHASCVT                          MAP THE SCVT                     122
         END                                                              123
```

Figure C.3 *(Continued)*

```
         MACRO                            MAP PREFIX FOR SVC FRONT-END      1
         HOOKPRE                                                           2
.*+-------------------------------------------------------------+          3
.*|      THIS DSECT MAPS THE PREFIX THAT BEGINS AN SVC FRONT-END |          4
.*|      INSTALLED WITH THE HOOKIN PROGRAM                       |          5
.*+-------------------------------------------------------------+          6
HOOKPRE  DSECT                                                             7
HOPLPRE  DS    F                          LENGTH OF THE PREFIX              8
HOPLSTG  DS    F                          LENGTH OF THIS MODULE             9
HOPORIG  DS    A                          ORIGINAL SVC ROUTINE ADDRESS     10
         DS    0D                                                          11
LHOOKPRE EQU   *-HOOKPRE                   LENGTH OF PARMLIST               12
         MEND                                                              13
```

Figure C.4 HOOKPRE.

```
*+----------------------------------------------------------------+   1
*|  FUNCTION:                                                     |   2
*|    SVC HOOK THAT RECEIVES CONTROL BEFORE AND AFTER AN SVC ROUTINE. | 3
*|    THIS HOOK IS INSTALLED WITH THE HOOKIN PROGRAM.            |   4
*|  LOGIC:                                                        |   5
*|    1) LOAD BASE REGISTER (NOT REGISTER 6) WITH PREFIX ADDRESS. |   6
*|    2) EXECUTE THE FRONT-END CODE.                             |   7
*|    3) SET UP REGISTERS FOR CALL TO ORIGINAL SVC ROUTINE.     |   8
*|    4) SAVE STATUS OF THIS MODULE ON THE LINKAGE STACK.       |   9
*|    5) BASSM TO THE ORIGNAL SVC ROUTINE.                      |  10
*|    6) POP THE STACK TO RESTORE STATUS OF THIS MODULE.        |  11
*|    7) EXECUTE THE BACK-END CODE.                             |  12
*|  INPUTS:                                                       |  13
*|    REGISTERS SET BY SVC FLIH BEFORE ENTRY TO AN SVC ROUTINE. |  14
*|    PARAMETERS FOR ORIGINAL SVC ROUTINE IN REGISTERS 0,1,15 . |  15
*|  OUTPUTS:                                                      |  16
*|    DEPENDS ON SVC ROUTINE THAT IS HOOKED.                    |  17
*|  ATTRIBUTES:                                                   |  18
*|    REENTERABLE                                                 |  19
*|  TO USE THIS CODE:                                             |  20
*|    1) SET AMODE, RMODE AND COMMENT ON THE MODULE MACRO.      |  21
*|    2) ADD CODE WHERE INDICATED TO BE EXECUTED BEFORE        |  22
*|       AND/OR AFTER THE CALL TO ORIGINAL SVC ROUTINE.        |  23
*|       MAKE SURE ORIGINAL SVC ROUTINE RECEIVES APPROPRIATE   |  24
*|       REGISTER VALUES.                                       |  25
*|    3) EXECUTE THE HOOKIN PROGRAM TO INSTALL THIS MODULE     |  26
*|       AS A FRONT-END/BACK-END FOR AN EXISTING SVC ROUTINE.  |  27
*+----------------------------------------------------------------+  28
*                                                                    29
*----------------------------------------------------------------*  30
*         HOOK PREFIX BUILT WHEN MODULE IS INSTALLED BY HOOKIN  *  31
*----------------------------------------------------------------*  32
HOOKSVC  CSECT                      FIRST CSECT IS PREFIX          33
         DS    CL(LHOOKPRE)         PREFIX                         34
*----------------------------------------------------------------*  35
*         ENTRY POINT                                           A  36
*----------------------------------------------------------------*  37
         MODULE HOOKSV2,BASE=6,ENTRY=SVC,                      X  38
               AMODE=24,RMODE=24,TEXT='SVC FRONT-END/BACK-END'    39
         LR    R12,R6               LOAD R12 WITH BASE REGISTER    40
         LA    R9,LHOOKPRE          .. SUBTRACT LENGTH OF PREFIX   41
         SLR   R12,R9               .. FROM BASE REGISTER          42
         USING HOOKPRE,R12          SET ADDRESSING ON PREFIX       43
*        *----------------------------------*                     44
*        *   CODE EXECUTED BEFORE          *                     45
*        *   ORIGINAL SVC ROUTINE          *                     46
*        *----------------------------------*                     47
******** ADD FRONT-END CODE HERE *************************************  48
         WTO   'SVC FRONT-END CODE EXECUTED'                     49
*        *----------------------------------*                     50
*        *   LOAD REGISTERS WITH VALUES    *                     51
*        *   FOR THE ORIGINAL SVC ROUTINE  *                     52
*        *----------------------------------*                     53
******** LOAD REGISTERS FOR ORIGINAL SVC HERE ***********************  54
         EREG  15,1                 RESTORE R15,R0,R1 FROM STACK   55
```

Figure C.5   HOOKSVC.

```
*          *----------------------------------------*                    56
*          *    CALL THE ORIGINAL SVC ROUTINE   *                        57
*          *----------------------------------------*                    58
           LA    R14,AFTERSVC        .. MAKE STACK-STATE ENTRY WITH       59
           BAKR  R14,0               .. PSW AFTER CALL TO ORIGINAL        60
           ICM   R6,15,HOPORIG       GET A(ORIGINAL SVC) FROM PREFIX      61
           BASSM R14,R6              INVOKE THE ORIGINAL SVC              62
           PR                        POP THE STACK                        63
AFTERSVC   DS    0H                  RECEIVES CONTROL AFTER PR            64
*          *----------------------------------------*                    65
*          *    CODE EXECUTED AFTER            *                         66
*          *    ORIGINAL SVC ROUTINE           *                         67
*          *----------------------------------------*                    68
******** ADD BACK-END CODE HERE ****************************************   69
           WTO   'SVC BACK-END CODE EXECUTED'                             70
           B     EXIT00                                                   71
*----------------------------------------------------------------------* 72
*          COMMON EXIT                                               *    73
*----------------------------------------------------------------------* 74
EXIT00     DS    0H                                                       75
           LA    15,X'00'                                                 76
******** ADD EXIT ROUTINES HERE ****************************************   77
EXIT       DS    0H                                                       78
           ENDMOD                                                         79
*----------------------------------------------------------------------* 80
*          WORK AREA                                                 *    81
*----------------------------------------------------------------------* 82
WHOOKSV2   DSECT                     ACQUIRED STORAGE FOR REENTRABLE      83
LHOOKSV2   EQU   *-WHOOKSV2          LENGTH OF WORK AREA                  84
*----------------------------------------------------------------------* 85
*          OTHER DSECTS                                              *    86
*----------------------------------------------------------------------* 87
           HOOKPRE                   MAP HOOK MOD PREFIX                  88
           END                                                           89
```

Figure C.5 *(Continued)*

```
*+--------------------------------------------------------------------+   1
* | FUNCTION:                                                          |   2
* |   ATTACHES A SUBTASK AND SCHEDULES AN IRB ROUTINE TO THE SUBTASK.  |   3
* |   . SINCE THIS PROGRAM ISSUES NO SVCS, IT COULD BE CALLED FROM     |   4
* |     AN SRB ROUTINE.  BRANCH-ENTRY INTO THE STAGE 1 AND 2 EXIT      |   5
* |     EFFECTORS REQUIRES THAT THE LOCAL LOCK BE OBTAINED.            |   6
* | LOGIC:                                                             |   7
* |     1) ATTACH A NON-DISPATCHABLE SUBTASK.                          |   8
* |     2) LOAD THE IRB ROUTINE.                                       |   9
* |     3) GET THE LOCAL LOCK.                                         |  10
* |     4) ISSUE CIRB TO CREATE AN IRB AND OBTAIN AN IQE WORK AREA.    |  11
* |        THIS IS THE STAGE 1 EXIT EFFECTOR                           |  12
* |     5) INITIALIZE THE IQE SO THAT IT CONTAINS IRB AND TCB ADDRESSES.|  13
* |     6) INVOKE CVTOEF00, THE STAGE 2 EXIT EFFECTOR.                 |  14
* |     7) RELEASE THE LOCAL LOCK.                                     |  15
* |     8) MAKE THE SUBTASK DISPATCHABLE.                              |  16
* |     9) WAIT UNTIL POSTED BY THE SUBTASK.                           |  17
* |    10) DETACH THE SUBTASK.                                         |  18
* | INPUTS:                                                            |  19
* |   NONE                                                             |  20
* | OUTPUTS:                                                           |  21
* |   CONSOLE MESSAGES                                                 |  22
* | ATTRIBUTES:                                                        |  23
* |   AMODE 24, RMODE 24, REENTRANT, REQUIRES APF AUTHORIZATION        |  24
*+--------------------------------------------------------------------+  25
          MODULE BLDIRB,BASE=12,LOC=BELOW,AMODE=24,RMODE=24,        X  26
                 TEXT=' ',SP=0                                         27
*         *----------------------------------------*                   28
*         *     ATTACH THE SUBTASK                 *                   29
*         *----------------------------------------*                   30
          LA    R3,MAINECB              ADDR ECB THIS TASK             31
          ATTACH EP=SUBTSK,            ATTACH SUBTASK              X  32
                 ECB=(R3),             WTTACH SUBTASK              X  33
                 DISP=NO,              NON-DISPATCHABLE            X  34
                 SF=(E,ATTLIST)        PARMLIST FOR ATTACH            35
          ST    R1,ADDRTCB             SAVE SUBTASK TCB ADDRESS        36
          WTO   'SUBTASK ATTACHED'                                    37
*         *----------------------------------------*                   38
*         *     LOAD THE IRB ROUTINE               *                   39
*         *----------------------------------------*                   40
          LOAD  EP=IRBRTN,ERRET=EXIT08 LOAD THE IRB ROUTINE           41
          LR    R3,R0                                                 42
*         *----------------------------------------*                   43
*         *     GET THE LOCAL LOCK                 *                   44
*         *----------------------------------------*                   45
          MODESET KEY=ZERO,MODE=SUP    GET A SUPERVISOR/KEY ZERO PSW   46
          SETLOCK OBTAIN,TYPE=LOCAL,MODE=UNCOND,                   X  47
                 REGS=USE,RELATED=REQUIRED                            48
*         *----------------------------------------*                   49
*         *     CREATE AN IRB                      *                   50
*         *----------------------------------------*                   51
          L     R4,ADDRTCB             LOAD ADDR OF SUBTASK TCB        52
          CIRB  EP=(R3),               ENTRY POINT OF IRB ROUTINE  X  53
                 KEY=PP,MODE=PP,       IRB RTN RUNS IN PROB STAT/TCBKEYX 54
                 SVAREA=YES,           SAVE AREA FOR IRB ROUTINE   X  55
                 RETIQE=NO,            GET AN IQE, NOT AN RQE      X  56
                 STAB=(DYN),           FREE THE IRB AT EXIT        X  57
```

Figure C.6 BLDIRB.

```
                WKAREA=10,              80 BYTES OF WORK AREA         X   58
                BRANCH=YES              BRANCH ENTER THE CIRB ROUTINE     59
          LR    R3,R1                   IRB ADDRESS TO R3                 60
          USING RBBASIC,R3              MAP THE IRB                       61
*         *------------------------------------------*                   62
*         *     INITIALIZE THE IQE                   *                    63
*         *------------------------------------------*                   64
          L     R5,RBNEXAV              ADDRESS OF THE IQE WORK AREA      65
          USING IQESECT,R5              MAP THE IQE                       66
          ST    R3,IQEIRB               IRB ADDRESS TO IQE                67
          L     R4,ADDRTCB              LOAD ADDR OF SUBTASK TCB          68
          ST    R4,IQETCB               TARGET TCB ADDRESS TO IQE         69
*         *------------------------------------------*                   70
*         *     INVOKE THE STAGE 2 EXIT EFFECTOR. *                      71
*         *------------------------------------------*                   72
          LCR   R1,R5                   COMPLEMENT IQE ADDR => R1         73
          L     R15,CVTPTR              ADDRESS OF THE CVT                74
          L     R15,CVT0EF00-CVT(R15)   ADDRESS OF STAGE 2 ROUTINE        75
          BALR  R14,R15                 CALL THE ROUTINE                  76
*         *------------------------------------------*                   77
*         *     RELEASE THE LOCAL LOCK               *                   78
*         *------------------------------------------*                   79
          SETLOCK RELEASE,TYPE=ALL,                                   X  80
                REGS=USE,RELATED=REQUIRED                                 81
          MODESET KEY=NZERO,MODE=PROB   GET A SUPERVISOR/KEY ZERO PSW     82
*         *------------------------------------------*                   83
*         *     MAKE THE SUBTASK DISPATCHABLE        *                   84
*         *------------------------------------------*                   85
          LA    R1,ADDRTCB              LOAD SUBTASK TCB ADDRESS          86
          STATUS START,TCB=(R1)        MAKE THE SUBTASK DISPATCHABLE     87
*         *------------------------------------------*                   88
*         *     WAIT UNTIL POSTED BY SUBTASK         *                   89
*         *------------------------------------------*                   90
          LA    R1,MAINECB              ..WAIT UNTIL                      91
          WAIT  ECB=(R1)                ..POSTED BY SUBTASK               92
          WTO   'MAIN TASK POSTED BY SUBTASK'                            93
*         *------------------------------------------*                   94
*         *     DETACH THE SUBTASK                   *                   95
*         *------------------------------------------*                   96
          LA    R1,ADDRTCB              LOAD ADDR OF SUBTASK TCB ADDR     97
          DETACH (R1)                   DETACH THE SUBTASK               98
          WTO   'SUBTASK DETACHED'                                       99
          B     EXIT00                                                   100
*------------------------------------------------------------*           101
*         EXIT ROUTINES                                      *           102
*------------------------------------------------------------*           103
EXIT00    DS    0H                      SUCCESSFUL                       104
          LA    15,X'00'                                                 105
          B     EXIT                                                     106
EXIT08    DS    0H                      LOAD FOR IRB ROUTINE FAILED      107
          LA    15,X'08'                                                 108
          B     EXIT                                                     109
*------------------------------------------------------------*           110
*         COMMON EXIT                                        *           111
*------------------------------------------------------------*           112
EXIT      DS    0H                                                       113
          ENDMOD                  RESTORE REGISTERS AND RETURN           114
```

Figure C.6 *(Continued)*

```
*-------------------------------------------------------------*   115
*          WORK AREA                                          *   116
*-------------------------------------------------------------*   117
WBLDIRB  DSECT                                                    118
ATTLIST  ATTACH ,SF=L           PARMLIST FOR ATTACH              119
ADDRTCB  DS    A                ADDRESS OF NEW TCB FROM ATTACH   120
MAINECB  DS    F                ECB FOR THIS TASK                121
LBLDIRB  EQU   *-WBLDIRB                                         122
*-------------------------------------------------------------*   123
*          OTHER DSECTS                                       *   124
*-------------------------------------------------------------*   125
         CVT    DSECT=YES,LIST=NO    MAP THE CVT                126
         IHAPSA DSECT=YES,LIST=NO    MAP THE PSA                127
         IHAIQE                      MAP THE IQE                128
         IHARB                       MAP THE RB                 129
         END                                                   130
```

Figure C.6   *(Continued)*

```
*+-------------------------------------------------------------+   1
* | FUNCTION:                                                  |   2
* |   SUBTASK OF SUBTSK TO TEST IRB SCHEDULING                 |   3
* | INPUTS:                                                    |   4
* |   NONE                                                     |   5
* | OUTPUTS:                                                   |   6
* |   CONSOLE MESSAGE                                          |   7
*+-------------------------------------------------------------+   8
         MODULE SUBTSK,BASE=12,AMODE=24,RMODE=24,            X   9
               TEXT=' ',SP=0                                     10
         WTO   'HELLO FROM THE SUBTASK'                         11
         B     EXIT00                                           12
*-------------------------------------------------------------*  13
*          EXIT ROUTINES                                      *  14
*-------------------------------------------------------------*  15
EXIT00   DS    OH                    SUCCESSFUL                 16
         LA    15,X'00'                                         17
         B     EXIT                                             18
*-------------------------------------------------------------*  19
*          COMMON EXIT                                        *  20
*-------------------------------------------------------------*  21
EXIT     DS    OH                                               22
         ENDMOD                                                 23
*-------------------------------------------------------------*  24
*          WORK AREA                                          *  25
*-------------------------------------------------------------*  26
WSUBTSK  DSECT                                                  27
LSUBTSK  EQU   *-WSUBTSK                                        28
*-------------------------------------------------------------*  29
*          OTHER DSECTS                                       *  30
*-------------------------------------------------------------*  31
         END                                                    32
```

Figure C.7   SUBTSK.

```
*+-----------------------------------------------------------------+    1
*| FUNCTION:                                                       |    2
*|   TEST IRB ROUTINE                                              |    3
*| INPUTS:                                                         |    4
*|   R0  - ADDRESS OF THE IQE                                      |    5
*|   R1  - ADDRESS OF PARAMTER LIST (IEQPARAM)                     |    6
*|   R13 - ADDRESS OF REGISTER SAVE AREA (IF IRB : SVAREA=YES)     |    7
*|   R14 - RETURN ADDRESS (CVTEXIT)                                |    8
*| OUTPUTS:                                                        |    9
*|   CONSOLE MESSAGE                                               |   10
*| ATTRIBUTES:                                                     |   11
*|   AMODE 24, RMODE 24, REENTRANT                                 |   12
*+-----------------------------------------------------------------+   13
          MODULE IRBRTN,BASE=12,AMODE=24,RMODE=24,              X   14
                 TEXT=' '                                           15
          WTO   'HELLO FROM IRBRTN'                                 16
          B     EXIT00                                             17
*-----------------------------------------------------------------*   18
*         EXIT ROUTINES                                          *   19
*-----------------------------------------------------------------*   20
EXIT00    DS    0H                    SUCCESSFUL EXIT              21
          LA    15,X'00'                                           22
          B     EXIT                                               23
*-----------------------------------------------------------------*   24
*         COMMON EXIT                                            *   25
*-----------------------------------------------------------------*   26
EXIT      DS    0H                                                 27
          ENDMOD                                                   28
*-----------------------------------------------------------------*   29
*         WORK AREA                                              *   30
*-----------------------------------------------------------------*   31
WIRBRTN DSECT                                                      32
LIRBRTN EQU    *-WIRBRTN                                           33
*-----------------------------------------------------------------*   34
*         OTHER DSECTS                                           *   35
*-----------------------------------------------------------------*   36
          END                                                      37
```

Figure C.8 IRBRTN.

```
*+------------------------------------------------------------------+   1
*|  FUNCTION:                                                        |   2
*|    ADD OR REPLACE MODULE ANCHORED IN LPAQ CDE.                    |   3
*|  LOGIC:                                                           |   4
*|    1) GET MODULE NAME FROM PARM=                                  |   5
*|    2) CALL UNANCH SERVICE TO UNANCHOR ANY EXISTING MODULE         |   6
*|    3) LOAD TARGET MODULE INTO PRIVATE STORAGE TO GET LENGTH       |   7
*|    4) DELETE MODULE FROM PRIVATE STORAGE                          |   8
*|    5) CALL ANCHOR SERVICE TO GET LPAQ ANCHORED STORAGE FOR MODULE |   9
*|    6) ISSUE LOAD ADRNAPF FOR MODULE INTO LPAQ ANCHORED STORAGE    |  10
*|  INPUTS:                                                          |  11
*|    EXEC PARM=                                                     |  12
*|  OUTPUTS:                                                         |  13
*|    R15 - RETURN CODE                                             |  14
*|          0 - SUCCESSFUL ROUTINE                                   |  15
*|          8 - PARM= NOT SUPPLIED                                   |  16
*|         16 - VARIOUS LOAD ERRORS                                  |  17
*|         20 - UNANCH SERVICE FAILED                                |  18
*|         24 - LOAD OF NEW MODULE FAILED                            |  19
*|  ATTRIBUTES:                                                      |  20
*|    AMODE 31, RMODE ANY, APF-AUTHORIZED, REENTERABLE               |  21
*+------------------------------------------------------------------+  22
          MODULE REPMOD,BASE=12,LOC=BELOW,AMODE=31,RMODE=ANY,      X  23
                 TEXT='BUILD A MODULE IN LPAQ'                        24
*------------------------------------------------------------------*  25
*          GET MODULE NAME FROM PARM=                              *  26
*------------------------------------------------------------------*  27
          LA    R5,ANKLIST                A(PARMLIST) => R5           28
          USING ANKPRM,R5                 MAP PARMLIST                29
          MVI   ANKNAME,X'40'               ..SET MODULE NAME         30
          MVC   ANKNAME+1(L'ANKNAME-1),ANKNAME ..TO SPACES            31
          L     R1,0(R1)                  ADDRESS OF PARM= STRING     32
          XR    R2,R2                     CLEAR R2                     33
          ICM   R2,B'0011',0(R1)          LENGTH OF PARM= STRING      34
          BZ    EXIT08                    =0; PROGAM NAME NOT GIVEN   35
          BCTR  R2,0                      LESS 1 FOR EXECUTE          36
          EX    R2,MV1                    MOVE NAME TO GETASCB PARMLIST 37
          B     EX1                       BRANCH AROUND EXECUTE       38
MV1       MVC   ANKNAME(0),2(R1)          ** EXECUTE ONLY ***          39
EX1       DS    0H                                                    40
*------------------------------------------------------------------*  41
*          CALL UNANCH - UNANCHOR CONTROL BLOCK FROM LPAQ          *  42
*------------------------------------------------------------------*  43
          MVI   ANKSP,@ANKSP              SET DEFAULT SUBPOOL          44
          OI    ANKFLAG1,@ANKFREE         SET TO FREEMAIN STORAGE      45
          LOAD  EP=UNANCH,ERRET=EXIT10 LOAD UNANCH SERVICE ROUTINE    46
          LR    R15,R0                    ENTRYPOINT TO R15            47
          LA    R1,ANKLIST                A(PARMLIST) => R1            48
          BASSM R14,R15                   INVOKE SERVICE               49
          C     R15,=F'8'                 DID ANCHOR SERVICE FAIL ?    50
          BH    EXIT14                    YES; EXIT PERCOLATING RC     51
          DELETE EP=UNANCH                DELETE UNANCH SERVICE ROUTINE 52
*------------------------------------------------------------------*  53
*          LOAD THE MODULE INTO PRIVATE STORAGE TO DETERMINE       *  54
*          LENGTH, AMODE AND RMODE.  THEN DELETE THE MODULE.       *  55
*------------------------------------------------------------------*  56
```

Figure C.9 REPMOD.

```
        LOAD  EPLOC=ANKNAME,ERRET=EXIT10                                  57
        N     R1,=A(X'00FFFFFF')    TURN OFF NON-LENGTH BITS              58
        SLL   R1,3                  MULTIPLY LENGTH BY 8                  59
        ST    R1,ANKLEN             LENGTH TO ANCHOR PARMLIST             60
        NI    ANKFLAG1,X'00'        CLEAR FLAGS BYTE                      61
        STCM  R0,B'1000',TESTBYTE   HIGH ORDER ADDRESS BYTE               62
        TM    TESTBYTE,B'01111111'  IS IT RMODE 24 ?                      63
        BNZ   T31                   NO; DO NOT GETMAIN 24-BIT             64
        OI    ANKFLAG1,@ANKBEL      SET ANCHOR TO GETMAIN 24BIT          65
        TM    TESTBYTE,B'10000000'  IS IT AMODE 31 ?                      66
        BZ    T31                   NO; LET CDE ENTRYPOINT BE 24 BIT      67
        OI    ANKFLAG1,@ANK31       MAKE SURE CDE HAS 31 BIT EP.          68
T31     DS    0H                                                         69
        DELETE EPLOC=ANKNAME        DELETE MODULE FROM PRIVATE            70
*--------------------------------------------------------------------*   71
*         GET STORAGE ANCHORED ON LPAQ FOR MODULE                    *   72
*--------------------------------------------------------------------*   73
        MVC   ANKEYE(L'ANKEYE),EYE  TABLE EYECATCHER TO PARMLIST          74
        XC    ANKEP(L'ANKEP),ANKEP  INITIALIZE ENTRYPOINT TO X'00'        75
        LOAD  EP=ANCHOR,ERRET=EXIT10 LOAD ANCHOR SERVICE ROUTINE          76
        LR    R15,R0                ENTRYPOINT TO R15                     77
        LA    R1,ANKPRM             ADDRESS OF PARMLIST => R1             78
        BASSM R14,R15               INVOKE SERVICE                        79
        C     R15,=F'8'             DID ANCHOR SERVICE FAIL ?             80
        BH    EXIT14                YES; EXIT PERCOLATING RC              81
        DELETE EP=ANCHOR            DELETE ANCHOR SERVICE ROUTINE         82
*--------------------------------------------------------------------*   83
*         LOAD MODULE INTO ANCHORED STORAGE                          *   84
*--------------------------------------------------------------------*   85
        MVC   LOADLIB(LDCBD),LOADLIBD COPY DCB TO RENT STORAGE            86
        MVC   OLIST(LOLIST),MOLIST  COPY OPEN LIST TO RENT STORAGE        87
        L     R2,ANKEP              ADDRESS OF ANCHORED CONTROL STG       88
        LA    R3,LOADLIB            ADDRESS OF LOADLIB DCB                89
        LA    R4,ANKNAME            NAME OF THE MODULE IN LOADLIB         90
        OPEN  (LOADLIB,INPUT),MF=(E,OLIST)  OPEN THE LOADLIB             91
        MODESET MODE=SUP            GET A SUPERVISOR STATE PSW            92
        LOAD  EPLOC=(R4),ERRET=EXIT18,    ..LOAD THE MODULE INTO      X   93
              ADRNAPF=(R2),DCB=(R3),SF=(E,LLIST) ..ANCHORED STORAGE       94
        MODESET MODE=PROB           GO BACK INTO PROBLEM STATE            95
        CLOSE MF=(E,OLIST)          CLOSE THE LOADLIB DCB                 96
        L     R0,ANKEP              LOAD THE MODULE ADDRESS => R0         97
        L     R1,ANKLEN             LOAD THE MODULE LENGTH  => R1         98
        MSTA  0                     PUT REGS R0 AND R1 INTO STACK         99
        B     EXIT00                                                    100
*--------------------------------------------------------------------*  101
*         EXIT ROUTINES                                              *  102
*--------------------------------------------------------------------*  103
EXIT00  DS    0H                    SUCCESSFUL                          104
        LA    15,X'00'                                                  105
        B     EXIT                                                      106
EXIT08  DS    0H                    PARM= NOT SUPPLIED                  107
        LA    15,X'08'                                                  108
        B     EXIT                                                      109
EXIT10  DS    0H                    ONE OF VARIOUS LOADS FAILED         110
        PERCRC RC=X'10'                                                 111
        B     EXIT                                                      112
```

Figure C.9 *(Continued)*

```
EXIT14   DS    OH                        UNANCHOR SERVICE FAILED           113
         PERCRC RC=X'14'                                                   114
         B     EXIT                                                        115
EXIT18   DS    OH                        LOAD OF NEW MODULE FAILED         116
         PERCRC RC=X'18'                                                   117
         B     EXIT                                                        118
*-------------------------------------------------------------------*     119
*        COMMON EXIT                                                 *     120
*-------------------------------------------------------------------*     121
EXIT     DS    OH                                                         122
         ENDMOD                                                           123
*-------------------------------------------------------------------*     124
*        CONSTANTS                                                   *     125
*-------------------------------------------------------------------*     126
EYE      DC    C'NULL'                   EYECATCHER REQUIRED BY ANCHOR     127
*-------------------------------------------------------------------*     128
*        DCB AND OPEN/CLOSE PARMLIST MODELS                          *     129
*-------------------------------------------------------------------*     130
LOADLIBD DCB   DSORG=PS,MACRF=GL,EODAD=EXIT,LRECL=256,                 X  131
               BLKSIZE=256,RECFM=FB,DDNAME=LOADLIB                        132
LDCBD    EQU   *-LOADLIBD                LENGTH OF DCB                     133
MOLIST   OPEN  (,),MF=L                  OPEN/CLOSE PARMLIST               134
LOLIST   EQU   *-MOLIST                  LENGTH OF OPEN/CLOSE PARMLIST     135
*-------------------------------------------------------------------*     136
*        WORK AREA                                                   *     137
*-------------------------------------------------------------------*     138
WREPMOD  DSECT                                                            139
LOADLIB  DS    OF,CL(LDCBD)              LOADLIB DCB                       140
ANKLIST  DS    CL(LANKPRM)               PARMLIST FOR ANCHOR SERVICE       141
OLIST    DS    CL(LOLIST)                OPEN/CLOSE PARMLIST               142
TESTBYTE DS    X                         A BYTE FOR TEST                   143
LLIST    LOAD  ,SF=L                     PARMLIST FOR LOAD                 144
LREPMOD  EQU   *-WREPMOD                                                  145
*-------------------------------------------------------------------*     146
*        OTHER DSECTS                                                *     147
*-------------------------------------------------------------------*     148
         ANKPRM                          MAP ANCHOR SERVICE PARMS          149
         END                                                              150
```

Figure C.9 *(Continued)*

```
*+----------------------------------------------------------------------+    1
*|  FUNCTION:                                                            |    2
*|      REMOVE A CONTROL BLOCK ANCHORED IN AN LPAQ CDE.                  |    3
*|  LOGIC:                                                               |    4
*|      1)  SEARCH CDE'S ON LINK-PACK-AREA-QUEUE CHOSEN CDE.             |    5
*|      2)  IF NOT FOUND, EXIT.                                          |    6
*|      3)  VERIFY THAT ENTRY POINT MODULE CHOSEN.                       |    7
*|      4)  GET THE LOCAL AND CMS LOCKS TO SERIALIZE LPAQ.              |    8
*|      4)  SCAN THE LPAQ FOR THE CDE PREVIOUS IN THE CHAIN             |    9
*|      5)  UNCHAIN THE CDE FROM THE LPAQ.                              |   10
*|      6)  (FREEMAIN STORAGE FOR TABLE, CDE AND XL)                    |   11
*|      7)  RELEASE ALL LOCKS                                           |   12
*|  INPUTS:                                                              |   13
*|      R1 - ADDRESS OF PARMLIST MAPPED BY ANKPRM MACRO.               |   14
*|  OUTPUTS:                                                             |   15
*|      R15 - RETURN CODE                                               |   16
*|            0 = CDE HAS BEEN UNCHAINED OR DOES NOT EXIST             |   17
*|            8 = EYECATCHER VERIFICATION FAILED                       |   18
*|           12 = FREEMAIN FAILED FOR MODULE.                          |   19
*|           16 = FREEMAIN FAILED FOR CDE                              |   20
*|           20 = FREEMAIN FAILED FOR EXTENT LIST                     |   21
*|  ATTRIBUTES:                                                          |   22
*|      AMODE 31, RMODE ANY, REENTRANT                                  |   23
*|      CALLER MUST BE IN PRIMARY SPACE MODE                           |   24
*+----------------------------------------------------------------------+   25
          MODULE UNANCH,BASE=12,LOC=BELOW,AMODE=31,RMODE=ANY,        X   26
                 TEXT='UNCHAIN CONTROL BLOCK ON LPAQ'                    27
*         *------------------------------------*                        28
*         *     MAP CONTROL BLOCKS USED        *                        29
*         *------------------------------------*                        30
          USING CVT,R3                 MAP CVT                          31
          USING CDENTRY,R4             MAP CDE                          32
          USING XTLST,R6               MAP EXTENT LIST                  33
          USING ANKPRM,R10             MAP PARMLIST                     34
          LR    R10,R1                 A(PARMLIST) => R10               35
*----------------------------------------------------------------------*   36
*      SCAN LINK PACK AREA QUEUE FOR CDE CONTAINING MODULE ANCHOR    *   37
*----------------------------------------------------------------------*   38
          L     R3,CVTPTR              A(CVT) => R3                     39
          LA    R9,ANKNAME             A(MODULE NAME) => R9             40
          L     R8,CVTQLPAQ            HEAD OF LPAQ => R8               41
          L     R15,CVTQCDSR           A(LPAQ SCAN ROUTINE)            42
          BALR  R14,R15                INVOKE LPAQ SCAN ROUTINE        43
          B     FNDCDE                 CDE FOUND; BRANCH TO PROCESS CDE 44
          B     EXIT00                 CDE NOT FOUND; EXIT             45
*----------------------------------------------------------------------*   46
*      IF CDE FOUND, CHECK STORAGE IT POINTS TO FOR EYECATCHER       *   47
*----------------------------------------------------------------------*   48
FNDCDE    DS    0H                                                      49
          LR    R4,R11                 A( CDE ) FROM CVTQCDSR ROUTINE  50
          ST    R11,ADCDE              SAVE ADDRESS OF CDE             51
          TM    ANKFLAG1,@ANKVFY       VERIFY THE STORAGE ?           52
          BNO   NOVFY                  NO; SKIP VERIFICATION           53
          L     R5,CDENTPT             ENTRY POINT FROM CDE => R5      54
          CLC   0(L'ANKEYE,R5),ANKEYE  IS EYECATCHER FIRST BYTES IN STG? 55
          BNE   EXIT08                 NO; EXIT                        56
```

Figure C.10   UNANCH.

```
NOVFY   DS    0H                                                       57
              MODESET MODE=SUP,KEY=ZERO   GET SUPERVISOR/KEY 0 PSW      58
*       *-------------------------------------*                        59
*       *       GET THE LOCAL LOCK          *                          60
*       *-------------------------------------*                        61
              SETLOCK OBTAIN,                                        X 62
                MODE=UNCOND,                                         X 63
                TYPE=LOCAL,                                          X 64
                REGS=USE,                                           X 65
                RELATED=REQUIRED                                      66
*       *-------------------------------------*                        67
*       *       GET CMS LOCK              *                            68
*       *-------------------------------------*                        69
              SETLOCK OBTAIN,                                        X 70
                MODE=UNCOND,                                         X 71
                TYPE=CMS,                                           X 72
                REGS=USE,                                           X 73
                RELATED=REQUIRED                                      74
*----------------------------------------------------------------*     75
*          FIND PREVIOUS CDE IN LPAQ                             *      76
*----------------------------------------------------------------*     77
        L     R4,CVTQLPAQ               HEAD OF LPAQ => R8             78
        LA    R5,CDCHAIN-CDENTRY        .. BACK UP FOR DISPLACEMENT    79
        SLR   R4,R5                     .. IN CDE TO CHAIN FIELD       80
SCDLP   DS    0H                                                       81
        CLC   CDCHAIN(L'CDCHAIN),ADCDE DOES THIS POINT TO OUR CDE?     82
        BE    FNDPREV                   YES; THIS IS THE PREVIOUS CDE  83
        ICM   R4,15,CDCHAIN             POINT AT NEXT CDE              84
        BNZ   SCDLP                     CHECK CHAIN FIELD IN NEXT CDE  85
        ABEND 123                                                      86
*----------------------------------------------------------------*     87
*          UNCHAIN CDE FROM LPAQ                                 *      88
*----------------------------------------------------------------*     89
FNDPREV DS    0H                                                       90
        L     R5,ADCDE                  ADDRESS OF TARGET CDE          91
        L     R5,CDCHAIN-CDENTRY(R5) CHAIN POINTER FROM TARGET CDE     92
        ST    R5,CDCHAIN                SAVE IN PREVIOUS ENTRY CHAIN FLD 93
*       *-------------------------------------*                        94
*       *       RELEASE ALL LOCKS          *                           95
*       *-------------------------------------*                        96
              SETLOCK RELEASE,                                       X 97
                TYPE=ALL,                                           X 98
                REGS=USE,                                           X 99
                RELATED=REQUIRED                                     100
*----------------------------------------------------------------*    101
*       VERIFY THAT THE OLD MODULE IS ALLOCATED IN THE RIGHT SUBPOOL * 102
*       IF SO, FREEMAIN OLD MODULE, CDE AND EXTENT LIST ENTRY       * 103
*----------------------------------------------------------------*    104
        TM    ANKFLAG1,@ANKFREE         FREE OLD MODULE STORAGE  ?    105
        BNO   EXIT00                    NO; EXIT                      106
        L     R4,ADCDE                  ADDRESS OF TARGET CDE         107
        L     R6,CDXLMJP                A(EXTENT LIST)                108
        L     R8,CDENTPT                A(ENTRY POINT)                109
        XR    R7,R7                                                   110
        ICM   R7,B'0111',XTLMSBLN       LENGTH OF THE MODULE          111
        VSMLOC SQA,AREA=((R8),(R7)) TEST SQA ALLOCATION               112
        LTR   R15,R15                   ALLOCATED ?                   113
```

Figure C.10 *(Continued)*

```
         BZ    CKSP              YES; CHECK SUBPOOL                 114
         VSMLOC CSA,AREA=((R8),(R7)) TEST CSA ALLOCATION            115
         LTR   R15,R15           ALLOCATED ?                        116
         BNZ   NOFREE            NO; DO NOT FREEMAIN                117
CKSP     DS    0H                                                   118
         STCM  0,B'0001',TESTSP  SAVE SUBPOOL NUMBER IN TEST        119
         CLC   TESTSP(L'ANKSP),ANKSP  IS THE STORAGE IN THIS SUBPOOL? 120
         BNE   NOFREE            NO; DO NOT FREEMAIN                121
         XR    R5,R5             .. SUBPOOL NUMBER                  122
         ICM   R5,B'0001',TESTSP .. FOR FREEMAIN                    123
         FREEMAIN RC,LV=(7),A=(8),SP=(5)                            124
         LTR   R15,R15           FREEMAIN SUCCESSFUL ?              125
         BNZ   EXITOC            NO; EXIT WITH ERROR                126
         LA    R0,LCDE           LENGTH OF A CDE                    127
         FREEMAIN RC,LV=(0),A=(4),SP=245  FREE THE CDE              128
         LTR   R15,R15                                              129
         BNZ   EXIT10                                               130
         LA    R0,LXTNT          LENGTH OF AN EXTENT LIST           131
         FREEMAIN RC,LV=(0),A=(6),SP=245  FREE THE XTENT LIST       132
         LTR   R15,R15                                              133
         BNZ   EXIT14                                               134
NOFREE   DS    0H                                                   135
         MODESET MODE=PROB,KEY=NZERO                                136
         B     EXIT00                                               137
*----------------------------------------------------------------* 138
*        EXIT ROUTINES                                           * 139
*----------------------------------------------------------------* 140
EXIT00   DS    0H                SUCCESSFUL                         141
         LA    15,X'00'                                             142
         B     EXIT                                                 143
EXIT08   DS    0H                STORAGE VERIFICATION FAILED        144
         LA    15,X'08'                                             145
         B     EXIT                                                 146
EXITOC   DS    0H                FREEMAIN FAILED FOR MODULE         147
         LA    15,X'0C'                                             148
         B     EXIT                                                 149
EXIT10   DS    0H                FREEMAIN FAILED FOR CDE            150
         LA    15,X'10'                                             151
         B     EXIT                                                 152
EXIT14   DS    0H                FREEMAIN FAILED FOR XL             153
         LA    15,X'14'                                             154
         B     EXIT                                                 155
         EJECT                                                      156
*----------------------------------------------------------------* 157
*        COMMON EXIT                                             * 158
*----------------------------------------------------------------* 159
EXIT     DS    0H                                                   160
         MODESET MODE=PROB,KEY=NZERO                                161
         ENDMOD                                                     162
*----------------------------------------------------------------* 163
*        WORK AREA                                               * 164
*----------------------------------------------------------------* 165
WUNANCH DSECT                                                       166
ADCDE    DS    A                 A( CDE )                           167
TESTSP   DS    X                 TEST SUBPOOL BYTE                  168
LUNANCH  EQU   *-WUNANCH                                            169
```

Figure C.10 *(Continued)*

```
*-------------------------------------------------------------------*   170
*        OTHER DSECTS                                               *   171
*-------------------------------------------------------------------*   172
         ANKPRM                   MAP PARMLIST                          173
         IHACDE                   MAP CDE                               174
LCDE     EQU   *-CDENTRY          LENGTH OF CDE                         175
         IHAXTLST                 MAP EXTENT LIST                       176
LXTNT    EQU   *-XTLST            LENGTH OF EXTENT LIST                 177
         CVT   DSECT=YES,LIST=YES MAP CVT                              178
         IHAPSA DSECT=YES,LIST=YES MAP PSA FOR SETLOCK                 179
         END                                                          180
```

Figure C.10 *(Continued)*

```
*+----------------------------------------------------------------------+     1
*|  FUNCTION:                                                            |     2
*|    DYNAMICALLY ALLOCATE/DEALLOCATE A DATSET.                          |     3
*|  LOGIC:                                                               |     4
*|    1)  INVOKE FINDPARM ROUTINE AGAINST USER-SUPPLIED PARMS            |     5
*|        BUILDING TEXTUNITS FOR DYNALLOC IN USER STORAGE.               |     6
*|    2)  ISSUE SVC 99                                                   |     7
*|  INPUTS:                                                              |     8
*|    R1 - PARMLIST MAPPED BY DYNPRM MACRO.                              |     9
*|  OUTPUTS:                                                             |    10
*|    R1 - PARMLIST MAPPED BY DYNPRM MACRO.                              |    11
*|    R15 - RETURN CODE                                                  |    12
*|         0 = SVC99 PROCESSING HAS BEEN SUCCESSFUL.                     |    13
*|         4 = NOT USED                                                  |    14
*|         8 = NOT USED                                                  |    15
*|        12 = NOT USED                                                  |    16
*|        16 = USER PARMLIST ERROR - R0 CONTAINS:                        |    17
*|              4 = ERROR IN FUNCTION CODE                               |    18
*|              8 = ERROR IN DISP=                                       |    19
*|             12 = ERROR IN SPACE=(XXX(                                 |    20
*|             16 = ERROR IN SPACE=(...(XXX,                             |    21
*|             20 = ERROR IN SPACE=(...(,,XXX                            |    22
*|                 24 = ERROR IN DCB=RECFM                               |    23
*|                 28 = ERROR IN DCB=LRECL                               |    24
*|        20 = SVC 99 FAILED - R0 CONTAINS:                              |    25
*|             +-----------+-----------+                                 |    26
*|             | S99ERROR  | S99INFO   |                                 |    27
*|             +-----------+-----------+                                 |    28
*|             0    1    2    3                                          |    29
*|             IF RC = 20, THE FOLLOWING PARMLIST FIELDS                 |    30
*|             ARE ALSO RETURNED:                                        |    31
*|                 DYRETURN  = 14                                        |    32
*|                 DYREASON  = THE CONTENTS OF R0                        |    33
*|                 DY99ERR   = RETUNED BY SVC 99 (SEE MANUAL)            |    34
*|  ATTRIBUTES:                                                          |    35
*|    AMODE 24, AMODE 24, REENTRANT                                      |    36
*+----------------------------------------------------------------------+    37
          MODULE DYNAL,BASE=12,LOC=BELOW,AMODE=24,RMODE=24,           X    38
                TEXT='DYNAMIC ALLOCATION/UNALLOCATION OF A DATASET'        39
          L     R8,0(R1)           A(PARMLIST) => R8                       40
          USING DYNPRM,R8          MAP INPUT PARMLIST                      41
*----------------------------------------------------------------------*    42
*         BUILD DYNALLOC RB AND ANCHOR TEXT UNITS                 *        43
*----------------------------------------------------------------------*    44
          LA    R3,RB99            ADDRESS OF SVC 99 RB                    45
          USING S99RB,R3           MAP SVC 99 RB                          46
          ST    R3,RBPT99          PUT A(SVC 99 RB) INTO RB POINTER        47
          OI    RBPT99,S99RBPND    SET FLAG IN RB POINTER                 48
*                                  SET SVC 99 RB TO X'00'                 49
          XC    S99RB(S99RBLEN),S99RB                                     50
          MVI   S99RBLN,S99RBLEN   PUT LENGTH IN RB                       51
*         *----------------------------------------*                      52
*         *   SET FUNCTION CODE                *                          53
*         *----------------------------------------*                      54
          LA    R9,DYFUNCT         A(INPUT PARM)                          55
          LA    R1,FUNCTB          A(TABLE OF VALID PARMS)                56
          BAL   R14,FINDPARM       SEARCH TABLE OF VALID PARMS            57
```

Figure C.11 DYNAL.

```
            LTR    R15,R15             IS L'OUTPUT PARM = 0                      58
            BNZ    SETFUNCT            NO; PARM IS IN TABLE                      59
*                                      DEFAULT FUNCTION IS ALLOCATE             60
            MVC    DYFUNCT(L'DYFUNCT),AL                                        61
            LA     R9,DYFUNCT          A(INPUT PARM)                            62
            LA     R1,FUNCTB           A(TABLE OF VALID PARMS)                  63
            BAL    R14,FINDPARM        SEARCH TABLE OF VALID PARMS              64
SETFUNCT    DS     0H                                                           65
*                                      MOVE PARM FROM TABLE                     66
            MVC    S99VERB(L'S99VERB),0(R9)                                     67
            LA     R4,TXPT99           A(FIRST TEXT POINTER)                    68
            ST     R4,S99TXTPP         PUT IN RB                                69
            LA     R4,TXPT99-4         POINT 4 BYTES BEFORE FIRST POINTER       70
            USING  S99TUPL,R4          MAP POINTER LIST ENTRY                   71
            LA     R5,TXTUNITS         A(TEXT UNITS) IN REENTERABLE STG         72
*--------------------------------------------------------------------*        73
*          MOVE TEXT UNIT MODELS TO REENTERABLE STORAGE              *         74
*              AND FILL IN FIELDS FROM INPUT PARMLIST                *         75
*--------------------------------------------------------------------*        76
            CLC    DYFUNCT(L'DYFUNCT),AL IS THIS AN ALLOCATE FUNCTION          77
            BNE    NOTALLOC            NO; USE OTHER TEXT UNITS                 78
*--------------------------------------------------------------------*        79
*          TEXT UNITS FOR ALLOCATE FUNCTION                         *         80
*--------------------------------------------------------------------*        81
*          *------------------------------------------*                        82
*          *   DISP=(XXX,                             *                        83
*          *------------------------------------------*                        84
DISPOK      DS     0H                                                           85
            LA     R9,DYDISP           A(INPUT PARM)                            86
            LA     R1,STATB            A(TABLE OF VALID PARMS)                  87
            BAL    R14,FINDPARM        SEARCH TABLE OF VALID PARMS              88
            LTR    R15,R15             IS L'OUTPUT PARM = 0                     89
            BNZ    SETSTAT             NO; PARM IS IN TABLE                     90
*                                      SET DEFAULT TO SHR                       91
            MVC    DYDISP(L'DYDISP),SHRDISP                                     92
            LA     R9,DYDISP           A(INPUT PARM)                            93
            LA     R1,STATB            A(TABLE OF VALID PARMS)                  94
            BAL    R14,FINDPARM        SEARCH TABLE OF VALID PARMS              95
SETSTAT     DS     0H                                                           96
            LA     R7,STATS            TEXTUNIT MODEL                           97
            BAL    R14,MOVEPARM        BUILD TEXTUNIT                           98
*          *------------------------------------------*                        99
*          *   DDNAME                                 *                       100
*          *------------------------------------------*                       101
            LA     R9,DYDDNAME         ADDRESS OF FIELD IN INPUT PARMLIST      102
            LA     R7,DDNAM            TEXTUNIT MODEL                          103
            BAL    R14,MOVEPARM        BUILD TEXTUNIT                          104
*          *------------------------------------------*                       105
*          *   DSNAME                                 *                       106
*          *------------------------------------------*                       107
            LA     R9,DYDSN            ADDRESS OF FIELD IN INPUT PARMLIST      108
            LA     R7,DSNAM            TEXTUNIT MODEL                          109
            BAL    R14,MOVEPARM        BUILD TEXTUNIT                          110
*          *------------------------------------------*                       111
*          *   ABNORMAL TERM DISPOSTITION             *                       112
*          *------------------------------------------*                       113
            LA     R9,DYCDISP          A(INPUT PARM)                           114
```

Figure C.11 *(Continued)*

```
          LA    R1,DISPTB          A(TABLE OF VALID PARMS)                    115
          BAL   R14,FINDPARM       SEARCH TABLE OF VALID PARMS                116
          LTR   R15,R15            IS L'OUTPUT PARM = 0                        117
          BZ    NOCDISP            YES; SKIP THIS                             118
          LA    R7,CDISP           TEXTUNIT MODEL                             119
          BAL   R14,MOVEPARM       BUILD TEXTUNIT                             120
NOCDISP   DS    0H                                                            121
*                                  IS IT DISP=(NEW,     ?                     122
          CLC   DYDISP(L'DYDISP),NEWDISP                                      123
          BE    ISNEW                                                         124
*         *------------------------------------------*                        125
*         *     NORMAL TERM DISPOSTITION             *                        126
*         *------------------------------------------*                        127
          LA    R9,DYNDISP         A(INPUT PARM)                              128
          LA    R1,DISPTB          A(TABLE OF VALID PARMS)                    129
          BAL   R14,FINDPARM       SEARCH TABLE OF VALID PARMS                130
          LTR   R15,R15            L'OUTPUT PARM ^= 0                         131
          BNZ   NONDISP            YES; USE FROM PARMLIST                     132
*                                  DEFAULT IS CATLG                           133
          MVC   DYNDISP(L'DYNDISP),KEEP                                       134
          LA    R9,DYNDISP         A(INPUT PARM)                              135
          LA    R1,DISPTB          A(TABLE OF VALID PARMS)                    136
          BAL   R14,FINDPARM       SEARCH TABLE OF VALID PARMS                137
NONDISP   DS    0H                                                            138
          LA    R7,NDISP           TEXTUNIT MODEL                             139
          BAL   R14,MOVEPARM       BUILD TEXTUNIT                             140
          B     ENDUNITS           NO ; SKIP OTHER TEXT UNITS                 141
ISNEW     DS    0H                                                            142
*-------------------------------------------------------------------*         143
*         ALLOCATION UNITS FOR DISP=(NEW,  DATASETS              *            144
*-------------------------------------------------------------------*         145
*         *------------------------------------------*                        146
*         *     NORMAL TERM DISPOSTITION             *                        147
*         *------------------------------------------*                        148
          LA    R9,DYNDISP         A(INPUT PARM)                              149
          LA    R1,DISPTB          A(TABLE OF VALID PARMS)                    150
          BAL   R14,FINDPARM       SEARCH TABLE OF VALID PARMS                151
          LTR   R15,R15            L'OUTPUT PARM ^= 0                         152
          BNZ   NONDISP1           YES; USE FROM PARMLIST                     153
*                                  DEFAULT IS CATLG                           154
          MVC   DYNDISP(L'DYNDISP),CATLG                                      155
          LA    R9,DYNDISP         A(INPUT PARM)                              156
          LA    R1,DISPTB          A(TABLE OF VALID PARMS)                    157
          BAL   R14,FINDPARM       SEARCH TABLE OF VALID PARMS                158
NONDISP1  DS    0H                                                            159
          LA    R7,NDISP           TEXTUNIT MODEL                             160
          BAL   R14,MOVEPARM       BUILD TEXTUNIT                             161
*         *------------------------------------------*                        162
*         *     UNIT=                                 *                       163
*         *------------------------------------------*                        164
          LA    R9,DYUNIT          ADDRESS OF FIELD IN INPUT PARMLIST         165
          CLI   0(R9),X'00'        IS FIRST BYTE X'00' ?                      166
          BE    SETUNITD           YES; SET UNIT DEFAULT                      167
          CLI   0(R9),X'40'        IS FIRST BYTE X'40' ?                      168
          BNE   UNITOK             NO ; USE INPUT PARM AS IS                  169
SETUNITD  DS    0H                                                            170
          MVC   DYUNIT(L'DYUNIT),UDFLT    SET DEFAULT                         171
```

Figure C.11 *(Continued)*

```
UNITOK    DS   OH                                                         172
          LA   R7,UNIT           TEXTUNIT MODEL                          173
          BAL  R14,MOVEPARM      BUILD TEXTUNIT                          174
*         *-----------------------------------------*                    175
*         *    VOL=SER=                             *                    176
*         *-----------------------------------------*                    177
          CLI  0(R9),X'00'       IS FIRST BYTE X'00' ?                   178
          BE   NOVOL             YES; BYPASS THIS TEXT UNIT              179
          CLI  0(R9),X'40'       IS FIRST BYTE X'40' ?                   180
          BE   NOVOL             YES; BYPASS THIS TEXT UNIT              181
          LA   R9,DYVOLSER       ADDRESS OF FIELD IN INPUT PARMLIST      182
          LA   R7,VLSER          TEXTVLSER MODEL                         183
          BAL  R14,MOVEPARM      BUILD TEXTVLSER                         184
NOVOL     DS   OH                                                        185
*         *-----------------------------------------*                    186
*         *    CYL OR TRK                           *                    187
*         *-----------------------------------------*                    188
          LA   R9,DYATYPE        A(INPUT PARM)                           189
          LA   R1,CTRKTB         A(TABLE OF VALID PARMS)                 190
          BAL  R14,FINDPARM      SEARCH TABLE OF VALID PARMS             191
          LTR  R15,R15           IS L'OUTPUT PARM = 0                    192
          BNZ  SETATYPE          NO; PARM IS IN TABLE                    193
          L    R15,ETYPE         REASON CODE                            194
          B    EXIT10            PEROCOLATE REASON CODE                  195
SETATYPE  DS   OF                                                        196
          XR   R9,R9                                                     197
          LA   R7,CYL            TEXTUNIT MODEL                          198
          BAL  R14,MOVEPARM      BUILD TEXTUNIT                          199
*                                MOVE CYL OR TRK FROM PARMLIST           200
          CLC  DYATYPE(L'DYATYPE),TRACKS IS THIS TRACK ALLOCATION?       201
          BNE  NOTRK             NO; LEAVE CYLINDER DEFAULT              202
          L    R15,0(R4)         A(TEXT UNIT IN USER STORAGE)            203
          MVC  0(2,R15),=AL2(DALTRK) INDICATE TRACK ALLOCATION           204
NOTRK     DS   OH                                                        205
*         *-----------------------------------------*                    206
*         *    PRIMARY ALLOCATION                   *                    207
*         *-----------------------------------------*                    208
          XR   R9,R9                                                     209
          ICM  R9,B'0111',DYPRIM+1                                       210
          BNZ  PALOK             ^=0; USE VALUE                          211
          L    R15,EPRIME        REASON CODE                            212
          B    EXIT10            PEROCOLATE REASON CODE                  213
PALOK     DS   OH                                                        214
          LA   R9,DYPRIM+1       ADDRESS OF FIELD IN INPUT PARMLIST      215
          LA   R7,PRIME          TEXTUNIT MODEL                          216
          BAL  R14,MOVEPARM      BUILD TEXTUNIT                          217
*         *-----------------------------------------*                    218
*         *    SECONDARY ALLOCATION                 *                    219
*         *-----------------------------------------*                    220
          XR   R9,R9                                                     221
          ICM  R9,B'0111',DYSEC+1                                        222
          BZ   NOSECND           ^=0; USE VALUE                          223
          LA   R9,DYSEC+1        ADDRESS OF FIELD IN INPUT PARMLIST      224
          LA   R7,SECND          TEXTUNIT MODEL                          225
          BAL  R14,MOVEPARM      BUILD TEXTUNIT                          226
NOSECND   DS   OH                                                        227
```

Figure C.11 *(Continued)*

```
*              *----------------------------------------*              228
*              *      DSORG                             *              229
*              *----------------------------------------*              230
               LA    R9,DYDSORG       A(INPUT PARM)                    231
               LA    R1,DSORGTB       A(TABLE OF VALID PARMS)          232
               BAL   R14,FINDPARM     SEARCH TABLE OF VALID PARMS      233
               LTR   R15,R15          IS L'OUTPUT PARM = 0             234
               BNZ   SETDSORG         NO; PARM IS IN TABLE             235
*                                     SET DEFAULT TO PS                236
               MVC   DYDSORG(L'DYDSORG),DSORGPS                        237
SETDSORG DS    0H                                                      238
               LA    R7,DSORG         TEXTUNIT MODEL                   239
               BAL   R14,MOVEPARM     BUILD TEXTUNIT                   240
*              *----------------------------------------*              241
*              *      DIRECTORY BLOCKS IF DSORG=PO       *             242
*              *----------------------------------------*              243
               CLC   DYDSORG(L'DYDSORG),DSORGPO  DSORG = PO?           244
               BNE   NOTPO            NO; DO NOT SET DIRECTORY BLOCKS   245
               XR    R9,R9                                             246
               ICM   R9,B'0111',DYDIR+1                                247
               BNZ   PDIROK                                            248
               L     R15,EDIR         REASON CODE                      249
               B     EXIT10           PEROCOLATE REASON CODE           250
PDIROK   DS    0H                                                      251
               LA    R9,DYDIR+1       ADDRESS OF FIELD IN INPUT PARMLIST 252
               LA    R7,DIR           TEXTUNIT MODEL                   253
               BAL   R14,MOVEPARM     BUILD TEXTUNIT                   254
NOTPO    DS    0H                                                      255
*              *----------------------------------------*              256
*              *      RECFM                             *              257
*              *----------------------------------------*              258
               LA    R9,DYRECFM       A(INPUT PARM)                    259
               LA    R1,RECFMTB       A(TABLE OF VALID PARMS)          260
               BAL   R14,FINDPARM     SEARCH TABLE OF VALID PARMS      261
               LTR   R15,R15          IS L'OUTPUT PARM = 0             262
               BNZ   SETRECFM         NO; PARM IS IN TABLE             263
               L     R15,ERECFM       REASON CODE                      264
               B     EXIT10           PEROCOLATE REASON CODE           265
SETRECFM DS    0H                                                      266
               LA    R7,RECFM         TEXTUNIT MODEL                   267
               BAL   R14,MOVEPARM     BUILD TEXTUNIT                   268
*              *----------------------------------------*              269
*              *      BLKSIZE                           *              270
*              *----------------------------------------*              271
               XR    R9,R9                                             272
               ICM   R9,B'0011',DYBLKSIZ                               273
               BZ    NOBLKSZ                                           274
               LA    R9,DYBLKSIZ      ADDRESS OF FIELD IN INPUT PARMLIST 275
               LA    R7,BLKSZ         TEXTUNIT MODEL                   276
               BAL   R14,MOVEPARM     BUILD TEXTUNIT                   277
NOBLKSZ  DS    0H                                                      278
*              *----------------------------------------*              279
*              *      LRECL                             *              280
*              *----------------------------------------*              281
               XR    R9,R9                                             282
               ICM   R9,B'0011',DYLRECL                                283
               BNZ   PLRECLOK                                          284
```

Figure C.11   *(Continued)*

```
              L      R15,ELRECL         REASON CODE                              285
              B      EXIT10             PEROCOLATE REASON CODE                   286
PLRECLOK  DS   OH                                                               287
              LA     R9,DYLRECL         ADDRESS OF FIELD IN INPUT PARMLIST       288
              LA     R7,LRECL           TEXTUNIT MODEL                           289
              BAL    R14,MOVEPARM       BUILD TEXTUNIT                           290
              B      ENDUNITS                                                    291
NOTALLOC  DS   OH                                                               292
*----------------------------------------------------------------------*        293
*         TEXT UNITS FOR DEALLOCATE FUNCTION                           *        294
*----------------------------------------------------------------------*        295
*         *--------------------------------------------*                         296
*         *     DDNAME                                  *                         297
*         *--------------------------------------------*                         298
              LA     R9,DYDDNAME        ADDRESS OF FIELD IN INPUT PARMLIST       299
              CLI    0(R9),X'00'        IS FIRST BYTE X'00' ?                    300
              BE     SETDNAMU           YES; SET UNIT DEFAULT                    301
              CLI    0(R9),X'40'        IS FIRST BYTE X'40' ?                    302
              BE     SETDNAMU           YES; SET UNIT DEFAULT                    303
              LA     R9,DYDDNAME        ADDRESS OF FIELD IN INPUT PARMLIST       304
              LA     R7,DDNAMU          TEXTUNIT MODEL                           305
              BAL    R14,MOVEPARM       BUILD TEXTUNIT                           306
SETDNAMU  DS   OH                                                               307
*         *--------------------------------------------*                         308
*         *     DSNAME                                  *                         309
*         *--------------------------------------------*                         310
              LA     R9,DYDSN           ADDRESS OF FIELD IN INPUT PARMLIST       311
              CLI    0(R9),X'00'        IS FIRST BYTE X'00' ?                    312
              BE     SETDSNU            YES; SET UNIT DEFAULT                    313
              CLI    0(R9),X'40'        IS FIRST BYTE X'40' ?                    314
              BE     SETDSNU            YES; SET UNIT DEFAULT                    315
              LA     R9,DYDSN           ADDRESS OF FIELD IN INPUT PARMLIST       316
              LA     R7,DSNAMU          TEXTUNIT MODEL                           317
              BAL    R14,MOVEPARM       BUILD TEXTUNIT                           318
SETDSNU   DS   OH                                                               319
*         *--------------------------------------------*                         320
*         *     END OF TEXT UNITS                       *                         321
*         *--------------------------------------------*                         322
ENDUNITS  DS   OH                                                               323
              OI     S99TUPTR,S99TUPLN  SET FLAG IN LAST POINTER LIST ENTRY      324
*----------------------------------------------------------------------*        325
*         DYNAMICALLY ALLOCATE DATASET                                 *        326
*----------------------------------------------------------------------*        327
              LA     R1,RBPT99          A(RB POINTER)                           328
              DYNALLOC                                                          329
              LTR    R15,R15            RC = 0 ?                                330
              BZ     EXIT00             YES ;EXIT                               331
              XR     R0,R0                                                      332
              ICM    R0,B'1100',S99ERROR   SET ERROR CODE                       333
              ICM    R0,B'0011',S99INFO    SET ERROR INFO CODE                  334
              B      EXIT14                                                     335
```

Figure C.11 *(Continued)*

```
*-------------------------------------------------------------*  336
*        FINDPARM ROUTINE                                      *  337
* FUNCTION:                                                    *  338
*   SEARCHES TABLE OF VALID PARMS USER-SUPPLIED PARM.          *  339
*   IF FOUND, RETURNS PARM FOR DYNALLOC TEXT UNIT.             *  340
* INPUTS:                                                      *  341
*        R1 = A(TABLE OF VALID PARMS)                          *  342
*        R9 = A(INPUT PARM)                                    *  343
* OUTPUTS:                                                     *  344
*        R9 = A(OUTPUT PARM)                                   *  345
*        R15 = L'(OUTPUT PARM) OR 0 IF NOT FOUND               *  346
*-------------------------------------------------------------*  347
FINDPARM DS    0H                                                 348
         STM   R4,R8,SAVE1      SAVE WORK REGISTERS              349
         XR    R15,R15          DEFAULT LENGTH = 0               350
         LM    R4,R7,0(R1)      LOAD TABLE REGS                  351
         LA    R1,16(R1)        POINT AT FIRST ENTRY             352
FILOOP   DS    0H                                                353
         EX    R4,FICLC         COMPARE INPUT PARM TO TABLE VALUE 354
         B     AFI                                               355
FICLC    CLC   0(0,R1),0(R9)    *** EXECUTE ONLY ***             356
AFI      DS    0H                                                357
         BE    FIFOUND          EXIT IF FOUND                    358
         LA    R1,0(R6,R1)      POINT AT NEXT ENTRY              359
         BCT   R7,FILOOP        CHECK NEXT PARM                  360
         B     FIEXIT                                            361
FIFOUND  DS    0H                                                362
         LR    R15,R5           OUTPUT PARM LENGTH               363
         LA    R9,1(R4,R1)      OUTPUT PARM ADDRESS              364
FIEXIT   DS    0H                                                365
         LM    R4,R8,SAVE1      RESTORE WORK REGISTERS           366
         BR    14               RETURN                           367
*-------------------------------------------------------------*  368
*                                                             *  369
*-------------------------------------------------------------*  370
MOVEPARM DS    0H                                                371
         LA    R4,4(R4)         BUMP TO NEXT SLOT IN POINTER LIST 372
         ST    R5,0(R4)         PUT A(TEXT UNIT) IN POINTER LIST 373
         ICM   R6,B'1111',0(R7) LENGTH FOR MOVE                  374
         EX    R6,MVIT          MOVE MODEL TO TEXTUNIT SLOT      375
         B     AFT1                                              376
MVIT     MVC   0(0,R5),4(R7)    *** EXECUTE ONLY ***             377
AFT1     DS    0H                                                378
*        *---------------------------------------*              379
*        *     LOOP THRU TEXTUNIT PARMS           *              380
*        *---------------------------------------*              381
         XR    R1,R1            CLEAR R1                         382
         LA    R5,4(R5)         POINT AT FIRST PARM IN TEXTUNIT  383
         ICM   R1,B'0011',6(R7) NUMBER OF PARMS                  384
         BZ    NOPARM                                            385
PARMLOOP DS    0H                                                386
         ICM   R6,B'0011',0(R5) LENGTH OF PARM IN TEXT UNIT      387
         BCTR  R6,0             LESS 1 FOR EXECUTE               388
         EX    R6,MVIT1         MOVE PARMLIST FIELD TO TEXTUNIT  389
         B     AFT2                                              390
MVIT1    MVC   2(0,R5),0(R9)    *** EXECUTE ONLY ***             391
AFT2     DS    0H                                                392
```

Figure C.11 *(Continued)*

```
            LA    R5,3(R6,R5)           POINT TO NEXT SPACE FOR TEXT UNIT    393
            LA    R9,1(R6,R9)           POINT TO NEXT PARM IN INPUT          394
            BCT   R1,PARMLOOP                                                395
NOPARM      DS    OH                                                         396
            BR    R14                                                        397
*-----------------------------------------------------------------*         398
*           EXIT ROUTINES                                          *         399
*-----------------------------------------------------------------*         400
EXIT00      DS    OH                    DATASET ALLOCATED OR UNALLOCATED     401
            LA    15,X'00'                                                   402
            B     EXIT                                                       403
EXIT10      DS    OH                    ERROR IN PARMLIST                    404
            PERCRC RC=X'10'                                                  405
            B     EXIT                                                       406
EXIT14      DS    OH                    SVC 99 FAILED                        407
            PERCRC RC=X'14'                                                  408
            B     EXIT                                                       409
*-----------------------------------------------------------------*         410
*           COMMON EXIT                                            *         411
*-----------------------------------------------------------------*         412
EXIT        DS    OH                                                         413
            STCM  R15,B'0011',DYRETURN                                       414
            STCM  R0,B'0011',DYREASON                                        415
            STCM  R1,B'1111',DY99ERR                                         416
            ENDMOD                                                           417
*-----------------------------------------------------------------*         418
*           CONSTANTS                                              *         419
*-----------------------------------------------------------------*         420
MAXUNITS    EQU   50                    MAXIMUM TEXT UNITS                   421
AL          DC    CL(L'DYFUNCT)'AL'     ALLOCATION FUNCTION                  422
NEWDISP     DC    CL(L'DYDISP)'NEW'                                          423
SHRDISP     DC    CL(L'DYDISP)'SHR'                                          424
CATLG       DC    CL(L'DYNDISP)'CATLG'                                       425
KEEP        DC    CL(L'DYNDISP)'KEEP'                                        426
UDFLT       DC    CL(L'DYUNIT)'SYSDA'   DEFAULT FOR UNIT=                    427
DSORGPO     DC    CL(L'DYDSORG)'PO'                                          428
DSORGPS     DC    CL(L'DYDSORG)'PS'     DEFAULT FOR DSORG                    429
TRACKS      DC    CL(L'DYATYPE)'TRK'    TRACK ALLOCATION                     430
EFUNCT      EQU   X'04'                 PARMLIST ERROR: FUNCTION CODE        431
EDISP       EQU   X'08'                 PARMLIST ERROR: DISP=(XXX            432
ETYPE       EQU   X'0C'                 PARMLIST ERROR: SPACE=(XXX(          433
EPRIME      EQU   X'10'                 PARMLIST ERROR: SPACE=(...(XXX,      434
EDIR        EQU   X'14'                 PARMLIST ERROR: SPACE=(...(,,XXX     435
ERECFM      EQU   X'18'                 PARMLIST ERROR: RECFM                436
ELRECL      EQU   X'1C'                 PARMLIST ERROR: LRECL                437
*-----------------------------------------------------------------*         438
*           TABLES OF VALID PARMS                                  *         439
*-----------------------------------------------------------------*         440
*           *-------------------------------------------*                   441
*           *    FUNCTIONS                              *                   442
*           *-------------------------------------------*                   443
FUNCTB      DS    OF                                                         444
            DC    AL4(L'DYFUNCT-1)              L'INPUT PARM -1              445
            DC    AL4(L'S99VERB)               LENGTH OF OUTPUT PARM        446
            DC    AL4(L'DYFUNCT+L'S99VERB)     LENGTH OF AN ENTRY           447
*                                              NUMBER OF ENTRIES            448
            DC    AL4(((EFUNCTB-FUNCTB)-16)/(L'DYFUNCT+L'S99VERB))          449
```

Figure C.11 *(Continued)*

```
        DC    CL(L'DYFUNCT)'AL',AL(L'S99VERB)(S99VRBAL)              450
        DC    CL(L'DYFUNCT)'UN',AL(L'S99VERB)(S99VRBUN)              451
        DC    CL(L'DYFUNCT)'CC',AL(L'S99VERB)(S99VRBCC)              452
        DC    CL(L'DYFUNCT)'DC',AL(L'S99VERB)(S99VRBDC)              453
        DC    CL(L'DYFUNCT)'RI',AL(L'S99VERB)(S99VRBRI)              454
        DC    CL(L'DYFUNCT)'DN',AL(L'S99VERB)(S99VRBDN)              455
        DC    CL(L'DYFUNCT)'IN',AL(L'S99VERB)(S99VRBIN)              456
EFUNCTB EQU   *                                                      457
*       *-----------------------------------*                        458
*       *     STATUS                         *                       459
*       *-----------------------------------*                        460
STATB   DS    0F                                                     461
        DC    AL4(L'DYDISP-1)              L'INPUT PARM -1            462
        DC    AL4(L'PSTATS)               LENGTH OF OUTPUT PARM      463
        DC    AL4(L'DYDISP+L'PSTATS)      LENGTH OF AN ENTRY         464
*                                         NUMBER OF ENTRIES          465
        DC    AL4(((ESTATB-STATB)-16)/(L'DYDISP+L'PSTATS))           466
        DC    CL(L'DYDISP)'OLD',AL(L'PSTATS)(X'01')                  467
        DC    CL(L'DYDISP)'MOD',AL(L'PSTATS)(X'02')                  468
        DC    CL(L'DYDISP)'NEW',AL(L'PSTATS)(X'04')                  469
        DC    CL(L'DYDISP)'SHR',AL(L'PSTATS)(X'08')                  470
ESTATB  EQU   *                                                      471
*       *-----------------------------------*                        472
*       *     DISP                           *                       473
*       *-----------------------------------*                        474
DISPTB  DS    0F                                                     475
        DC    AL4(L'DYCDISP-1)            L'INPUT PARM -1            476
        DC    AL4(L'PCDISP)              LENGTH OF OUTPUT PARM      477
        DC    AL4(L'DYCDISP+L'PCDISP)     LENGTH OF AN ENTRY         478
*                                         NUMBER OF ENTRIES          479
        DC    AL4(((EDISPTB-DISPTB)-16)/(L'DYCDISP+L'PCDISP))        480
        DC    CL(L'DYCDISP)'UNCATLG',AL(L'PCDISP)(X'01')             481
        DC    CL(L'DYCDISP)'CATLG',AL(L'PCDISP)(X'02')               482
        DC    CL(L'DYCDISP)'DELETE',AL(L'PCDISP)(X'04')              483
        DC    CL(L'DYCDISP)'KEEP',AL(L'PCDISP)(X'08')                484
EDISPTB EQU   *                                                      485
*       *-----------------------------------*                        486
*       *     ALLOCATION UNIT                *                       487
*       *-----------------------------------*                        488
CTRKTB  DS    0F                                                     489
        DC    AL4(L'DYATYPE-1)            L'INPUT PARM -1            490
        DC    AL4(2)                     LENGTH OF OUTPUT PARM      491
        DC    AL4(L'DYATYPE+2)            LENGTH OF AN ENTRY         492
*                                         NUMBER OF ENTRIES          493
        DC    AL4(((ECTRKTB-CTRKTB)-16)/(L'DYATYPE+2))               494
        DC    CL(L'DYATYPE)'TRK',AL(2)(X'0007')                      495
        DC    CL(L'DYATYPE)'CYL',AL(2)(X'0008')                      496
ECTRKTB EQU   *                                                      497
*       *-----------------------------------*                        498
*       *     DSORG                          *                       499
*       *-----------------------------------*                        500
DSORGTB DS    0F                                                     501
        DC    AL4(L'DYDSORG-1)            L'INPUT PARM -1            502
        DC    AL4(L'PDSORG)              LENGTH OF OUTPUT PARM      503
        DC    AL4(L'DYDSORG+L'PDSORG)     LENGTH OF AN ENTRY         504
*                                         NUMBER OF ENTRIES          505
        DC    AL4(((EDSORGTB-DSORGTB)-16)/(L'DYDSORG+L'PDSORG))      506
```

Figure C.11 *(Continued)*

```
                DC    CL(L'DYDSORG)'PS',AL(L'PDSORG)(X'4000')              507
                DC    CL(L'DYDSORG)'DA',AL(L'PDSORG)(X'2000')              508
                DC    CL(L'DYDSORG)'PO',AL(L'PDSORG)(X'0200')              509
EDSORGTB  EQU   *                                                         510
*               *-------------------------------------*                   511
*               *    RECFM                            *                   512
*               *-------------------------------------*                   513
@F        EQU   X'80'              FIXED   LENGTH RECORDS                  514
@V        EQU   X'40'              VARIABLE LENGTH RECORDS                 515
@U        EQU   X'C0'              VARIABLE LENGTH RECORDS                 516
@B        EQU   X'10'              BLOCKED RECORDS                         517
@A        EQU   X'04'              RM=XXA (ASA CONTROL CHARACTERS)         518
@M        EQU   X'02'              RM=XXM (MACHINE CONTROL   CHARACTERS    519
RECFMTB   DS    0F                                                        520
          DC    AL4(L'DYRECFM-1)                   L'INPUT PARM -1        521
          DC    AL4(L'PRECFM)                      LENGTH OF OUTPUT PARM  522
          DC    AL4(L'DYRECFM+L'PRECFM)            LENGTH OF AN ENTRY     523
*                                                  NUMBER OF ENTRIES      524
          DC    AL4(((ERECFMTB-RECFMTB)-16)/(L'DYRECFM+L'PRECFM))         525
          DC    CL(L'DYRECFM)'F  ',AL(L'PRECFM)(@F)                       526
          DC    CL(L'DYRECFM)'FA ',AL(L'PRECFM)(@F+@A)                    527
          DC    CL(L'DYRECFM)'FM ',AL(L'PRECFM)(@F+@M)                    528
          DC    CL(L'DYRECFM)'FB ',AL(L'PRECFM)(@F+@B)                    529
          DC    CL(L'DYRECFM)'FBA',AL(L'PRECFM)(@F+@B+@A)                 530
          DC    CL(L'DYRECFM)'FBM',AL(L'PRECFM)(@F+@B+@M)                 531
          DC    CL(L'DYRECFM)'V  ',AL(L'PRECFM)(@V)                       532
          DC    CL(L'DYRECFM)'VA ',AL(L'PRECFM)(@V+@A)                    533
          DC    CL(L'DYRECFM)'VM ',AL(L'PRECFM)(@V+@M)                    534
          DC    CL(L'DYRECFM)'VB ',AL(L'PRECFM)(@V+@B)                    535
          DC    CL(L'DYRECFM)'VBA',AL(L'PRECFM)(@V+@B+@A)                 536
          DC    CL(L'DYRECFM)'VBM',AL(L'PRECFM)(@V+@B+@M)                 537
          DC    CL(L'DYRECFM)'U  ',AL(L'PRECFM)(@U)                       538
ERECFMTB  EQU   *                                                         539
*-------------------------------------------------------------------*     540
*          TEXT UNIT MODELS FOR FUNCTION DSNAME ALLOCATION (AL)     *     541
*-------------------------------------------------------------------*     542
*               *-------------------------------------*                   543
*               *    UNIT                             *                   544
*               *-------------------------------------*                   545
UNIT      DC    AL4((PUNIT-UNIT)+L'PUNIT-5)                               546
          DC    AL2(DALUNIT)                                              547
          DC    AL2(1)                                                    548
LUNIT     DC    AL2(L'PUNIT)                                              549
PUNIT     DC    CL8' '            < === PRODDA AFTER TEST                  550
*               *-------------------------------------*                   551
*               *    VOL=SER=                         *                   552
*               *-------------------------------------*                   553
VLSER     DC    AL4((PVLSER-VLSER)+L'PVLSER-5)                            554
          DC    AL2(DALVLSER)                                             555
          DC    AL2(1)                                                    556
LVLSER    DC    AL2(L'PVLSER)                                             557
PVLSER    DC    CL6' '            < === PRODDA AFTER TEST                  558
*               *-------------------------------------*                   559
*               *    SPECIFICATION                    *                   560
*               *-------------------------------------*                   561
STATS     DC    AL4((PSTATS-STATS)+L'PSTATS-5)                            562
          DC    AL2(DALSTATS)                                             563
```

Figure C.11 *(Continued)*

```
          DC    AL2(1)                                            564
LSTATS    DC    AL2(L'PSTATS)                                     565
PSTATS    DC    X'04'                   DISP=(NEW,)               566
*         *-------------------------------------------*          567
*         *     NORMAL DISPOSITION               *               568
*         *-------------------------------------------*          569
NDISP     DC    AL4((PNDISP-NDISP)+L'PNDISP-5)                    570
          DC    AL2(DALNDISP)                                     571
          DC    AL2(1)                                            572
LNDISP    DC    AL2(L'PNDISP)                                     573
PNDISP    DC    X'02'                   DISP=(,CATLG)             574
*         *-------------------------------------------*          575
*         *     CONDITIONAL DISPOSITION          *               576
*         *-------------------------------------------*          577
CDISP     DC    AL4((PCDISP-CDISP)+L'PCDISP-5)                    578
          DC    AL2(DALCDISP)                                     579
          DC    AL2(1)                                            580
LCDISP    DC    AL2(L'PCDISP)                                     581
PCDISP    DC    X'04'                   DISP=(,,DELETE)           582
*         *-------------------------------------------*          583
*         *     DSORG                             *               584
*         *-------------------------------------------*          585
DSORG     DC    AL4((PDSORG-DSORG)+L'PDSORG-5)                    586
          DC    AL2(DALDSORG)                                     587
          DC    AL2(1)                                            588
LDSORG    DC    AL2(L'PDSORG)                                     589
PDSORG    DC    X'4000'                 DSORG=PS                  590
*         *-------------------------------------------*          591
*         *     RECFM                             *               592
*         *-------------------------------------------*          593
RECFM     DC    AL4((PRECFM-RECFM)+L'PRECFM-5)                    594
          DC    AL2(DALRECFM)                                     595
          DC    AL2(1)                                            596
LRECFM    DC    AL2(L'PRECFM)                                     597
PRECFM    DC    AL1(X'10'+X'80')                  RECFM=FB        598
*         *-------------------------------------------*          599
*         *     LRECL                             *               600
*         *-------------------------------------------*          601
LRECL     DC    AL4((PLRECL-LRECL)+L'PLRECL-5),AL2(DALLRECL)      602
          DC    AL2(1)                                            603
LLRECL    DC    AL2(L'PLRECL)                                     604
PLRECL    DC    AL2(0)                                            605
*         *-------------------------------------------*          606
*         *     BLOCKSIZE                         *               607
*         *-------------------------------------------*          608
BLKSZ     DC    AL4((PBLKSZ-BLKSZ)+L'PBLKSZ-5),AL2(DALBLKSZ)      609
          DC    AL2(1)                                            610
LBLKSZ    DC    AL2(L'PBLKSZ)                                     611
PBLKSZ    DC    AL2(0)                                            612
*         *-------------------------------------------*          613
*         *     PRIMARY ALLOCATION                *               614
*         *-------------------------------------------*          615
PRIME     DC    AL4((PPRIME-PRIME)+L'PPRIME-5),AL2(DALPRIME)      616
          DC    AL2(1)                                            617
LPRIME    DC    AL2(L'PPRIME)                                     618
PPRIME    DC    AL3(0)                                            619
```

Figure C.11   *(Continued)*

```
*           *----------------------------------------*               620
*           *      SECONDARY ALLOCATION              *               621
*           *----------------------------------------*               622
SECND    DC    AL4((PSECND-SECND)+L'PSECND-5),AL2(DALSECND)          623
         DC    AL2(1)                                                624
LSECND   DC    AL2(L'PSECND)                                         625
PSECND   DC    AL3(0)                                                626
*           *----------------------------------------*               627
*           *      DIRECTORY BLOCK ALLOCATION        *               628
*           *----------------------------------------*               629
DIR      DC    AL4((PDIR-DIR)+L'PDIR-5),AL2(DALDIR)                  630
         DC    AL2(1)                                                631
LDIR     DC    AL2(L'PDIR)                                           632
PDIR     DC    AL3(0)                                                633
*           *----------------------------------------*               634
*           *      ALLOCATION TYPE                   *               635
*           *----------------------------------------*               636
CYL      DC    AL4((ECYL-CYL)-5),AL2(DALCYL)                         637
         DC    AL2(0)                                                638
ECYL     EQU   *                                                     639
*           *----------------------------------------*               640
*           *      DDNAME                            *               641
*           *----------------------------------------*               642
DDNAM    DC    AL4((PDDNAM-DDNAM)+L'PDDNAM-5),AL2(DALDDNAM)          643
         DC    AL2(1)                                                644
LDDNAM   DC    AL2(L'PDDNAM)                                         645
PDDNAM   DC    CL8' '                                                646
*           *----------------------------------------*               647
*           *      DATASET NAME                      *               648
*           *----------------------------------------*               649
DSNAM    DC    AL4((PDSNAM-DSNAM)+L'PDSNAM-5),AL2(DALDSNAM)          650
         DC    AL2(1)                                                651
LDSNAM   DC    AL2(L'PDSNAM)                                         652
PDSNAM   DC    CL44' '                                               653
*           *----------------------------------------*               654
*--------------------------------------------------------------------* 655
*           TEXT UNIT MODELS FOR FUNCTION DSNAME UNALLOCATION (UN)  * 656
*--------------------------------------------------------------------* 657
*           *----------------------------------------*               658
*           *      DDNAME                            *               659
*           *----------------------------------------*               660
DDNAMU   DC    AL4((PDDNAMU-DDNAMU)+L'PDDNAMU-5),AL2(DUNDDNAM)       661
         DC    AL2(1)                                                662
LDDNAMU  DC    AL2(L'PDDNAMU)                                        663
PDDNAMU  DC    CL8' '                                                664
*           *----------------------------------------*               665
*           *      DATASET NAME                      *               666
*           *----------------------------------------*               667
DSNAMU   DC    AL4((PDSNAMU-DSNAMU)+L'PDSNAMU-5),AL2(DUNDSNAM)       668
         DC    AL2(1)                                                669
LDSNAMU  DC    AL2(L'PDSNAMU)                                        670
PDSNAMU  DC    CL44' '                                               671
*--------------------------------------------------------------------* 672
*           WORK AREA                                               * 673
*--------------------------------------------------------------------* 674
WDYNAL   DSECT                                                        675
SAVE1    DS    5F                    SUBROUTINE WORK REGISTERS        676
```

Figure C.11 *(Continued)*

```
S99RBLEN EQU   S99RBEND-S99RB         SVC 99 RB LENGTH              677
RBPT99   DS    A                      SVC 99 RB POINTER            678
RB99     DS    0F,CL(S99RBLEN)        SVC 99 RB                    679
TXPT99   DS    0F,CL((MAXUNITS)*4)    SVC 99 TEXT POINTERS         680
TXTUNITS DS    CL500                  TEXT UNITS                   681
LDYNAL   EQU   *-WDYNAL                                            682
*----------------------------------------------------------------*  683
*        OTHER DSECTS                                            *  684
*----------------------------------------------------------------*  685
         DYNPRM                MAP INPUT PARMS                      686
         PRINT NOGEN                                                687
         IEFZB4D0                                                   688
         IEFZB4D2                                                   689
         END                                                        690
```

Figure C.11 *(Continued)*

```
          MACRO                     MAPS PARMLIST DYNAL              1
          DYNPRM                                                    2
   .*+----------------------------------------------------------+   3
   .*|     PARMLIST FOR DYNAL - DYNAMIC ALLOCATION ROUTINE      |   4
   .*+----------------------------------------------------------+   5
DYNPRM    DSECT                                                     6
*         +-----------------------------------+                     7
*         |     USED BY ALL ALLOCATIONS       |                     8
*         +-----------------------------------+                     9
DYPLEN    DS    H                   LENGTH OF PARMLIST             10
DYRETURN  DS    H                   RETURN CODE                    11
DYREASON  DS    H                   REASON CODE                    12
DYFUNCT   DS    CL2                 FUNCTION REQUESTED             13
DYDDNAME  DS    CL8                 DDNAME                         14
DYDSN     DS    CL44                DATASET NAME                   15
DYDISP    DS    CL4                 DISP=(XXX,)     (NEW, MOD, SHR, OLD)  16
DYNDISP   DS    CL6                 DISP=(,XXX)                    17
DYCDISP   DS    CL6                 DISP=(,,XXX)                   18
*         +-----------------------------------+                    19
*         |     USED BY DISP=(NEW, ALLOCATIONS |                   20
*         +-----------------------------------+                    21
DYATYPE   DS    CL4                 ALLOCATION TYPE         (TRK, CYL)  22
DYPRIM    DS    F                   PRIMARY ALLOCATION             23
DYSEC     DS    F                   SECONDARY ALLOCATION           24
DYDIR     DS    F                   DIRECTORY BLOCKS FOR DSORG = PO  25
DYRECFM   DS    CL4                 RECFM  (F ,FB ,V, VB, FBA, VBM, ETC.)  26
DYLRECL   DS    H                   LRECL                          27
DYBLKSIZ  DS    H                   BLOCKSIZE                      28
DYDSORG   DS    CL2                 DSORG              (PS, DA, PO)  29
DYUNIT    DS    CL8                 UNIT TYPE                      30
DYVOLSER  DS    CL6                 VOL=SER=                       31
DY99ERR   DS    CL4                 ERROR DATA FROM S99            32
*         +-----------------------------------+                    33
*         |     RESERVED FOR EXANSION         |                    34
*         +-----------------------------------+                    35
          DS    CL(200-(*-DYNPRM)) AVAILIBLE FOR EXPANSION         36
LDYNPRM   EQU   *-DYNPRM            LENGTH OF PARMLIST             37
          MEND                                                    38
```

Figure C.12 DYNAL.

Assembly and Link Edit JCL

```
//*---------------------------------------------------------------------*
//* THIS JOB CONTAINS INSTREAM PROCEDURES AND STEPS TO ASSEMBLE         *
//* AND LINK EDIT THE PROGRAMS IN "MVS POWER PROGRAMMING".              *
//* BEFORE EXECUTING THIS JOB:                                          *
//*   1) ADD A JOB CARD.                                                *
//*   2) CHANGE EVERY LINE MARKED:  "<== " .                            *
//* COPY ANY PROGRAM LINKED WITH PARM='AC=1' INTO AN APF-AUTHORIZED     *
//* LIBRARY BEFORE EXECUTING IT.                                        *
//*---------------------------------------------------------------------*
//*          *----------------------------*
//*          *  ASSEMBLY PROCEDURE        *
//*          *----------------------------*
//ASSEM    PROC MEMBER=,
//         PARM1=,
//         UNIT=SYSDA,                 <== CHANGE IF NECESSARY
//         MACLIB='MACLIB',            <== NAME OF MACRO  LIBRARY
//         SOURCE='SOURCE',            <== NAME OF SOURCE LIBRARY
//         OBJECT='OBJECT'             <== NAME OF OBJECT LIBRARY
//ASSEM    EXEC PGM=IEV90,
//              PARM='NOOBJECT,DECK,XREF(SHORT),&PARM1'
//SYSLIB   DD DISP=SHR,DSN=&MACLIB
```

```
//         DD DISP=SHR,DSN=SYS1.AMODGEN
//         DD DISP=SHR,DSN=SYS1.MACLIB
//*        DD DISP=SHR,DSN=SYS1.MODGEN
//SYSUT1   DD UNIT=&UNIT,SPACE=(1700,(600,100))
//SYSUT2   DD UNIT=&UNIT,SPACE=(1700,(600,100))
//SYSUT3   DD UNIT=&UNIT,SPACE=(1700,(600,100))
//SYSPRINT DD SYSOUT=*
//SYSLIN   DD DUMMY
//SYSIN    DD DISP=SHR,DSN=&SOURCE(&MEMBER)
//SYSPUNCH DD DISP=SHR,DSN=&OBJECT(&MEMBER)
//         PEND
//*        *----------------------------*
//*        * LINK EDIT PROCEDURE         *
//*        *----------------------------*
//LKED     PROC PARM1=,
//         UNIT=SYSDA,              <== CHANGE IF NECESSARY
//         OBJECT='OBJECT',         <== NAME OF OBJECT LIBRARY
//         LOAD='LOAD'              <== NAME OF LOAD   LIBRARY
//LKED     EXEC PGM=IEWL,
//              PARM='XREF,LET,LIST,NCAL,&PARM1'
//SYSPRINT DD SYSOUT=*
//SYSUT1   DD UNIT=&UNIT,SPACE=(1024,(50,20))
//OBJ      DD DSN=&OBJECT,DISP=SHR
//SYSLMOD  DD DSN=&LOAD,DISP=SHR
//SYSLIN   DD DDNAME=SYSIN
//         PEND
//*----------------------------------------------------------------*
//* EACH OF THE FOLLOWING STEPS ASSEMBLES AND LINK EDITS A PROGRAM  *
//* CALLED BY OTHER PROGRAMS (APPENDIX B)                           *
//*----------------------------------------------------------------*
//*
//*----------------------------------------------------------------*
//*        GETASCB                                                  *
//*----------------------------------------------------------------*
//GETASCB  EXEC ASSEM,MEMBER=GETASCB,PARM1='RENT'
//LGETASCB EXEC LKED,PARM1='RENT'
//LKED.SYSIN DD *
         ENTRY GETASCB
         INCLUDE OBJ(GETASCB)
         NAME  GETASCB(R)
/*
```

```
//*---------------------------------------------------------------------*
//*         HEXPRT                                                      *
//*---------------------------------------------------------------------*
//HEXPRT   EXEC ASSEM,MEMBER=HEXPRT,PARM1='RENT'
//LHEXPRT  EXEC LKED,PARM1='RENT'
//LKED.SYSIN DD *
         ENTRY HEXPRT
         INCLUDE OBJ(HEXPRT)
         NAME  HEXPRT(R)
/*
//*---------------------------------------------------------------------*
//*         PGMNAME                                                     *
//*---------------------------------------------------------------------*
//PGMNAME  EXEC ASSEM,MEMBER=PGMNAME,PARM1='RENT'
//LPGMNAME EXEC LKED,PARM1='RENT'
//LKED.SYSIN DD *
         ENTRY PGMNAME
         INCLUDE OBJ(PGMNAME)
         NAME  PGMNAME(R)
/*
//*---------------------------------------------------------------------*
//*  EACH OF THE FOLLOWING STEPS ASSEMBLES AND LINK EDITS PROGRAMS      *
//*  RELATED TO ONE OF THE CHAPTERS IN "MVS POWER PROGRAMMING"          *
//*---------------------------------------------------------------------*
//*
//*---------------------------------------------------------------------*
//*         NCRYPT                                                      *
//*---------------------------------------------------------------------*
//NCRYPT   EXEC ASSEM,MEMBER=NCRYPT,PARM1='RENT'
//LNCRYPT  EXEC LKED,PARM1='RENT'
//LKED.SYSIN DD *
         ENTRY NCRYPT
         INCLUDE OBJ(NCRYPT)
         NAME  NCRYPT(R)
/*
//*---------------------------------------------------------------------*
//*         EDEBUG                                                      *
//*---------------------------------------------------------------------*
//EDEBUG   EXEC ASSEM,MEMBER=EDEBUG,PARM1='RENT'
//LEDEBUG  EXEC LKED,PARM1='RENT'
//LKED.SYSIN DD *
         ENTRY EDEBUG
         INCLUDE OBJ(EDEBUG,HEXPRT)
         NAME  EDEBUG(R)
/*
```

```
//*----------------------------------------------------------------------*
//*        SVCLIST                                                       *
//*----------------------------------------------------------------------*
//SVCLIST  EXEC ASSEM,MEMBER=SVCLIST,PARM1='RENT'
//LSVCLIST EXEC LKED,PARM1='RENT'
//LKED.SYSIN DD *
         ENTRY SVCLIST
         INCLUDE OBJ(SVCLIST)
         NAME  SVCLIST(R)
/*
//*----------------------------------------------------------------------*
//*        ESAMOVE                                                       *
//*----------------------------------------------------------------------*
//ESAMOVE  EXEC ASSEM,MEMBER=ESAMOVE,PARM1='RENT'
//XTALK    EXEC ASSEM,MEMBER=XTALK,PARM1='RENT'
//PRTMOD   EXEC ASSEM,MEMBER=PRTMOD,PARM1='RENT'
//LESAMOVE EXEC LKED,PARM1='RENT,AC=1'
//LKED.SYSIN DD *
         ENTRY ESAMOVE
         INCLUDE OBJ(ESAMOVE,XTALK,GETASCB,PRTMOD)
         NAME  ESAMOVE(R)
/*
//*----------------------------------------------------------------------*
//*        XAMOVE                                                        *
//*----------------------------------------------------------------------*
//XAMOVE   EXEC ASSEM,MEMBER=XAMOVE,PARM1='RENT'
//LXAMOVE  EXEC LKED,PARM1='RENT,AC=1'
//LKED.SYSIN DD *
         ENTRY XAMOVE
         INCLUDE OBJ(XAMOVE,GETASCB,PRTMOD)
         NAME  XAMOVE(R)
/*
//XASAC    EXEC ASSEM,MEMBER=XASAC,PARM1='RENT'
//LXASAC   EXEC LKED,PARM1='RENT'
//LKED.SYSIN DD *
         ENTRY XASAC
         INCLUDE OBJ(XASAC)
         NAME  XASAC(R)
/*
```

```
//*----------------------------------------------------------------------*
//*          ANCHOR                                                      *
//*----------------------------------------------------------------------*
//ANCHOR    EXEC ASSEM,MEMBER=ANCHOR,PARM1='RENT'
//LANCHOR   EXEC LKED,PARM1='RENT,AC=1'
//LKED.SYSIN DD *
          ENTRY ANCHOR
          INCLUDE OBJ(ANCHOR)
          NAME   ANCHOR(R)
/*
//*----------------------------------------------------------------------*
//*          SCHDSRB                                                     *
//*----------------------------------------------------------------------*
//SCHDSRB   EXEC ASSEM,MEMBER=SCHDSRB,PARM1='RENT'
//LSCHDSRB EXEC LKED,PARM1='RENT,AC=1'
//LKED.SYSIN DD *
          ENTRY SCHDSRB
          INCLUDE OBJ(SCHDSRB,GETASCB)
          NAME   SCHDSRB(R)
/*
//NSWPRTN   EXEC ASSEM,MEMBER=NSWPRTN,PARM1='RENT'
//LNSWPRTN EXEC LKED,PARM1='RENT'
//LKED.SYSIN DD *
          ENTRY NSWPRTN
          INCLUDE OBJ(NSWPRTN)
          NAME   NSWPRTN(R)
/*
//*----------------------------------------------------------------------*
//*          PCSET                                                       *
//*----------------------------------------------------------------------*
//PCSET     EXEC ASSEM,MEMBER=PCSET,PARM1='RENT'
//LPCSET    EXEC LKED,PARM1='RENT,AC=1'
//LKED.SYSIN DD *
          ENTRY PCSET
          INCLUDE OBJ(PCSET)
          NAME   PCSET(R)
/*
//PCPERM    EXEC ASSEM,MEMBER=PCPERM,PARM1='RENT'
//PCPERM    EXEC LKED,PARM1='RENT'
//LKED.SYSIN DD *
          ENTRY PCPERM
          INCLUDE OBJ(PCPERM)
          NAME   PCPERM(R)
/*
```

```
//CKXTALK  EXEC ASSEM,MEMBER=CKXTALK,PARM1='RENT'
//LCKXTALK EXEC LKED,PARM1='RENT'
//LKED.SYSIN DD *
          ENTRY CKXTALK
          INCLUDE OBJ(CKXTALK,XTALK,ANCHOR)
          NAME  CKXTALK(R)
/*
//*       *----------------------------*
//*       * ESAMOVE: PC VERSION        *
//*       *----------------------------*
//ESAMVPC  EXEC ASSEM,MEMBER=ESAMVPC,PARM1='RENT'
//LESAMVPC EXEC LKED,PARM1='RENT'
//LKED.SYSIN DD *
          ENTRY ESAMVPC
          INCLUDE OBJ(ESAMVPC,PRTMOD)
          NAME  ESAMVPC(R)
/*
//*--------------------------------------------------------------------*
//*       DSPACE                                                       *
//*--------------------------------------------------------------------*
//DSPACE   EXEC ASSEM,MEMBER=DSPACE,PARM1='RENT'
//LDSPACE  EXEC LKED,PARM1='RENT,AC=1'
//LKED.SYSIN DD *
          ENTRY DSPACE
          INCLUDE OBJ(DSPACE,PGMNAME,ANCHOR)
          NAME  DSPACE(R)
/*
//DSPUT    EXEC ASSEM,MEMBER=DSPUT,PARM1='RENT'
//DSPFIND  EXEC ASSEM,MEMBER=DSPFIND,PARM1='RENT'
//LDSPUT   EXEC LKED,PARM1='RENT,AC=1'
//LKED.SYSIN DD *
          ENTRY DSPUT
          INCLUDE OBJ(DSPUT,DSPFIND)
          NAME  DSPUT(R)
/*
```

```
//*------------------------------------------------------------------------*
//*  EACH OF THE FOLLOWING STEPS ASSEMBLES AND LINK EDITS PROGRAMS     *
//*  IN APPENDIX C (ADDITIONAL PROGRAMS)                               *
//*------------------------------------------------------------------------*
//*
//*------------------------------------------------------------------------*
//*        REPMOD                                                      *
//*------------------------------------------------------------------------*
//REPMOD   EXEC ASSEM,MEMBER=REPMOD,PARM1='RENT'
//LREPMOD  EXEC LKED,PARM1='RENT,AC=1'
//LKED.SYSIN DD *
         ENTRY REPMOD
         INCLUDE OBJ(REPMOD)
         NAME   REPMOD(R)
/*
//UNANCH   EXEC ASSEM,MEMBER=UNANCH,PARM1='RENT'
//LUNANCH  EXEC LKED,PARM1='RENT,AC=1'
//LKED.SYSIN DD *
         ENTRY UNANCH
         INCLUDE OBJ(UNANCH)
         NAME   UNANCH(R)
/*
//*------------------------------------------------------------------------*
//*        HOOKDRV                                                     *
//*------------------------------------------------------------------------*
//HOOKDRV  EXEC ASSEM,MEMBER=HOOKDRV,PARM1='RENT'
//LHOOKDRV EXEC LKED,PARM1='RENT,AC=1'
//LKED.SYSIN DD *
         ENTRY HOOKDRV
         INCLUDE OBJ(HOOKDRV)
         NAME   HOOKDRV(R)
/*
//HOOKIN   EXEC ASSEM,MEMBER=HOOKIN,PARM1='RENT'
//LHOOKIN  EXEC LKED,PARM1='RENT,AC=1'
//LKED.SYSIN DD *
         ENTRY HOOKIN
         INCLUDE OBJ(HOOKIN,REPMOD)
         NAME   HOOKIN(R)
/*
```

```
//HOOKSVC  EXEC ASSEM,MEMBER=HOOKSVC,PARM1='RENT'
//LHOOKSVC EXEC LKED,PARM1='RENT,AC=1'
//LKED.SYSIN DD *
          ENTRY HOOKSVC
          ORDER HOOKSVC,HOOKSV2
          INCLUDE OBJ(HOOKSVC)
          NAME  HOOKSVC(R)
/*
//*------------------------------------------------------------------*
//*        BLDIRB                                                    *
//*------------------------------------------------------------------*
//BLDIRB    EXEC ASSEM,MEMBER=BLDIRB,PARM1='RENT'
//LBLDIRB   EXEC LKED,PARM1='RENT,AC=1'
//LKED.SYSIN DD *
          ENTRY BLDIRB
          INCLUDE OBJ(BLDIRB)
          NAME  BLDIRB(R)
/*
//SUBTSK    EXEC ASSEM,MEMBER=SUBTSK,PARM1='RENT'
//LSUBTSK   EXEC LKED,PARM1='RENT'
//LKED.SYSIN DD *
          ENTRY SUBTSK
          INCLUDE OBJ(SUBTSK)
          NAME  SUBTSK(R)
/*
//IRBRTN    EXEC ASSEM,MEMBER=IRBRTN,PARM1='RENT'
//LIRBRTN   EXEC LKED,PARM1='RENT'
//LKED.SYSIN DD *
          ENTRY IRBRTN
          INCLUDE OBJ(IRBRTN)
          NAME  IRBRTN(R)
/*
//*------------------------------------------------------------------*
//*        DYNAL                                                     *
//*------------------------------------------------------------------*
//DYNAL     EXEC ASSEM,MEMBER=DYNAL,PARM1='RENT'
//LDYNAL    EXEC LKED,PARM1='RENT'
//LKED.SYSIN DD *
          ENTRY DYNAL
          INCLUDE OBJ(DYNAL)
          NAME  DYNAL(R)
/*
```

To execute each program, add a JOB card and make the indicated changes in the following JCL:

```
//*-----------------------------------------------------------------*
//*        NCRYPT  - ENCRYPT OR DEENCRYPT A FILE                    *
//*-----------------------------------------------------------------*
//NCRYPT   EXEC PGM=NCRYPT,PARM='KKKKKKK'        <==== ENCRYPTION KEY
//STEPLIB  DD DISP=SHR,DSN=LOADLIB
//IN       DD DISP=SHR,DSN=DDDDDDD               <=== FILE TO ENCRYPT


//*-----------------------------------------------------------------*
//*        SVCLIST - PRINT THE CONTENTS OF THE SVC TABLE            *
//*-----------------------------------------------------------------*
//SVCLIST  EXEC PGM=SVCLIST
//STEPLIB  DD DISP=SHR,DSN=LOADLIB
//PRINT    DD SYSOUT=*


//*-----------------------------------------------------------------*
//*        ESAMOVE - PRINTS THE NAMES OF MODULES LOADED IN ANOTHER  *
//*                  ADDRESS SPACE. (ACCESS REGISTER MODE VERSION)  *
//*-----------------------------------------------------------------*
//ESAMOVE  EXEC PGM=ESAMOVE,PARM='NNNNNNNN' <=TARGET ADDRESS SPACE NAME
//STEPLIB  DD DISP=SHR,DSN=LOADLIB
//PRINT    DD SYSOUT=*


//*-----------------------------------------------------------------*
//*        XAMOVE  - PRINTS THE NAMES OF MODULES LOADED IN ANOTHER  *
//*                  ADDRESS SPACE (DUAL ADDRESS SPACE VERSION)     *
//*-----------------------------------------------------------------*
//XAMOVE   EXEC PGM=XAMOVE,PARM='NNNNNNNN'  <=TARGET ADDRESS SPACE NAME
//STEPLIB  DD DISP=SHR,DSN=LOADLIB
//PRINT    DD SYSOUT=*


//*-----------------------------------------------------------------*
//*        TSCHD1  - CALL SCHDSRB TO SCHEDULE A LOCAL SRB           *
//*-----------------------------------------------------------------*
//SCHDSRB  EXEC PGM=TSCHD1
//STEPLIB  DD DISP=SHR,DSN=LOADLIB
//LOADLIB  DD DISP=SHR,DSN=LOADLIB            <== SRB ROUTINE RESIDES HERE
```

```
//*----------------------------------------------------------------------*
//*        ESAMVPC - PRINTS THE NAMES OF MODULES LOADED IN ANOTHER    *
//*                  ADDRESS SPACE.  THIS VERSION, REFERRED TO IN      *
//*                  CHAPTER 10 AS ESAMOVE(PC), INVOKES A PC ROUTINE.  *
//*        PCSET, THE SERVICE ADDRESS SPACE THAT CONTAINS THE PC       *
//*        ROUTINE,  MUST BE ACTIVE BEFORE THIS PROGRAM CAN EXECUTE.   *
//*----------------------------------------------------------------------*
//ESAMVPC  EXEC PGM=ESAMVPC,PARM='NNNNNNNN' <=TARGET ADDRESS SPACE NAME
//STEPLIB  DD DISP=SHR,DSN=LOADLIB
//PRINT    DD SYSOUT=*


//*----------------------------------------------------------------------*
//*        DSPUT   - MOVES DATA AMONG DATASPACES.                     *
//*                  BEFORE EXECUTING THIS PROGRAM, START THE DSPACE   *
//*                  TASK AND ISSUE CONSOLE MODIFY COMMANDS TO CREATE  *
//*                  DATASPACES "DSP1" AND "DSP2" (SEE CHAPTER 11).    *
//*----------------------------------------------------------------------*
//DSPUT    EXEC PGM=DSPUT
//STEPLIB  DD DISP=SHR,DSN=LOADLIB


//*----------------------------------------------------------------------*
//*        HOOKSVC - FRONT-END OR BACK-END AN SVC.                    *
//*                  AFTER EXECUTING THIS PROGRAM, ANY CALL TO THE     *
//*                  SVC WILL ALSO INVOKE THE FRONT/BACK-END CODE      *
//*----------------------------------------------------------------------*
//HOOKSVC  EXEC PGM=HOOKDRV
//STEPLIB  DD DISP=SHR,DSN-LOADLIB
//LOADLIB  DD DISP=SHR,DSN=LOADLIB    <=== SVC HOOK MODULE RESIDES HERE


//*----------------------------------------------------------------------*
//*        BLDIRB - EXECUTE AN IRB UNDER A SUBTASK.                   *
//*----------------------------------------------------------------------*
//BLDIRB   EXEC PGM=BLDIRB
//STEPLIB  DD DISP=SHR,DSN=LOADLIB
```

Bibliography

These IBM Manuals are all for MVS Version 3 (ESA). See MVS Library Guide (GC28-1563) for the equivalent manuals in MVS/XA.

370 Architecture

IBM ESA/370 Principles of Operation	SA22-7200

MVS Configuration and Operations

MVS SPL: Initialization and Tuning	GC28-1828
MVS Operations: System Commands	GC28-1826

Using MVS Component Services

MVS SPL: System Modifications	GC28-1831
MVS SPL: User Exits	GC28-1836
MVS Application Dev. Guide	GC28-1821
MVS Application Dev. Macro Reference	GC28-1822
MVS SPL: Application Dev. Guide	GC28-1852
MVS SPL: Application Dev. Macro Reference	GC28-1857
MVS SPL: Application Dev. 31-bit Addressing	GC28-1820
MVS SPL: Application Dev.-Extended Addressability	GC28-1854
MVS SPL: Callable Services for High Level Language	GC28-1843

MVS Internals

MVS/XA: Overview (no ESA version available)	CC28-1348
MVS Diagnosis: Data Areas Vol. 1	LY28-1043
MVS Diagnosis: Data Areas Vol. 2	LY28-1044
MVS Diagnosis: Data Areas Vol. 3	LY28-1045
MVS Diagnosis: Data Areas Vol. 4	LY28-1046
MVS Diagnosis: Data Areas Vol. 5	LY28-1047
Component Logic Manuals	LY28-xxxx

Assembly Language/Link Editor

Link Editor and Loader User's Guide	SC26-4510
Assembler H Language Reference	GC26-4037

Abbreviations

ABEND	Abnormal End
AKM	Authorization Key Mask
ALB	Access Lookaside Buffer
ALET	Access List Entry Token
AMODE	Addressing Mode
APF	Authorized Program Facility
ARR	Associated Recovery Routine
ART	Access Register Translation
ASC	Address Space Control (Addressing Mode)
ASCB	Address Space Control Block
ASID	Address Space Identifier
ASN	Address Space Number
ASTE	Address Space Second Table Entry
ASVT	Address Space Vector Table
AX	Authorization Index
BSAM	Basic Sequential Access Method
CDE	Contents Directory Entry
CESD	Common External Symbol Dictionary
CIB	Command Information Block
CLPA	Construct Link Pack Area

CSA	Common Service Area
CSCB	Command Scheduling Control Block
CSECT	Control Section
CVT	Communications Vector Table
DAS	Dual Address Space
DASD	Direct Access Storage Device
DAT	Dynamic Address Translation
DCB	Data Control Block
DEB	Data Extent Block
DIV	Data-In-Virtual
DSECT	Dummy Section
DSN	Data Set Name
EAX	Extended Authorization Index
ECB	Event Control Block
ESA	Enterprise System Architecture
ESD	External Symbol Dictionary
ETE	Entry Table Entry
FLIH	First Level Interrupt Handler
FLPA	Fixed Link Pack Area
FRR	Functional Recovery Routine
GRS	Global Resource Serialization
ILC	Instruction Length Code
IOQ	Input/Output Queue
IOS	Input/Output Supervisor
IPL	Initial Program Load
IQE	Interrupt Queue Element
IRB	Interruption Request Block
JCL	Job Control Language
JES	Job Entry Subsystem
JFCB	Job File Control Block
JPAQ	Job Pack Area Queue
JSCB	Jobstep Control Block
LCCA	Logical Communications Control Area
LLE	Load List Element
LPAQ	Link Pack Area Queue
LPDE	Link Pack Directory Entry
LSQA	Local System Queue Area
LX	Linkage Index

MLPA	Modified Link Pack Area
MVS	Multiple Virtual Storage
MVT	Multiple Virtual Tasks
PASN	Primary Address Space Number
PDS	Partitioned Data Set
PER	Program Event Recording
PFRA	Page Frame Real Address
PGTE	Page Table Entry
PKM	PSW Key Mask
PLPA	Pageable Link Pack Area
PLPAQ	Pageable Link Pack Area Queue
PRB	Program Request Block
PSA	Prefixed Save Area
PSW	Program Status Word
PTF	Program Temporary Fix
PVR	Prefix Value Register
QCB	Queue Control Block
QEL	Queue Element
QSAM	Queued Sequential Access Method
RACF	Resource Access Control Facility
RB	Request Block
RCE	Real Storage Manager Control and Enumeration Area
RCT	Region Control Task
RLD	Relocation Dictionary
RMODE	Residency Mode
RSM	Real Storage Manager
RTM	Recovery Termination Manager
SAF	System Authorization Facility
SASN	Secondary Address Space Number
SCB	STAE Control Block
SCBX	STAE Control Block Extension
SCVT	Secondary CVT
SDWA	Schedular Diagnostic Work Area
SFT	System Function Table
SGTE	Segement Table Entry
SLIH	Second Level Interrupt Handler
SMF	System Management Facility
SQA	System Queue Area

SRB	Service Request Block
SRM	System Resource Manager
SSCT	Subystem Control Table
STC	Started Task Control
STD	Segement Table Designator
STCB	Secondary TCB
STOKEN	Space Token
SVC	Supervisor Call
SVRB	Supervisor Call Request Block
SVS	Single Virtual Storage
TCB	Task Control Block
TIOT	Task Input/Output Table
TLB	Translation Lookaside Buffer
TMP	Terminal Monitor Program
TSO	Time Sharing Option
UCB	Unit Control Block
VIO	Virtual Input/Output
VLF	Virtual Lookaside Facility
VSAM	Virtual Storage Access Method
VSM	Virtual Storage Manager
VTAM	Virtual Terminal Access Method
XA	Extended Architecture
XMS	Cross Memory Services
XPGTE	External Page Table Entry
XSB	Extended Status Block

Glossary

Absolute address. The unique address of a byte of physical main storage in the range of 0 to 1 less than the quantity of physical storage installed.

Access Register (AR) Mode. Cross memory synchronous communication using ESA architectural feature of access registers. Can logically treat the total storage addressed as a single address space. Cannot use SVCs except for ABEND.

Access Register Translation (ART). Used in conjunction with Dynamic Address Translation (DAT) to translate virtual addresses in AR Addressing Mode. ESA only. Locates the correct access list entry, performs a validation check, locates the Segment Table Designator (STD) for the target address space, and passes it to DAT for virtual address translation.

Address Space Number (ASN). Assigned during address space creation by MVS. Serves as an index into Address Space Vector Table (ASVT) and is stored in the Address space control Block (ASCB).

Address Space Number Second Table Entry (ASTE). A virtual storage control structure that contains the essential control information describing a virtual storage space (address space, dataspace, hiperspace). Has been expanded from 4 fullwords to 16 fullwords in ESA.

Addressing mode (AMODE). A module specific attribute that determines whether an address is interpreted by Dynamic Address Translation (DAT) as 24 bit or 31 bit.

Associated Recovery Routine (ARR). Recovery routines used by stacking PC routines. Used instead of an ESTAE. Its address is located in the Entry Table Entry (ETE) rather than an MVS control block.

Authority Index (AX). The indexes into the target address space's authority table. Not used in ESA.

Authority Table. The table an address space uses to restrict other address spaces from making it the target of a Cross Memory Services (XMS) operation.

Auxiliary Storage Manager (ASM). The MVS component that manages page slots. Moves data to expanded storage and DASD in page and swap operations.

Communications Vector Table (CVT). The MVS control block that contains pointers (vectors) to most other MVS control structures.

Component. A group of services with related functions and control structures.

Contents Directory Entry (CDE). The control block built by Program Manager to keep track of a module once it has been brought into virtual storage.

Cross Memory Services (XMS).   Those services that move data from one address space to another. Synchronous XMS uses 370 architecture rather than MVS software. Dual Address Space (DAS) and Access Register (AR) mode accomplish interaddress space communication with instructions and execute without a program interrupt.

Dual Address Space (DAS).   A synchronous cross memory facility using 370 architecture. Employs two special instructions, MVCP and MVCS, for moving data from one address space to another. Employs secondary space mode, which allows a program in one address space to use ordinary instructions to manipulate data in another address space.

Dynamic Address Translation (DAT).   Hardware/microcode that translates a virtual address to a real address in storage before an instruction can be fetched and executed.

Exit.   A place in MVS or JES code with a specific assigned name where control may be transferred to a user-written program.

Extended Specify Task Abnormal Exit (ESTAE).   User-written exit routines for RMT2 task recovery.

First Level Interrupt Handler (FLIH).   Provides the interface between hardware and software by saving registers, copying the Old PSW from low storage to a control block related to the type of interrupt, routing control to Second Level Interrupt Handler (SLIH) routines that complete the processing of the interrupt.

Frame.   The 4K unit into which physical storage is organized.

Global Resource Serialization (GRS).   The MVS component that serializes the use of resources among tasks.

Hook.   User-written code that front-ends an MVS service.

Interrupt.   The mechanism by which hardware can communicate with software. When hardware detects an event that requires handling by the operating system, a signal is sent to the processor which causes the Program Status Word (PSW) and registers to be saved and replaced by the Old PSW associated with the specific type of interrupt.

Linkage stack.   Last-in-first-out (LIFO) stack containing entries that describe the contents of general registers, access registers, the PSW, and cross-memory information from control registers.

Load module.   One or more source code modules that have been linked together by the linkage editor in such a way as to make the source code executable by the operating system.

Lock.   An MVS mechanism used to serialize control blocks. Each lock regulates a specific group of MVS control blocks.

Lock Manager.   The MVS component that obtains, tests, and releases all locks.

Lockword.   The fullword in storage for every lock that contains a value describing the holder of the lock. If the lock is "free," the value in the lockword will be x'00000000'.

Macro.   Instruction level interface to components.

Module.   The basic unit of software.

Operating system.   A collection of software programs that manages computer hardware for the benefit of applications programs.

Page.   A 4k block of data.

Paging.   Refers to the movement of 4k blocks of data (pages) into and out of real storage frames during the execution of a program.

PC Routine.   A program that receives control when the PC instruction is executed. PC routines are defined in Entry Table Entries and can be basic or stacking (ESA-only) and space-switching or nonspace switching.

PCAUTH.   MVS component that manages cross memory structures. Facilitates interaddress space data movement and program execution.

Prefixed Value Register (PVR).   A 4-byte area that contains the absolute address of the frame of storage allocated as the prefixed area for that processor.

Primary Address Space Number (PASN). The address space number of the primary address space, found in control register 4. Used as an index into the Address Space First and Second Tables to locate the Segment Table Designator (STD), which is loaded into control register 1 for Dynamic Address Translation.

Program Manager. MVS component also known as Contents Supervision. Locates load modules in load libraries, brings them into virtual storage, and manages the modules once they are in virtual storage.

Real address. The same as an absolute address with the exception of the low core range of 0 to x'FFF'.

Real Storage Manager (RSM). The MVS component that keeps track of all real storage frames. Satisfies frame requests.

Recovery Termination Manager (RTM). MVS component responsible for normal/abnormal task termination and cleanup, as well as global recovery. RTM1 is responsible for global recovery; RTM2 is responsible for task level recovery and termination. Reentrant. A linkage editor attribute identifying a module that has been written in such a way that multiple users can execute a single copy of the module simultaneously.

Refreshable. A linkage editor attribute identifying a module that is able to support multiple users executing simultaneously. In addition, the module can be reloaded while users are actively executing the code.

Residency mode (RMODE). A linkage editor attribute that determines if a load module can reside in below-the-line storage (24 bit addressing) or above-the-line storage (31 bit addressing).

Secondary Address Space Number (SASN). Located in control register 3. A change to the SASN initiates Address Space Number (ASN) translation. The Segment Table Designator (STD) that is located will be loaded into control register 7.

Segment Table Designator (STD). The real address of the first byte of a segment table.

Slot. The 4k unit in expanded storage or DASD where data is paged by Auxiliary Storage Manager (ASM).

STOKEN. Identifiers used by RASP to keep track of each address space, dataspace, hiperspace. RASP matches each STOKEN with an ASTE. Exists only in software not in 370 architecture.

Supervisor Call (SVC). An interrupt that is initiated by a program to transfer control to another program, often with higher authority.

System Authorization Facility (SAF). MVS component that serves as a central interface to resource security systems (RACF, etc.).

System Management Facility (SMF). The MVS component that collects data on system events. Writes data to MANx files.

Task Control Block (TCB). The control block that defines a task, or unit of work, to MVS. Anchors queues of control blocks that describe individual resource elements owned by the unit of work represented by the TCB.

Task Manager. MVS component that is responsible for creating and initializing tasks in response to ATTACH macro. Manages Request Block (RB) queue. Removes tasks in response to DETACH macro. Controls serialization and authority.

Virtual address. An algorithm used by Dynamic Address Translation (DAT) to locate a byte in real storage.

Virtual Storage Manager (VSM). The MVS component that allows programs to allocate and free ranges of virtual addresses by keeping track of which virtual addresses within pages of storage have been allocated by Getmain or Storage macros and which addresses within pages have not yet been allocated.

Virtual Lookaside Facility (VLF). Esa only. A variation on the concept of Virtual I/O (VIO). Load modules, clists, or frequently used data files can be defined as virtual objects that are paged into real storage rather than read into storage with an access method.

Index